First Published in the United States of America in 2012

By Gingko Press in association with Kill Your Idols

Third Printing

Gingko Press, Inc.
1321 Fifth Street
Berkeley, CA 94710, USA
www.gingkopress.com

Kill Your Idols
PO Box 48888
Los Angeles, CA 90048
www.killyouridols.com

ISBN: 978-1-58423-488-3

LCCN: 2012948076

Printed in China

© 2012, © 2013 Jeff Gold // Kill Your Idols, Inc.

Author: Jeff Gold
Art Director: Bryan Ray Turcotte
Design: Clint Woodside
Copy Editor: Chelsea Hodson
Cover Design: YYES
Cover Photo: Dan Monick

For further information: www.101essentialrecords.com

101
ESSENTIAL
ROCK
RECORDS

**The Golden Age of Vinyl
From The Beatles to the Sex Pistols**

Jeff Gold

CONTENTS

THE ALBUMS

ESSAYS BY GENE SCULATTI

CONTENTS

This experimental disc of Scheherazade, Part 2, Movements 3 & 4 (pressed on February 27, 1946) is the first LP record ever made. It was a gift to Jac Holzman from the developer of the long-play record, Dr. Peter Goldmark.

ENGINEERING RESEARCH & DEVELOPMENT DEPARTMENT
COLUMBIA BROADCASTING SYSTEM
EXPERIMENTAL RECORD NO.
DATE 2/27/46
DESCRIPTION
33 1/3 RPM
SCHEHERAZADE, PART 2
movements 3 & 4
referp. 56755 Book I
To Jac from
Peter Goldmark

THE RECORD OBSESSION

by Jeff Gold

Maybe I spend too much time thinking about records. For more than 40 years, as a collector, record executive, and now music historian and dealer, they've been my obsession.

Why do we lust after this outdated, obsolete format—this outmoded 12" square in an era of downloads and CDs? And why are sales of turntables and vinyl actually up in the past few years? It's true that vinyl records *sound* better, but that can't be the only reason.

Writing in a 1977 issue of *Zimmerman Blues*, journalist Pete Howard noted, "When a collector plays an original copy of Bob Dylan's first album, he knows that record was made when Dylan was 20 years old. That record has survived through the years in the same way Dylan himself has. On the other hand, if someone goes to a store and buys Dylan's first album today, all he has is a replica. It's almost like the difference between owning an original Rembrandt painting and a print."

If a reissue album is like a reproduction, how could anyone possibly get excited about owning a *download*?

You hold in your hands a tribute to the humble vinyl album, the format that just won't die. While technology evolves at warp speed, the LP (long playing) record survives, even thrives, inspiring collectors around the world. And while 21st century life would be just fine without one more list of the best or most important anythings, this book exists to shine a light on 101 rock albums, well known and obscure, that changed music forever.

The focus here is on rock albums. For this book, rock means music that's generally guitar driven and song based, with a verse-chorus-verse structure, but often incorporating elements of other kinds of music. Sub-genres of rock, such as psychedelic, blues, folk, and punk are included, but I've steered clear of other full-fledged genres (we'll cover those in future volumes).

I've concentrated on records that are seminal, a word defined as *highly original and influencing the developments of future events*. Albums that in some way, large or small, influenced the music that followed.

As this book is titled *101 Essential Rock Records*, it begins with the group that changed everything, The Beatles, and their British debut album, *Please Please Me*.

Record executive Jeff Ayeroff observed, "Elvis' cool was milk that had soured. I told my mom, 'Some day Elvis is going to be Frank Sinatra.' So when The Beatles came on Ed Sullivan, it was shattering. They had great songs, long hair, tight pants, Beatles boots. They were cute--every girl could have their own Beatle; but guys wanted to be like them too. They were funny and had *English accents*. They were like us, but not us. They were the other. And we wanted to be them. It was the waking up of youth culture; a phenomenon like nothing else."

It may be less obvious to end with the Sex Pistols' *Never Mind The Bollocks*, but like The Beatles, the Pistols were one of a handful of artists who set off a revolution that indelibly affected not just music, but fashion, art, and youth culture as a whole. As critic Ira Robbins put

it, "Their importance—both to the direction of contemporary music and more generally to pop culture—can hardly be overstated."

In 1979, two years after *Never Mind The Bollocks*, Sony introduced the Walkman, and not long after that, cassettes began outselling LPs. The decline of vinyl—at least as a mainstream format for music—began. Vinyl's Golden Age was over.

Flash forward 30 years. As probably no one in the major-label music business would have predicted, we're in the midst of a vinyl resurgence. In 2010, vinyl was the fastest growing music format, and in 2011, U.S. vinyl sales topped 3.6 million units, 37 percent more than the previous year.

CDs and downloads may have their advantages—they're easier to find than records, theoretically never wear out, and as anyone who's ever moved a large record collection knows, they're a whole lot easier to transport than vinyl. But for some ineffable reason, there are many of us who just don't care. We want and we need that cardboard-sheathed slab of black plastic in our hands. Now.

If you are one of those people, this book is dedicated to you.

Notes on format

All record collectors, no matter how compulsive, have rules limiting what they collect. For the purpose of this book, here are ours.

Albums were chosen based on quality, originality, and influence. While these criteria and what constitutes a *rock* album are entirely subjective, I was fortunate to have the trusted counsel of Geoffrey Weiss, Jon Savage, Gene Sculatti, Gary Johnson, and a number of others as a reality check.

The albums illustrated are the earliest pressings from each artist's country of origin. In the case of someone like Jimi Hendrix, who was American, but formed his group and signed his record contract with a British company, we've chosen the country most often identified with that artist—in the case of The Jimi Hendrix Experience, England.

All albums are presented chronologically, with release dates largely sourced from Wikipedia.

We've tried to include as much album cover art as possible; where there are alternate covers or inserts we have pictured them as space allows, or when merited. Both mono and stereo albums are illustrated.

While it would have been ideal to include only one album per artist, some, particularly The Beatles and Bob Dylan, were regularly reinventing themselves and their music, with successive records. Hence, a decision was made to limit artists to a maximum of four albums.

If we've left out your favorite album, we invite you to write about it or post your own list of records at www.101essentialrecords.com

DREAMS OF VINYL

by Jac Holzman

The story of the LP (long playing) record lies at the heart of recording history.

The first widely available pre-recorded music device was the player piano and rolls—large punched paper rolls, cumbersome to load, apt to tear but they brought "recorded" music into homes throughout America and the world.

The most renowned pianists, in all musical genres, played in your parlor at the touch of a button or pull of a lever. The notes and timing were identical to their original performance but the subtleties of emphasis and shading could not be captured. Player piano rolls were a simplified, early hint of our digital system of ones and zeros. The key was struck when a row of feelers, very lightly pressed against the paper roll, found an opening and activated the corresponding key on the piano; "on"/"off" with no nuance.

In 1877, Thomas Edison invented the first pre-recorded, home playback system with his tin foil (and later, wax) cylinder—shaped and looking somewhat like a narrow roll of black toilet paper. The cylinder was driven by a mechanical windup motor which rotated the wax at a more-or-less constant speed while an acoustic playback head nested in the groove picked up minor changes in depth and converted these hills and dales into acoustic energy which was, in turn, fed into the familiar acoustic horn. Previewing the slugfest with the Columbia LP versus the 7" 45 RCA Disc, Edison had competition and lawsuits with his rivals (including Alexander Graham Bell) who had "invented" their own cylinder systems. You guessed it—none of these systems were compatible with each other.

The most significant and best-conceived advance came 10 years later, in 1887, with a one-two punch of thoughtful invention by Emile Berliner. Berliner's basic concept would be incorporated into every physical record produced since that time, up to and including the CD, DVD and Blu-Ray.

Berliner, clearly aware of the cylinder's limitations -- complicated to record and produce in quantity—chose to record on a flat disc which offered significant advantages. The disc's grooves would form a compact spiral, one of the most efficient means for information storage. The fragile shellac 78 rpm records, the vinyl LP disc which succeeded them and the CDs/DVDs are all music and image carriers that took advantage of the efficiencies of a compact spiral. In addition to the compact spiral, flat discs were far easier to mold and to ship. A shellac (and later, vinyl) biscuit of raw material would be slipped into the press between the A-Side and B-Side record labels and switches thrown, the press itself resembled a large, round waffle iron, only with far more pressure and heat. The press closed, and there was a lot of steam. When the press popped open, the molded record would be removed and the rough circular edge would be trimmed or beveled.

The first LP to come off a press at the CBS laboratory was made on February 27, 1946. It took two additional years for problems with mastering, cutterhead mechanics, corrective equalization for the inner grooves (where the same amount of information is squeezed into ever shorter spaces), and vinyl formulations to be resolved. The first LPs, released in time for Christmas 1948, were already quieter and contained a fidelity and dynamic range far better than their recent shellac 78 RPM parents.

Mastering engineers, like Peter Bartok, modified existing equipment to ensure a cleaner, more powerful dynamic range to the cutterhead. Experimentation was everywhere, and audio engineers shared their techniques because it improved the breed.

Milestones in LP disc development included the "hot stylus." A resistive tungsten wire, very much like the filament of a light bulb, was tightly wound around the stylus' metal shank and current run though it. Thus heated, the stylus cut smoothly through the acetate coated aluminum disc and made for a much quieter master disc.

Equally important was the installation of an extra playback head, reading the tape a few seconds ahead of the music. It previewed the music, looking for high-energy passages. When a loud section was detected, a message was sent to the servo controlled lathe screw urging the lathe to hurry up and widen the "land" between adjacent grooves, thus preventing them from running into each other and making possible longer, long playing records.

In 1956, Westrex invented a method of encoding two substantially separate signals into a single groove, which offered vastly improved imaging of the original performance via stereo. The vinyl LP and high quality analog tape recording lived joyously together from 1948 until 1983 when the first CD's came to market.

The success of the vinyl LP allowed small labels to record unusual repertoire and ship it without fear of breakage all over the world. The LP, together with high quality microphones and truly portable tape recorders said you didn't need a studio to make sonically competitive recordings. You could do it as well as the majors, maybe better. And you could do it *yourself*. Independent record entrepreneurs were to broaden the range and direction of the music during more than 35 years of LP dominance.

In 1970 I worked with Peter Goldmark who led the LP technology development at CBS labs. Peter told me that the notion for the LP came from his constantly interrupted listening to a Mozart symphony. Every four to five minutes the music stopped, another record would plop from the top of the changer onto the turntable below and the interruption and changer noises drove him crazy. Why can't we get it all in one record he wondered?

The LP, for all of its influence and prominence, was more of an adaptation than a from-the-ground-up new thing. 33 1/3 had been a standard playback speed in every radio station worldwide, used for playing recorded transcriptions of radio broadcasts and commercials, though on much larger 16-inch discs.

To achieve a longer playing time the LP was slowed down from 78 rpm to 33 1/3 (approx. 57%) and by narrowing the playback stylus by 2/3rds, (to .001 in.) the LP was born.

It takes smarts and a controlled ego not to reinvent everything. After the war, 78 rpm standard groove vinyl discs were available to the serious collector. The vinyl LP could be molded in the same presses as the older 78's. Yes, a new disc player was necessary, but Columbia accelerated LP acceptance by giving away a rather nifty player in a solid bakelite shell equipped with a gentle cobra-like playing arm, *if* you purchased just five LP's. It worked and millions of serious music listeners were the winners… and so was I.

The coming together of circumstance—the invention of the unbreakable LP, easy to press and ship, the need of the major labels to keep their factories pressing records, even for us indies, high quality portable mics and tape recorders, the relocation in the broadcast spectrum for a permanent FM band at 88-108 MHz—all together gave more music to a wider variety of tastes and interests.

The LP was the single most important of these factors for, without IT, my life and Elektra Records would never have happened.

Happily, the LP is alive again and doing well. Serious music fans appreciate its warmer, more sensual sound, the heavier pressings (180 grams) and the delicious tactile feel of the vinyl. Established equipment manufacturers are turning out updated turntables with both conventional RCA plugs for analog listening but also with built-in analog/digital convertors and a standard USB connector to plug directly into your computer. Your analog vinyl LP is now welcome in the digital universe, while still retaining its soul.

Jac Holzman founded Elektra Records and Nonesuch Records, and is a recording technology pioneer. The acts he signed and nurtured include The Doors, Love, Queen, The Stooges, Judy Collins and Carly Simon.

PLEASE PLEASE ME ★ THE BEATLES   stereo

PARLOPHONE

THE BEATLES

PLEASE PLEASE ME

with Love Me Do and 12 other songs

Photo: Angus McBean

THE BEATLES | Please Please Me

March 1963 | Parlophone

Modern popular music starts with this voyage of discovery. The Beatles' debut is, was and forever shall be, startling in its originality. The expedition begins with "I Saw Her Standing There" and proceeds through a sustained high of eight band originals and a half dozen covers. Not only does the megawatt brilliance of Lennon & McCartney's melodies impress (the title track, "P.S. I Love You," "Do You Want to Know a Secret," "There's a Place"). The songwriting expertise is matched by performances that powerfully illuminate even the non-originals; the Isley Brothers and Arthur Alexander recede in the distance against Lennon's intense revamping of "Twist and Shout" and "Anna." *Please Please Me* introduced the one group that yoked rock 'n' roll's pioneer past to its soaring future: the Beatles were, with the Beach Boys, the first self-contained band since Buddy Holly's Crickets to write, perform and record their own material, and they alone are the artists who, for almost

half a century, have inspired others to push harder and go farther to show what a once-derided genre could be and say and do. Initial copies of *Please Please Me* bore the traditional Parlophone Records label design, with logo and lettering printed in gold on a black background. Within a few weeks of its release, Parlophone changed their label design to a yellow pound symbol insignia on a black background, and today, gold Parlophone first pressings are among the most collectible of all rock albums.

Please Please Me
THE BEATLES

■ **GEORGE HARRISON** (lead guitar) ■ **JOHN LENNON** (rhythm guitar)
■ **PAUL McCARTNEY** (bass guitar) ■ **RINGO STARR** (drums)

PCS
3042

SIDE ONE

1. I SAW HER STANDING THERE
   (McCartney-Lennon)
2. MISERY
   (McCartney-Lennon)
3. ANNA (GO TO HIM)
   (Alexander)
4. CHAINS
   (Goffin-King)
5. BOYS
   (Dixon-Farrell)
6. ASK ME WHY
   (McCartney-Lennon)
7. PLEASE PLEASE ME
   (McCartney-Lennon)

SIDE TWO

1. LOVE ME DO
   (McCartney-Lennon)
2. P.S. I LOVE YOU
   (McCartney-Lennon)
3. BABY IT'S YOU
   (David-Williams-Bacharach)
4. DO YOU WANT TO KNOW A SECRET
   (McCartney-Lennon)
5. A TASTE OF HONEY
   (Scott-Marlow)
6. THERE'S A PLACE
   (McCartney-Lennon)
7. TWIST AND SHOUT
   (Medley-Russell)

Recording first published 1963

Pop picking is a fast 'n' furious business these days whether you are on the recording studio side listening out, or on the disc-counter side listening in. As a record reviewer I find myself installed halfway in-between with an ear cocked in either direction. So far as Britain's record collecting public is concerned, The Beatles broke into earshot in October, 1962. My natural hometown interest in the group prevented me taking a totally unbiased view of their early success. Eighteen months before their first visit to the EMI studios in London, The Beatles had been voted Merseyside's favourite outfit and it was inevitable that their first Parlophone record, LOVE ME DO, would go straight into the top of Liverpool's local hit parade. The group's chances of national chart entry seemed much more remote. No other team had joined the best-sellers via a début disc. But The Beatles were history-makers from the start and LOVE ME DO sold enough copies during its first 48 hours in the shops to send it soaring into the national charts. In all the busy years since such pop singles first shrank from ten to seven inches I have never seen a British group leap to the forefront of the scene with such speed and energy. Within the six months which followed the Top Twenty appearance of LOVE ME DO, almost every leading deejay and musical journalist in the country began to shout the praises of The Beatles. Readers of the *New Musical Express* voted the boys into a surprisingly high place via the 1962/63 popularity poll . . . on the strength of just one record release. Pictures of the group spread themselves across the front pages of three national music papers. People inside and outside the record industry expressed tremendous interest in the new vocal and instrumental sounds which The Beatles had introduced. Brian Matthew (who has since brought The Beatles to many millions of viewers and listeners in his "Thank Your Lucky Stars", "Saturday Club" and "Easy Beat" programmes) describes the quartet as *visually and musically the most exciting and accomplished group to emerge since The Shadows.*
Disc reviewing, like disc producing, teaches one to be wary about making long-term predictions. The hit parade isn't always dominated by the most worthy performances of the day so it is no good assuming that versatility counts for everything. It was during the recording of a Radio Luxembourg programme in the *EMI Friday Spectacular* series that I was finally convinced that The Beatles were about to enjoy the type of top-flight national fame which I had always believed that they deserved. The teen-audience didn't know the evening's line-up of artists and groups in advance, and before Muriel Young brought on The Beatles she began to read out their Christian names. She got as far as John . . . Paul . . . and the rest of her introduction was buried in a mighty barrage of very genuine applause. I cannot think of more than one other group — British or American — which would be so readily identified and welcomed by the announcement of two Christian

names. To me, this was the ultimate proof that The Beatles (and not just one or two of their hit records) had arrived at the uncommon peak-popularity point reserved for discdom's privileged few. Shortly afterwards The Beatles proved their pop power when they by-passed the lower segments of the hit parade to scuttle straight into the nation's Top Ten with their second single, PLEASE PLEASE ME.

This brisk-selling disc went on to overtake all rivals when it bounced into the coveted Number One slot towards the end of February. Just over four months after the release of their very first record The Beatles had become triumphant chart-toppers!

Producer George Martin has never had any headaches over choice of songs for The Beatles. Their own built-in tunesmith team of John Lennon and Paul McCartney has already tucked away enough self-penned numbers to maintain a steady output of all-original singles from now until 1975! Between them The Beatles adopt a do-it-yourself approach from the very beginning. They write their own lyrics, design and eventually build their own instrumental backdrops and work out their own vocal arrangements. Their music is wild, pungent, hard-hitting, uninhibited . . . and personal. The do-it-yourself angle ensures complete originality at all stages of the process. Although so many people suggest (without closer definition) that The Beatles have a trans-Atlantic style, their only real influence has been from the unique brand of Rhythm and Blues folk music which abounds on Merseyside and which The Beatles themselves have helped to pioneer since their formation in 1960.
This record comprises eight Lennon-McCartney compositions in addition to six other numbers which have become firm live-performance favourites in The Beatles' varied repertoire.
The group's admiration for the work of The Shirelles is demonstrated by the inclusion of BABY IT'S YOU (John taking the lead vocal with George and Paul supplying the harmony), and BOYS (a fast rocker which allows drummer Ringo to make his first recorded appearance as a vocalist). ANNA, ASK ME WHY, and TWIST AND SHOUT also feature stand-out solo performances from John, whilst DO YOU WANT TO KNOW A SECRET hands the audio spotlight to George. MISERY may sound as though it is a self-duet created by the multi-recording of a single voice . . . but the effect is produced by the fine matching of two voices belonging to John and Paul. There is only one 'trick duet' and that is on A TASTE OF HONEY featuring a dual-voiced Paul. John and Paul get together on THERE'S A PLACE and I SAW HER STANDING THERE: George joins them for CHAINS, LOVE ME DO and PLEASE PLEASE ME.

TONY BARROW

LONG PLAY 33⅓ R.P.M. • **E.M.I. RECORDS LIMITED**
(Controlled by Electric & Musical Industries Ltd.)
HAYES • MIDDLESEX • ENGLAND
Made and Printed in Great Britain

TRADE MARK OF
THE PARLOPHONE Co., Ltd.

Printed and Made by Ernest J. Day & Co. Ltd. London   PMC 1202   PCS 3042

Please Please Me was issued in the U.S. by the Vee Jay label, who retitled it *Introducing The Beatles*.

Only the earliest copies of *Please Please Me* featured black and gold labels; a month or two after release, Parlophone changed their label design and unwittingly created one of the rarest Beatles albums in existence. Stereo first pressings in excellent condition sell for $5,000. This version has the corrected publishing credits.

MONAURAL—CL 1986

COLUMBIA

THE FREEWHEELIN' BOB DYLAN

Blowin' in the Wind
Girl From the North Country
Masters of War
Down the Highway
Bob Dylan's Blues
A Hard Rain's A-Gonna Fall

Don't Think Twice, It's All Right
Bob Dylan's Dream
Oxford Town
Talkin' World War III Blues
Corrina, Corrina
Honey, Just Allow Me One More Chance
I Shall Be Free

© COLUMBIA RECORDS

GUARANTEED HIGH FIDELITY

BOB DYLAN | The Freewheelin' Bob Dylan　　　　**May 1963 | Columbia**

"We wondered, with him being this little white boy, how he could feel all those things we felt," said Mavis Staples, recalling the first time she heard "Blowin' in the Wind." "You know, all this pain and the hurt. How could he write those songs?" Staples' astonishment at Dylan's precociousness was shared by countless others. Just a year earlier, the 21-year-old singer had debuted with an album of folk and blues covers and one original composition. *Freewheelin'* counted one cover among a slate of Dylan tunes that effectively introduced one of the 20th century's greatest songwriters. Staples and dozens of other artists would record "Blowin' in the Wind" and likewise shine light on the album's pointedly topical material ("A Hard Rain's A-Gonna Fall," "Oxford Town"), its dark musings ("Masters of War") and deeply personal ruminations ("Girl from the North Country," "Don't Think Twice, It's All Right"). In some ways, the prominence of

social-protest material on *Freewheelin'* tended to obscure the record's other treasures and signposts. Even what appears to be the album's most trifling cut, "Talkin' World War III Blues," carries weight, its jumbled account of Abe Lincoln, Rocka-day Johnny, commies and psychiatrists' couches presaging the surreal wordplay that would later characterize *Bringing It All Back Home* and *Highway 61 Revisited*. As the title of the *Freewheelin'*'s successor would suggest, there were many other sides of Bob Dylan, and each would, in its turn, exert a profound influence on the direction of popular music for years to come. Extremely valuable are the few extant copies of an early alternate version of the LP that replaces four of the final version tracks with "John Birch Society Blues," "Let Me Die in My Footsteps," "Rambling Gambling Willie" and "Rocks and Gravel."

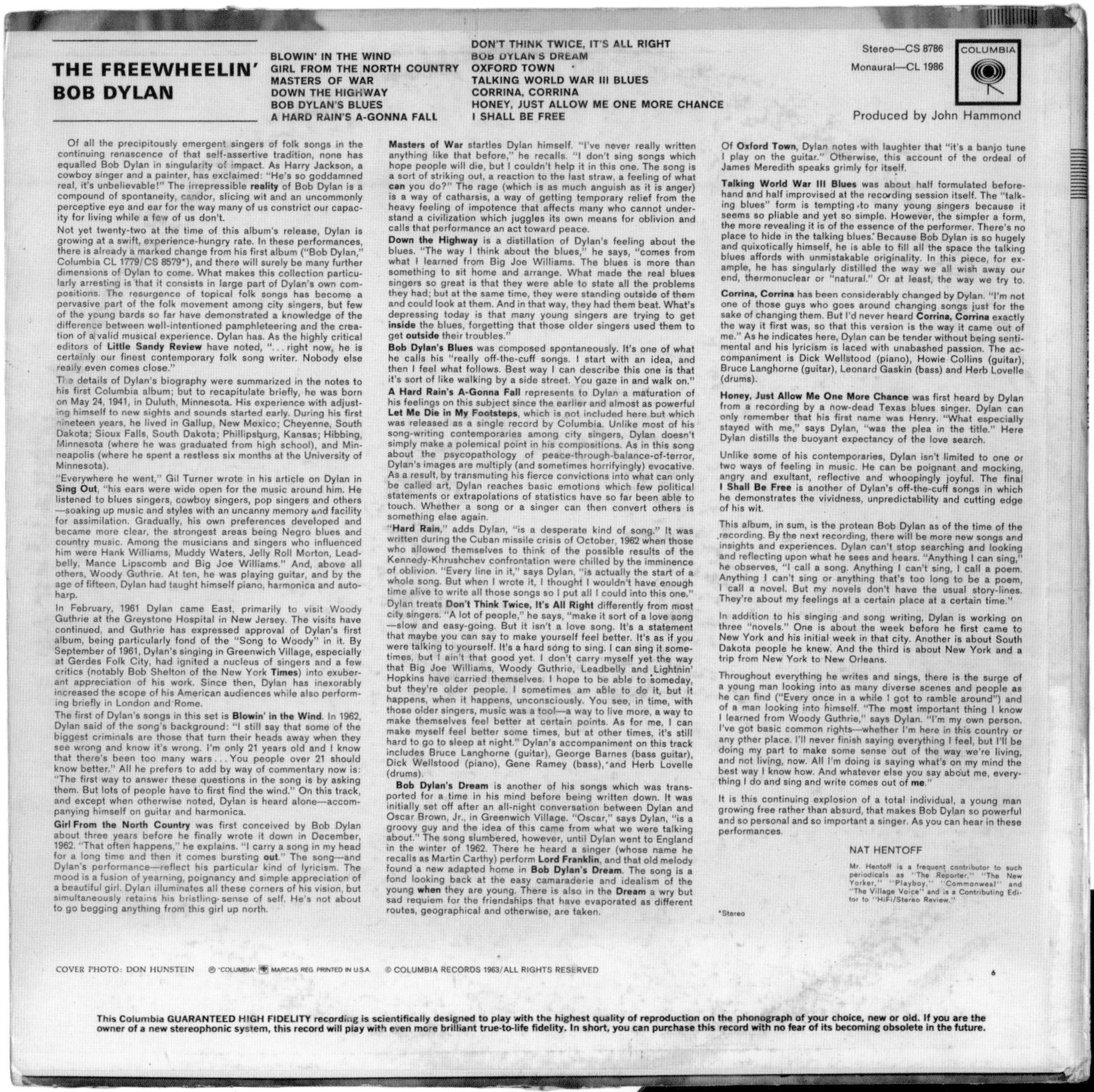

THE FREEWHEELIN' BOB DYLAN

BLOWIN' IN THE WIND
GIRL FROM THE NORTH COUNTRY
MASTERS OF WAR
DOWN THE HIGHWAY
BOB DYLAN'S BLUES
A HARD RAIN'S A-GONNA FALL
DON'T THINK TWICE, IT'S ALL RIGHT
BOB DYLAN'S DREAM
OXFORD TOWN
TALKING WORLD WAR III BLUES
CORRINA, CORRINA
HONEY, JUST ALLOW ME ONE MORE CHANCE
I SHALL BE FREE

Stereo—CS 8786
Monaural—CL 1986

COLUMBIA

Produced by John Hammond

Of all the precipitously emergent singers of folk songs in the continuing renascence of that self-assertive tradition, none has equalled Bob Dylan in singularity of impact. As Harry Jackson, a cowboy singer and a painter, has exclaimed: "He's so goddamned real, it's unbelievable!" The irrepressible **reality** of Bob Dylan is a compound of spontaneity, candor, slicing wit and an uncommonly perceptive eye and ear for the way many of us constrict our capacity for living while a few of us don't.

Not yet twenty-two at the time of this album's release, Dylan is growing at a swift, experience-hungry rate. In these performances, there is already a marked change from his first album ("Bob Dylan," Columbia CL 1779/CS 8579*), and there will surely be many further dimensions of Dylan to come. What makes this collection particularly arresting is that it consists in large part of Dylan's own compositions. The resurgence of topical folk songs has become a pervasive part of the folk movement among city singers, but few of the young bards so far have demonstrated a knowledge of the difference between well-intentioned pamphleteering and the creation of a valid musical experience. Dylan has. As the highly critical editors of **Little Sandy Review** have noted, "... right now, he is certainly our finest contemporary folk song writer. Nobody else really even comes close."

The details of Dylan's biography were summarized in the notes to his first Columbia album; but to recapitulate briefly, he was born on May 24, 1941, in Duluth, Minnesota. His experience with adjusting himself to new sights and sounds started early. During his first nineteen years, he lived in Gallup, New Mexico; Cheyenne, South Dakota; Sioux Falls, South Dakota; Phillipsburg, Kansas; Hibbing, Minnesota (where he was graduated from high school), and Minneapolis (where he spent a restless six months at the University of Minnesota).

"Everywhere he went," Gil Turner wrote in his article on Dylan in **Sing Out**, "his ears were wide open for the music around him. He listened to blues singers, cowboy singers, pop singers and others —soaking up music and styles with an uncanny memory and facility for assimilation. Gradually, his own preferences developed and became more clear, the strongest areas being Negro blues and country music. Among the musicians and singers who influenced him were Hank Williams, Muddy Waters, Jelly Roll Morton, Leadbelly, Mance Lipscomb and Big Joe Williams." And, above all others, Woody Guthrie. At ten, he was playing guitar, and by the age of fifteen, Dylan had taught himself piano, harmonica and autoharp.

In February, 1961 Dylan came East, primarily to visit Woody Guthrie at the Greystone Hospital in New Jersey. The visits have continued, and Guthrie has expressed approval of Dylan's first album, being particularly fond of the "Song to Woody" in it. By September of 1961, Dylan's singing in Greenwich Village, especially at Gerdes Folk City, had ignited a nucleus of singers and a few critics (notably Bob Shelton of the New York **Times**) into exuberant appreciation of his work. Since then, Dylan has inexorably increased the scope of his American audiences while also performing briefly in London and Rome.

The first of Dylan's songs in this set is **Blowin' in the Wind**. In 1962, Dylan said of the song's background: "I still say that some of the biggest criminals are those that turn their heads away when they see wrong and know it's wrong. I'm only 21 years old and I know that there's been too many wars... You people over 21 should know better." All he prefers to add by way of commentary now is: "The first way to answer these questions in the song is by asking them. But lots of people have to first find the wind." On this track, and except when otherwise noted, Dylan is heard alone—accompanying himself on guitar and harmonica.

Girl From the North Country was first conceived by Bob Dylan about three years before he finally wrote it down in December, 1962. "That often happens," he explains. "I carry a song in my head for a long time and then it comes bursting **out**." The song—and Dylan's performance—reflect his particular kind of lyricism. The mood is a fusion of yearning, poignancy and simple appreciation of a beautiful girl. Dylan illuminates all these corners of his vision, but simultaneously retains his bristling sense of self. He's not about to go begging anything from this girl up north.

Masters of War startles Dylan himself. "I've never really written anything like that before," he recalls. "I don't sing songs which hope people will die, but I couldn't help it in this one. The song is a sort of striking out, a reaction to the last straw, a feeling of what **can** you do?" The rage (which is as much anguish as it is anger) is a way of catharsis, a way of getting temporary relief from the heavy feeling of impotence that affects many who cannot understand a civilization which juggles its own means for oblivion and calls that performance an act toward peace.

Down the Highway is a distillation of Dylan's feeling about the blues. "The way I think about the blues," he says, "comes from what I learned from Big Joe Williams. The blues is more than something to sit home and arrange. What made the real blues singers so great is that they were able to state all the problems they had; but at the same time, they were standing outside of them and could look at them. And in that way, they had them beat. What's depressing today is that many young singers are trying to get **inside** the blues, forgetting that those older singers used them to get **outside** their troubles."

Bob Dylan's Blues was composed spontaneously. It's one of what he calls his "really off-the-cuff songs. I start with an idea, and then I feel what follows. Best way I can describe this one is that it's sort of like walking by a side street. You gaze in and walk on."

A Hard Rain's A-Gonna Fall represents to Dylan a maturation of his feelings on this subject since the earlier and almost as powerful **Let Me Die in My Footsteps**, which is not included here but which was released as a single record by Columbia. Unlike most of his song-writing contemporaries among city singers, Dylan doesn't simply make a polemical point in his compositions. As in this song about the psycopathology of peace-through-balance-of-terror, Dylan's images are multiply (and sometimes horrifyingly) evocative. As a result, by transmuting his fierce convictions into what can only be called art, Dylan reaches basic emotions which few political statements or extrapolations of statistics have so far been able to touch. Whether a song or a singer can then convert others is something else again.

"**Hard Rain**," adds Dylan, "is a desperate kind of song." It was written during the Cuban missile crisis of October, 1962 when those who allowed themselves to think of the possible results of the Kennedy-Khrushchev confrontation were chilled by the imminence of oblivion. "Every line in it," says Dylan, "is actually the start of a whole song. But when I wrote it, I thought I wouldn't have enough time alive to write all those songs so I put all I could into this one."

Dylan treats **Don't Think Twice, It's All Right** differently from most city singers. "A lot of people," he says, "make it sort of a love song —slow and easy-going. But it isn't a love song. It's a statement that maybe you can say to make yourself feel better. It's as if you were talking to yourself. It's a hard song to sing. I can sing it sometimes, but I ain't that good yet. I don't carry myself yet the way that Big Joe Williams, Woody Guthrie, Leadbelly and Lightnin' Hopkins have carried themselves. I hope to be able to someday, but they're older people. I sometimes am able to do it, but it happens, when it happens, unconsciously. You see, in time, with those older singers, music was a tool—a way to live more, a way to make themselves feel better at certain points. As for me, I can make myself feel better some times, but at other times, it's still hard to go to sleep at night." Dylan's accompaniment on this track includes Bruce Langhorne (guitar), George Barnes (bass guitar), Dick Wellstood (piano), Gene Ramey (bass), and Herb Lovelle (drums).

Bob Dylan's Dream is another of his songs which was transported for a time in his mind before being written down. It was initially set off after an all-night conversation between Dylan and Oscar Brown, Jr., in Greenwich Village. "Oscar," says Dylan, "is a groovy guy and the idea of this came from what we were talking about." The song slumbered, however, until Dylan went to England in the winter of 1962. There he heard a singer (whose name he recalls as Martin Carthy) perform **Lord Franklin**, and that old melody found a new adapted home in **Bob Dylan's Dream**. The song is a fond looking back at the easy camaraderie and idealism of the young **when** they are young. There is also in the **Dream** a wry but sad requiem for the friendships that have evaporated as different routes, geographical and otherwise, are taken.

Of **Oxford Town**, Dylan notes with laughter that "it's a banjo tune I play on the guitar." Otherwise, this account of the ordeal of James Meredith speaks grimly for itself.

Talking World War III Blues was about half formulated beforehand and half improvised at the recording session itself. The "talking blues" form is tempting to many young singers because it seems so pliable and yet so simple. However, the simpler a form, the more revealing it is of the essence of the performer. There's no place to hide in the talking blues. Because Bob Dylan is so hugely and quixotically himself, he is able to fill all the space the talking blues affords with unmistakable originality. In this piece, for example, he has singularly distilled the way we all wish away our end, thermonuclear or "natural." Or at least, the way we try to.

Corrina, Corrina has been considerably changed by Dylan. "I'm not one of those guys who goes around changing songs just for the sake of changing them. But I'd never heard **Corrina, Corrina** exactly the way it first was, so that this version is the way it came out of me." As he indicates here, Dylan can be tender without being sentimental and his lyricism is laced with unabashed passion. The accompaniment is Dick Wellstood (piano), Howie Collins (guitar), Bruce Langhorne (guitar), Leonard Gaskin (bass) and Herb Lovelle (drums).

Honey, Just Allow Me One More Chance was first heard by Dylan from a recording by a now-dead Texas blues singer. Dylan can only remember that his first name was Henry. "What especially stayed with me," says Dylan, "was the plea in the title." Here Dylan distills the buoyant expectancy of the love search.

Unlike some of his contemporaries, Dylan isn't limited to one or two ways of feeling in music. He can be poignant and mocking, angry and exultant, reflective and whoopingly joyful. The final **I Shall Be Free** is another of Dylan's off-the-cuff songs in which he demonstrates the vividness, unpredictability and cutting edge of his wit.

This album, in sum, is the protean Bob Dylan as of the time of the recording. By the next recording, there will be more new songs and insights and experiences. Dylan can't stop searching and looking and reflecting upon what he sees and hears. "Anything I can sing," he observes, "I call a song. Anything I can't sing, I call a poem. Anything I can't sing or anything that's too long to be a poem, I call a novel. But my novels don't have the usual story-lines. They're about my feelings at a certain place at a certain time."

In addition to his singing and song writing, Dylan is working on three "novels." One is about the week before he first came to New York and his initial week in that city. Another is about South Dakota people he knew. And the third is about New York and a trip from New York to New Orleans.

Throughout everything he writes and sings, there is the surge of a young man looking into as many diverse scenes and people as he can find ("Every once in a while I got to ramble around") and of a man looking into himself. "The most important thing I know I learned from Woody Guthrie," says Dylan. "I'm my own person. I've got basic common rights—whether I'm here in this country or any other place. I'll never finish saying everything I feel, but I'll be doing my part to make some sense out of the way we're living, and not living, now. All I'm doing is saying what's on my mind the best way I know how. And whatever else you say about me, everything I do and sing and write comes out of **me**."

It is this continuing explosion of a total individual, a young man growing free rather than absurd, that makes Bob Dylan so powerful and so personal and so important a singer. As you can hear in these performances.

NAT HENTOFF

Mr. Hentoff is a frequent contributor to such periodicals as "The Reporter," "The New Yorker," "Playboy," "Commonweal" and "The Village Voice" and is a Contributing Editor to "HiFi/Stereo Review."

*Stereo

COVER PHOTO: DON HUNSTEIN ® "COLUMBIA" MARCAS REG. PRINTED IN U.S.A. © COLUMBIA RECORDS 1963/ALL RIGHTS RESERVED

6

This Columbia GUARANTEED HIGH FIDELITY recording is scientifically designed to play with the highest quality of reproduction on the phonograph of your choice, new or old. If you are the owner of a new stereophonic system, this record will play with even more brilliant true-to-life fidelity. In short, you can purchase this record with no fear of its becoming obsolete in the future.

COLUMBIA
THE FREEWHEELIN'
BOB DYLAN
COLUMBIA RECORDS RADIO STATION SERVICE ■ NOT FOR RESALE CL 1986
SIDE 1
BLOWIN' IN THE WIND 2:46
M. Witmark & Sons (ASCAP)
ROCKS AND GRAVEL 2:21
M. Witmark & Sons (ASCAP)
LET ME DIE IN MY FOOTSTEPS 4:05
M. Witmark & Sons (ASCAP)
DOWN THE HIGHWAY 3:10
M. Witmark & Sons (ASCAP)
BOB DYLAN'S BLUES 2:19
M. Witmark & Sons (ASCAP)
A HARD RAIN'S A-GONNA FALL 6:48
M. Witmark & Sons (ASCAP)
21:54
SIDE 2
DON'T THINK TWICE, IT'S ALL RIGHT 3:37
M. Witmark & Sons (ASCAP)
GAMBLIN' WILLIE'S DEAD MAN'S HAND 4:11
Duchess Music Corp. (BMI)
OXFORD TOWN 1:47
M. Witmark & Sons (ASCAP)
CORRINA CORRINA 2:42
M. Witmark & Sons (ASCAP)
TALKIN' JOHN BIRCH BLUES 3:45
M. Witmark & Sons (ASCAP)
HONEY, JUST ALLOW ME ONE MORE CHANCE 1:57
M. Witmark & Sons (ASCAP)
I SHALL BE FREE 4:46
M. Witmark & Sons (ASCAP)
23:15

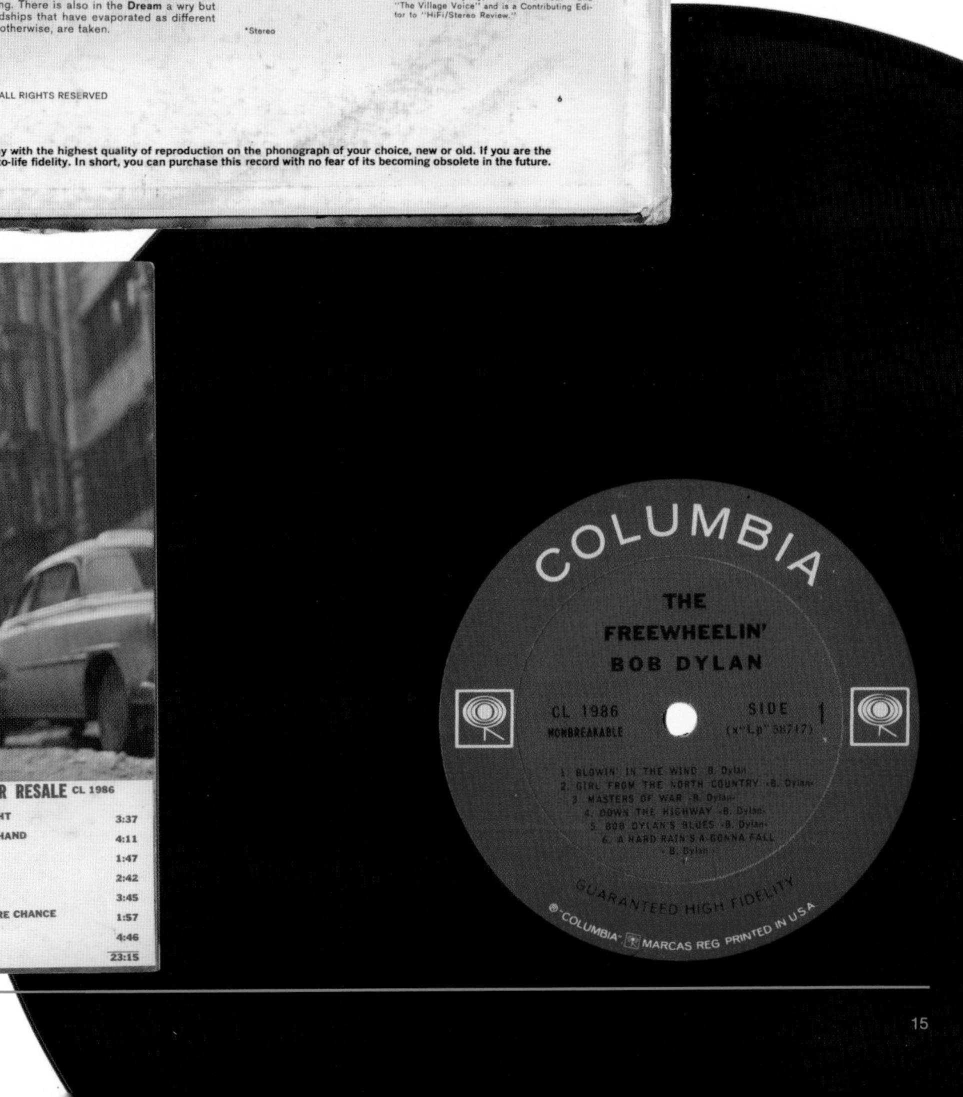
COLUMBIA
THE
FREEWHEELIN'
BOB DYLAN
CL 1986
NONBREAKABLE
SIDE 1
1. BLOWIN' IN THE WIND -B. Dylan
2. GIRL FROM THE NORTH COUNTRY -B. Dylan-
3. MASTERS OF WAR -B. Dylan-
4. DOWN THE HIGHWAY -B. Dylan-
5. BOB DYLAN'S BLUES -B. Dylan-
6. A HARD RAIN'S A-GONNA FALL
-B. Dylan-
GUARANTEED HIGH FIDELITY
® "COLUMBIA" MARCAS REG PRINTED IN U.S.A.

Mono copies of the rare version list correct song titles on the labels; stereo copies list the rare tracks. Only discs that actually play the rare tracks are valuable.

A promotional copy which lists the rare tracks, but plays the regular ones.

mono LK 4605

DECCA

THE ROLLING STONES | The Rolling Stones

April 1964 | Decca

Nearly fifty years on, Beatles versus Stones arguments seem like relics from a battlefield no one can quite locate anymore. And yet they hold some truth, for the Rolling Stones are, both by original intent and savvy brand embellishment, the first anti-pop band. Their debut LP provides only slight glimpses of what the Stones would become ("Tell Me" and "Little by Little" are the group's sole originals), but it does reveal much about who they thought they were: aspiring blues and soul men who dared to dream of being Muddy Waters, Bo Diddley and Jimmy Reed. Their relative failure to match the authenticity of their idols—they were only 4,000 miles, a culture and a generation removed from the source—nonetheless enabled them to invent something entirely their own. This is the most energetic and galvanizing rock 'n' roll since the '50s, including the radical makeover of the role of front-man and the whole idea of what a rock band could be. On

The Rolling Stones, the group isn't out to "please please" us. Their "I Just Want to Make Love to You" borders on the unhinged, and their "Carol" cuts Chuck Berry's original. In addition to establishing them as a major musical and cultural institution, the Stones' arrival chalks up two other achievements, one intended, the other purely accidental. It introduces pop-music audiences to the rich legacy of vintage black music (along the way revitalizing the careers of many of the band's heroes), and it inspires legions of young musicians to dream of being the Rolling Stones, thereby inventing garage and first-generation punk-rock.

The ROLLING STONES are more than just a group—they are a way of life. A way of life that has captured the imagination of the nation's teenagers, and made them one of the most sought after groups in Beatdom. For the Stones have their fingers on the pulse of the basic premise of "pop" music success—that its public buys sound, and the sound is what they give you with this their first album; a raw, exciting basic approach to Rhythm and Blues which, blended with their five own explosive characters, has given them three smash hits and an E.P. that stayed in the single charts for fifteen weeks. In the eight months since the Stones embarked on their pop career, they have not only chalked up major chart successes, but smashed attendance records on tours the length and breadth of the country. They have emerged as five well rounded intelligent talents, who will journey successfully far beyond the realms of pop music. And in this album there are twelve good reasons why.

Andrew Loog Oldham.

DECCA   MONO
LK 4605

Regd. Trade Mark
THE DECCA RECORD COMPANY LIMITED, LONDON, ENGLAND
© 1964, The Decca Record Company Limited, London

SIDE ONE
ROUTE 66 (Troup)
I JUST WANNA MAKE LOVE TO YOU (Dixon)
HONEST I DO (Hurran, Calvert)
MONA (McDaniels)
NOW I'VE GOT A WITNESS (Like Uncle Gene and Uncle Phil) (Phelge)
LITTLE BY LITTLE (Phelge, Spector)

SIDE TWO
I'M A KING BEE (Moore)
CAROL (Berry)
TELL ME (You're Coming Back) (Jagger, Richard)
CAN I GET A WITNESS (E. & B. Holland, Dozier)
YOU CAN MAKE IT YOU TRY (Jarrett)
WALKING THE DOG (Thomas)

Gene Pitney plays piano and Phil Spector maracas on *Little by Little*.
Ian Stewart plays piano on *Tell me, Can't I get a witness* and organ on *Now I've got a witness, You can make it*.

Cover photography by Nicholas Wright
Arrangements by the Rolling Stones
Produced by Andrew Loog Oldham and Eric Easton for Impact Sound Studio, Regent Sound, London.

THE ROLLING STONES

MICK JAGGER *Vocals and harmonica*   BRIAN JONES *Guitar, harmonica and vocals*   BILL WYMAN *Bass guitar and vocals*   CHARLIE WATTS *Drums*   KEITH RICHARD *Guitar*

Laminated with 'Claritfoil' made by British Celanese Limited   Printed in England by MacNeill Press, London, S.E.1.

The earliest copies mistakenly listed "I Need You Baby" as "Mona" on the back cover and record label.

London Records, the Stones U.S. label, added the title "England's Newest Hitmakers."

The earliest copies of The Rolling Stones mistakenly included a 2:52 demo version of "Tell Me," instead of the finished 4:06 version. These are highly collectible.

ENGLAND'S NEWEST HIT MAKERS
THE ROLLING STONES
LONDON ffrr
FREE full color photo
THE ROLLING STONES
inside
LL 3375 MONO

MONO-CL 2193
COLUMBIA

Another side of Bob Dylan

All I Really Want To Do
Black Crow Blues
Spanish Harlem Incident
Chimes Of Freedom
I Shall Be Free No. 10
To Ramona
Motorpsycho Nitemare
My Back Pages
I Don't Believe You
Ballad In Plain D
It Ain't Me Babe

GUARANTEED HIGH FIDELITY

CL 2193

BOB DYLAN | Another Side of Bob Dylan   **August 1964 | Columbia**

As swiftly as he transformed himself from the folk-blues interpreter of his debut LP to the most eloquent and forceful voice of protest music on *The Freewheelin' Bob Dylan*, Dylan leapt onto an even faster, potentially riskier freight on *Another Side*. He abandoned the politically-charged material that had been his calling card to dive deep into personal reflections on the vagaries of romance and whatever else piqued his interest. Against howls of anger from early fans who felt suddenly betrayed, *Another Side* connected him to a whole new listenership, as pop acts perked up to the presence of his unique, yet highly accessible, new material. "It Ain't Me Babe" was a hit for the Turtles, "All I Really Want to Do" was a hit for Cher. The Byrds also snagged the latter tune, plus "Chimes of Freedom" and "Spanish Harlem Incident" for their first album and, later, "My Back Pages." That song suggested that, at just 23, Dylan wasn't just perfecting his craft. He was developing a perspective on his own work that by all rights should

have been the exclusive province of much older artists. *Another Side* is a critical work in that it marks his transition from a figure who was principally seen as a songwriter to one who, with the release of *Bringing It All Back Home* barely six months later, would be viewed as a recording artist—and a hit-making one at that.

Some other kinds of songs...

Poems by Bob Dylan

PRODUCED BY
TOM WILSON

baby black's
been had
aint bad
smokestacked
chicken shacked
dressed in black
silver monkey
on her back
mammy ma
juiced pa
janitored
between the law
brothers ten
rat-faced
gravestoned
ditch dug
firescaped an substroked
choked
baby black
hits above
robs. pawns
lives by trade
sits an waits on fire plug
digs the heat
eyes meet
picket line
across the street
head rings
of bed springs
freedom's holler
you ask of order
she'd hock
the world
for a dollar an a quarter
baby black
dressed in black
gunny sack
about t crack
been gone
carry on
i'm givin you
myself t pawn

* * *

for françoise hardy
at the seine's edge
a giant shadow
of notre dame
seeks t grab my foot
sorbonne students
whirl by on thin bicycles
swirlin' lifelike colors of leather spin
the breeze yawns food
far from the bellies
of erhardt meetin johnson
piles of lovers
fishing
kissing
lay themselves on their books. boats.
old men
clothed in curly mustaches
float on the benches
blankets of tourists
in bright red nylon shirts
with straw hats of ambassadors
(cannot hear nixon's
dawg bark now)
will sail away
as the sun goes down
the doors of the river are open
i must remember that
i too play the guitar
it's easy t stand here
more lovers pass
on motorcycles
roped together
from the walls of the water then
i look across t what they call
the right bank
an envy
your
trumpet
player

* * *

"i could make you crawl
if i was payin attention"
he said munchin a sandwich
inbetween chess moves
"what d you wanna make
me crawl for?"
"i mean i just could"
"could make you crawl"
"yeah, make you crawl!"
"humm, funny guy you are"
"no, i just play t win,
that's all"
"well if you cant win me,
then you're the worst player
i ever played"

"what d you mean?"
"i mean i lose all the time"
his jaw tightened an he took
a deep breath
"humm, now i gotta beat you"

straight away an into the ring
juno takes twenty pills an
paints all day. life he says
is a head kinda thing. outside
of chicago, private come down
junkie nurse home heals countless
common housewives strung out
fully on drugstore dope, legally
sold t help clean the kitchen.
lenny bruce shows his seventh
avenue hand made movies, while a
bunch of women sneak little white
tablets into shoes, stockings, hats
an other hidin places. newspapers
tell earlier. irma goes t israel
an writes me that there, they
hate nazis much more n we over here
do. eichmann dies yes, an west
germany sends eighty year old
pruned out gestapo hermit off t
the penitentiary. in east berlin
renata tells me that i must wear
tie t get in t this certain place
i wanna go. back here, literate
old man with rebel flag above
home sweet home sign says he wont
vote for goldwater. "talks too
much. should keep his mouth shut"

i walk between back yards an see
little boy with feather in his hair
lyin dead on the grass. he gets
up an hands feather t another
little boy who immediately falls
down. "it's my turn t be the good
guy . . . take that, redskin" bang bang.
henry miller stands on other side
of ping pong table an keeps
talkin about me. "did you ask
the poet fellow if he wants
something t drink" he says t
someone gettin all the drinks.
i drop my ping pong paddle
an look at the pool. my worst
enemies dont even put me down
in such a mysterious way.
college student trails me with
microphone an tape machine.
what d you think a communist
party? what communist party?
he rattles off names an numbers.
he cant answer my question. he
tries harder. i say 'you dont
have t answer my question" he
gets all squishy. i say
there's no answer t my question
any more n there's an answer t
your question. ferris wheel runs
in california park an the sky trembles.
turns red. above hiccups an pointed
fingers. i tell reporter lady that yes
i'm monstrously against the house
unamerican activities committee
an also the cia an i beg her please
not t ask me why for it would take
too long t tell she asks me about
humanity an i say i'm not sure
i say what that word means. she wants me
t say what she wants me t say. she
wants me t say what she
can understand. a loose tempered fat
man in borrowed stomach slams wife
in the face an rushes off t civil
rights meeting, while some strange
girl chases me up smoky mountain
tryin t find out what sign i am.
i take allen ginsberg t meet fantastic
great beautiful artist an no trespassin

boards block up all there is t see.
eviction. infection gangrene an
atom bombs. both ends exist only
because there is someone who wants
profit. boy loses eyesight, becomes
airplane pilot. people pound their
chests an other people's chests an
interpret bibles t suit their own
means. respect is just a misinterpreted word
an if Jesus Christ, himself, came
down thru these streets, Christianity
would start all over again. standin
on the stage of all ground, insects
play in their own world. snakes
slide thru the weeds. ants come an
go thru the grass. turtles an lizards
make their way thru the sand. everything
crawls. everything. . . .
an everything still crawls

* * *

jack o' diamonds
jack o' diamonds
one eyed knave
on the move
hits the street
sneaks. leeps

between pillars of chips
springs on them like samson
thumps thumps
strikes
is on the prowl
you'll only lose
shouldnt stay
jack o' diamonds
is a hard t play

jack o' diamonds
wrecked my hand
left me here t stand
little tin men play
their drums now
upside my head
in the midst of cheers
flowers
four queens
with pawed out hearts
make make believe
they're stull good
but i should drop
fold
an dean martin should apologize
t the rolling stones
ho hum
wierd tablestakes
young babies horseback ride
their fathers' necks
two dudes in hopped up ford
for the tenth time
have rolled thru town
its your turn baby t
cut the deck
on you're goin under
stayed too long
chinese gong
down the way
says jack o' diamonds
(a high card)
jack o' diamonds
(but ain't high enough)

jack o' diamonds
is a hard card t play

jack o' diamonds used t laugh at me
now wants t collect from me
used t be ashamed of me
now wants t walk long side of me
jack o' diamonds
one armed prince
wears but a single glove
as he shoves
never loves
the moon's too bright
as he's fixed mirrors
round the room at nite
it's hard t think
there's probably somethin
in my drink
should pour it out
inside the sink
would throw it in his lap
but it'd do no good
give no pain
just leave a stain
jack o' diamonds
an all his crap
needs some acid
in his lap
what hour now
it feels late somehow
my hounddog plays
need more ashtrays
i cant even remember
the early days
please dont stay
gather your bells an go
jack o' diamonds
(can open for riches)
jack o' diamonds
(but then it switches)
a colorful picture but
beats only the ten
jack o' diamonds
is a hard card t play

(swingin wanda's
down in new orleans
rumbles across
brick written
swear word
vulgar wall
in new york city)

no they cant make it
off the banks of their river
i am in their river
(i wonder if he jumped
i really wonder if he jumped)
i turn corner
t get off river
an get off river
still goin up
i about face
an discover
that i'm on another river
(this time, king rex

jack o' diamonds
(a king's death)
jack o' diamonds
(at the ace's breath)
jack o' diamonds
is a hard card t play

* * *

run go get out of here
quick
leave joshua
split
go fit your battle
do your thing
i lost my glasses
cant see jerico
the wind is tyin knots
in my hair
nothin sneems
t be straight
out there
no i shant go with you
i cant go with you

on the brooklyn bridge
he was cockeyed
an stood on the edge
there was a priest talkin to him
i was shiftin myself around
so i could see from all sides
in an out of stretched necks
an things
cops held people back
the lady in back of me
burst into my groin
"sick sick some are so sick"
like a circus trapeze act
"oh i hope he dont do it"
he was on the other side of the railin
both eyes fiery wide
wet with sweat
the mouth of a shark
rolled up soiled sleeves
his arms were thick an tattoed
an he wore a silver watch
i could tell at a glance
he was uselessly lonely
i couldnt stay an look at him
i couldnt stay an look at him
because i suddenly realized that
deep in my heart
i really wanted
t see him jump

(a mob. each member knowin
that they all know an see the same thing
they have the same thing in common.
can stare at each other in total blankness
they do not have t speak an not feel guilty
about havin nothin t say. everyday boredom
soaked by the temporary happiness
of 'that their search is finally over
for findin a way t communicate' a leech cookout
giant cop out. all mobs i would think.
an i was in it an caught by the excitement of it)

an i walked away
i wanted t see him jump so bad
that i had t walk away an hide
uptown uptown
orchard street
thru all those people on
orchard street
pants' legs in my face
"comere! comere!"
i don't need no clothes
an cross the street
skull caps climb
by themselves out of manholes
an shoeboxes into
the cracks of the sidewalk
fishermen—
i've suddenly been turned into
a fish
but does anybody
wanna be a fisherman
any more 'n i
dont wanna be a fish

blesses me with plastic beads
a toot toot whistles
paper rings an things.
royal street
bourbon street
st. claude an esplanade
pass an pull
everything out of shape
joe b. stuart
white southern poet
holds me up
we charge thru casa
blazin jukebox
gumbo overflowin
get kicked out of colored bar
streets jammed
hypnotic stars explode
in louisiana murder nite
everything's wedged
arm in arm
stoned galore
must see you in mobile then
down governor nichel
an gone)

ok i can get off this river too
on bleeker street
i meet many friends
who look at me
as if they know something
i dont know

rocco an his brothers
say that some people
are worse hung up than me
i dont wanna hear it
a basketball drops thru
the hoop
an i recall that the
living theater's been busted

(has the guy jumped yet?)
intellectual spiders
weave down sixth avenue
with colt forty fives
stickin out of their
belly buttons
an for the first time
in my life
i'm proud that
i havent read into
any masterpiece books
(an why did i wanna see that
poor soul so dead?)

first of all two people get
together an they want their doors
enlarged. second of all, more
people see what's happenin an
come t help with the door
enlargement. the ones that arrive
however have nothin more than
"let's get these doors enlarged"
t say t the ones who were
there in the first place. it follows then that
the whole thing revolves around
nothing but this door enlargement idea.
third of all, there's a group now existin
an the only thing that keeps them friends
is that they all want the doors enlarged.
obviously, the doors're then enlarged
fourth of all,
after this enlargement
the group has t find
something else t keep
them together or
else the door enlargement
will prove t be
embarrassing

on fourteenth street
i meet someone
who i know in front
wants t put me
up tight
wants me t be on
his level
in all honesty
he wants t drag
me down there
i realize gravity
is my only enemy
loneliness has clutched
hands an squeezes you
into wrongin others
everybody has t do things
keep themselves occupied
the workin ones
have their minds on
the weekends
victims of the systerg
pack movie theaters
an who do of what
sadistic company is he
from that has the right
t condemn others as trivial
whose fault
an who really is t blame
for one man carryin a gun
that is impossible that
it's him

slaves are of no special color
an the links of chains
fall into no special order
how good an actor do you have to be
an play God

(in greece, a little old lady
a worker lady
looks at me
rubs her chin
an by sign language asks
how come i'm so unshaven
"the sea is very beautiful here"

i reply
pointin t my chin.
an she believes me
needs no other answer
i strum the guitar
she dances
laughs
her bandana flies
i too realize that
she will die here
on the side of this sea
her death is certain here
my death is unknown
an i come t think that
i love her)

i talk t people everyday
involved in some scene
good an evil are but words
invented by those
that are trapped in scenes

on what grounds are the
grounds for judgment
an i think also
that there is not
one thing anyplace
anywhere that makes any
sense. there are only tears
an there is only sorrow
there are no problems

i have seen what i've loved
slip away an vanish. i still
love what i've lost but i run
an try t catch it'd
be very greedy
for the rest of my life
i will never chase a livin soul
into the prison grasp
of my own self love

i cant believe that i have
t hate anybody
an when i do
it will only be out of fear
an i'll know it

i know no answers an no truth
for absolutely no soul alive
i will listen t no one
who tells me morals
there are no morals
an i dream alot

so go joshua
go fit your battle
i have t go t the woods
for awhile
i hope you understand
but if you dont
it doesnt matter
i will be with you
nex time around
dont think about me
i'll be ok
just go ahead out there
right out front
do what you say
you're gonna do
an who knows
someday
someone might even
write
     a song
          about you

Thank you t Bernard,
Marylou, Jean Pierre,
Gerard Philip an Monique
for the use of their house.

—BOB DYLAN

THE SELECTIONS—PUBLISHED BY M. WITMARK & SONS (ASCAP)—ARE FOLLOWED BY THEIR TIMINGS

SIDE I		SIDE II	
ALL I REALLY WANT TO DO	4:02	MOTORPSYCHO NITEMARE	4:31
BLACK CROW BLUES	3:12	MY BACK PAGES	4:20
SPANISH HARLEM INCIDENT	2:22	I DON'T BELIEVE YOU	4:20
CHIMES OF FREEDOM	7:09	BALLAD IN PLAIN D.	8:15
I SHALL BE FREE—No. 10	4:45	IT AIN'T ME BABE	3:30
TO RAMONA	3:50		

COVER PHOTO: SANDY SPEISER

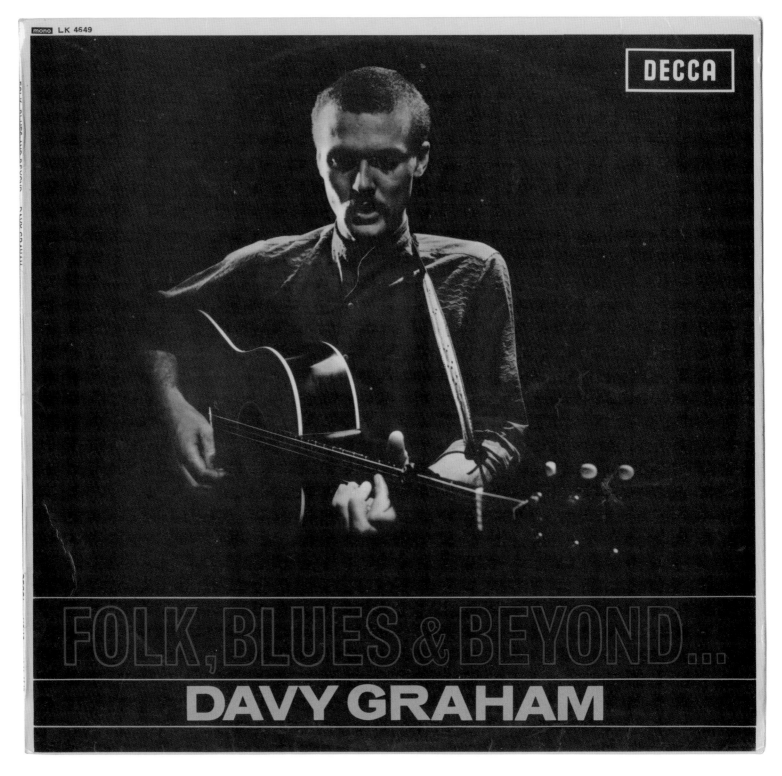

mono LK 4649

DECCA

FOLK, BLUES & BEYOND...

DAVY GRAHAM

DAVY GRAHAM | Folk Blues & Beyond...

January 1965 | Decca

Not only does the guitarist-singer's second solo album qualify as the true starting point of modern British folk music, it also creates the folk-instrumental genre, placing the late Graham on a par with American original John Fahey. *Folk, Blues and Beyond* wasn't just a groundbreaking record for the liberties Graham took with traditional forms, but also for the influence it exerted on a generation of guitarists; among them Bert Jansch, Jimmy Page, Eric Clapton, Nick Drake and Paul Simon (who covered Graham's "Anji" on *The Sounds of Silence* LP). Graham's unique tuning, which he termed "DADGAD," partly explains his appeal to other players, but non-musicians responded just as enthusiastically to his unbridled imagination and willingness to take such material as Leadbelly's "Leavin' Blues," the pianist Bobby Timmons' "Moanin'" and the Broadway-musical hit "Ballad of the Sad Young Men" to places they hadn't previously visited.

Graham's vocals are both warmly personal and coolly understated on "Cocaine" and "I Can't Keep From Cryin' Sometimes," and his playing throughout the album, supported by acoustic bass and subtle drumming, meshes jazz freedom and eclectic sources with a strong melodic sense. It's likely that *Folk, Blues and Beyond* will inspire and instruct musicians for a long time to come.

FOLK, BLUES & BEYOND...

**MONO
LK 4649**

DAVY GRAHAM

Ulysses was probably a restless man. After having fought against and finally conquered (by a trick) the city of Troy, he had a tough time getting back to his native land. And yet, reading between Homer's solemn, measured lines, one senses that the wily king actually *enjoyed* the many shipwrecks and chance adventures this involved. In fact, it is easy to understand the later portrait of him in Kazantzakis' Sequel to "The Odyssey"; a portrait of the man becoming bored with life as ruler of a small Greek kingdom and no more Trojans to fight against. Finally, he abdicates in favour of his son, kisses the ever-faithful Penelope "good-bye" and sets off in search of new adventures—which take him down to the Antarctic...

The Ulysses-type is always with us. Intelligent, but footloose and full of curiosity about a wide variety of *things,* insatiable for all the experiences of living: we meet him constantly at every level of society. However, the patterns of this twentieth century and its increasingly autonomised existence have made it very difficult for the Ulysses-type to be one in reality—and this is where an obsessive frustration creeps in.

Happily, both for himself and for his music, Davy Graham is a Ulysses-type without the frustration. A traveller (by compulsion), a panderer to his own curiosity and a natural musician with no particular problems of expression, he impresses one as being both intense and sincere in all these things. Certainly he is one of the more extraordinary artists that the world of folk has produced: the most *original* young guitarist in Europe, a gifted, natural arranger and a singer who sings as he feels. Moreover, he is too large a personality for the folk scene to entirely contain, although he is one of its favourite sons. By this, I mean that Davy is constantly drawing other musical forms into his own orbit: blues, modern jazz, Indian or Arabic forms, and so on. All have joined the basic folk repertoire he began with, colouring his overall output in a quite remarkable way. And because he is a traveller and curious and a musician, he is still collecting new ideas. (It's interesting to note that immediately after the sessions which resulted in this album, Davy began to plan a visit to Persia. One can pleasurably anticipate the results!)

Davy was born in England in 1940. His father, a Scot (from the Isle of Skye), taught Gaelic, was an amateur singer and—so Davy tells me—a considerable athlete. His mother is from Georgetown, British Guiana—and from her he inherits slight oriental and American Indian traces. He grew up mainly in England, and it was at a Kensington lycée that he suffered the accident which left him with only twenty per cent vision in his right eye. Since school he has lived only the itinerant musician's life...

At first, this life meant singing in cafés or for cinema queues. Later, as he became better known, it led to work in the London clubs (folk or smart-set diners), television and appearances at the Edinburgh Festival. And each year he travels...to some place that arouses his curiosity and offers the possibility of acquiring new musical ideas. In Paris he played for Elizabeth Taylor as well as spending four separate nights in jail for street-singing. Between Fréjus and St. Maxime he thumbed a lift on a camel; the result being that he prefers air-travel these days! In Malaga he rented an expensive apartment overlooking the Mediterranean until his money ran out, then moved to a cheap room in the Moorish part and sang for his suppers. In Tangier he worked for six months in a 'hole in the wall' eating-place whose speciality was a sweet, sticky cake flavoured with hashish.

Influences? A difficult one to answer, because apart from the guitar, he plays banjo, string-bass and harmonica (all with reasonable proficiency) and is tremendously enthusiastic about good drummers and every kind of rhythm. On the folk side, he likes Jack Elliott, Darrell Adams and Bob Dylan. From the blues and rhythm-and-blues areas, Leadbelly (his first influence, according to Davy), Bill Broonzy, Robert Johnson, King Solomon Hill and Howlin' Wolf. The first jazz musician he admired was Charlie Parker, but the strongest influences appear to come from Thelonious Monk and Mingus. In addition to these, he likes girl gospel groups, Mary Wells, flamenco (cante hondo) and fado, Indian sitars and sarodes, Rimsky-Korsakov, Miles Davis' modal pieces, Arabic compositions and Elizabethan lute music. (Also, incidentally, he studies the Koran and reads Henry Miller.)

RAY HORRICKS

© 1964, *The Decca Record Company Limited, London.*

Cover photography: Crispian Woodgate

Regd. Trade Mark
THE DECCA RECORD COMPANY LTD., LONDON.

Printed in England by Clout & Baker Ltd.
Laminated with 'Clarifoil' made by British Celanese Limited

Side One

1. **LEAVIN' BLUES**
   A Leadbelly composition. In Davy's version it has travelled via India on its way from Louisiana to London.
2. **COCAINE**
   The sick junkie's call for love (or pity!). Davy first heard it when Jack Elliott visited England.
3. **SALLY FREE AND EASY**
   A sailor's love-lament by Plymouth ex-sailor and singer Cyril Tawney.
4. **BLACK IS THE COLOUR OF MY TRUE LOVE'S HAIR**
   A folk song, originally from Norway.
5. **ROCK ME BABY**
   By Bill Broonzy. Davy picked it up from Alexis Korner, the pioneer of R & B in England.
6. **SEVEN GYPSIES**
   An English song, descended from *Raggle-Taggle Gypsies-O*.
7. **BALLAD OF THE SAD YOUNG MEN**
   From an off-Broadway show, *The Nervous Set*, by Landesman and Wolf. Davy sings only the first verse and chorus, which he thinks explains the dilemma of many young people.
8. Play-out piece: **MOANIN'**
   A Bobby Timmons composition with a very churchy feel.

Side Two

1. **SKILLET (GOOD 'N GREASY)**
   The song of a happy man. Originally learned from a banjo player who claimed it came from the Appalachian mountains.
2. **AIN'T NOBODY'S BUSINESS WHAT I DO**
   Davy says "In my lyrics, I've chosen to bring out the loneliness side of the song".
3. Guitar Solo: **MAAJUN (A Taste Of Tangier)**
   Davy plays a melody he found in Tangier.
4. **I CAN'T KEEP FROM CRYING SOMETIMES**
   A song by Blind Willie Johnson, the gospel growler.
5. **DON'T THINK TWICE, IT'S ALL RIGHT**
   Davy's favourite Bob Dylan composition. "I think Dylan must have lived all the words", he says.
6. **MY BABE**
   A well-known blues tune, to which Davy has added a Chico Hamilton-ish rhythmic feel.
7. **GOIN' DOWN SLOW**
   Davy's favourite blues number, learnt from Champion Jack Dupree.
8. Play-out piece: **BETTER GIT IN YOUR SOUL**
   A modern blues in 6/8 time by Charles Mingus.

Producer: RAY HORRICKS
Recording Engineer: GUS DUDGEON

mono LK 4700

DECCA

THEM | The Angry Young Them **June 1965 | Decca** 🇬🇧

Few debut albums manage such double-threat introductions as *The Angry Young Them*. The 1965 LP by the Belfast bluesmen not only officially announced the arrival of one of the modern era's most significant writer-performers in Van Morrison. It also unleashed the nascent strain of '60s garage-rock on an unsuspecting world in the near-psychotic raver, "Mystic Eyes," and the salacious, now venerable, punk anthem "Gloria"—the song that launched a thousand bands. Snarling and possessed, Morrison and his bandmates' performances out-tough the Stones vocally and instrumentally (compare their respective versions of "Route 66") and restore primitiveness to its rightful place: at the dead center of rock 'n' roll. The album's sustained intensity intimates something combustible at the band's core, as if it were bound to blow up after this brief shining moment. Following the sophomore set, *Them Again*, it did just that.

The "Angry" Young THEM !

This is a long playing record by "THEM".
No excuses...no highbrow explanations...no apologies, simply music and sounds that only THEM could produce. A collection of sounds and songs that mean a great deal to the artistes who poured their souls into the making of this L.P.
Of course they hope that you will like the sound — but the important thing is that when you play this L.P. you will be listening to the truth! Because these five young rebels are outrageously true to themselves. Defiant! Angry! Sad!
Reporters who try to interview them lament that they "don't care". Oh but they do!...they care about their music, they care about their fans, the people who appreciate their music. But above all, they are honest to the point of insult. When asked to produce a track that they considered "a pretty song", their answer was simply "NO! This is our music, you either like it or you don't". We think you will like it...

SIDE ONE
Track one expresses the sheer exuberance with which these boys got together. This number was intended simply as a non-vocal track — but on the session Van Morrison began to sing a few phrases towards the end — and suddenly the song came alive.
Van of course is not only the singer, he also plays harmonica and sax on some of these tracks. So alive and vibrant are the pure, basic thoughts that he writes, that it seems incredible that one man can have so much talent. His phrasing is so wonderful that in his hands even the most banal lyrics take on a new depth and meaning...and become touched with genius.
"JUST A LITTLE BIT" is of course one of the best R&B songs around today...this is THEM's new, modern version very unlike the predecessors.
A&R man, Tommy Scott, who produced most of the tracks on this album, enjoys working with THEM very much. "They have", he says, "a tremendous feel for this type of music, and I consider them to be the most individual group to emerge on the British scene."
"I GAVE MY LOVE A DIAMOND" was written by Bert Berns, who

wrote such hit songs as "Twist and Shout". He recorded THEM's first successful record, "Baby Please Don't Go", and followed this up with the dramatic "Here Comes The Night".
"GLORIA" was the 'B' side of "Baby Please Don't Go" and was released on its own merits in the States. It is without doubt an R&B standard of the future.
The final track on Side One, "YOU JUST CAN'T WIN" was also penned by Van Morrison. This is a contemporary blues set in London, lamenting a love lost to the "high life".
SIDE TWO
"GO ON HOME BABY" is a driving, up-tempo number, again written by Bert Berns.
John Lee Hooker, hailed as one of the greatest R&B singers in the world...the man behind the magic of "Boom Boom" and "Dimples", wrote "DON'T LOOK BACK". Perhaps it isn't so extraordinary that this soulful ballad sounds uncannily like a Van Morrison composition. Obviously, they have a great deal in common.
With "I LIKE IT LIKE THAT", Van again comes up with a superb rendering of his own composition.
"I'M GONNA DRESS IN BLACK" is once again a contemporary number comparable to the old Country Blues.
"BRIGHT LIGHTS, BIG CITY" introduces a song by Jimmy Reed ...since it was first written, "Bright Lights" has become an R&B classic.
"ROUTE 66" was recorded by the late, great Nat 'King' Cole. It loses none of it's impact on this track — although THEM have given it a very different tempo.
The boys' favourite track on this album is "IF YOU AND I COULD BE AS TWO". Of all the numbers that Van has written — this is his personal favourite.
A number of tracks on this L.P. were recorded by Tommy Scott, the brilliant young A&R man from Scotland. So this is probably a unique record in another sense...Irishmen, THEM, recorded by a Scot, "Tommy Scott", an American, Bert Berns, and an odd track by DICK ROWE, Head A&R man at Decca...and English.

© 1965, The Decca Record Company Limited, London.

SIDE ONE
1. MYSTIC EYES (Morrison)
2. IF YOU AND I COULD BE AS TWO (Morrison)
3. LITTLE GIRL (Morrison)
4. JUST A LITTLE BIT (Gordon)
5. I GAVE MY LOVE A DIAMOND (Berns) *
6. GLORIA (Morrison) †
7. YOU JUST CAN'T WIN (Morrison)

SIDE TWO
1. GO ON HOME BABY (Berns) *
2. DON'T LOOK BACK (Hooker)
3. I LIKE IT LIKE THAT (Morrison)
4. I'M GONNA DRESS IN BLACK (Gillon)
5. BRIGHT LIGHTS BIG CITY (Reed)
6. MY LITTLE BABY (Berns; Farrell) †
7. (Get Your Kicks On) ROUTE 66 (Troup)

Production of L.P. by Tommy Scott.
Except *Produced by Bert Berns. †Produced by Dick Rowe.

DECCA

THE DECCA RECORD COMPANY LTD., LONDON.

Laminated with 'Clarifoil' made by British Celanese Limited

Printed in England by James Upton Ltd. Birmingham & London.

THEM featuring HERE COMES THE NIGHT

Parrot

MONO

For the U.S. release, Parrot Records changed the cover and included the band name and the title of their first hit.

THE BYRDS | Mr. Tambourine Man

June 1965 | Columbia

Folk rock was invented on this record by the first and most persistent popularizers of Bob Dylan songs. Dense harmonies, electric 12-string and McGuinn's sibilant, semi-detached vocals place "Mr. Tambourine Man" and its 11 companion pieces among the most original pop music ever recorded. David Crosby would find greater fame with Stills & Nash, Chris Hillman would co-found the country-rock flagship Flying Burrito Brothers, and Gene Clark would become a respected writer-singer. Yet this album is where they all enter the major league—not just scoring hits ("Mr. Tambourine Man," "All I Really Want to Do")—but influencing everyone from the Beatles to Buffalo Springfield, Tom Petty and countless other artists over the decades. Nor did the Byrds' arrival just launch a thousand ships. It dramatically raised all boats by expanding the vocabulary of mid-'60s music beyond the Beatles' upbeat romanticism and the Stones' kinetic

blues—its modal chords and melancholy vocals projecting an offhanded, unsentimental coolness that, like the music of the Velvet Underground, seems eternally modern. Even now, more than 40 years later, the album's mix of Dylan (the title track and three others), folk-protest (Pete Seeger's "Bells of Rhymney"), pop (Jackie DeShannon's "Don't Doubt Yourself, Babe") and band originals ("I Knew I'd Want You") usher the listener into a world of captivating beauty and beautiful strangeness.

Produced by
Terry Melcher

Mr. Tambourine Man
THE BYRDS

CL 2372

MR. TAMBOURINE MAN
I'LL FEEL A WHOLE LOT BETTER
SPANISH HARLEM INCIDENT
YOU WON'T HAVE TO CRY
HERE WITHOUT YOU
THE BELLS OF RHYMNEY

ALL I REALLY WANT TO DO
I KNEW I'D WANT YOU
IT'S NO USE
DON'T DOUBT YOURSELF, BABE
CHIMES OF FREEDOM
WE'LL MEET AGAIN

BOB DYLAN VISITS THE BYRDS AT AN IN-PERSON PERFORMANCE: MIKE CLARK, DAVE CROSBY, GENE CLARK, DYLAN, CHRIS HILLMAN, JIM McGUINN.

Open Letter to a Friend:

Hey—have you heard The Byrds? Bob Dylan's **Mr. Tambourine Man** was their first Columbia single record, and it was a hit! (The way I got the story was that Dylan heard The Byrds' version, flipped and said nobody could do it as well, and they should record it.)

The Byrds are five guys who've been together for about eight months, but collectively have had years of experience. The leader of the group is Jim McGuinn, who toured for two years with The Chad Mitchell Trio and for a year with Bobby Darin when he had a folk act. McGuinn's done a bunch of other things, including writing and playing most of the arrangements for folk artists like Judy Collins.

David Crosby—who calls himself the "troublemaker" of the group because when he does this cute little smiling bit and crinkles his nose, the little girls flip—did the Macdougal Street thing for a while, and has been working as a solo singer-guitarist for five years.

Gene Clark played with The New Christy Minstrels for a little over a year and writes a lot. In a way, he's the foundation of the group: unruffled, with a kind of Grant Wood-ish, Bonner Springs, Kansas, background. Chris Hillman, who used to play a lot of Bluegrass mandolin, now plays bass guitar with the group. (I'm told he plays John Coltrane solos on the mandolin—does that wake you up?) Mike Clark, the drummer, is, well, he's Mike Clark—happy, dedicated, whose gods are drummers Joe Morello and Elvin Jones.

That's who they are, but what they are is special. Aside from singing Dylan's tunes better than anyone I've heard, they're taking the entire field in a new direction—and it's a direction that the public has been "burstingly" ready for: playing the new American music in an exciting way.

Leader McGuinn says: "What I'm doing now is a continuation of my love for music. Superficially, the form may have changed slightly, but the essence is the same. In other words, the harmonies—fourths, fifths—are the same, as well as the kinds of rhythms that are used and the chord changes. The instrumentation is changing somewhat to meet the nuclear expansion and jet age. I used to like folk music, just straight folk music without electric guitar, drums and bass. I think that although the folk instruments are changing, it's still folk music. Actually, you can call it whatever you like."

Of the English rock-and-roll groups he says: "They're a new package, a new presentation of music in which music finds a new form. Life is the same thing; it's just going through different manifestations—and music is life. We sent something over there and they're echoing it back to us with a slightly different flavor because they're different people. And now we can take what they gave us and echo it back to them with something else, another flavor added. There's an international music coming out;

it's kind of like halvah, you know, it has all these ingredients: it has Latin and blues and jazz flavors, Anglo-Saxon church music, Negro church music. It has a lot of different forms."

Of changing musical tastes Jim says: "I think the difference is in the mechanical sounds of our time. Like the sound of the airplane in the Forties was a rrrrrrrrooooooaaaaaaaahhhhhhhhh sound and Sinatra and other people sang like that with those sort of overtones. Now we've got the krrrriiiiiisssssssshhhhhhhh jet sound, and the kids are singing up in there now. It's the mechanical sounds of the era: the sounds are different and so the music is different. I trust everything will turn out all right."

I asked a couple of fans why they dug The Byrds. Here's one answer:

"They're bubbly and high and fast. They're rakish and raffish; there's a certain amount of irony in what they do; they're orange and green and yellow and near."

Got that? Here's another one:

"They play things no other group does. The music should have a strong beat, and the stronger the beat the stronger the emotions that can come out. Well, The Byrds play with a lot of emotion, but they do one more thing: they put true meaning across."

Their first nightclub appearance drew a rave review from "Daily Variety" which contained such Variety-ese as "Biz should perk once word is out, The Byrds, in for a week, are in full flight" and "At last—a rock 'n' roll group that's considerate of the listener as well as the gyrating, beat-happy terper."

The Byrds are a lot of things, with people filling in all kinds of reasons why they're special. The super-hippies find in them a perfect opportunity to trip out, to forget they're super-hippies. The folk singers flip because The Byrds have found a way to get to the beauty, the poetry, the love that's in the best of what's called folk—and they've found a way to get it onto Top Forty radio.

The rock-and-roll musicians—Major Lance, Little Richard, teentypes Sonny and Cher, and a few others—made it into Ciro's in Hollywood when The Byrds were there, and they dug that something new was happening. And Jackie De Shannon dug the way they did her tunes; Mary Travers was beautiful dancing to **Mr. Tambourine Man.** Judy Henske, Buffy Sainte-Marie, Barry McGuire and a bunch of other New Christy Minstrels all became Byrd watchers. Then there were Lloyd Thaxton, Mitch Reid (and Mitch was one of four disc jockeys who unanimously picked the **Mr. Tambourine Man** single on KFWB in Los Angeles), a great-looking chick named Mary Hughes and, of course, the "in" crowd's method-actor comer, Michael Pollard. And L. A.'s pop art crowd, too, and a flippy guy named Bobby Dale at KEWB in San Francisco, who was the first disc jockey in the country to play their single.

Art Seidenbaum did a piece on them in the Los Angeles *Times*, devoting most of the column to great descriptive prose on the

audience at Ciro's ("people who looked like they had just straggled out of Sherwood Forest"). His most significant line was: "But who can be sure what's happening?"

There's a young writer in Los Angeles who *is* sure. His name is Paul Jay Robbins and he contributes occasionally to the Los Angeles *Free Press*, a "Village Voice"-ish weekly. He wrote: "What The Byrds signify . . . is a concept deeply applied to unification and empathy and a rich joy of life—together with a positive recognition of the bulbous clusters of sickness around us. It represents a passing through negative apathy and an approach into involvement. . . . Dancing with The Byrds becomes a mystic loss of ego and tangibility; you become pure energy some place between sound and motion and the involvement is total." (Like the girl said, they're orange and green and yellow and near. Hmm.)

Besides **Mr. Tambourine Man,** the other Dylan tunes they do are **All I Really Want to Do, Chimes of Freedom** and **Spanish Harlem Incident.** Lately, when they do **Chimes** in a club, McGuinn announces: "We'd like to dedicate this next song to Donovan." **We'll Meet Again** they dedicate to Peter Sellers, Slim Pickens and Stanley Kubrick. **The Bells of Rhymney** is dedicated to Pete Seeger. Initially, you get a great shock hearing this song about a Welsh mine disaster being sung this way, as you watch a few dozen people doing the twistfrugwatusijerk and the endless, nameless variations. But soon you see how right it is as you see the words become the thoughts of people who would never have heard those words from any other source. Jackie De Shannon wrote **Don't Doubt Yourself, Babe.** Tunes in the album written by Gene Clark: **I'll Feel a Whole Lot Better, Here Without You. I Knew I'd Want You,** and in collaboration with Jim McGuinn: **You Won't Have to Cry** and **It's No Use.**

There's a new thing happening, and it probably started with Bob Dylan. He gave the audience a new vocabulary, a new set of symbols to fit the feelings exploding in and around them. The Byrds take his words and put them in the framework of the beat, and make imperative the meaning of those words. And there's an unseen drive, a soaring motion to their sound that makes it compelling, almost hypnotic sometimes. And when you listen, hear through the sound to the joy that propels it. I hope you enjoy the record and, as Jim McGuinn says, I trust everything will turn out all right.

Regards,

Billy Jones

The Byrds National Fan Club
Suite 805
9000 Sunset Boulevard
Los Angeles 69, California

5

THE SELECTIONS—TICKSON MUSIC CO. (BMI) EXCEPT WHERE NOTED—ARE FOLLOWED BY THEIR PUBLISHERS AND TIMINGS

SIDE I			SIDE II		
MR. TAMBOURINE MAN—M. Witmark & Sons (ASCAP)		2:20	ALL I REALLY WANT TO DO—M. Witmark & Sons (ASCAP)		2:02
I'LL FEEL A WHOLE LOT BETTER		2:31	I KNEW I'D WANT YOU		2:14
SPANISH HARLEM INCIDENT—M. Witmark & Sons (ASCAP)		1:58	IT'S NO USE		2:23
YOU WON'T HAVE TO CRY		2:07	DON'T DOUBT YOURSELF, BABE—Metric Music Co. (BMI)		2:46
HERE WITHOUT YOU		2:36	CHIMES OF FREEDOM—M. Witmark & Sons (ASCAP)		3:50
THE BELLS OF RHYMNEY—Ludlow Music, Inc. (BMI)		3:30	WE'LL MEET AGAIN—World Music, Inc. (ASCAP)		2:07

Cover photo: Barry Feinstein

® "COLUMBIA", ▥ MARCAS REG. PRINTED IN U.S.A.

COLUMBIA

MR. TAMBOURINE MAN
THE BYRDS

1. MR. TAMBOURINE MAN—Dylan

CS 9172   SIDE I
XSM 110187

2. I'LL FEEL A WHOLE LOT BETTER—G. Clark
3. SPANISH HARLEM INCIDENT—Dylan
4. YOU WON'T HAVE TO CRY
H. Clark-McGuinn
5. HERE WITHOUT YOU—G. Clark
6. THE BELLS OF RHYMNEY
Davies-Seeger

"360 SOUND" STEREO "360 SOUND"
® "COLUMBIA" ▥ MARCAS REG. PRINTED IN U.S.A.

BOB DYLAN | Highway 61 Revisited   **August 1965 | Columbia**

Less than five months earlier, *Bringing It All Back Home* had partially revealed Dylan's newly amplified style and invited scrutiny for its surreal cover and back-sleeve poetry. Here the roving gambler not only ups the ante but whips out a pistol to challenge anyone who might question his bets—which upend all accepted notions of song length and subject matter, interpretation and instrumentation (LP credits read "Bob Dylan: guitar, harmonica, piano and police car"). This is an album of uncompromising music, loud and spiteful from start to finish, perhaps no more so than on "Like a Rolling Stone," a single so unprecedented and singularly powerful that Top-40 radio was forced to play it in its six-minute entirety. Egged on by the fierce playing of guitarist Mike Bloomfield, organist Al Kooper and their cohorts, Dylan spits out many of the songs that would form

the cornerstone of his repertoire for years to come: "Ballad of a Thin Man," "Desolation Row," "Just Like Tom Thumb's Blues," "Highway 61 Revisited." Despite its brilliance, the album was but the opening act for what Dylan considered his masterwork, 1966's *Blonde on Blonde*. Like the music within, *Highway 61*'s cover photo confounded. Unstaged and oddly composed, it conferred additional mystery to the proceedings: What's with his hair? The Triumph Motorcycle shirt? The headless guy with the camera? Who knew?

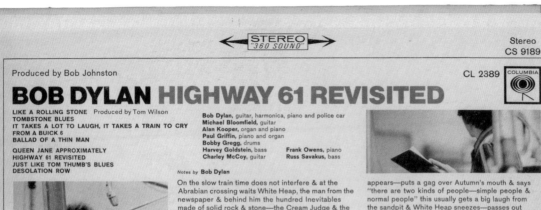

STEREO "360 SOUND"

Stereo
CS 9189

CL 2389 COLUMBIA

Produced by Bob Johnston

BOB DYLAN HIGHWAY 61 REVISITED

LIKE A ROLLING STONE   Produced by Tom Wilson
TOMBSTONE BLUES
IT TAKES A LOT TO LAUGH, IT TAKES A TRAIN TO CRY
FROM A BUICK 6
BALLAD OF A THIN MAN

QUEEN JANE APPROXIMATELY
HIGHWAY 61 REVISITED
JUST LIKE TOM THUMB'S BLUES
DESOLATION ROW

Bob Dylan, guitar, harmonica, piano and police car
Michael Bloomfield, guitar
Alan Kooper, organ and piano
Paul Griffin, piano and organ
Bobby Gregg, drums
Harvey Goldstein, bass   Frank Owens, piano
Charley McCoy, guitar   Russ Savakus, bass

Notes by Bob Dylan

On the slow train time does not interfere & at the Abrabian crossing waits White Heap, the man from the newspaper & behind him the hundred Inevitables made of solid rock & stone—the Cream Judge & the Clown—the doll house where Savage Rose & Fixable live simply in their wild animal luxury. . . . Autumn, with two zeros above her nose arguing over the sun being dark or Bach is as famous as its commotion & that she herself—not Orpheus—is the logical poet "I am the logical poet!" she screams "Spring? Spring is only the beginning!" she attempts to make Cream Judge jealous by telling him of down-to-earth people & while the universe is erupting, she points to the slow train & prays for rain and for time to interfere—she is not extremely fat but rather progressively unhappy. . . . the hundred Inevitables hide their predictions & go to bars & drink & get drunk in their very special conscious way & when tom dooley, the kind of person you think you've seen before, comes strolling in with White Heap, the hundred Inevitables all say "who's that man who looks so white?" & the bartender, a good boy & one who keeps a buffalo in his mind, says "I don't know, but I'm sure I've seen the other fellow someplace" & when Paul Sargent, a plainclothes man from 4th street, comes in at three in the morning & busts everybody for being incredible, nobody really gets angry—just a little illiterate most people get & Rome, one of the hundred Inevitables whispers "I told you so" to Madam John. . . . Savage Rose & Fixable are bravely blowing kisses to the Jade Hexagram-Carnaby Street & to all the mysterious juveniles & the Cream Judge is writing a book on the true meaning of a pear—last year, he wrote one on famous dogs of the civil war & now he has false teeth & no children. . . . when the Cream met Savage Rose & Fixable, he was introduced to them by none other than Lifelessness—Lifelessness is the Great Enemy & always wears a hip guard—he is very hipguard. . . . Lifelessness said when introducing everybody "go save the world" & "involvement! that's the issue" & things like that & Savage Rose winked at Fixable & the Cream went off with his arm in a sling singing "summertime & the Livin is easy". . . . the Clown

appears—puts a gag over Autumn's mouth & says "there are two kinds of people—simple people & normal people" this usually gets a big laugh from the sandpit & White Heap sneezes—passes out & rips open Autumn's gag & says "What do you mean youre Autumn and without you there'd be no spring! you fool! without spring, there'd be no you! what do you think of that???." then Savage Rose & Fixable come by & kick him in the brains & color him pink for being a phony philosopher—then the Clown comes by and screams "You phony philosopher!" & jumps on his head—Paul Sargent comes by again in an umpire's suit & some college kid who's read all about Nietzsche comes by & says "Nietzsche never wore an umpire's suit" & Paul says "You wanna buy some clothes, kid?" & then Rome & John come out of the bar & they're going up to Harlem. . . . we are singing today of the WIPE-OUT GANG—the WIPE-OUT GANG buys, owns & operates the Insanity Factory—if you do not know where the Insanity Factory is located, you should hereby take two steps to the right, paint your teeth & go to sleep . . . . the songs on this specific record are not so much songs but rather exercises in tonal breath control. . . . the subject matter—tho meaningful as it is—has something to do with the beautiful strangers . . . . the beautiful strangers, Vivaldi's green jacket & the holy slow train

you are right john cohen—quazimodo was right—mozart was right . . . . I cannot say the word eye any more . . . . when I speak this word eye, it is as if I am speaking of somebody's eye that I faintly remember . . . . there is no eye—there is only a series of mouths—long live the mouths—your rooftop —if you don't already know—has been demolished . . . . eye is plasma & you are right about that too—you are lucky—you don't have to think about such things as eyes & rooftops & quazimodo.
                                            © Bob Dylan 1965/All rights reserved.

Other albums by Bob Dylan you will enjoy:
Bringing It All Back Home . . . CL 2328/CS 9128*
Another Side of Bob Dylan . . . CL 2193/CS 8993*
The Times They Are A-Changin' . . . CL 2105/CS 8905*
                                                            *Stereo

SIDE I	LIKE A ROLLING STONE	THE SELECTIONS—M. WITMARK & SONS (ASCAP)—ARE FOLLOWED BY THEIR TIMINGS	SIDE II	QUEEN JANE APPROXIMATELY	4:57
	LIKE A ROLLING STONE	5:59		QUEEN JANE APPROXIMATELY	4:57
	TOMBSTONE BLUES	5:53		HIGHWAY 61 REVISITED	3:15
	IT TAKES A LOT TO LAUGH, IT TAKES A TRAIN TO CRY	3:25		JUST LIKE TOM THUMB'S BLUES	5:08
	FROM A BUICK 6	3:06		DESOLATION ROW	11:18
	BALLAD OF A THIN MAN	5:48			

Cover photo: Daniel Kramer   5   ® "COLUMBIA" MARCAS REG. PRINTED IN U.S.A.

COLUMBIA

BOB DYLAN
HIGHWAY 61 REVISITED

RADIO STATION COPY · NOT FOR RESALE

CL 2389   SIDE 1
               XLP 110638

1. LIKE A ROLLING STONE 5:59
2. TOMBSTONE BLUES 5:53
3. IT TAKES A LOT TO LAUGH, IT TAKES
   A TRAIN TO CRY 3:25
4. FROM A BUICK 6 3:06
5. BALLAD OF A THIN MAN 5:48

® "COLUMBIA". MARCAS REG. PRINTED IN U.S.A.

The earliest copies included this "Striking portrait suitable for framing."

This rare white label promotional copy was made for radio stations.

The bold colors, stenciled graphics, and bassist John Entwhistle's Union Jack jacket telegraph the band's pop art approach.

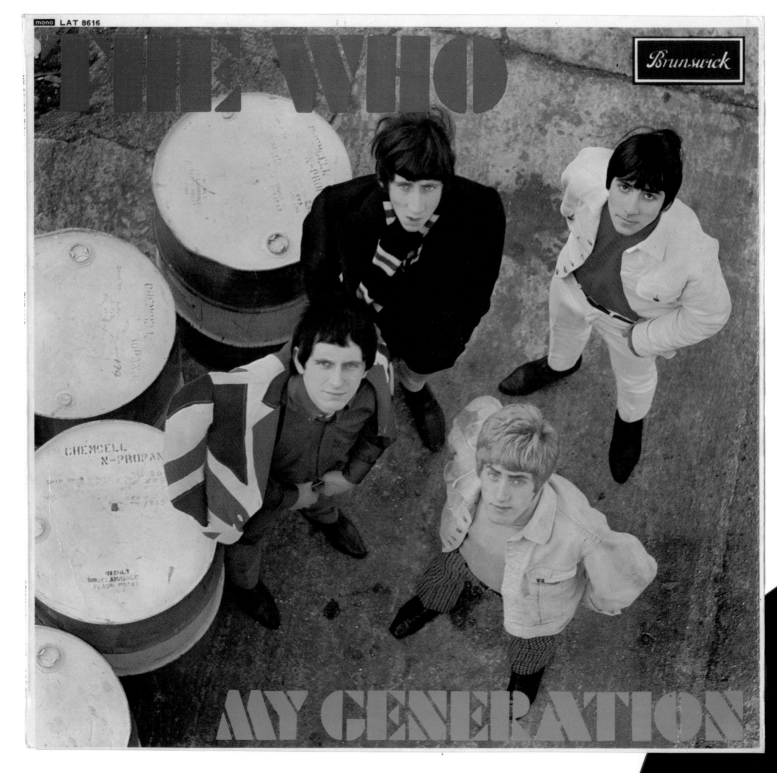

THE WHO | My Generation

December 1965 | Brunswick

One of the louder, more significant splashes of the later British Invasion, The Who's debut put into play several elements that would define rock throughout the '60s and '70s. Sporting the first pop-art cover sleeve, *My Generation* bristles with energy, Keith Moon's drumming and Pete Townshend's slashing, distortion-drenched guitar work unleashing a barely contained instrumental style that virtually battles Roger Daltrey's vocals for center stage. If the program is all over the map—the Townshend pop gems "Circles," "A Legal Matter," James Brown and Bo Diddley covers, the group

instrumental "The Ox"— the band's aggressive performance bashes it into something resembling a coherent LP. The presentation of Townshend as a fully-formed songwriter may not even be the record's crowning achievement; the title track and "The Kids Are Alright" represent the first serious acknowledgment of a generational consciousness, without which the '60s could not have become The Sixties.

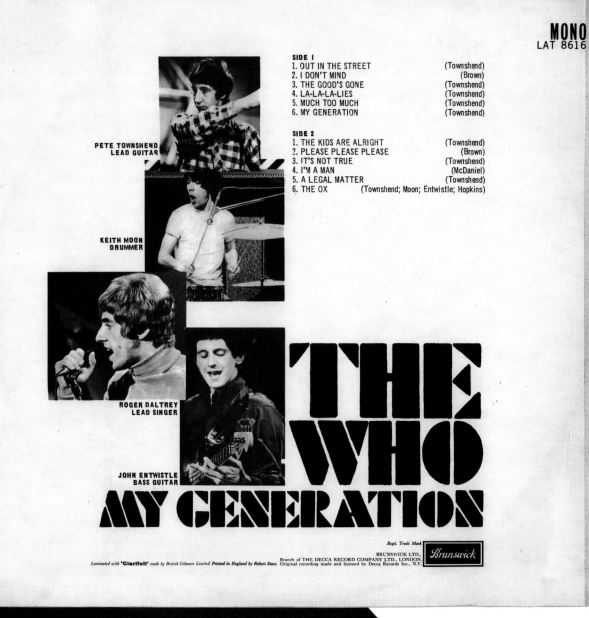

SIDE 1

1. OUT IN THE STREET   (Townshend)
2. I DON'T MIND   (Brown)
3. THE GOOD'S GONE   (Townshend)
4. LA-LA-LA-LIES   (Townshend)
5. MUCH TOO MUCH   (Townshend)
6. MY GENERATION   (Townshend)

SIDE 2

1. THE KIDS ARE ALRIGHT   (Townshend)
2. PLEASE PLEASE PLEASE   (Brown)
3. IT'S NOT TRUE   (Townshend)
4. I'M A MAN   (McDaniel)
5. A LEGAL MATTER   (Townshend)
6. THE OX   (Townshend; Moon; Entwistle; Hopkins)

PETE TOWNSHEND LEAD GUITAR

KEITH MOON DRUMMER

ROGER DALTREY LEAD SINGER

JOHN ENTWISTLE BASS GUITAR

THE WHO
MY GENERATION

MONO
LAT 8616

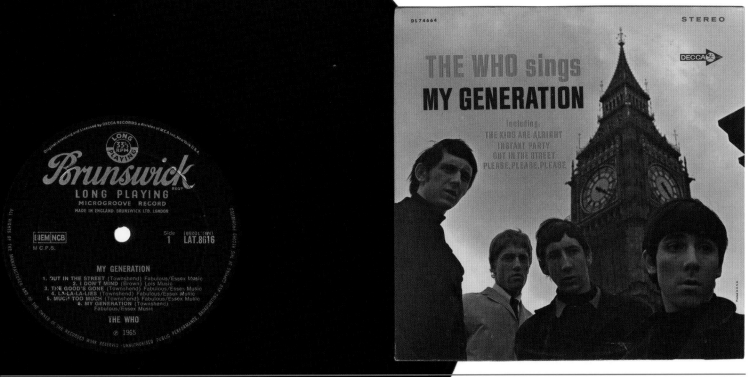

STEREO

DL74664

DECCA

THE WHO sings
MY GENERATION

including:
THE KIDS ARE ALRIGHT
INSTANT PARTY
OUT IN THE STREET
PLEASE, PLEASE, PLEASE

U.S. label Decca
designed a new
cover with the band
posing next to Big
Ben.

SIMON & GARFUNKEL | Sounds of Silence

January 1966 | Columbia

The Sounds of Silence qualifies as one of the more curious career jump-starts in the history of popular music. After their debut album flopped and the duo split up, producer Tom Wilson (Dylan's "Like a Rolling Stone") took their original acoustic track and, without Simon or Garfunkel's participation, overdubbed electric instruments and turned the track into a #1 pop hit. *The Sounds of Silence* made pop stars of the two college-grad folk singers, and its track list disclosed the pair's interests and ambitions as wider and deeper than those of the typical Top-40 act. Subjects included loss of faith, suicide, the consequences of poverty, and the isolation of individuals in modern society. Simon emerges here as a concise, literate songwriter with a unique temperament ("Kathy's Song," "I Am a Rock," "April Come She Will") capable of rocking out as well as reflecting. This can be seen in the the haunted mini-story "Somewhere They Can't Find

Me," the duo's adaptation of Edward Arlington Robinson's poem "Richard Cory," whose subject "went home last night and put a bullet through his head." Also included is the instrumental "Angie," Simon's adaptation of the tune by British folk guitarist Davy Graham, a key influence on Fairport Convention, Nick Drake, Bert Jansch and others. Original editions of *The Sounds of Silence* bore just the album's title and artist, while subsequent pressings listed the songs on the left side.

When their single
"I Am A Rock"
became a hit,
Columbia added
that song's title and
the rest of the track
listing to the front
cover.

stereo SKL 4786

DECCA

THE ROLLING STONES | Aftermath

April 1966 | Decca

If Lennon & McCartney saw themselves as songwriters from the start, Jagger & Richards had to be forced into the act. "We had never thought of it," recalled Keith Richards in David Dalton's book *Rolling Stones: In Their Own Words*. "Andrew [Loog Oldham] locked Mick and me up in a room about the size of a kitchen and said, 'You've got a day off, I want to hear a song when you come out.' 'He's got to be joking,' we said." The punch line: Oldham's challenge forced not just the public, but the band itself, to realize it was much more than a collection of blues acolytes. *Aftermath* was the first Stones album to feature all Jagger-Richards material, and its stunning evidence of just how fruitful the team's relationship would become. The record simultaneously introduced such favored Stones tunes as "Under My Thumb," "Stupid Girl" and "Mother's Little Helper" and showed that Mick and Keith could work credibly in modes as diverse as

courtly ballads ("Lady Jane"), first-generation rock 'n' roll ("Flight 505"), pop R&B ("Out of Time") and country ("High and Dry," "What to Do"). *Aftermath* is where the modern notion of the Rolling Stones emerges. And it's the writing, as much as the band's playing, that allows them to stake their claim to being not just the unkempt anti-Beatles or the flame-keepers of the Chess Records legacy, but to often being referred to as "the world's greatest rock 'n' roll band."

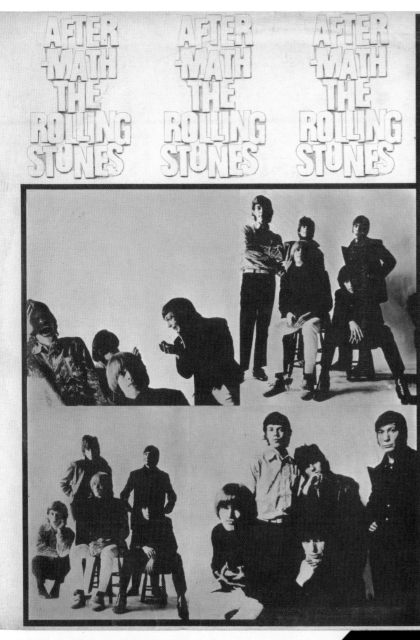

AFTER MATH THE ROLLING STONES

STEREO SKL 4786

In July 1964, I was engineering a session for Jack Nitzsche at RCA in Hollywood; the song was "Yes sir, that's my baby" In walked the Rolling Stones and Andrew Oldham, who had stopped by to say hello to Jack, a friend they had met thru Phil Spector. In December of 1964, we did our first session together. Andrew had phoned me from England, and wanted to do a session en route to Australia. I was thrilled; since then, we have worked together thru "The Last Time"; "Satisfaction"; "Cloud"; "Breakdown" and a number of albums, in a way that has been rewarding both artistically and professionally, for working with the Stones is extremely exhilarating. They never go the easy route;—from the moment Mick and Keith run a song down to the rest of the group,—to Brian deciding on an acoustic or electric guitar, or something more bizarre,— to Bill sorting out a bass pattern,—to Charlie laying down the tempo;—to their friend Jack Nitzsche (always on the dates) or Road Manager Stu picking out chords on piano, organ, harpsichord or anything else that happens to be lying around. To some many hours later, at a final take,—it's all great. In this business of dubious standards, it's been great working with the Stones, who, contrary to the countless jibes of mediocre comedians all over the world, are real professionals, and a gas to work with.

Dave Hassinger, Engineer

SIDE ONE
MOTHERS LITTLE HELPER 2:40
STUPID GIRL 2:52
LADY JANE 3:06
UNDER MY THUMB 3:20
DONCHA BOTHER ME 2:35
GOIN' HOME 11:35

SIDE TWO
FLIGHT 505 3:25
HIGH AND DRY 3:06
OUT OF TIME 5:15
IT'S NOT EASY 2:52
I AM WAITING 3:10
TAKE IT OR LEAVE IT 2:47
THINK 3:10
WHAT TO DO 2:30

Vocals: Mick Jagger, Keith Richard
Guitars: Keith Richard, Brian Jones
Bass: Bill Wyman
Drums: Charlie Watts
Percussion: Charlie Watts, Jack Nitzsche, Mick Jagger
Marimbas, Bells:
Brian Jones, Charlie Watts, Bill Wyman
Dulcimer, Sitar: Brian Jones
Piano, Organ, Harpsichord:
Jack Nitzsche, Ian Stewart, Brian Jones, Bill Wyman
Lighting: Mick Jagger

Photography: Guy Webster Jerrold Schatzberg
Cover Design: Sandy Beach

Songs by Mick Jagger and Keith Richard
Arranged by The Rolling Stones
Engineer: Dave Hassinger
Recorded at RCA Studios, Hollywood
Producer: Andrew Loog Oldham

DECCA *Regd. Trade Mark*

THE DECCA RECORD COMPANY LTD. LONDON
© 1966, The Decca Record Company Limited, London.

Laminated with 'Clarifoil' made by British Celanese Limited
Printed in England by Robert Stace.

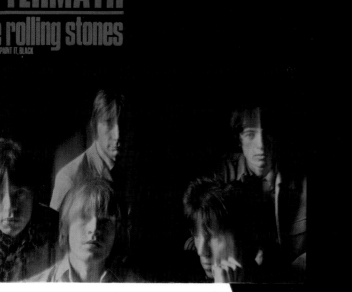

AFTERMATH
the rolling stones
INCLUDING PAINT IT, BLACK

STEREO PS 476   LONDON

The band's U.S. label issued the album with a different—and equally striking—cover.

File Under: The Beach Boys   T 2458

The Beach Boys Pet Sounds

Sloop John B. / Caroline No
Wouldn't It Be Nice / You Still Believe In Me
That's Not Me / Don't Talk (Put Your Head on My Shoulder)
I'm Waiting For The Day / Let's Go Away For Awhile
God Only Knows / I Know There's An Answer / Here Today
I Just Wasn't Made For These Times / Pet Sounds

Capitol RECORDS

THE BEACH BOYS | Pet Sounds

May 1966 | Capitol

The Beach Boys had left clues to where their ambition might lead as far back as 1965's moody, ballad-rich *Today* album. But the more conventional cars-and-girls cast of *Summer Days (and Summer Nights!!)* and the good-natured goofiness of *Beach Boys Party!* made the group appear anachronistic just as the rest of rock was starting to grow up and out. *Pet Sounds*' arrival announced the full maturing of Brian Wilson's prodigious talent and shattered notions about how much might be attempted in the LP format. The uncommon sophistication of the writing, orchestration and performances put across an introspective song cycle brimming with love, loss and regret that, apart from the single hits "Wouldn't It Be Nice" and "Sloop John B," sailed over the heads of many pop music fans. Meanwhile, the Beatles credited *Pet Sounds*' scope and structure as the inspiration for *Sgt. Pepper's Lonely Hearts Club Band*. "It may be going overboard to

say it's the classic of the century," Paul McCartney has said, "but to me it certainly is a total, classic record that is unbeatable in many ways ... I've often played *Pet Sounds* and cried." In time, audiences, critics and most other artists have come to acknowledge the album's exalted place in the canon of rock albums—an achievement rendered all the more notable for the fact that Wilson, like his chief inspiration Phil Spector, chose to cut the album in mono rather than stereo.

Pet Sounds and the other early Beach Boys albums were mastered in mono; group mastermind Brian Wilson preferred mono, and was almost totally deaf in one ear.

The gatefold cover featured a blurry photograph by Jerry Schatzberg, who noted "The frame he [Dylan] chose for the cover is blurred and out of focus. Of course everyone was trying to interpret the meaning, saying it must represent getting high on an LSD trip. It was none of the above; we were just cold and the two of us were shivering."

BOB DYLAN | Blonde On Blonde

Dylan routinely revolutionized popular music on an annual or even semi-annual basis during his heyday. He worked the controls of a creative bullet train that shot from *Freewheelin'* (1963) and *The Times They Are-A-Changin'* and *Another Side* (both 1964) through *Bringing It All Back Home* and *Highway 61 Revisited* (both 1965). Less than a year after the latter LP, he delivered *Blonde on Blonde*, the first double album of the rock era. What's remarkable about *Blonde on Blonde* is not its format-shattering size, but the fact that all four sides were needed to contain the range and breadth of its contents—none of it was filler or extraneous. *Highway 61 Revisited* had first put Dylan's surreal rock 'n' roll on the table, but in a more chaotic and experimental context. Here is where songs, singing and accompaniment hit the perfect note, in what he himself described as "that thin, wild mercury sound. It's metallic and bright and gold, with whatever that conjures up." *Blonde on Blonde* conjures a multitude of moods, images and associations that invite endless speculation, and reward the listener with an experience that manages to be fresh and dynamic some 40 years on. "Just Like a Woman," "Visions of Johanna," "Stuck Inside of Mobile with the Memphis Blues Again," "Sad Eyed lady of the Lowlands" and every other track here became a standard in the repertoire of pop music's most non-standard artist.

May 1966 | Columbia

Rainy Day Women #12 & 35 / Pledging My Time / Visions of Johanna / One of Us Must Know / I Want You / Memphis Blues Again / Leopard-skin Pill-box Hat / Just Like a Woman

Most Likely You Go Your Way and I'll Go Mine / Temporary Like Achilles / Absolutely Sweet Marie / 4th Time Around / Obviously 5 Believers / Sad Eyed Lady of the Lowlands

Recorded at Columbia Recording Studios, Nashville, Tennessee / Bob Dylan, Harmonica & Lead Guitar (on "Leopard-skin Pill-box Hat") / Charlie McCoy, Harmonica (on "Obviously 5 Believers") / Musicians:

Wayne Moss, Charlie McCoy, Kenneth Buttrey, Hargus Robbins, Jerry Kennedy, Joe South, Al Kooper, Bill Aikins, Henry Strzelecki, Jaime Robertson / Produced by Bob Johnston

The original inside gatefold featured a photo of Italian actress Claudia Cardinale chosen by Dylan, from Schatzberg's portfolio. Cardinale's representatives threatened to sue, and it was replaced. Dylan included a self-portrait of Schatzberg instead of a printed photo credit.

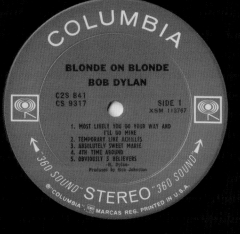

COLUMBIA
BLONDE ON BLONDE
BOB DYLAN
C2S 841
CS 9317   SIDE 1
                XSM 113767

1. MOST LIKELY YOU GO YOUR WAY AND
   I'LL GO MINE
2. TEMPORARY LIKE ACHILLES
3. ABSOLUTELY SWEET MARIE
4. 4TH TIME AROUND
5. OBVIOUSLY 5 BELIEVERS
   —B. Dylan—
   Produced by Bob Johnston

STEREO "360 SOUND" 360 SOUND
"COLUMBIA" MARCAS REG. PRINTED IN U.S.A.

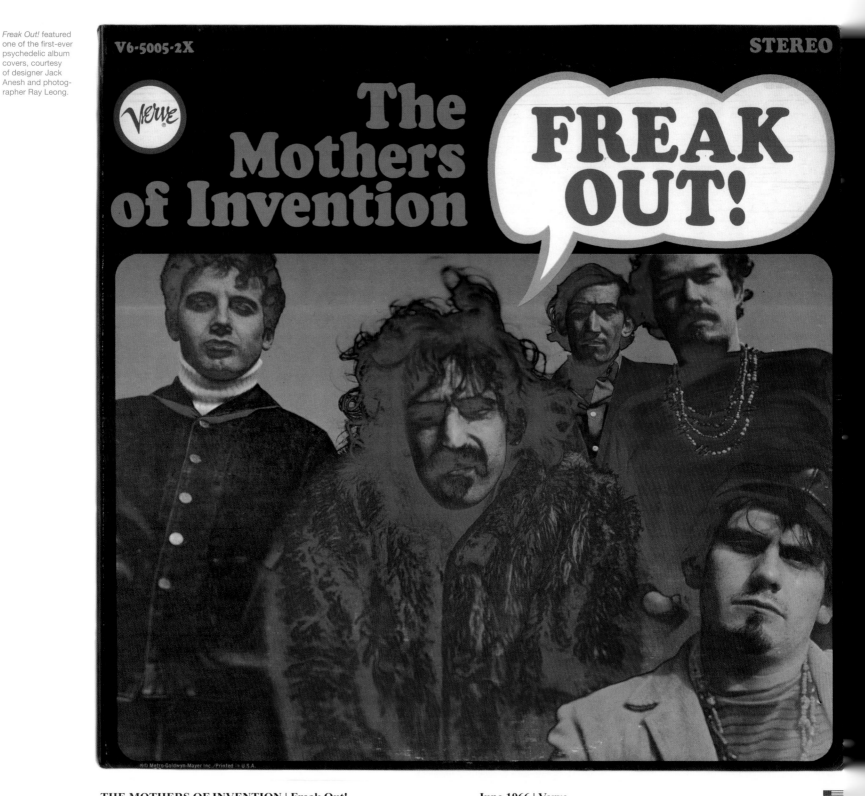

THE MOTHERS OF INVENTION | Freak Out!

June 1966 | Verve

"If anyone owns this album, perhaps he can tell me what in the hell is going on," wrote the *L.A. Times*' pop critic upon encountering *Freak Out!* This "talented but warped quintet has fathered an LP that could be the greatest stimulus to the aspirin industry since the income tax." New wonders appeared almost weekly in 1966, but few record buyers were prepared for rock's second double-album (after *Blonde on Blonde*), its eye-popping solarized cover, or its improbable mix of deftly arranged, hook-filled songs and spooky dissonance. *Freak Out!* contains all of the elements that would define Frank Zappa's unique musical universe through three decades, from send-ups that savaged both '50s doowop and '60s counterculture, to uncompromising social protest ("Trouble Every Day") and extended improvisations and sound collages that sampled avant-classical sources. A concept album that critiques mid-century California and much of American culture, *Freak Out!* almost didn't get made. MGM/Verve executives thought producer Tom Wilson, scouting talent in Los Angeles, had signed a white blues band. They learned otherwise, persuaded by Wilson's rep (he'd produced "Like a Rolling Stone" and "Sounds of Silence") and his unshakable belief in the Mothers. "He was so impressed," wrote Zappa in *Hit Parader* magazine, "that he got on the phone and called New York, and, as a result, I got a more or less unlimited budget to do this monstrosity."

The first copies of *Freak Out !* included this offer inside the gatefold cover –

PLANNING ON VISITING L.A. THIS SUMMER ? Send for your copy of the special map we have prepared for you: "Freak-Out Hot Spots" shows how to get to **Canters**, **Ben Franks's**, **Fred C. Dobbs**, **The Trip**, **The Whiskey A-Go-Go**, **The Brave New World**, **It's Boss**, **Bido Lito's**, and many more interesting places. Also shows where the heat has been busting frequently with tips on safety in police-terror situations. Only $1.00 in magnificent color (mostly black)…Hurry ! This map has no commercial potential !

Few must have taken advantage of the offer, as original *Freak Maps* are extremely rare and sought after.

#1 The Cinematheque 16 still happens on a psychedelic level with rare and interesting films from the Great Underground. Located at 8815-1/2 Sunset Bl. (657-6815)

#2 The Trip used to be the center of the Freak Scene See it now: 8572 Sunset Blvd.

#3 Ben Franks used to be the place to go after the dancing stopped. The atomic blast denotes a bust (overall) by the L. A. heat. 8585 Sunset Blvd. (phone 655-7410)

#4 Whisky a Go-Go still happens every night with top Pop Music Acts (and occasionally, lesser known fill-in groups like us). Yay, gang! Lotsa fun! 8901 Sunset Blvd. (phone 652-4202)

#5 Gazzarri's still happens on a hard rock custom pompadour sport coat level. Don't miss it at 9039 W. Sunset Blvd. (phone 273-6606)

#6 The Troubadour gives you not only folk music, but folk-rock music, rock music itself, and other hybrids, all IN CONCERT. Stunning in its concept at 9083 Santa Monica Blvd. (phone 276-6168)

#7 West L.A. Sheriff's Station nestled in the heart of the outskirts of the fringe of where everything is happening, this moral arsenal provides shelter and sanctuary for that proud and magnificent beast we call THE WEST L.A. SHERIFF'S DEPUTY/ servant & protector OR, more commonly, THE MAN. See the hapless trustees in their stenciled shirts washing HIS cars. Hear bold Aryan operatives rave about long hair freakos and the last John Birch meeting at 720 N. San Vincente Blvd. (phone... only as a last resort if you have long hair or a beard 652-3525)

#8 Barney's Beanery is still there. It is a matter of opinion whether it is still (or ever was) HAPPENING. Fun to visit: 8447 W. Santa Monica Blvd. (phone 654-9240)

#9 The Chez which used to be The Action which was the first place we worked when we emerged from the sticks and came to Hollywood is now High Class. A must: 8265 Santa Monica Blvd. (phone 656-3576)

#10 P.J.'s is now, as it was, and always (most likely but I'll check it out for you a coupla times) will be, the greatest place in town to see Trini Lopez in action. Located at 8151 W. Santa Monica Blvd. (phone 656-8000)

#11 The Sea Witch is one of the teenie-bopper (no offense, gang) IN SPOTS, featuring the new local bands in performances of psychedelic music b/w Cokes and Coffee, ...8514 Sunset Blvd. (phone 652-9160)

#12 FRED C. DOBBS Memorial Shrine... it used to be the best place to go to meet friends and dig the juke box until the heat blew it for us... or was it that bunch of outside idiots that started hanging around towards the end there, unable to maintain their coolness? The ruins are located at 8537 Sunset Blvd.

#13 IT'S BOSS is teenie-bopper heaven. You only have to be 15 to get in. Located at 8433 Sunset Blvd. (phone 654-9900)

#14 Nikki's Too is a day-time spot with an outdoor thing where you can ingest surprisingly good hamburgers in the company of a lot of really creepy people who sit there next to you while you're eating and hope that somebody driving by owes them money so they can scream and yell at them and make a scene so the people walking by will notice that they're sitting there and how groovy their sunglasses are... 8355 Sunset Blvd. (phone 656-9244)

#15 The Colonial West Motel is a nice place to visit, but I wouldn't care to live there. My views, however, were not shared by The Paul Butterfield Blues Band, Sammy Davis Jr., or any of the other 18 million hippies who have made this their place to crash over the past few years. Conveniently located next to Nikki's Too at 8351 Sunset Blvd. (phone for reservations 656-4120)

#16 The Stripcombers is HAPPENING for black leather jackets and motorcycle boots if that is your bag. Keen fun at 8301 Sunset Blvd. (for pertinent information phone the West Hollywood Sheriff's Station)

#17 The Fifth Estate is one of those places that refuses to quit .. even after a whole series of scenes with the heat, bravely situated at 8226 Sunset Blvd. (phone 656-7673)

#18 PANDORA'S BOX is another teenie-bop underground stronghold...a defiant little island at the top of the strip with a picket fence around it and cops and ingenue freakos and lots of atmosphere, but tiny. Try sitting at Frascati's across the street and watching the heat surround the place while the kids scramble for cover. Keen fun. Located at 8118 Sunset Blvd. (phone 656-9192)

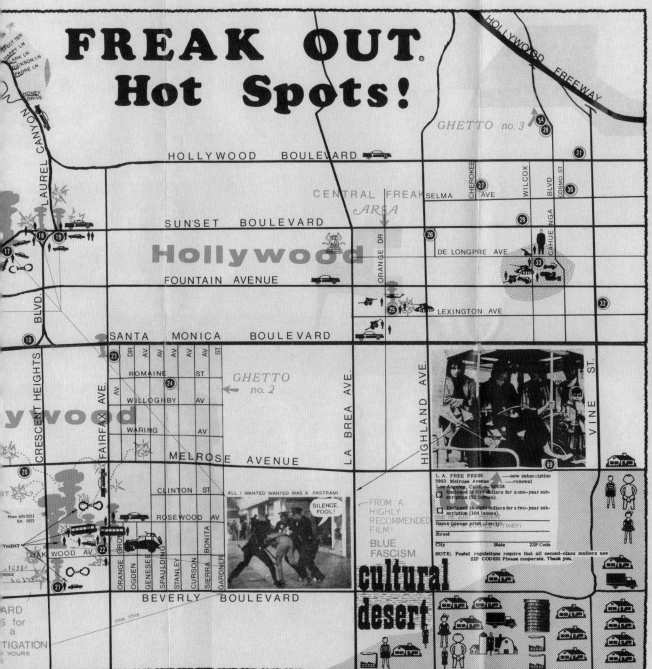

FREAK OUT. Hot Spots!

#19 GEE GEE'S was a scene until it was mysteriously forced out of business. It is, at this moment, for rent... 8100 Sunset Blvd., next to Schwab's drug store, across the street from Ah Fong's and Greenblatts Deli.

#20 The Ash Grove features ETHNIC ETHNICAL ETHNOCENTRIC Folqie Musique ... I remember when Bud & Travis used to work there and Ed Pearl used to do Ethnopolitical Greasing for the newly founded cabaret at the idyllic old Folk Freak Sanctuary in 1958, Before Hal Zeiger invented the HOOTENANNY. Check it out at 8162 Melrose Ave. (phone 653-2070)

#21 VITO'S STUDIO & store & cult HQ & sanctuary & genetic laboratory which is REALLY THE PLACE TO SEE is located at 303 N. Laurel (the bomb blast tells us that the status quo agents have made it known that they are checking Vito out)

#22 CANTERS Fairfax Restaurant is THE TOP FREAKO WATERING HOLE AND SOCIAL HQ, scene of more blatant Gestapo practices than the peaceful natives care to recollect, it is a good place to go as soon as you arrive in town. If a black bus (or two) pulls up in front and you see your fellows, brethren and kinfolk being loaded into them (as if it were off to Auschwitz), do not flip out. Do something constructive: something positive... unfortunately, I'm not allowed to offer any suggestions, except to say, perhaps, that the silverware is cheap and easy to replace. You may cautiously approach it at 419 N. Fairfax (safer to phone 651-2030) Canters is across the street from the Kazoo. (See #69)

#23 The Blue Grotto coffee house used to be nice and quiet until it got busted in the middle of the night. Meet and talk with the survivors at 1010 N. Fairfax.

#24 CARL'S HOUSE is where Carl lives. It wouldn't be right to give EVERYBODY the address... he would never get any sleep, poor fella.

#25 SITE OF A GIGANTIC & FESTIVE BUST wherein much brutality and authoritarian B S was perpetrated with the result that all parties involved served a lot of DEAD TIME (time before trial) and got acquited (causing them great physical and mental discomfort & status loss).

#26 TTG RECORDING STUDIOS where we cut our album.

#27 THE BRAVE NEW WORLD is a very IN sort of late-teen Freak spot, Visit 1644 N. Cherokee, near M'Goos on Hollywood Blvd.

#28 The Omnibus is a coffee house next door to the WILD THING at 1835 Cahuenga (phone 462-0473)

#29 The Red Velvet is HQ for the plastic & pompadour set with lotsa hard rock & blue-eyed soul to TURN YOU ON, BABY Located at 6507 Sunset Blvd. (466-0861)

#30 BIDO LIDO'S (formerly Cosmo Alley, one of our beloved manager's old coffee houses) is another underground teen-freako hot spot that launched the group LOVE "into orbit in the top pop hit charts with many smash numbers" (some of them performed on their employers). The Bido Lido's ain't quite the same ... but still sort of happening & atmospheric at 1608 N. Cosmo St.

#31 The Haunted House is fulla go-go & snappy ensembles & hair-dos & a genuine fire-breathing bandstand. Must be seen to be believed at 6315 Hollywood Blvd.

#32 The Hollywood Ranch Market never closes and is a good place to see some REAL FREAKS. 1248 N. Vine (phone 464-0156)

#33 The Hollywood Police Station, a masterpiece of Etruscan architecture in the heart of primitive Hollywood.

#34 WILD THING is a dance place I never been to yet which is next door to the Omnibus on Cahuenga near Yucca, which has featured such groups as The West Coast Experimental Pop Art Band, The Knack and The Eastside Kids (who, I am led to believe, are funky).

#35 THE TROPICANA MOTEL is groupies' paradise ... that's where most of the touring groups who play the Whisky a Go-Go stay when they hit town, as well as many members of active local groups like The Doors and The Byrds. Located at 8585 Santa Monica Blvd. (phone 652-5720)

#69 (by request) THE LOS ANGELES FREE PRESS OFFICE, cognoscenti HQ, beacon of truth, champion of teen & otherwise justice, nice people, and more at 5903 Melrose Avenue. You would be wise to subscribe immediately upon arrival to town or you will never really know what's going on ... socially or politically. THEY ALSO SELL BOOKS, MAGAZINES, BUMPERSTICKERS & BUTTONS THAT WILL MAKE YOU LAUGH & HAVE STATUS at 424-1/2 Fairfax, across from Canter's, #22. Behold the enclosed subscription blank.

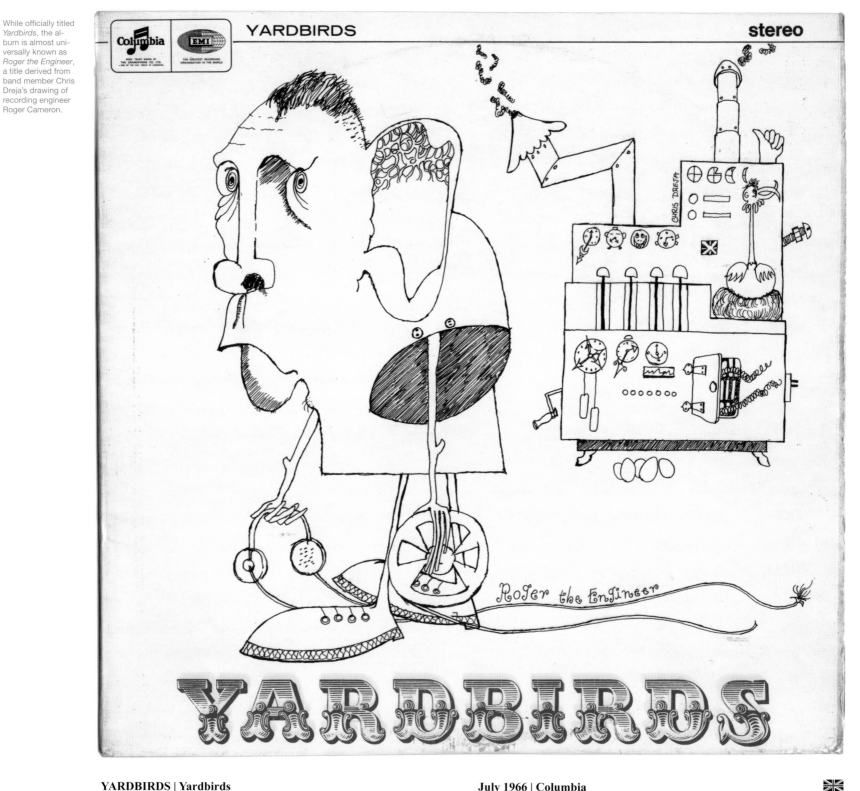

YARDBIRDS | Yardbirds

July 1966 | Columbia

Despite having hits in both the U.S. and U.K. since the spring of 1965, the Yardbirds didn't get a proper studio album release until the summer of 1966. That LP was *Yardbirds*, commonly known as *Roger the Engineer* in reference to guitarist Chris Dreja's cover drawing of the album's audio engineer, Roger Cameron. The record contained only the group's most recent hit, "Over, Under, Sideways, Down," but it's nonetheless a noteworthy debut, one that features some of the earliest examples of several motifs that would become popular in rock throughout the late '60s. Among them are the first prominent use of fuzz guitar ("Over, Under, Sideways, Down"), Middle Eastern exotica ("Hothouse of Omagararshid") and the official start of the boogie-rock craze that, in lesser hands than Jeff Beck's, bullied rock for the remainder of the decade ("Jeff's Boogie"). The album's historical significance lies in the fact that it marked the first appearance of music that came to be called psychedelic. The mid-song breakdown of "Lost Woman" resembles San Francisco's then as-yet-unrecorded ballroom blitzes, while "Rack My Mind" presages any number of Cream rave-ups. The case for the Yardbirds' influence on California acid rock is strong: the band played the Fillmore more than once in 1966, the year that scene broke. Bassist Paul Samwell-Smith's production gives *Roger the Engineer* an emphatic presence, keeping guitars in the foreground without letting them run the game.

The back cover features more drawings from Yardbirds rhythm guitarist Dreja.

The album was retitled *Over Under Sideways Down* in the U.S., Germany and France, after the Yardbirds' hit of the same name. This is the U.S. cover.

Blues Breakers is known as *The Beano Album*, as Eric Clapton is pictured on the cover reading an issue of *The Beano*, a British children's comic. Clapton wrote in his autobiography that he was reading the comic as he felt like being "uncooperative" during the photo session.

JOHN MAYALL WITH ERIC CLAPTON | Blues Breakers

July 1966 | Decca

No one can fault Eric Clapton for inconsistency. He'd joined the Yardbirds with the understanding that it would remain the blues group it had started out as. He left the band when it began tightening its instrumental belt and pulling on its pop togs, and signed on with Mayall's Chicago-styled outfit. Clapton's co-billing with Mayall on *Blues Breakers* let the cat out of the bag: the prominence of his lead work and the eloquence of his solos signaled the approach of the guitar hero, a cultural figure that has traveled farther than Link Wray or Duane Eddy could ever have imagined. Clapton here sketches out a whole landscape for future guitarists: blues-anchored, jazz-inspired stretching that would reshape the previously constricted contours of pop. The album deserves credit, along with the first Paul Butterfield Band LP and John Hammond's Band-backed *So Many Roads*, for taking up the torch handed off by the Stones and Animals and

igniting the blues revival that burned so strongly through the '60s and '70s. Clapton's incandescent playing on such cuts as "Steppin' Out" and "All Your Love" inspired the once omnipresent graffiti-scrawl "Clapton is God." Chas Chandler's promise to introduce Jimi Hendrix to the emerging deity was part of the reason the young American agreed to decamp for Britain.

RED-MONO   LK 4804
BLUE-STEREO   SKL 4804

U.K. Patents Applications No. 43212/68

BLUES BREAKERS   JOHN MAYALL   ERIC CLAPTON

In John Mayall and Eric Clapton we have the two most dedicated blues musicians in this country. Together with John McVie and Hughie Flint, they make up John Mayall and the Bluesbreakers. To hear them play can be a thrilling experience. Playing the blues is such a complex business, involving so many personal and external conditions, that it is never certain how well you are going to play until the first number of the evening is over. Watching the Bluesbreakers perform, you are immediately aware of their intense search for new ways in which to interpret their material. In fact, it is surprising to learn how little of their music is arranged and how much is improvised. It is because of this phenomenal ability to improvise that John Mayall and the Bluesbreakers are the premier blues group in England. On this record we have captured some of their best performances on numbers which they feature regularly in their club appearances.

The person responsible for much of the improvisation is Eric Clapton. Two years ago I stuck my neck out to say that Eric would become one of the top blues guitarists in the country. Now I know I was right – he is the best, damn it. A lot of people wondered why Eric left the Yardbirds just as they were hitting big. But Eric had an inevitable course to follow, and at the time it led him to the Bluesbreakers, as no doubt it will lead him elsewhere in the future. Since joining the group, his technique has improved beyond recognition, and on his best nights Eric can make time stand still. Some idea of this can be gained by listening to his solo on "Have You Heard". But even without stopping the clock his playing can be both breathtakingly beautiful and savage, as on "All Your Love", "Double Crossin' Time", and his two instrumental features, "Hideaway" and "Steppin' Out". As if this wasn't enough, this record marks the first occasion on which the Clapton voice has been aired on disc. For his debut, Eric chose the Robert Johnson number, "Ramblin' On My Mind", which has a very sympathetic piano backing from John.

Because a lot of the spotlight is thrown on Eric, we tend to overlook the fact that John himself is a most capable musician. Besides doing all of the singing (well almost), his piano, organ and harmonica playing provide much of the driving force of the group. His flair for composition, with some unusual chord progressions, is also shown to good advantage on "Little Girl" and "Key To Love". The two harmonica features on this record, "Another Man" and "Parchman Farm", usually develop into tours-de-force in a club performance, but here John remains short, sharp, but very much to the point.

It is a measure of this group's capabilities that they can inject new life into such cobwebbed numbers as "What'd I Say", and make them sound even more vital than the original. And perhaps this is why John Mayall and the Bluesbreakers are such an exciting group to watch and hear, and why they are the only group in Britain today whose music closely parallels that being produced by the blues bands of Chicago.

© 1966, The Decca Record Company Limited, London.   NEIL SLAVEN

DECCA   *Regd. Trade Mark*

Printed in England by MacNeill Press, London, S.E.1.

THE DECCA RECORD COMPANY LIMITED,
Decca House, 9 Albert Embankment, London S.E.1

SIDE ONE
1. ALL YOUR LOVE (Rush;Dixon)
2. HIDEAWAY (King;Thompson)
3. LITTLE GIRL (Mayall)
4. ANOTHER MAN (arr. Mayall)
5. DOUBLE CROSSING TIME (Mayall;Clapton)
6. WHAT'D I SAY (Charles)

SIDE TWO
1. KEY TO LOVE (Mayall)
2. PARCHMAN FARM (Allison)
3. HAVE YOU HEARD (Mayall)
4. RAMBLIN' ON MY MIND (Johnson)
5. STEPPIN' OUT (L.C. Frazier)
6. IT AIN'T RIGHT (Jacobs)

JOHN MAYALL, vcl/piano/organ/harmonica.
ERIC CLAPTON, vcl/guitar.
JOHN McVIE, bass-guitar.
HUGHIE FLINT, drums.
on Tracks 1, 2, 3, 6, 12.

Augmented by: JOHN ALMOND, baritone sax on Track 5

ALAN SKIDMORE, tenor sax; JOHN ALMOND, baritone sax;
DENNIS HEALEY, trumpet
on Tracks 7, 9, 11.

Layout: JOHN MAYALL.
Sleeve photography by Decca Publicity Art Department.
Produced by MIKE VERNON.
Engineer: GUS DUDGEON.

Laminated with 'Clarifoil' made by British Celanese Limited

MADE IN ENGLAND BY THE DECCA RECORD CO. LTD LONDON

DECCA (Regd.)
FULL FREQUENCY STEREOPHONIC SOUND

SPEED 33⅓   Side   1   ZAL 7297
BIEM NCB   SKL 4804
GEMA

BLUESBREAKERS
1. ALL YOUR LOVE (Rush) Jewel Music
2. HIDEAWAY (King, Thompson) P. Maurice
3. LITTLE GIRL (Mayall) Gunnell Music
4. ANOTHER MAN (arr. Mayall) Gunnell Music
5. DOUBLE CROSSIN' TIME (Mayall, Clapton) Gunnell Music
6. WHAT'D I SAY (Charles) Carlin Music

JOHN MAYALL with ERIC CLAPTON
℗ 1966

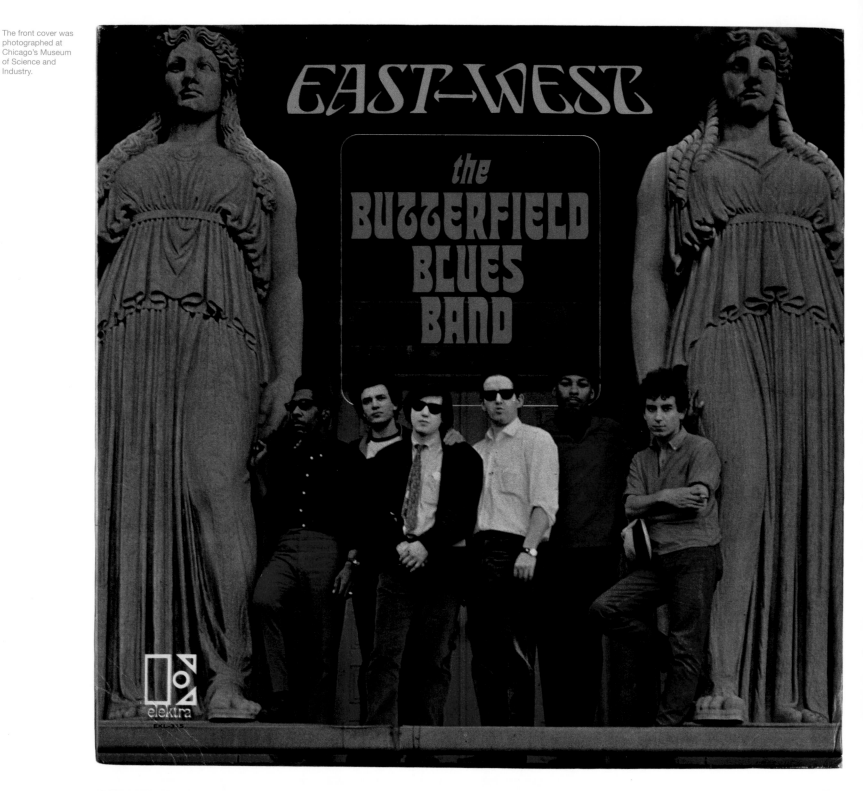

THE BUTTERFIELD BLUES BAND | East-West

August 1966 | Elektra

In 1964 and '65, Paul Butterfield's Chicago band had spearheaded the post-Stones amplified blues movement in the States, as John Mayall had in the U.K. By the summer and fall of 1966, the quintet had left the South Side clubs of its hometown and taken its powerful playing and still-traditional set list on the road. The rapidly growing psychedelic ballroom circuit is where the band, and particularly star guitarist Mike Bloomfield, started to stretch instrumentally, which is precisely where *East-West* finds them. With "Paint It Black" and "Love You To," the Stones and Beatles had flirted with Middle Eastern sounds, but until Butterfield's group committed all 13 minutes of "East-West" to wax, no one had attempted a sustained melding of such "foreign" elements with traditional blues rock. Bloomfield, who had animated Dylan's *Highway 61 Revisited* and backed him at Newport, steps out with what can only be termed a jazz approach: thinking on his

feet and translating his thoughts into astonishing feats of dexterity as the band roils around him. Not surprisingly, the track, which also features soloing from guitarist Elvin Bishop and Butterfield, inspired a wave of improvisation that left few young guitarists untouched, especially on the West Coast, where free-form dancers were only too happy to welcome extended accompaniment. *East-West* was most assuredly not a pop record, but it was influential, lodging on *Billboard*'s Top Albums chart for more than half a year.

the BUTTERFIELD BLUES BAND

left to right   **MIKE BLOOMFIELD**   **PAUL BUTTERFIELD**   **ELVIN BISHOP**   **JEROME ARNOLD**   **MARK NAFTALIN**   **BILLY DAVENPORT**
guitar   harmonica & vocal   guitar   bass   organ & piano   drums

EAST   # WEST

Be sure to hear
the first Paul Butterfield
Blues Band album
EKL-294 · EKS-7294

"We don't want any liner notes; we'll do our own notes, hey," they said — they being the Paul Butterfield Blues Band, the Marat/ Sade of blues — now all draped in, on, over, and around navy-blue canvas chairs in Elektra's Engineering (renamed Pioneering) A, doing a sound mix for this album..."We gotta do our own notes, maybe with a flashlight, little Tom Wolfe blips, you know"..."Naw, Pop Art: pictures of Bach, Beethoven, and Brahms—the 3 B's. We've got the 3 B's too, the 3 B's of blues — Butterfield, Bloomfield, and Bishop — plus the A-N-D—Arnold, Naftalin, and Davenport. Pop Art"..."Just print our names and pictures, that's all. We like to see our names"... "Not a word about the music, even though this record's got a lot of different sounds on it. Nothing about the music"..."We should all write about each other. We'll draw names out of a hat to keep it fair" ..."Two paragraphs of insanity, the notes can't be longer than that" ..."People call us all sorts of things—blues, pop, folk-rock—but we're mainly a blues band: everything we touch turns into blues in some way"..."Brahms!"..."Three things the notes can't be: (1) 'The blues came up the Mississippi River many years ago on the back of a . . .'; (2) 'This song was learned from a Muddy Waters record on which he . . .'; or the fan approach (3) 'Handsome, blue-eyed so-and-so covered his eyes from the cruel glare of the spotlights.' Also, no scholarship, no superlatives, no 'best of' or any of that crap"... "No notes, period. Just run our photos. We like to see ourselves"... "We're gonna have to write our own notes, otherwise we're gonna hate 'em. We'll put ink on dogs' feet and let 'em run on white paper" ... "No, use rats. They lead a rougher home life, more suitable environment"... "We're gonna all get together and hate the notes"...

PAUL NELSON

Producers • MARK ABRAMSON & PAUL ROTHCHILD
Cover photos & design • WILLIAM S. HARVEY

ELEKTRA RECORDS 51 WEST 51st STREET NEW YORK CITY 10019 U.S.A • 7, POLAND STREET LONDON W.1 ENGLAND

SIDE ONE
1. WALKIN' BLUES 3:15
2. GET OUT OF MY LIFE, WOMAN 3:13
3. I GOT A MIND TO GIVE UP LIVING 4:57
4. ALL THESE BLUES 2:18
5. WORK SONG 7:53
   (order of solos: Mike Bloomfield, Paul Butterfield, Mark Naftalin, Elvin Bishop)

SIDE TWO
1. *MARY, MARY 2.48
2. *TWO TRAINS RUNNING 3.50
3. NEVER SAY NO (Vocal: Elvin Bishop) 2:57
4. EAST-WEST 13:10
   (order of solos: Elvin Bishop, Paul Butterfield, Mike Bloomfield)

*Produced by Barry Friedman

Production Supervisor JAC HOLZMAN

elektra

PROMOTION
PREVIEW
COPY

elektra

NOT
FOR
SALE

EKL-315-A
SIDE ONE

PAUL BUTTERFIELD BLUES BAND
EAST-WEST

1. WALKIN' BLUES (Robert Johnson, ASCAP) 3:15
2. GET OUT OF MY LIFE, WOMAN
   (A. Toussaint, Marsaint Music BMI) 3:13
3. I GOT A MIND TO GIVE UP LIVING 4:57
4. ALL THESE BLUES 2:18
5. WORK SONG (N. Adderly, Upam Music BMI) 7:53
   Recording first published August 1966

This white label
promotion copy
was made for
reviewers, retailers
and radio stations.

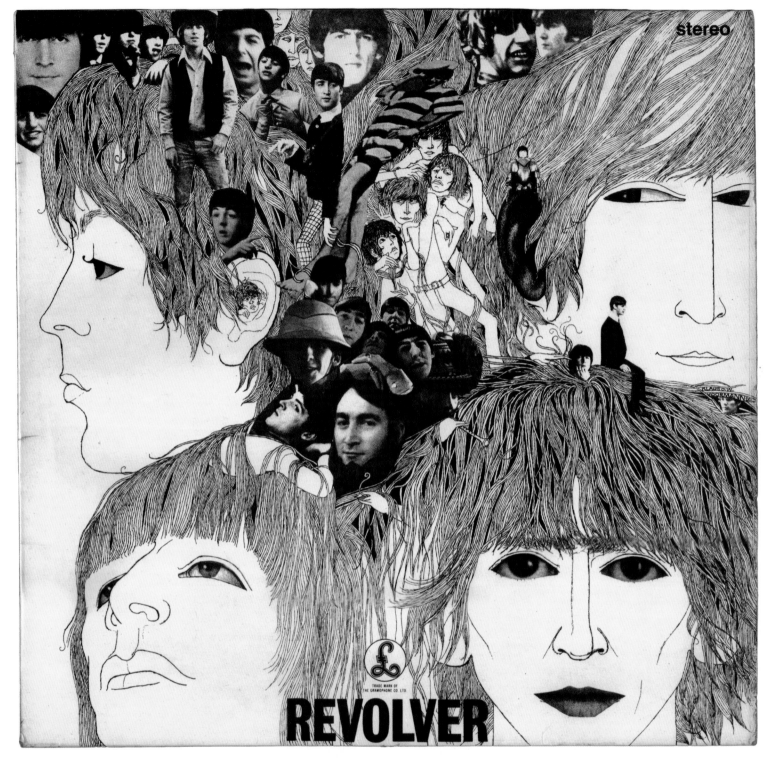

THE BEATLES | Revolver

August 1966 | Parlophone

The velocity with which pop music moved in the mid-'60s now seems hard to comprehend, when current bands' releases are likely to be announced with advertisements that tout, "Their first new recording in seven years!" Because artistic ambitions and commercial tastes were so perfectly aligned during that period, the most successful acts were obliged to grow up in public, setting forth fresh new feasts for a monstrously hungry audience every few months—or cede ground to the competition. *Revolver* is the most experimental of all the Beatles' albums. Released in August of 1966, it followed *Rubber Soul* by just eight months and preceded *Sgt. Pepper's Lonely Hearts Club Band* by nine months, a period during which some of rock's most frenetic and fruitful innovation occurred. *Revolver* is the sound of a band trying out new things: strings and social observation in "Eleanor Rigby," unapologetic pop optimism in "Good Day Sunshine,"

electronic collage in "Tomorrow Never Knows," Indian sounds in "Love You To," and varying shades of psychedelia—from Harrison's acid-tongued "Taxman" to Lennon's narcoleptic "I'm Only Sleeping" and "Doctor Robert," who dispenses feel-good medicine from "his special cup." With simpatico production and their usual good instincts, the Beatles make the crazy-quilt repertoire cohere and compel. Acknowledged as one of the Beatles' most adventurous LPs, *Revolver* topped the U.S. and U.K. charts, where it remained for six and seven weeks, respectively.

PCS
7009

SIDE ONE

1. **TAXMAN** (Harrison)
2. **ELEANOR RIGBY** (Lennon-McCartney)
3. **I'M ONLY SLEEPING** (Lennon-McCartney)
4. **LOVE YOU TO** (Harrison) Tabla - Anil Bhagwat.
5. **HERE, THERE AND EVERYWHERE** (Lennon McCartney)
6. **YELLOW SUBMARINE** (Lennon-McCartney)
7. **SHE SAID SHE SAID** (Lennon-McCartney)

LEAD SINGER

George Harrison
Paul McCartney
John Lennon
George Harrison
Paul McCartney
Ringo Starr
John Lennon

Recording Produced by GEORGE MARTIN
Cover Designed by KLAUS VOORMANN
Back cover photo by ROBERT WHITAKER ℗ 1966

THE BEATLES

REVOLVER

SIDE TWO

1. **GOOD DAY SUNSHINE** (Lennon-McCartney)
2. **AND YOUR BIRD CAN SING** (Lennon McCartney)
3. **FOR NO ONE** (Lennon-McCartney) Horn - Alan Civil
4. **DR. ROBERT** (Lennon-McCartney)
5. **I WANT TO TELL YOU** (Harrison)
6. **GOT TO GET YOU INTO MY LIFE** (Lennon McCartney)
7. **TOMORROW NEVER KNOWS** (Lennon-McCartney)

LEAD SINGER

Paul McCartney
John Lennon
Paul McCartney
John Lennon
George Harrison
Paul McCartney
John Lennon

LONG PLAY 33⅓ R.P.M.

TRADE MARK OF
THE GRAMOPHONE CO. LTD.

E.M.I. RECORDS
(The Gramophone Company Ltd.)
HAYES · MIDDLESEX · ENGLAND
Made and Printed in Great Britain

Use **NEW**
EMITEX
RECORD CLEANER
The use of NEW EMITEX
provides an effective means of
ensuring groove cleanliness so
essential to good reproduction.
Its regular use will lengthen the
life of the record and reduce
the static charge. *Available
from Record Dealers.*

IMPORTANT This record is intended for use only on special stereophonic reproducers. If you are doubtful of the suitability
of your reproducer for playing this record, we recommend you to consult your record dealer.
Most equipment designed for playing stereophonic records may, however, be used with perfect safety for playing normal 33⅓ r.p.m. and 45 r.p.m. microgroove records.

Printed and made by Garrod & Lofthouse Ltd. Patents pending   PMC 7009   PCS 7009

LSP-3584 STEREO

JEFFERSON AIRPLANE

TAKES OFF

RCA VICTOR DYNAGROOVE RECORDING

JEFFERSON AIRPLANE | Jefferson Airplane Takes Off　　　　　**September 1966 | RCA**

Once the British Invasion washed ashore, America's initial retort was the strummed, chiming folk-rock of the Byrds and the Lovin' Spoonful. It took a sextet from the unlikeliest pop outpost on the San Francisco coast to light the spark of the next big sound heard 'round the world: psychedelic music. *Jefferson Airplane Takes Off* is not the high-dose rave-up that the Grateful Dead's later debut LP is, but it introduces many elements that pull rock farther from its traditionally lighthearted Top-40 tether: minor-key melodies, Marty Balin and Signe Anderson's vocals, the fluid, almost dreamlike meshing of bass and dual guitars, and the casual frankness of the subject material. Oblique drug references in "Runnin' 'Round This World" caused nervous RCA Records executives to pull the song from the album at the last minute (fewer than five copies of *Takes Off* with the track have surfaced, making it the rarest of all American rock albums.) Subsequent

pressings featured censored versions of two other songs, "Run Around" and the similarly "controversial" "Let Me In." This underappreciated record also gets credit for fitting rock with its first non-plural-noun band name, springing the idiosyncratic Skip Spence on the world (the Airplane drummer subsequently founded Moby Grape, and cut the cult-fave solo album *Oar*), and bringing serious mainstream attention to pop. Well before *Time* magazine gushed over *Sgt. Pepper's Lonely Hearts Club Band*, respected jazz critic Ralph Gleason's championing of the Airplane drew attention to the creative contours of the emerging underground. RCA Records heard him and anted up the previously unthinkable advance of $25,000 for the relatively unproved, pre-Grace Slick edition of the band to sign on the dotted line.

Rare versions of *Jefferson Airplane Takes Off* contain 12 songs; common ones only eleven.

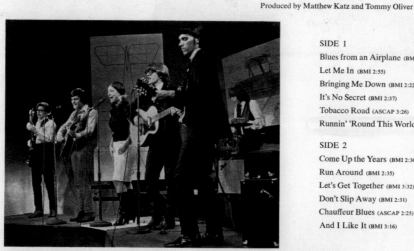

JEFFERSON AIRPLANE TAKES OFF Mono LPM-3584
Produced by Matthew Katz and Tommy Oliver Stereo LSP-3584

SIDE 1

Blues from an Airplane (BMI 2:10)

Let Me In (BMI 2:55)

Bringing Me Down (BMI 2:22)

It's No Secret (BMI 2:37)

Tobacco Road (ASCAP 3:26)

Runnin' 'Round This World (BMI 2:20)

SIDE 2

Come Up the Years (BMI 2:30)

Run Around (BMI 2:35)

Let's Get Together (BMI 3:32)

Don't Slip Away (BMI 2:31)

Chauffeur Blues (ASCAP 2:25)

And I Like It (BMI 3:16)

A JET AGE SOUND

"We like to put the music down like a big hand and grab you and shake you. We like the excitement of the rock."

"We" is Jefferson Airplane and the statement is from their leader and spokesman, Marty Balin.

Jefferson Airplane was the first of the new rock groups to emerge from San Francisco, the Liverpool of the U.S.A. Its fame spread, even before this LP and the first RCA Victor single, far enough so that Donovan, the British songwriter and singer, wrote a song about them, *Ride Jefferson Airplane*, in which he refers to "trans-love airlines."

It's no accident that Donovan links love and Jefferson Airplane. "All the material we do is about love," Marty Balin says. "A love affair or loving people. Songs about love. Our songs all have something to say, they all have an identification with an age group and, I think, an identification with love affairs, past, beginning or wanting…finding something in life…explaining who you are.

"When we play, we're involved and I think that really communicates to an audience…something, the power of creating, you can feel it. To anyone who is involved, who really believes in what he's doing, it really comes across. Everyone in our group is very involved with what we're doing, enjoys doing it and really believes in it. No matter how many times we do it, we've never, ever, once been on stage when we didn't become one person.

"We're terrific fans of everything that happens and we experiment. Sometimes a tune is completely finished and I give it to the rest of the guys…they start working on it and have ideas… it starts happening differently and we completely change the tune…

"I never have to explain my songs to my age group," Marty said when we talked about this LP. There's an instant communication that goes on once you are familiar with Jefferson Airplane's language. It's loud like the world we live in and it's strong, too. But it is also romantic and lyrical. When Marty sings, he says, "I feel like I'm talking. It's the greatest way to communicate."

Listening to rock bands has convinced me—and I'm old enough to have teen-aged children of my own—that we are in the process of evolving a new kind of electronic music. The sound of Jefferson Airplane is a jet-age sound, but its music speaks for all time, once you open your ears to it. I played this LP one afternoon, heard three rock bands that night, Muddy Waters the next night, Ray Charles the next, the Clancy Brothers the next and I still had *Come Up the Years* sounding in my ears. That's my standard for good music, when it sticks in your mind.

RALPH J. GLEASON
San Francisco Chronicle

The Crew:

Marty Balin, twenty-three, leader and singer. Eighteen years in San Francisco (born in Ohio), a former folk singer ("but I was always rock"), writer of most of the Airplane's material.

Paul Kantner, twenty-four, rhythm guitar and vocal. A native of San Francisco, he sings *Let Me In*. "Paul didn't think he could do it," Marty says. "I went through a million different guys till I saw Paul. He was walking into a folk club. I just knew it. He had a twelve string, a banjo, his hair down to here and an old cap. I just went up to him and said, 'Let's get together.' I hadn't heard him but I knew he was good."

Jorma Ludwik Kaukonen, solo guitar; has a degree in sociology from Santa Clara University.

Signe Toly Anderson, from the Pacific Northwest; a former folk singer. Her high, strong voice gives an unusual quality to the ensemble and is a great solo vehicle.

Alex (Skip) Spence, drummer, from Canada. "I saw him sitting in a club one day and I said 'THAT'S my drummer.' Skip had never played drums in his life." (Marty speaking.)

Jack Casady, bass, from Washington, D.C. Marty says, "He carries it. He's been with James Brown and other groups and he knows."

Recorded in RCA Victor's Music Center of the World, Hollywood, California.
Recording Engineer: Dave Hassinger.

DYNAGROOVE

Dynagroove records are the product of RCA Victor's newly developed system of recording which provides a spectacular improvement in the *sound quality.*

CHARACTERISTICS:

1. *Brilliance and clarity*—the original sound in startling definition.
2. *Realistic presence*—sound projected in "photographic" perspective.
3. *Full-bodied tone*—even when you listen at low level.
4. *Surface noise virtually eliminated!*
5. *Inner-groove distortion virtually eliminated!*

To solve these old and obstinate problems in disc recording, highly ingenious computers—"electronic brains"—have been introduced to audio for the first time. These remarkable new electronic devices and processes grew out of an intense research program which produced notable advances in virtually every step of the recording science.

The final test of any record is in the listening—*compare* the sound of Dynagroove recordings!

Dynagroove recordings are mastered on RCA Magnetic Tape.

· 4

© 1966, Radio Corporation of America · Printed in U.S.A.

"Runnin' Round This World" is the last song on Side One.

THE KINKS | Face To Face

October 1966 | Pye

It's almost hard to believe that, a mere two years before *Face to Face*, the Kinks had debuted behind the magnificent bone-cruncher "You Really Got Me." Over the course of three more long-players, Ray Davies' songwriting enabled the band not only to hammer out a signature instrumental style, but to fashion a distinctly Kinks-ian point of view that could be applied to virtually any song subject. Nowhere is the latter achievement better displayed than on *Face to Face*. Unaffected by the psychedelic trend tempting every other group in 1966, the Kinks maintain their distance by making

ironic observations and moody ruminations on everything from idle tax-cheats ("Sunny Afternoon") and careerism ("Session Man") to carefree fops ("Dandy") and familial estrangements ("Rosie Won't You Please Come Home"). Few pop writers before or since have communicated ennui or loss of faith as effectively as Davies does here on "Too Much on My Mind" and "Rainy Day in June."

SIDE ONE: PARTY LINE/ROSY WON'T YOU PLEASE COME HOME/DANDY/TOO MUCH ON MY MIND/SESSION MAN/RAINY DAY IN JUNE/HOUSE IN THE COUNTRY.

SIDE TWO: HOLIDAY IN WAIKIKI/MOST EXCLUSIVE RESIDENCE FOR SALE/FANCY/LITTLE MISS QUEEN OF DARKNESS/YOU'RE LOOKIN' FINE/SUNNY AFTERNOON/I'LL REMEMBER.

NPL 18149

FACE TO FACE
KINKS

It has been said by mercenary-minded persons that upon setting out along life's road the bread, the filthy lucre of W. Shakespeare of highly regarded memory would seem to be the thing to go for.
So if you accept the opinion of these aforesaid persons in the spirit in which it is given and get cracking you get the loot.
So what next?
So far on your passage through this vale of tears you have been a hick, a nothing and an unheralded nobody.
To be a well respected man must be your next aim, and with the loot in your pocket and the wicked world being what it is,
You become a well respected personage ere you know it.
Then comes dedication to the dictates of fashion. The Carnaby Street. The striped natty suiting. Touches of velvet upon the collar. Touches of lace upon the underwear.
And of course, ties of polka dot and Persian—originated Paisley pattern.
Next? Country house, yacht, powered by sail and/or steam, with the motor car in lurid colour and with white walls to its wheels smiling in the golden gravel drive.
Ladies of course. Ladies with long legs and little bosom, hair the colour of corn, very mini, very skinny dresses.
Status symbol ladies with rich dark sheen in the depths of the skin.
Dwindling in the end to one lady, one Special who gets in among the soul.
The trouble being that the perfect woman becomes a bore, like having Venus de Milo constantly upon one's hands.
So angry words are spoken, and she of golden hair and mini skirt, half woman, half thighs leaves. With car. Back to ma and pa. With tales of drunkeness and cruelty.
As if this is not enough, fate flings its last custard pie.
The taxman cometh.
And you are left with the glass of ice cold beer, and the sun on the uplands with dappled shadows and all, which is much better, as the poet has it than a poke up the nostril with a burnt stick.
(Now read on.).
Raymond Douglas Davies, a musician, not forgetting David, his kith and kin,
Peter Quaife, bass guitar who once wrote a story about an embarrasing affliction from which Rays grandfather suffered for over forty years.
And Michael Avory, drummer and the possessor of four shoes, two for each foot,
Have continued the story. And stories parallel to his sad one.
About the frustrations of the telephone, About rainy days and sunny days, about sessions men and dark ladies, about P.V.C. grass skirts in Waikiki, about memories, and dandies, and most of all about the breadwinner who was in the beginning, who lost all, sold his most exclusive residence, and passed into the bosom of his fathers.
Frank Smyth, Autumn 1966.

MUSICAL DIRECTION	RAYMOND DAVIES
ARRANGEMENTS	RAYMOND DAVIES
	DAVID DAVIES
RECORDED BY	SHEL TALMY
ENGINEERS	ALAN Mc KENZIE
	IRISH
HARPSICHORD	NICK HOPKINS

MR DAVID DAVIE'S COSTUMES BY GAIL OF BLACKBURN

© Pye Records Ltd., 1966;
Distributed by Pye Records (Sales) Ltd.,
A.T.V. House,
Gt. Cumberland Place
London, W.1.
"Pye" is the trademark of
Pye Limited, Cambridge, England.

Printed and made by Garrod & Lofthouse Ltd. Patents pending

33⅓ RPM

STEREO
SIDE 1

NSPL.18149

℗ 1966
NSPL.18149-A

FACE TO FACE
1. Party Line (R. & D. Davies)
2. Rosy Won't You Please Come Home (R. Davies)
3. Dandy (R. Davies)
4. Too Much On My Mind (R. Davies)
5. Session Man (R. Davies)
6. Rainy Day In June (R. Davies)
7. House In The Country (R. Davies)
THE KINKS
A Shel Talmy Production
CARLIN MUSIC CORP. (1-7)

Graham Nash

on The Beatles: *Please Please Me* and Joni Mitchell: *Blue*

The Beatles: *Please Please Me*

I started buying records in 1956. The first one I bought was *Be-Bop-A-Lula* by Gene Vincent—it was on a 78 disk and I was heartbroken when I sat on it and broke it to pieces. I bought it from a record store on Regent Road in Salford near Manchester, where I lived.

There was a radio program being broadcast from Luxembourg in Europe on a Sunday evening, it would be faint but listenable. My family had just gotten a radio and I used to hear it through my bed-post when I was supposed to be sleeping and getting ready to go to school the next day. I was riveted to this new sound and raved about this new music at school with my friend Freddy Marsden who knew more than I did about rock and roll.

I first heard the Beatles' single, "Please Please Me," on an acetate in the offices of Dick James, a publisher of their music. It was an obvious smash hit record. Everyone knew it. Everyone.

I first met the lads in November of 1959 at a talent show at the Ardwick Empire Theater in Manchester. I wish I had a copy of that show. On it were me and Allan Clarke who later formed the Hollies, a man named Freddy Garrity who formed Freddy and the Dreamers, a guy called Ron Wycherley who became Billy Fury and a group from Liverpool called Johnny and the Moondogs, later of course to become The Beatles. At this point Allan and I had not started the Hollies, we didn't begin until '62.

Everybody, certainly every girl, knew the Beatles were going to be outrageously successful. When I worked in a coffee bar called the 2 Jays (later to be named The Oasis), every girl wanted them. They walked into the door and it was over. They all looked like James Dean in black leather.

One evening the Hollies were playing at the Twisted Wheel Club and the Beatles were at the Oasis. After the show we all went to an after hours club where liquor was served—very hush, hush in those days, especially for teenagers. The lads were going down to London to record their first album and John had forgotten the words to "Anna" by Arthur Alexander, so I showed him the words.

It was the first time I'd ever seen anyone eat a flower. The bass player for the Big Three, Johnny Gustafson, who I think opened for the Beatles was a little drunk and at one point I remember that he actually ate a large rose and a cigarette.

The Beatles' album *Please Please Me* was incredible to listen to—new, fantastically energetic. As with the Beatles, the Hollies' first album was also a recording of our "set." We did the 30-minute set twice and made the record from that. Up to this point, long-playing records were basically a bunch of singles put out to capitalize on the success of the singles. But John realized that they could actually be a collection of music that made a statement, and after *Please Please Me*, that's what they did. Of course it affected every band; the Beatles opened up the door and we all ran through it.

I remember at a show in the Kings Hall, in Stoke-on-Trent in the North of England. They had only just written "Misery" for a British singer called Helen Shapiro (who I later took on a dinner date) and the Hollies were opening for the Beatles. Just before the sound check, John and Paul sang their new song for me, one voice in each ear—quite a musical moment for me.

How could you not be affected by their energy and song writing abilities? They, and Bob Dylan, showed us the way to create music that meant something other than "moon, june" lyrics, and it was when I was writing "deeper" songs that the Hollies became disenchanted with me and it was the start of the end. I'd written "King Midas in Reverse" and, although it was a critical success, it failed to get us into the top ten. They didn't trust me anymore and that hastened my departure.

Joni Mitchell: *Blue*

I first met Joan in Ottawa, Canada, in 1967. The Hollies were playing a show there and Joni was playing at a local club. There was a party thrown for us after our show, and when I entered the room I noticed a beautiful woman sitting down with what appeared to be a large bible on her knees. I kept staring at her and our manager at the time, Robin Britten, was saying something into my ear and distracting me from my quest. I asked him to be quiet as I was checking Joni out. He said, "If you'd just listen to me I'm trying to tell you that she wants to meet you." David Crosby had told me earlier that year to look out for Joni should I ever get the chance to meet her. Joni and I hit it off immediately, and I ended up in her room at the Chateau Laurier and she beguiled me with 15 or so of the most incredible songs I'd ever heard. Obviously I fell in love right there and then. She touched my heart and soul in a way that they had never been touched before.

It's well known that Joni and I were boyfriend and girlfriend for a couple of years. It was a ridiculously wonderful time for us both; people said that we "lit up a room" when we entered. But good things sometimes come to an end, and our relationship did.

Listening to *Blue* is quite difficult for me personally. It brings back many memories and saddens me greatly. It is, by far, my most favorite solo album, and the thought that I spent much time with this fine woman and genius of a writer is incredible to me. I watched her write some of those songs and I believe that one or two of them were about me, but who really knows?

Blue will be, and really deserves to be, her best work… so stark, so deep… so *Blue*…

Graham Nash is a singer and songwriter who co-founded The Hollies and Crosby, Stills and Nash. Twice inducted into the Rock and Roll Hall of Fame, he is also well known for his photography.

Iggy Pop

on Them: *The Angry Young Them* & The Mothers Of Invention: *Freak Out!*

Them: *The Angry Young Them*

I bought my first record in 1960; I was 13. I had one dollar of my own money and I bought *Red River Rock*, an album by Johnny and The Hurricanes, at the Woolworth's in the first mall opened in southern Michigan.

I found out about music and groups from my friend in junior high school, Jim McLaughlin. He had a guitar and amp, because his dad was a ham radio nut. He played me his Ray Charles records, and Elvis, too. We formed a duo for the school talent show; I called it the Megaton 2. We played "What I'd Say," and "Let There Be Drums," which was a record I owned by Sandy Nelson. Later Jim and I started The Iguanas.

The radio in Detroit wasn't that great, but nowhere near as bad as it is now. You could hear the Beatles, Stones, Ronnettes, Wailers, Booker T, early Motown, Jackie Wilson, the Kinks, and other good stuff on CKLW, the Detroit AM station, but you had to be patient and listen to lots of shit like Peter and Gordon, Freddie and the Dreamers, Lesley Gore, Frankie Avalon, etc. to hear what you liked. When I later got a job at a record store, it really opened up my knowledge of music. The other people who worked there were experts in classical music, avant-garde, R&B and blues as well as rock, and I took it all in. The store was loosely organized, so when I wanted to hear a record, I just opened it up and played it right there.

I probably first heard "Gloria" by Them. When I bought the album it was the American version of *The Angry Young Them*, the same album, but with a hideous ugly orange cover, and it just said "Them." Now I have a vinyl copy of the original. It still blows my mind. I would listen over and over and over to "Mystic Eyes," and "One Two Brown Eyes." Those two cuts really influenced my ideas of what The Stooges could be.

At about that time, I was listening to all the good English groups plus Bob Dylan plus anything that came from San Francisco plus Love, plus tons of garage rock. Them was by far the most experimental, but also had a kind of doomed quality that I liked, because I could see that these guys weren't cute, didn't know how to dress and did not have a commercial touch except for the one hit, "Gloria." "Gloria" at the time was completely inescapable, all over the University of Michigan campus and at any club, anywhere with live music. Every band covered it, including my own. I think the liner notes were really pathetic. What a great example of a repressed, apologetic, neurotic show-biz bullshitter. I never saw Them, but I saw Van [Morrison] play once at the Troubadour in LA. It was around the time of "Moondance." He was very stern, and the group members all looked ill. He was so cool, the best thing he did was pick up a chair with one hand and wave it over his head while he screamed. I saw him do the same thing on TV on *American Bandstand*. I guess it was his one stage move. I've always wondered where he got it. The way Van's voice ripped through the mic, and the simple arrangements and spirit of experiment was a huge deal for me. I still listen to the record in the early mornings and when I want to get worked up.

The Mothers Of Invention: *Freak Out!*

The first time I heard *Freak Out!* by the Mothers of Invention was on headphones, smoking an early joint in my drug career, at the house of SRC, a Michigan band of the 60's. That night I kind of knew they were asking [Stooges guitarist] Ron [Asheton] to leave our group and join up with them, so I was hanging around to see what was going to happen. Rather than waste my time, I saw a copy of *Freak Out!* and listened to it on the phones. I thought it was very, very funny. I particularly loved "Help, I'm a Rock," "Who Are The Brain Police" and the cameo of Suzie Creamcheese. I had already seen the Fugs live on stage, with Tuli Kupferberg changing costumes out of a large bag in a humorous way, so I was somewhat prepared. I liked the Mothers' conceptualism and humor, although the music didn't really do much for me. My own experiments were more influenced by Bob Ashley, Harry Partch, and Berlioz.

The first time I saw The Mothers, I was opening for them. It was the second or third gig the Stooges had ever done, so I remember us more than them. I think playing with them so early in our career pushed me to be weirder faster, and also to be stranger to look at, earlier than I would have been otherwise. That night I did my first stage dive. I knew the Mothers were on after us and I didn't want people to forget about us.

Years later, I got to know Frank a little bit, and he was very decent to me. We went out for a burger once in Berlin, to a brightly-lit cheap and greasy joint with David Bowie. That was pretty funny and unusual. Frank was kind of a wry person, and as he made clear in his film "200 Motels," he had a certain ambivalence about English rock stars. I went along with Frank later that night and kept him company for a while at the Hilton hotel until his Berlin girlfriend showed up. For no exact reason, I remember feeling that Frank was a very lonely cat. He was all alone, and the suite was so dark and cold. The girl who came over later was kind of a troubled type, but I think he enjoyed the company and that was about it. Earlier that night at his show, Frank played one of his incredibly long guitar solos while his hired lead guitarist, Adrian Belew, had to wait his turn. That was the moment when David Bowie basically hired Adrian away for his own next projects, in a conversation behind the PA stack. I thought that was pretty funny.

Earlier in my life, when the Stooges went to LA in 1970 to record *Fun House*, we were staying at the Tropicana Motel. I walked up the hill to [legendary Hollywood coffee shop] Ben Franks to get something to eat, and there, sitting at the counter expressionless, with his hair and mustache and weird beard, was Frank Zappa. What a vision. I might as well have seen Aristotle. I was very impressed.

Iggy Pop is a singer, songwriter, and member of the Rock and Roll Hall of Fame whose band The Stooges virtually invented punk rock.

Robyn Hitchcock

on Pink Floyd: *The Piper at the Gates of Dawn* & Bob Dylan: *Highway 61 Revisited* & The Beatles: *Revolver*

Pink Floyd: *The Piper at the Gates of Dawn*

I found out about *The Piper At The Gates Of Dawn* because my cousin had a copy of "Arnold Layne," which was the first Pink Floyd single, produced by Joe Boyd. I'd just got hold of a guitar—I hadn't quite learned to tune it, but I noticed that the guitar solo on the B side, "Candy and a Currant Bun," was pretty much all on the bottom string, and I did learn to play that. I borrowed his copy of "Arnold Layne" and I was quite drawn into it. I wasn't sure about it, but it lodged in my head. I could see that both songs were written by someone named Syd Barrett, and there was a reference to "[It's All Over Now] Baby Blue" and I thought, "OK, he's obviously a Dylan fan." I was attracted but uncertain. This was August '67—the cover of this album, *Piper At The Gates of Dawn*, was in the window of the local music shop in Winchester which is called Whitwams, and I thought, "Oh, they've made an LP."

I saw this and thought, "Oh right, it's that Syd Barrett chap and his group, I wonder what that's like." Soon enough I got back to school, where all the records were; the other guys would come in with their records so you could all hear them. I was at a sort of upscale penitentiary for bright kids in the home counties. But, of course, it was 1967 so Brian Eno was wandering through the water meadows in his secular blue sunglasses, releasing balloons that were blown up with gas from hydrogen from the school science department. Anyway, there were about four or five copies of *Piper* floating around the house when I got back to school. "Astronomy Domine" was there, you could hear those voices, which I later found out were [band manager] Peter Jenner and Barrett reciting the…I don't know what they were—planets, astronomical… you know, Pluto, Libra, Scorpio… heavenly bodies. And everything was in mono.

We had a mono gramophone in the hall at school with terrific sound. And there it was, you had that morse code kind of sound, that bup, bup, bup bup bup bup. I just sort of accepted it as a fact of life. I thought, "This is good, I prefer The Incredible String Band, and I prefer Bob Dylan, this is OK, but…" It was autumn '67 and so leaves are inevitably falling off the trees, the nights were getting darker, I started getting up at 4 o'clock in the morning and going down a trap

door in a neighboring Stalag because that was the only time you could have some unmonitored time. So my dissident friends and I would sit under the floorboards eating whiskey cake. One of these friends is my legendary friend Fletcher, and we would listen to *Signs of the Zodiac* by Cosmic Sounds, and a Messiaen album, and then this thing *Piper* appeared. I didn't even have a copy but it would sit there on this portable gramophone, which I found out belonged to me in the end. But there it was. It was going on.

I didn't actually buy *Piper* until 1972, but I did buy it from Whitwams. I actually bought it after I'd bought the two Barrett solo albums. My Syd Barrett epiphany was delayed. I was aware of it all, but I thought, "I'm not sure about this guy, fancies himself a bit." I don't know what it was, I remember somebody playing the descent from "Astronomy Domine" in 1970, so we bought the live record, *Ummagumma,* and learned to play "Astronomy Domine." I got very depressed and sorry for myself when I was about 18, and I coincidentally bought the second Barrett album, and I just thought it was me. So I entered Barrett from the end of his career and worked my way back to this record from five years previously, and I memorized every note: I still hear my telecaster playing and I think "Oh, that sounds like Syd." They became involuntary mannerisms.

To me, *Piper* means a condensed intensity… it means talent squeezed like oil paint or toothpaste into a compressed state. There's more talent, more creativity in the record than there's actually room for. Barrett packs what most of us do in 40 years, he just squeezed it into six months. There's obviously some psychotic magic at work, but you just listen to this stuff and there's nothing else like it. This gave me something to aim at and miss, I suppose like all my musical heroes. It means I've done what I've done, but I don't think I've equaled them at their peak, but then they've never equaled themselves at their peak, either, and at least I'm still working. I got "Astronomy Domine" and it's such a great thing to play, you can play it on the piano and it sounds good.

It's been a huge influence. The only track I'm not that keen on is the Roger Waters song, "Take Up Thy Stethoscope and Walk." I mean, Roger eventually wrote good songs, but this wasn't really one of them. "Interstellar Overdrive" I

think goes on a bit, but I never actually listened to music on acid, so I don't know. I think Side One is really psychedelic R&B; it's sort of British nursery rhymes meets Bo Diddley over The Beatles. But it's also very rock, and a pioneer of the heavy metal sound with all those Telecaster riffs playing down the bottom. You know, skin-curdling genius. "Lucifer Sam," true dark metal. So Side One kinda takes off… "Interstellar Overdrive" is the plateau, and then Side Two comes down into the more acoustic-y stuff, and then it goes out on another kind of burst of psychosis with "Bike."

Bob Dylan: *Highway 61 Revisited*

Again, I was in the upscale penitentiary for the bright sons of wealthy characters and this was March 1966. I went off to this boarding school; I had lived with my parents and sisters and a cat for 12 years, and suddenly I was in this weird, quasi-medieval gothic Victorian but vaguely enlightened, intellectual environment where they produced kids who come out with the mental age of 60 and an emotional age of 12. You pretty much emotionally freeze as soon as you get in there. They say that thing about the child lost in the forest, the first thing it sees, it thinks it's his parents. So I was in this school and I thought, "What the fuck, I'm completely on my own, I just hope nobody finishes me off." So I very quickly made people laugh. I had to make people laugh and I adopted mannerisms of a PG Woodhouse character, I started stuttering. And so they wouldn't hit me because I made them laugh.

And coming out of the jukebox in this Victorian gothic medieval Stalag wherein we dwelt— they'd only just put doors on the toilets—they didn't even charge extra for that, it was amazing. What should come out of the jukebox every day but "Like A Rolling Stone." Now, I'd never heard Dylan; for some reason, they'd never had him on *Top of the Pops*. I'd heard of him, but I didn't know what it was. And I just heard this voice going, "How does it feel to be on your own?" And I thought, "Wow, what does he know?" Everyone thought Dylan was talking to them personally, and so within about six weeks I just thought Dylan was my mum and dad. I thought, "OK, this is where I'm going. I wanna suffer from curly hair and sunglasses, too." I didn't realize there were problems in getting there, I just thought, "I'll do that."

And lo and behold, there was an American kid who was also incarcerated there—he was a couple of years older—and he had a copy of *Highway 61 Revisited*. Every so often, we would be treated to not only "Like A Rolling Stone," but to one of the sides of *Highway 61* and one night he put on Side Two, and it had "Queen Jane Approximately" and I thought, "God, what's this?" And then "Just Like Tom Thumb's Blues" and I was hypnotized. And then "Highway 61" itself with all those lines—"Mack The Finger said to Louie the King." I was laughing at the words because they were so sharp. Then finally "Desolation Row," which I thought was "Destination Roll." I remember my job that evening was to sweep up the hall, and the song had that thing about Cinderella sweeping up, and I remember it was getting dark, it was about 6 o'clock or something in March, and I suppose, the same story as lots of Dylan fans, I just felt like this applied to me. And the same, I think, when I got into Syd Barrett, I just thought, "This is me." You know, the line between me and the music blurred, but I know that happened with Dylan universally. Especially young men of that age. So that was it.

I went off and I got some money at the end of the term and and bought my first copy of *Highway 61*. I've had so far four copies on vinyl, I've had it on cassette and CD. Now, well-wishers and potentates send me sensurround versions. And interestingly enough, the American import had an extra "Ballad of a Thin Man" that carries on for about half a minute, and so does "It Takes a Lot to Laugh." Much longer than the British pressings. I was in a thrift store in Seattle about ten years ago with [record collector and music executive] Geoffrey Weiss and I said, "Wow, look! An early copy of *Highway 61*, are you gonna buy it?" and he said, "No, but you are." And I did.

The Beatles: *Revolver*

I remember reading in August '66 an interview with John Lennon and Paul McCartney in something like *The Daily Mirror* and one of them said, "Our new LP is going to shock a lot of people." And I thought, "Ooh, really?"

So back in the Stalag, the penitentiary, comes September 1966. I've already been fully Dylanified at this point. It was a very interesting thing that year, the beginning of the year, the hipsters were all listening to Coltrane and Dylan, and the jocks were listening to the Beach Boys, and the Beatles were sort of in between. By September, the hipsters and the jocks were all playing the new Beatles record. The real crossover moment came when Beach Boys' "Good Vibrations" came out in November, and the hipsters and the jocks were freaked out because they were both listening to the same thing. The guys who had muscles and drank beer, you know, things we hipsters didn't get into for years. But I got back in September of '66 and we'd heard "Yellow Submarine" on the radio, but everybody was playing *Revolver*.

Musically, of the three records, *Highway 61*, *Piper*, and *Revolver*, *Revolver* is the one that has most continued to influence me as I've been a professional musician and a songwriter. Whereas I feel that whatever Barrett and Dylan did musically was great for them, it has its limitations. I think for all of us musicians, unless you happen to not like the Beatles, *Revolver* is the eternal grail, a fount of where music, of where pop music comes from. If you talk to Jon Brion or Elvis Costello or Glenn Tilbrook or Andy Partridge, especially that generation, but right from the Stones onwards—even Brian Wilson and Dylan and Barrett and all were all listening to it. I don't think they could have made it if they'd known how it was going to be seen.

When they made *Revolver*, they were still a pop group. By the time they'd done *Sgt. Pepper's*, they were a rock band, and they also knew how good they were, critically. Whereas when *Revolver* came out, there was still no rock criticism, it was just, you know, you get two pages, two paragraphs in the *New Musical Express* or *Melody Maker*. There was no *Rolling Stone*. There was nobody to give you these musical superlatives about the fact that you had sitars or orchestra or anything, they'd just say, "Well, the boys are throwing in some funny effects on this one." All the songs are under three minutes, practically. The fact that they let George do three songs and they're bloody good—I think this is their high water mark. After this, Paul took over. It was John's band to begin

with, then it was Paul's band, and John was falling apart on acid and he never forgave Paul for kind of taking it over. But someone had to when [Beatles manager] Brian Epstein died.

It was also the fruits of The Beatles and Dylan cross-pollination. They copulated. Dylan literally turned The Beatles on, and they begat The Byrds. But then both Dylan and The Beatles listened very closely to The Byrds and that seemed to influence what they then did. There's that lovely sort of McGuinn-Harrison thing of riffs being mutated and going across records. I never took acid much, maybe four or five times, but I do remember taking it once and playing an electric guitar and you get this wire between the ears, that spangle, that's my only kind of drug influence. You hear it on "Interstellar Overdrive" and you hear it in… a lot of this is a kind of high clanging, pinging thing. It was one of Jim McGuinn's trademark sounds, and Syd's too.

I guess LSD enhances an awareness of that. It makes you want a wire between your ears, so you can floss your brain. *Revolver* is rich with that. But the other great thing about *Revolver* is that all the McCartney songs are great. After this, McCartney went into parody, and that was another reason the Beatles were doomed. Because people liked "When I'm 64" he then came out with "Your Mother Should Know" and "Honey Pie" and "Maxwell's Silver Hammer." And for John and George, it was like salt on a slug for them. But on this, Paul's songs are "For No One." It's sad, but it's quite cruel in a way. "Good Day Sunshine" is up without being cheesy. On *Revolver*, John and George and Paul are all really good, and they're still working as a team. You don't feel them going in different directions.

Robyn Hitchcock is an English singer and songwriter, writer, artist and founder of the much loved punk era psychedelic band The Soft Boys. Oscar winning director Jonathan Demme's 1996 film "Storefront Hitchcock" captures him performing his songs standing inside a derelict New York City shop window.

Nels Cline

on The Jimi Hendrix Experience: *Are You Experienced* & The Jimi Hendrix Experience: *Electric Ladyland*

The Jimi Hendrix Experience: *Are You Experienced*

I remember hearing "Manic Depression" on what I believe was KHJ on a Saturday afternoon, in the back room of my parents' house on the Garrard Hi-Fi. Somehow my brother Alex and I knew it was Jimi Hendrix, having never heard him before, but somehow we figured it out. We'd stared at the cover of *Are You Experienced?* as soon as it came out, but didn't buy it. We used to buy records every two weeks with our allowance. But we didn't buy it because we'd been burned in the past by records that looked super cool, and we'd buy them without hearing them sometimes, and generally they just weren't very good. There maybe was a single that we liked on the record, but the rest of the albums would be very filler-heavy in those days. So we were a little wary and wanted to hear a track first, and we knew right away from the vibe of that song and from the voice that it was a black guy. And we were literally jumping up and down 'cause you could tell it was a trio, and I have to say, it was like being jolted with electricity. It was like being sent to another planet in that moment, and we were literally jumping up and down, running around the Hi-Fi. That was really the moment when I decided I was going to play guitar for the rest of my life, and that's not an exaggeration. And it still sounds magical when he sings that ascending line leading to the guitar solo, along with the guitar and then plays that solo, I still feel like I'm being jolted with electricity, like I'm in the presence of pure magic.

We went out and bought it of course. "Third Stone From The Sun" was on it, the song "Are You Experienced?," "Love or Confusion"… these are tracks which I guess are probably underrated because of "Foxy Lady," which is great. It's remarkable, in retrospect, to think that "Manic Depression" was the first song we heard, because it wasn't the single. "Foxy Lady" and "Purple Haze" were the singles. I don't know why they played "Manic Depression" that day and not "Purple Haze" or "Foxy Lady" or some other song, but that's what they played and it changed my life forever.

We were listening to everything that was going on at that time. I guess the disappointing records we bought at the time, based on how cool

they looked, were records like Blues Magoos' *Electric Comic Book*. It looked so awesome that I thought the record would be awesome, but it wasn't. Similarly, my brother had bought the West Coast Pop Art Experimental Band's *Volume 2*, with the silver bathroom on the cover, and that record didn't exactly hold up to the cover, in spite of the fact it had "Smell of Incense" on it. The song my brother liked so much, the opening track, "In The Arena," we had seen them do on TV, on the "Groovy" TV show. They didn't even try to lip synch. I remember one of the guys in the band stuffed an acoustic guitar full of fake dollar bills and lit it on fire during the song.

The other irony is that my brother had bought the first Velvet Underground record just because it had Andy Warhol's banana on the cover and he was a huge Warhol fan. And we were really disappointed in that album (laughing). Because we thought the whole album was going to sound like "European Son," which we just thought was the greatest thing ever. We thought the whole record was going to be really extreme, so ballads like "Femme Fatale" were lost on us at that time. It wasn't because we were so radical and into noise, because I was also listening to at that time The Left Banke, The Lovin' Spoonful, you know, I wasn't Mr. Hardcore Noise or anything. My brother was more hardcore than me at that time. Some of the pop stuff of the day, The Yardbirds' "Happenings Ten Years Time Ago" was another seminal song, as was "7 and 7 Is" by Love, so "Manic Depression" just fit right into the galvanic rock songs.

I never saw Hendrix live because we were too young and no one would drive us. The two gigs I remember, The Forum and Devonshire Downs, that one was way out in the North Valley, and there's no way we could get to that. The first time I saw Hendrix perform was probably [the film] *Monterey Pop*. From the very first sighting of *Are You Experienced* with that jacket with the eyes on it, that was like looking at a wizard or something. That was so powerful that nothing he wore surprised me, nothing he did surprised me, because all the potential for all that magical, flamboyant showmanship and vision was there in that photograph for me.

Having listened to the *Band of Gypsys* album for years and years and years, and not being on the

cutting edge of the bootleg world, I didn't know that there was this sort of surveillance-camera video recording of it. So years and years ago, my friend Gregg Bendian, I was staying with him in New Jersey, and he said, "I have this video cassette, I can't believe you've never seen this." He put it on and I literally wept. After listening to this for so long, to actually be seeing it, and this was a very heavy thing with Band of Gypsys, because Hendrix was just going to stand still, you know. I remember it even being announced that that was supposed to be the deal, that he was not going to jump around, that he wanted to be taken seriously and work harder on his guitar playing. So we all read about this and this video was of one of the two nights, so I got verification of what I'd read about. But to see it, and whether he's standing still or not, just to be able to see the actual thing happening, was so overwhelming. Particularly "Machine Gun." That's when I lost it. It's just like, all these years of listening to every note of this song over and over and over again, and then to see him doing it… I don't know why I never got to see Hendrix…

The Jimi Hendrix Experience: *Electric Ladyland*

Electric Ladyland is certainly one of my favorite records of all time. *Electric Ladyland*, of course, highly anticipated, 'cause I'd just come out as a complete Hendrix fanatic. In junior high school, arguments used to rage between these guys, some of whom were about a year older, and who were becoming decent musicians and rock 'n' roll dudes. They would have arguments about who was better—Beck, Page, or Clapton. They would get into really really heated arguments at recess, and then I would walk by, and they would say, "Nels! Nels! You play guitar!" Which was basically very kind of them to say… I was horrible then. "Nels, who's better: Page, Beck, or Clapton?" and I'd say "Hendrix" and they'd go, "gimmick!" Hendrix was not taken all that seriously by this kind of core of blues rock aficionados, because they thought all the psychedelia and feedback and all his flamboyant stage behavior was some kind of jive thing, which I always just thought was completely ridiculous because there was so much poetry. I mean, of those three that they asked me about, I would have said Jeff Beck, if I hadn't heard Hendrix, being a Jeff Beck fanatic also. But the fact that Hendrix wasn't taken seriously because of his flamboyance was one of the things that led him to form the Band of Gypsys, and this standing still thing. I think he, strangely, seemed to be oversensitive to how people perceived him, which is interesting for someone so flamboyant and visionary.

When *Electric Ladyland* was released, there was great excitement—not just because there was a new Hendrix album, but also we read it had guests. Stevie Winwood [of Traffic], one of my idols at that time, and [Jefferson Airplane bassist] Jack Cassidy was one of our idols… but it was a daunting proposition because it was a double album. Double albums were basically unaffordable. I remember how long it took for my brother to get the Mothers of Invention's *Freak Out!* because it was a double album. It was $5.49, it was printed right on the cover. But that was too much, because that meant you'd have to wait four weeks to get the record--for our next allowance period--and we were too impatient. So, in order to get around it, of course the object was to get the cheapest possible copy, and the cheapest price that we could find anywhere was at a store called Music Odyssey. This place was legendary to us because they seemed to only sell defective albums. My copy of *Electric Ladyland,* which I still have, the one I bought there, always skipped in the same place, which is about two or three times during Mitch Mitchell's drum break on "Voodoo Chile" when they start that amazing drone and ramp up to that kind of Irish melody. Steve Winwood comes in with this Irish melody and Hendrix echoes it and they go into this amazing swing, I've got chills just talking about it. The drums always skipped in that section. I gave up by the third copy; I still have it and it still skips in the same place.

It basically lived up to everything we could possibly imagine a double Jimi Hendrix record to be because it had everything on it. Obviously, you had songs like "House Burning Down," which is super psychedelic. "Crosstown Traffic" is classic sort of *Axis* style. The long jams, certainly "Voodoo Chile," still, not only one of the greatest blues jams of all time, the pure chemistry in evidence, but also a great recording. The sound of it is spectacular, it just feels… not just because it has people going "Yeah yeah" and clapping, but it just feels truly like there's

live electricity in the air when you're playing it. Songs like "Rainy Day Dream Away"… this kind of swing thing going on, funky organ…it just goes on and on. And of course in "1983" and "Moon Turn the Tides," for us, perhaps, besides the two "Voodoo Childs," the absolute centerpieces of the record, and everything we were looking for in music at that time was, how far out can you take it? That was kind of what we were interested in… within reason, with it being articulate and lucid and, I guess the word might be "artistic." So, absolutely stunning on every level.

There was something a little disappointing about the album design, which is funny in light of what the British album cover was. The U.S. cover looked kind of like it could have been the first album. The portrait on the cover of them looked so retro, it didn't really look like we thought they looked at that time. So we were looking at it and going, "God, it doesn't seem they put a lot of thought into this cover," but then when you opened it up, and it had all the tiny black and white photos of the session, and the picture of Hendrix with the cigarette in his mouth at the organ… for some reason that photo really stands out to me.

We scrutinized album covers…it was a time when we knew every title and all kinds of minutiae about records… the producer's name, the studio, all kinds of stuff, because that's what we did. You'd sit there with this big object in your hand, and read it over and over again, not necessarily while you were listening, but sometimes. It was something you could really sink your teeth into.

I'm not sure when I first saw the British cover, with the naked women. I think it might have been on our trip to Europe in 1968, but I don't have a recollection of the exact moment. I remember in those days I was so stupid about sex, I think that I had to have been one of the most innocent 13 year olds. But I remember being quite compelled by it (laughing). And I didn't understand then, but you look at all these women and they're so kind of made up, you kind of look at them and now I can see that they're not exactly the girl next door. I remember the British version being really perplexing to me because in a way, there was something really

unsexy about it, and on some other level it is kind of sensual.

I still listen to my Hendrix records. Like I said before, hearing "Manic Depression" has the same effect on me now as it did upon hearing it for the first time. I've talked with young musicians, there's a lot of water under the bridge and a lot of people imitating the sounds of all the innovators, which in some ways, for people coming up, can make it more difficult for them to feel the impact of these masters on our minds and hearts. So I've heard young people say, like, "Eh, Hendrix always sounded a little wimpy to me, I much prefer so-and-so…" and I just think, "Are you insane?"

I didn't try to play like Hendrix, ever. I thought it was impossible, in fact. I never really had a normal guitar style; I was kind of this weird primitive. I always thought it was kind of like sacrilege to try and play like Hendrix because he seemed like, there was something shamanistic about Hendrix to me, and I'm not prone to that kind of hyperbole. It wasn't really until later that I started; years and years later I would look back, stylistically, out of necessity. Like Mike Watt saying, "We're going to do 'Maggot Brain' for 15 minutes. Go." Where, basically, rather than channel Eddie Hazel, specifically, I'm really channeling my version of Hendrix and trying to take it as far as possible out of reverence. I never took anything specifically from Hendrix until later, when I realized it was at my fingertips, because I had learned how to play normal blues rock guitar along the road. Now I can hear it in my head, and I can go there in some ways, in my own style, but, in another way, I am kind of imitating Hendrix because it's in my head. It's like, deep in my system.

Nels Cline is a guitarist and composer who plays with Wilco and The Nels Cline Singers, and has performed with artists including Mike Watt, Yoko Ono, The Geraldine Fibbers, Thurston Moore, Charlie Haden, and Vinny Golia. He has played on over 150 albums in the jazz, pop, rock, country, and experimental music genres.

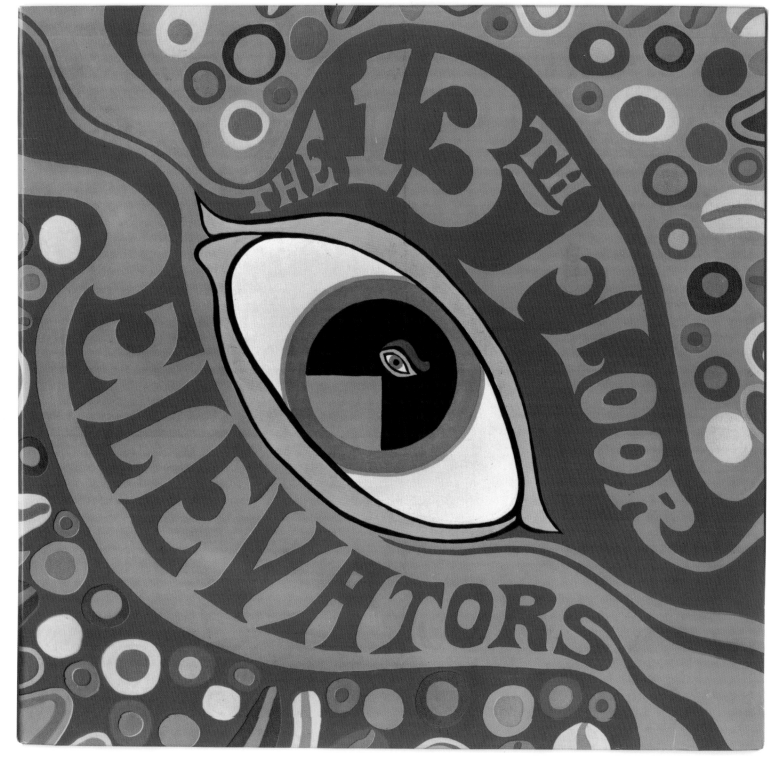

THE 13TH FLOOR ELEVATORS | The Psychedelic Sounds Of　　　**November 1966 | International Artists**

Of all the strange encounters that characterized '60s rock, the coming together of elements that produced the 13th Floor Elevators ranks high. It didn't look good on paper, but it worked: this meeting of garage-rock primitivism, LSD, spaced-out lyrics, a leader who played amplified jug and a singer who'd be declared insane and committed to a mental facility—the whole enterprise taking place under the hot glare of ultra-conservative Texas. And The Elevators' debut isn't merely the first album to feature the word "psychedelic" in its title. Released well before *The Doors* or *The Grateful Dead*, it's clearly the first to deserve that often misapplied handle. *The Psychedelic Sounds* is a roaring, intense, at times frightening record that does come close to conjuring the rollercoaster run of moods of the drug trip. Roky Erickson's banshee wailing and the band's breakneck playing made "You're Gonna Miss Me" a near hit. More importantly, the

track was featured on Lenny Kaye's *Nuggets* compilation of forgotten mid-'60s gems, which led directly to punk rock's back-to-basics triumph of the late-'70s. Tracks like the ominous "Fire Engine" and "Reverberation" and the almost delicate "Splash 1" make *Psychedelic Sounds* one of those unprecedented records whose inexplicable beauty obliges the listener to make frequent repeat visits.

THE PSYCHEDELIC SOUNDS OF:
The 13th Floor Elevators

Since Aristotle, man has organized his knowledge vertically in separate and unrelated groups---Science, Religion, Sex, Relaxation, Work, etc. The main emphasis in his language, his system of storing knowledge, has been on the identification of objects rather than on the relationships between objects. He is now forced to use his tools of reasoning separately and for one situation at a time. Had man been able to see past this hypnotic way of thinking, to distrust it (as did Einstein), and to resystematize his knowledge so that it would all be related horizontally, he would now enjoy the perfect sanity which comes from being able to deal with his life in its entirety.

It has recently become possible for man to chemically alter his mental state and thus alter his point of view (that is, his own basic relation with the outside world which determines how he stores his information). He then can restructure his thinking and change his language so that his thoughts bear more relation to his life and his problems, therefore approaching them more sanely.

It is this quest for pure sanity that forms the basis of the songs on this album.

YOU DON'T KNOW HOW YOUNG YOU ARE
explains the difference between persons using the old and the new reasoning. The old reasoning, which involves a preoccupation with objects, appears to someone using the new reasoning, as childishly insane. The old system keeps man blind to his animal-like emotional reactions.

THROUGH THE RHYTHM
shows the results of applying the old system and its ramifications. The new system involves a major evolutionary step for man. The new man views the old man in much the same way as the old man views the ape.

MONKEY ISLAND
expresses the position of a person who has just discovered that he no longer belongs to the old order.

ROLLER COASTER
describes the discovery of the new direction and purpose to man's life, the movement in that direction, and the results. The pleasures of the quest are made concrete in FIRE ENGINE.

REVERBERATION
is the root of all inability to cope with environment. Doubt causes negative emotions which reverberate and homper all constructive thought. If a person learns and organizes his knowledge in the right way---with perfect cross-reference--- he need not experience doubt or hesitation.

TRIED TO HIDE
was written about those people who for the sake of appearances take on the superficial aspects of the quest. The dismissal of such a person is expressed in YOUR GONNA MISS ME.

I'VE SEEN YOUR FACE BEFORE — (Splash 1)
describes a meeting with a person who radiates the essence of the quest. There is an outpour of warmth and understanding at the instant of meeting between two such persons, just as if they have been friends for life.

DON'T FALL DOWN
refers to the care that must be taken to retain and reinforce this state.

THE KINGDOM OF HEAVEN IS WITHIN YOU
The Bible states in "Proverbs" that man's only escape from the end foretold in "Revelations" lies in his reinterpreting and redefining God.

"ELEVATORS"

This space is reserved for a word of thanks to all those people who have made the success of the Thirteenth Floor Elevators record "You're Gonna Miss Me" possible.

DENNY ZEITLER and the staff at Independent Music Sales in San Francisco. DENNY being one of the greatest promotion men to ever pick up a phonograph record.

GORDON BYNUM, a young, up-and-coming record producer who has a by-word which is "right, right". When told the record by the Elevators was a smash, he simply stated "right, right".

CHUCK DUNAWAY of Radio KILT, Houston, a D. J. and Music Director with enough forethought to realize when the group was on Contact Records, a local company, that they had that certain something to put them in the class of HIT artists.

GARY STITES and JOE STANZIONE of Campus Record Distributors, Miami, Florida, who almost ended up with a nervous breakdown trying to break this record and keep it.

CAROL DALING at Concord Distributors, Cleveland, Ohio, whose persistence with her own radio stations finally paid off: and ARMEN BOLADIAN and his crew of Record Distributors, Detroit, who despite the tight play list, found a way: and JERRY LOVE of Alpha Distributors, of New York City, who tried - God knows he tried: and DON ANTI, Radio Station KFWB, Los Angeles, who tried twice and CHIC SILVERS in Washington who did everything in his power, even top ten and to JAY-KAY Distributors in Dallas who continually yelled "It's a smash everywhere" except in Dallas and kept right on trans-shipping and to ERNIE LEANER and his son BILL who knew I was over-due and tried and to CAROL at Tempo in San Francisco who was the very first to believe DENNY ZEITLER and gave us the Wizard Pick and last but not least to BILL GAVIN of the Gavin Reporter who believed in the record and stuck with us to the very end and to the many D. J.'s whom we have never met personally but who kept asking "What is that funny little noise in that record?"

Lelan Rogers

INTERNATIONAL ARTIST

INTERNATIONAL ARTIST PRODUCING CORP.
Houston, Texas

STEREO L. P. - 1 A - No.1

YOU'RE GONNA MISS ME
(Rocky Ericson)

ROLLER COASTER
(T. Hall - R. Ericson)

SPLASH 1
(C. Hall - R. Ericson)

REVERBERATION (Doubt)
(T. Hall-S. Sutherland-R. Ericson)

DON'T FALL DOWN
(T. Hall - R. Ericson)

CREDITS:

YOU'RE GONNA MISS ME
Produced by: GORDON BYNUM

All other tunes Produced by:
LELAN ROGERS

Engineer: BOB SULLIVAN at
Summit Sound Studio
Dallas, Texas

Cover Design: JOHN CLEVELAND
Austin, Texas

All tunes in this L.P. Published by:
TAPIER MUSIC CORP. B.M.I.
Houston, Texas

FIRE ENGINE
(T. Hall-S. Sutherland-R. Ericson)

THRU THE RHYTHM
(T. Hall-S. Sutherland)

YOU DON'T KNOW
(John St. Powell)

KINGDOM OF HEAVEN
(John St. Powell)

MONKEY ISLAND
(John St. Powell)

TRIED TO HIDE
(T. Hall - S. Sutherland)

PRINTING BY TANNER 'N' TEXAS, INC. - 1422 WEST POPLAR STREET - SAN ANTONIO, TEXAS 78207

INTERNATIONAL ARTIST
INTERNATIONAL ARTIST PRODUCING CORP.
Houston, Texas

THIRTEENTH FLOOR ELEVATORS

1A-LP-1 - Stereo
Side 1

Tapier Music
Corporation -BMI

1. YOU'RE GONNA MISS ME - 2:24 (R. Erickson)
Produced by Gordon Bynum
2. ROLLER COASTER - 5:00 - (T. Hall-R. Erickson)
3. SPLASH 1 (Now I'm Home) - 3:50
(Clementine Hall-R. Erickson)
4. REVERBARATION - 2:46
(T. Hall-S. Sutherland-R. Erickson)
5. DON'T FALL DOWN - 3:00
(T. Hall-R. Erickson)
Produced by:
LELAN ROGERS

LAURA NYRO | More Than A New Discovery

January 1967 | Verve Folkways

The title of Laura Nyro's first album suggests how strongly her label felt about her talent and the impact it would have. In a business accustomed to hype, *More Than a New Discovery* proved more than justified, since, for all intents and purposes, the singer-songwriter tradition starts with this record. In the space between Dylan and Gordon Lightfoot's emergence as folksingers and Neil Young and Van Morrison's '70s solo careers—and three full years before James Taylor's *Sweet Baby James*—Nyro produced one of the most original debuts in pop music history. By the time of her June 1967 performance at the Monterey Pop Festival, *More Than a New Discovery* had already been wowing rock cognoscenti for six months with its resonant mixing of Brill Building girl-group pop and deeply autobiographical, even mystical lyrics. The evidence that a major artist and composer had burst upon the scene was hard to refute. No less than four

songs from this record went on to become hit singles and radio staples: "Wedding Bell Blues" and "Blowing Away" (both for the Fifth Dimension), "And When I Die" (Blood, Sweat & Tears) and "Stoney End" (Barbra Streisand, who also covered the album's "Flim Flam Man").

Laura Nyro

More Than A New Discovery

Verve FOLKWAYS

All of the above compositions written by Laura Nyro (BMI)
Arranged and Conducted by: Herb Bernstein
Produced by: MILT OKUN
Production Supervisor: Jerry Schoenbaum
Production Assistant: Jean Goldhirsch
Director of Engineering: Val Valentin
Engineer: Harry Yarmark
Cover Design: Michael Malatak
Cover Photo: Murray Laden

FT/FTS-3020

SIDE I:
1. Goodbye Joe 2:36
2. Billy's Blues 3:16
3. And When I Die 2:37
4. Stoney End 2:41
5. Lazy Susan 3:50
6. Hands Off The Man 2:25

SIDE II:
1. Wedding Bells Blues 2:46
2. Buy And Sell 3:34
3. He's A Runner 3:37
4. Blowin' Away 2:20
5. I Never Meant To Hurt You 2:49
6. California Shoe-Shine Boys 2:43

After you've listened to even part of this debut LP by Laura Nyro, you will know why it is called "More Than a New Discovery."

Wouldn't it almost be enough for a young woman to sing this well, to shape and interpret musical lines and lyrics with the style, the grace and the power she does? It would be enough for most singers, but think for a moment that Laura Nyro wrote every song on this record! If that isn't enough to cause excitement, be advised that these are the first twelve songs she ever wrote professionally.

Laura Nyro is a study in contrasts. She is shy, quiet, an almost humble person. She seems contemplative and reserved. Then she starts to write, and sing, and a whole world of emotion and feeling starts to flow. If ever there was truth to the concept that some musicians speak best through their music, Laura Nyro is living proof.

The singer-songwriter featured here was discovered by two of the most astute figures in the music industry: Arthur Mogull and Paul Barry. If Artie needs any introduction, let's just drop the name of one songwriter that Mogull was the first to sign for publishing, a fellow from Hibbing, Minnesota, named Bob Dylan. Working along with Mogull and Barry on this session was Milt Okun, the musical director for Peter, Paul and Mary, The Mitchell Trio and The Brothers Four. When Messrs. Mogull and Okun get excited about a new singing star, everyone ought to get excited.

But the work of Laura Nyro speaks for itself, more than the praise of fans or co-workers. Here is a young stylist who deals in a type of song and a type of delivery that she describes as "polished soul." Here is reined passion in pop music, a passion that catches the listener and moves him, as the best of artists alone can do.

Laura Nyro was born in New York 19 years ago. She graduated from the High School of Music and Art in Manhattan in 1965. For a year thereafter, she recalls, "I kind of moved around. I saw publishers and I saw other music people. But none could offer me what I was really looking for, a certain freedom, a real freedom." She found

what she was looking for when she met Artie Mogull and Paul Barry, and then things began to happen.

Her single of "Wedding Bells Blues" on Verve/Folkways immediately won the praise of all the trade papers in the business. And it caught on with radio listeners and fans around the country. Peter, Paul and Mary recorded her gospel-driving joyful song, "And When I Die," and that is rather a quick trip to the moon for a new songwriter.

All of this was in the fall of 1966. Actually, Laura started singing when she was just a baby, then continued in elementary school. As nearly as she can recall, she started trying to write songs about the age of eleven. "My first few songs were very bad," she says today, although with her modesty, one wonders how true that is.

Later, she had some fun rewriting pop songs of the day with her own racy lyrics, just for kicks. Around the time Laura turned fourteen she joined up with a few Puerto Rican groups, singing and riffing in subway stations and on street corners. There were "about four guys and me doing rock 'n' roll."

Laura's father was a jazz trumpeter and worked in the piano business; her mother "digs" the classical scene, so she has always been immersed in music in and away from home. Laura is still living at home with her brother and three cats.

In describing her music as "polished soul," Laura indicates that she does a lot of thinking about what goes into a performance and into writing a song. "Anybody can sing soul if they've got it. I think some classical music is soul music," she added, referring to works by Orff and others. "Soul," she continued, "is honesty, for one thing."

Laura is wisely avoiding being put into any pigeonholes, in line with her "I want to be free" philosophy. Although some of her musical roots are folk ("I sort of grew up with Bob Dylan's music") she loves the work of Nancy Wilson and Sarah Vaughan and the Vibrations in live concert.

Although she would rather sing and write music than talk about it, Laura has given it a lot of thought, "I sing mostly to life, to people that I may have known and loved, if only for an hour. I try to have a little bit of hope in even the saddest of blues."

So, here is a phenomenon named Laura Nyro. Still a girl, a young woman, and yet she writes and sings and feels like a woman. There is depth here and a sense of musicality that one rarely encounters. The album was produced by Milt Okun, (to Laura, "A good folk") with arrangements by Herb Bernstein (Laura calls him "a genius and a pussycat"). A group of three studio singers who call themselves The High Fashions help out. But the album is pure Laura Nyro, and that is pure gold.

—Bob Shelton

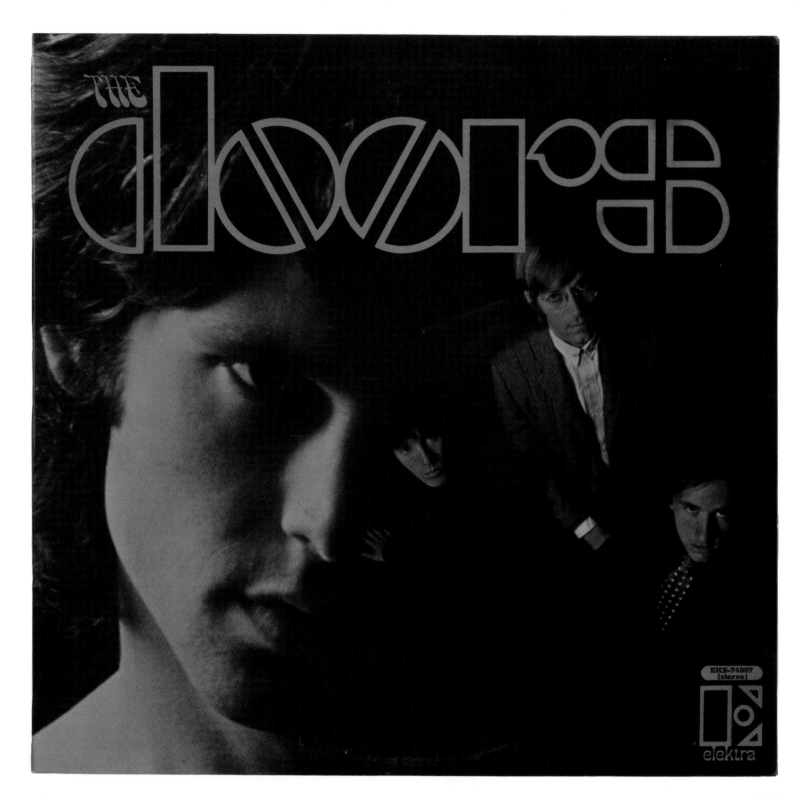

EKS-74007
(stereo)

elektra

THE DOORS | The Doors

January 1967 | Elektra

When it comes to abundant riches, few periods in popular music can compete with 1967. The year's creative bumper crop included *Sgt. Pepper's, Surrealistic Pillow, The Piper at the Gates of Dawn, Younger Than Yesterday, The Velvet Underground & Nico, I Never Loved a Man the Way I Love You, Moby Grape, Procol Harum, Cold Sweat, Forever Changes, Disraeli Gears…* and *The Doors*. Few considered the L.A. quartet the Most Likely to Succeed among the class of '67 once its first single, "Break on Through," flopped. But *The Doors* also contained "Light My Fire," guitarist Robby Krieger's partially completed response to an early Jim Morrison challenge that each member of the band write a song over the weekend. Released as a single, the melodic rocking ode to romantic and hallucinogenic ecstasy became the hit of the Summer of Love, a global standard that launched a thousand covers. "Light My Fire" was

the entry point to a provocative album dense with ideas and atmosphere, most notably the otherworldly "Crystal Ship," "Soul Kitchen," "Break on Through" and the group's iconic versions of Willie Dixon's "Back Door Man" and Kurt Weill's "Alabama Song." Neither the initial controversy engendered by the profane, 11-minute "The End" nor subsequent criticism of Morrison as tragic rock god could obscure the album's achievements. It provided a perfect introduction to one of rock's most important bands and remains both an artifact of its age and a time-transcending classic.

Side One
1. BREAK ON THROUGH
   (To The Other Side) 2:25
2. SOUL KITCHEN 3:30
3. THE CRYSTAL SHIP 2:30
4. TWENTIETH CENTURY FOX 2:30
5. ALABAMA SONG (Whisky Bar)
   (Weill-Brecht, Witmark ASCAP) 3:15
6. LIGHT MY FIRE 6:50

Side Two
1. BACK DOOR MAN
   (W. Dixon & C. Burnett, Arc Music BMI) 3:30
2. I LOOKED AT YOU 2:18
3. END OF THE NIGHT 2:49
4. TAKE IT AS IT COMES 2:13
5. THE END 11:35

Words & music to all songs
by The Doors (unless otherwise indicated)
© Copyright Nipper Music ASCAP

THE DOORS

JIM MORRISON vocals

RAY MANZAREK organ, piano, bass

ROBBY KRIEGER guitar

JOHN DENSMORE drums

EKS-74007
(stereo)

elektra

Produced by PAUL A. ROTHCHILD Production Supervisor · JAC HOLZMAN
Engineering · BRUCE BOTNICK, Sunset Sound Recorders, Hollywood
Front Cover Photo · GUY WEBSTER   Back Cover Photo · JOEL BRODSKY
Art Direction & Design · WILLIAM S. HARVEY
ELEKTRA RECORDS · 1855 Broadway · New York, N.Y. 10019 · 2, Dean Street · London W.1

STEREO elektra STEREO

EKS-74007-A
SIDE ONE

THE DOORS

1. BREAK ON THROUGH (To The Other Side) 2:25
2. SOUL KITCHEN 3:30
3. THE CRYSTAL SHIP 2:30
4. TWENTIETH CENTURY FOX 2:30
5. ALABAMA SONG (Whiskey Bar)
   (Weill-Brecht, Witmark ASCAP) 3:15
6. LIGHT MY FIRE 6:30
Words & music to all songs by The Doors
(unless otherwise indicated)
© Copyright Nipper Music ASCAP
Recording first published January 1967

LPM-3766

JEFFERSON AIRPLANE | Surrealistic Pillow

February 1967 | RCA

The breakthrough album for San Francisco's fertile psychedelic-rock scene came late. *Surrealistic Pillow* was released a year after the Fillmore opened its doors and six months after the Airplane's modestly-selling debut, by which time the band had issued four unsuccessful singles and changed drummers and female lead singers. But Signe Anderson's replacement by Grace Slick, who brought "White Rabbit" and "Somebody to Love" to the group, made all the difference. The two 45s shot a hole through prevailing notions of how loud and forceful singles might sound and still gain Top-40 acceptance, and it shattered conventional wisdom about how much women could rock. "Rabbit" and "Somebody" dominated the spring and Summer of Love, put San Francisco on the minds of the world and boosted *Surrealistic Pillow* to No. 3 on *Billboard*'s album chart, where it remained for over a year. And there's more to the LP than Slick. Marty Balin shines on the pummeling,

quasi-electronica of "Plastic Fantastic Lover" and the delicate ballad "Today," and the musicians, in particular lead guitarist Jorma Kaukonen and bassist Jack Casady, are endlessly inventive yet precisely focused on "She Has Funny Cars" and "3/5 of a Mile in 10 Seconds." *Surrealistic Pillow* is the Jefferson Airplane that remade pop music history.

SURREALISTIC PILLOW   Mono LPM-3766
Jefferson Airplane   Stereo LSP-3766

SIDE 1

She Has Funny Cars (3:03)
Somebody to Love (2:54)
My Best Friend (2:59)
Today (2:57)
Comin' Back to Me (5:18)

SIDE 2

3/5 of a Mile in 10 Seconds (3:39)
D. C. B. A. — 25 (2:33)
How Do You Feel (3:26)
Embryonic Journey (1:51)
White Rabbit (2:27)
Plastic Fantastic Lover (2:33)

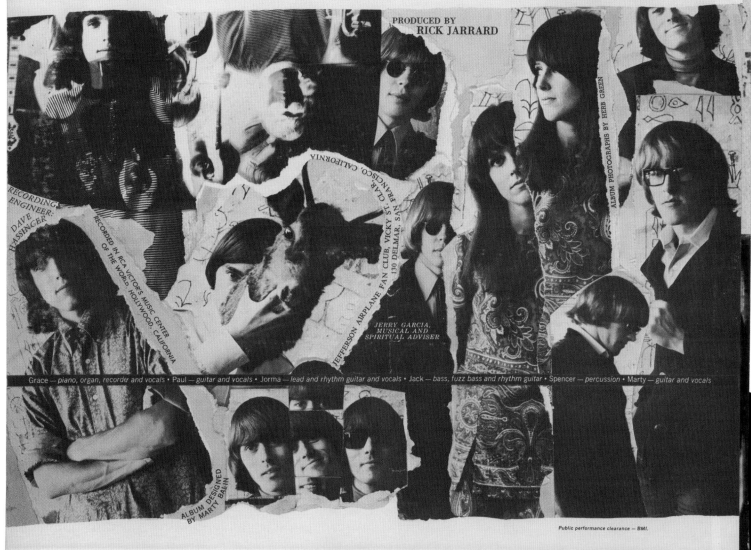

PRODUCED BY
RICK JARRARD

RECORDING ENGINEER: DAVE HASSINGER

RECORDED IN RCA VICTOR'S MUSIC CENTER OF THE WORLD, HOLLYWOOD, CALIFORNIA

JEFFERSON AIRPLANE FAN CLUB, VICKY ST., CLAIR, 130 DELMAR, SAN FRANCISCO, CALIFORNIA

ALBUM PHOTOGRAPHS BY HERB GREEN

JERRY GARCIA, MUSICAL AND SPIRITUAL ADVISER

ALBUM DESIGNED BY MARTY BALIN

Grace — piano, organ, recorder and vocals • Paul — guitar and vocals • Jorma — lead and rhythm guitar and vocals • Jack — bass, fuzz bass and rhythm guitar • Spencer — percussion • Marty — guitar and vocals

Public performance clearance — BMI.

RCA VICTOR

SURREALISTIC PILLOW
Jefferson Airplane

LPM 3766   SIDE 1
(TPRM-480?)

1—SHE HAS FUNNY CARS (Jorma Kaukonen-Marty Balin)
2—SOMEBODY TO LOVE (Darby Slick)
3—MY BEST FRIEND (Skip Spence)
4—TODAY (Marty Balin-Paul Kantner)
5—COMIN' BACK TO ME (Marty Balin)

MONAURAL

◀ PEEL SLOWLY AND SEE

Andy Warhol

THE VELVET UNDERGROUND & NICO |
The Velvet Underground & Nico

March 1967 | Verve

Producer Tom Wilson, who'd helmed Bob Dylan's "Like a Rolling Stone" and the Mothers' *Freak Out!*, deserves some kudos, but the bulk of the credit for this audacious debut goes to the New York quartet rightly regarded as the godparents of punk and alternative rock. Founder Lou Reed thought popular music undertook themes usually reserved for fiction, yielding several songs about drug addiction and sex fetishism, sung by Reed and Warhol-appointed vocalist Nico, in droll, deadpan tones that, to some critics, read as endorsement. All this from a band that took its name from a pornographic paperback and featured a cello in its rhythm section (played by bassist/pianist John Cale). Perhaps even more radical was the musical approach espoused by *The Velvet Underground and Nico*. When most rock was gravitating toward technical mastery and virtuoso showmanship, the Velvet Underground practiced primitivism, Maureen Tucker's drumming and Reed and Sterling Morrison's nuance-free guitar

work rendering "I'm Waiting for the Man" and "Heroin" and "There She Goes Again" powerful in a direct, elemental way far removed from the music of the band's contemporaries. Ironically, time has proven the album's low-rent approach more deserving of the appellation "art" than dozens of more accomplished and self-conscious records of the era.

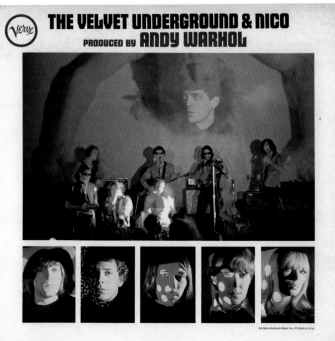

THE VELVET UNDERGROUND & NICO
PRODUCED BY ANDY WARHOL

V-5008

The back cover featured an upside down image of actor Eric Emerson, from Warhol's film *Chelsea Girls*, his face projected over Lou Reed's. Emerson claimed it had been included without his permission and sought to be paid; MGM withdrew the album and airbrushed out his image, causing further delays.

THE VELVET UNDERGROUND & NICO

LOU REED . . . . Lead Guitar, Ostrich Guitar, Vocal
JOHN CALE . . . . Electric Viola, Piano, Bass Guitar
STERLING MORRISON . . . . . . Rhythm Guitar, Bass Guitar
MAUREEN TUCKER . . . . Percussion
NICO . . . . Chanteuse

PRODUCED BY: ANDY WARHOL

THE VELVET UNDERGROUND & NICO

The Exploding Plastic Inevitable was a show created by Andy Warhol to introduce THE VELVET UNDERGROUND & NICO. The group opened in New York and toured the United States and Canada. This was the way some critics responded:

"Suddenly the Intermedia shows are all over town. The Velvet Underground performances at the Dom during the month of April provided the most violent, loudest and most dynamic exploration platform for this new art. Theirs remains the most dramatic expression of the contemporary generation. The place where its needs and desperations are most dramatically split open. At the Plastic Inevitable it is all Here and Now and the Future."
—Jonas Mekas, Village Voice

"Not since the Titanic ran into that iceberg has there been such a collision as when Andy Warhol's Exploding Plastic Inevitable burst upon the audiences at The Trip Tuesday. For once a Happening really happened, and it took Warhol to come out from New York to show how it's done. The Velvet Underground is so far out that it makes the tremendous thumping beat of the great, groovy group which opened the program sound passé."
—Los Angeles Times

"Screeching rock 'n roll - reminded viewers of nothing so much as Berlin in the decadent 30's."
—Los Angeles Magazine

"A Three-ring psychsafe that assaults the senses with the sights and sounds of the total environment syndrome... Discordant music, throbbing cadences, pulsating tempo."
—Variety

Edited and Remixed under the Supervision of Tom Wilson by Gene Radice & David Greene
Recording Engineers: Omi Haden—T.T.G. Hollywood
All arrangements by THE VELVET UNDERGROUND
*Produced by Tom Wilson
All songs written by Lou Reed except the following two:
THE BLACK ANGEL'S DEATH SONG—Lou Reed & John Cale
EUROPEAN SON to DELMORE SCHWARTZ—Lou Reed, John Cale, Sterling Morrison & Maureen Tucker

SIDE I:
1. SUNDAY MORNING* 2:53
2. I'M WAITING FOR THE MAN 4:37
3. FEMME FATALE 2:35
4. VENUS IN FURS 5:07
5. RUN RUN RUN 4:18
6. ALL TOMORROW'S PARTIES 5:55
SIDE II:
1. HEROIN 7:05
2. THERE SHE GOES AGAIN 2:30
3. I'LL BE YOUR MIRROR 2:01
4. THE BLACK ANGEL'S DEATH SONG 3:10
5. EUROPEAN SON 7:40

COVER DESIGN: Acy R. Lehman
DIRECTOR OF ENGINEERING: Val Valentin
LINER PHOTOS BY: Nat Finkelstein & Billy Linich
COLOR SHOW PHOTO BY: Hugo
PORTRAITS BY: Paul Morrissey
Cover Painting BANANA by: ANDY WARHOL

"Warhol's brutal assemblage—non-stop horror show. He has indeed put together a total environment, but it is an assemblage that actually vibrates with menace, cynicism, and perversion. To experience it is to be brutalized, helpless—you're in any kind of horror you want to imagine, from police state to mad house. Eventually the men-oberations in your ears stop. But what do you do with what you still hear in your brain? The flowers of evil are in full bloom with the Exploding Plastic Inevitable."
—Michaela Williams, Chicago Daily News

"Shatteringly contemporary—the electronic music, loud enough to make the vision and the mind vibrate in unison—Nico, the beautiful flaxen-haired girl, the noise, the lights, the film and the dances build to a screeching crescendo."
—San Francisco Chronicle

"The Velvet Underground, a group whose howling, throbbing beat is amplified and extended by electronic dist-twiddling, has a sound hard to describe, even harder to duplicate, but haunting in its uniqueness. And with the Velvets come the blonde, bland, beautiful Nico, another cooler Detrich for another cooler generation. Art has come to the discotheque and it will never be the same again."
—John Wilcock, East Village Other

"The sound is a savage series of atonal thrusts and electronic feedback. The lyrics combine Sado-Masochistic imagery. The whole sound seems to be the product of a secret marriage between Bob Dylan and The Marquis de Sade."
—Richard Goldstein, New York World Journal-Tribune

"The rock 'n roll music gets louder, the dancers get more frantic, and the lights start going on and off like crazy. And there are spotlights blinking in our eyes, and car horns beeping, and Gerard Malanga and the dancers are shaking like mad, and you don't think the noise can get any louder, and then it does, until there is one big rhythmic tidal wave of sound, pressing down around you, just impure enough so you can still get the beat, the audience, the dancers, the music and the movies, all of it fused together into one magnificent moment of hysteria."
—George English, Fire Island News

"Nico, astonishing—the macabre face—so beautifully mournful it mesmerizes a moment: next, the marvelous deathlike voice coming from the lovely blind head."
—David Antim, Art News

VERVE Records

THE VELVET UNDERGROUND & NICO

Prod. By Andy Warhol
*Prod. By Tom Wilson
All Arrangements By The Velvet Underground

V-5008
(MG-55B)

*1. SUNDAY MORNING—2:53 (Reed) Three Prong Music
2. I'M WAITING FOR THE MAN—4:37 (Reed) Three Prong Music
3. FEMME FATALE—2:35 (Reed) Three Prong Music
4. VENUS IN FURS—5:07 (Reed) Three Prong Music
5. RUN, RUN, RUN—4:18 (Reed) Three Prong Music
6. ALL TOMORROW'S PARTIES—5:55 (Reed) Three Prong Music
All Selections BMI

MGM RECORDS—A DIVISION OF METRO-GOLDWYN-MAYER, INC.—Made in U.S.A.

Side 1

V/V6-5008

The cryptic lettering at the top of the cover reads, "In the land of the dark the ship of the sun is driven by the," followed by the easily readable, "Grateful Dead." The original design was easy to read and the band asked for it to be changed. Dead leader Jerry Garcia told Ralph J. Gleason, "We didn't like it because we thought it was a tad pretentious. So we talked to Stanley [Mouse] and said, 'Could you do something that almost says something but doesn't quite?' The result of that has been that all the places we've been where people have had the album, we've been able to hear their translations."

GRATEFUL DEAD | Grateful Dead

March 1967 | Warner Bros.

The first truly psychedelic album from the San Francisco scene is loud, fast and rooted in as many conventions as it breaks. The same record that allots almost a full side to an extended freak-out ("Viola Lee Blues") by way of introducing what its manager called "the world's ugliest band" also relies on a wellspring of musical traditions that sustained the group's 40-year career. Though Jerry Garcia and company would later contribute their share of standards to the rock-song canon, this debut features just two Dead originals, the crazed, Dylanesque "Cream Puff War" and the would-be pop single "The Golden Road." The remainder of the track list is grounded in the folk, blues and old-timey material the band played before it went electric and long after it evolved into a respected American institution: Jesse Fuller's "Beat It on Down the Line," Noah Lewis' "Viola Lee Blues" and "[New] New Minglewood Blues," the bluegrass staple "Cold Rain and

Snow" popularized by Bill Monroe, Junior Wells' arrangement of Sonny Boy Williamson's "Good Morning Little Schoolgirl." *The Grateful Dead* also features one of the first real psychedelic covers, by San Francisco poster artists Stanley Mouse and Alton Kelley.

SAN FRANCISCO'S *GRATEFUL DEAD:*
Bob Weir, Pigpen, Bill The Drummer,
Jerry ("Captain Trips") Garcia, and Phil Lesh

SIDE ONE:
The Golden Road
(To Unlimited Devotion)
(2:07)
Beat It on Down the Line
(2:27)
Good Mornin' Little School Girl
(5:56)
Cold Rain and Snow
(2:25)
Sittin' on Top of the World
(2:01)
Cream Puff War
(2:25)

SIDE TWO:
Morning Dew
(5:00)
New, New Minglewood Blues
(2:31)
Viola Lee Blues
(10:01)

PRODUCED BY DAVE HASSINGER
Engineer: Dick Bogert / Cover Design: Mouse
Studios / Collage: Kelly / Cover Photo: Herb
Greene / Liner Photo: Gene Anthony

The Grateful Dead Fan Club
P.O. Box 31201, San Francisco, California

WARNER BROS. RECORDS, INC., A SUBSIDIARY AND LICENSEE OF WARNER BROS. PICTURES, INC., 4000 WARNER BOULEVARD, BURBANK, CALIFORNIA; 321 W. 44TH STREET, NEW YORK, NEW YORK.   MADE IN U.S.A.

ELT

WARNER BROS.
RECORDS

WB

PROMOTION   NOT FOR SALE
Playing   Time - 17:21

THE GRATEFUL DEAD
Produced by Dave Hassinger
Arranged by The Grateful Dead

W 1689
(9233)

SIDE
1

1. Ice Nine Pub. Co.   4. Ice Nine Pub. Co.
   BMI - 2:07   BMI - 2:25
2. Contemporary   5. Mayfair Music
   Music BMI - 2:27   ASCAP - 2:01
3. Jewel Music Pub.   6. Ice Nine Pub. Co.
   Co. Ltd. ASCAP -   BMI - 2:25
   5:56

1. THE GOLDEN ROAD (To Unlimited Devotion)
   (McGannahan Skjellyfetti)
2. BEAT IT ON DOWN THE LINE
   (Jesse Fuller)
3. GOOD MORNING, LITTLE SCHOOL GIRL
   (H.G. Demarais)
4. COLD RAIN AND SNOW
   (McGannahan Skjellyfetti)
5. SITTING ON TOP OF THE WORLD
   (Jacobs-Carter)
6. CREAM PUFF WAR
   (Jerry Garcia)

VITAPHONIC

33⅓   HIGH FIDELITY

This rare mono
promotional copy
was made for radio
stations.

THE JIMI HENDRIX EXPERIENCE | Are You Experienced   **May 1967 | Track**

Jimi Hendrix's debut was an album of inestimable importance, and a key pivot in a musical success story whose arc now reads as inevitable as the solar system itself. Clapton may have claimed the crown as rock's original guitar hero, but Hendrix, in front of a band bearing his name and playing his songs, was the music's first—and truest—guitar star. If proof was needed of his unfathomable depths of talent and imagination, *Are You Experienced* provided it. The album appeared four months after "Hey Joe" became a global smash and barely a month before Hendrix awed audiences at the Monterey Pop Festival. An instant staple of the then new rock-FM radio, it was a cornerstone experience of the counterculture and remains a potent signifier of the era more than four decades later. Hendrix's performances here comprise ineradicable portions of the rock canon, with "Fire" and "Foxy Lady,"

"Purple Haze," "Third Stone from the Sun" and the rest expressing everything that the music had ever been and might become: sex, blues, sci-fi and psychedelia, technology and spiritual liberation all roll and tumble across its 40 amazing minutes.

THE JIMI HENDRIX EXPERIENCE

JIMI HENDRIX
Guitar and Vocal
Born Seattle, Washington, November 27, 1947. Left school early and joined the Army-Airborne, but was invalided out with a broken ankle and an injured back. Started hitching around the Southern States, guitar pickin'.
One night one of the Isley Brothers heard him playing and offered him a place in their band.
"Yeah, I'll gig. May as well, man, sleeping outside between them tall tenements was hell. Rats running all across your chest, cockroaches stealin' your last candy bar from your very pockets".
But he soon turned in his silk stage suit and matching patent boots and headed once more for Nashville.
A tour came through town headed by B. B. King, Sam Cooke, Solomon Burke, Chuck Jackson, and Jackie Wilson. Jimi managed to join the show and toured all over the States, backing these great artistes, learning much of *his* artistry on the way. One day he missed the tour bus and found himself stranded in Kansas City, penniless. He scraped together enough money to make it to Atlanta, Georgia, where he joined the Little Richard package tour, again touring all over, finally playing with Ike and Tina Turner on the West Coast. When the tour arrived in New York Jimi left Little Richard and became one of Joey Dee's Starliters, at a time when this band was big news internationally. In August 1966 Jimi went solo with a backing band, playing in Greenwich Village for the princely sum of fifteen dollars a night.
Ex-Animal Chas Chandler and Mike Jeffrey, the Animal's Manager persuaded him to come to England, and he arrived in September, since which time he has already excited many audiences up and down the country.
"I came to England, picked out the two best musicians, the best equipment, and all we are trying to do now is create, create, create, music, our own personal sound, our own personal being . . ."

MITCH MITCHELL
Drummer
Nineteen year old Mitch is a product of Acts Educational and The Corona Stage School. He first joined the Coronets, Chris Sandfords' backing group. "Not Too Little, Not Too Much" became a hit but the group disbanded due to Chris's many acting commitments. Mitch then had a year's spell with Georgie Fame's Blue Flames, which lasted until October 1966. A chance meeting with Chas Chandler in November last year resulted in Mitch joining The Experience. Young and refreshing in ideas but truly a well seasoned professional drummer Mitch plays a key role in the sound of this exciting trio.

NOEL REDDING
Bass Guitar and Vocal
21 year old ex-art student Noel has been playing guitar with various groups since he left school five years ago. Noel formed "The Loving Kind" in October 1965. Unhappy at the group's lack of recording success, and being not a little ambitious, Noel went his own way and attended an audition Jimi was holding in October 1966. He was persuaded to change from guitar to bass guitar, which he has managed to do very successfully, making a strong contribution to the driving rhythm behind Jimi's extraordinary lead guitar.

Track Record
POLYDOR RECORDS LTD.
612 001

Printed and made by Ernest J. Day & Co. Ltd., London, W.1. Patent Pending.

U.S. label Reprise released the album with a psychedelic cover, featuring a fish eye photo by Karl Ferris.

U.K. label Track Records released the album in mono only.

THE BEATLES | Sgt. Pepper's Lonely Hearts Club Band   **June 1967 | Parlophone**   🇬🇧

With the exception of their *Please Please Me* debut, this must be considered the Beatles' most significant album, and thus one of the most important in all of popular music. While McCartney and Lennon openly acknowledged the inspiration of the Beach Boys' *Pet Sounds* of a year earlier, there's no denying that *Sgt. Pepper's Lonely Hearts Club Band* represented the most dramatic leap forward in rock's steadily escalating ambitions. The conceit behind the record along with the Beatles' imaginative execution pulled off something extraordinary. In almost one fell swoop, the divide between high and popular art was breached, and a medium previously considered ephemeral suddenly stood the chance of being taken seriously, like classical or jazz, as deserving of study and scholarship as literature or painting or dance. There really was no precedent for tracks as experimental and fully realized as "A Day in

the Life," "Fixing a Hole" or "Lucy in the Sky with Diamonds," just as there had never been an album that unified such wildly diverse selections into a cohesive whole. The response to *Sgt. Pepper's* was overwhelming commercial and critical success, and it left a lasting impression on culture in general. The album may be the ultimate example of what literary critic Harold Bloom identified as "the anxiety of influence": after *Sgt. Pepper's*, no artist would be able to avoid the shadow of its achievement.

Mono copies like this one featured a different sound mix.

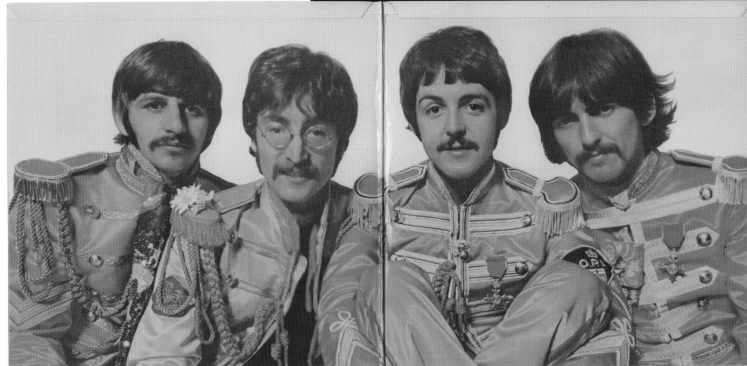

Inside the gatefold, The Beatles appeared as Sgt. Pepper's band, in silk military style outfits.

The back cover included the lyrics to every song; a first for a rock album.

An insert, with Sgt. Pepper Cut-Outs.

The album cover photo featured drummer Don Stevenson giving "the finger;" it was airbrushed out for the second pressing. Original copies also included a poster of the album art. Photograph by Jim Marshall.

PETER LEWIS

JERRY MILLER

SKIP SPENCE

DON STEVENSON

BOB MOSLEY

MOBY GRAPE | Moby Grape   **June 1967 | Columbia**

The band that delivered what many observers have called the best debut album ever had so much going for it, yet so much went wrong. But not here, where the San Francisco quintet is revealed in all its melodic, multi-threat glory. Five great musicians, all of whom contribute vocals and write—no small accomplishment on a music scene rife with bands deficient in one or more of those departments. The Grape's garage, surf and bar-band roots provide the foundation for an album that is at once psychedelic and focused, idiosyncratic yet broadly appealing, and dynamic from start to finish. Jerry Miller's lead guitar playing on "Hey Grandma" and "Indifference" is incandescent, bright and burning with ideas that utterly transform these basic shuffles. "Fall on You" predates punk's pogo tempo by a decade, Bob Mosley tenderizes tough soul on "Mr. Blues," and Skip Spence's infectious "Omaha" gleefully erases all previous

distinctions between "pop" and "rock." The album's quieter tunes are just as impressive, Miller and Don Stevenson's "8:05" and Peter Lewis' melancholy "Sitting by the Window" besting the ballads of most of their West Coast contemporaries. The wrong stuff: while *Moby Grape* sold respectably, the group never recovered from early, self-inflicted wounds (a widely publicized drug bust following its album-launch party) and the sins of their label, which, in a fit of hype, issued 10 of the album's 13 cuts on singles at the same time.

A scarce mono pressing.

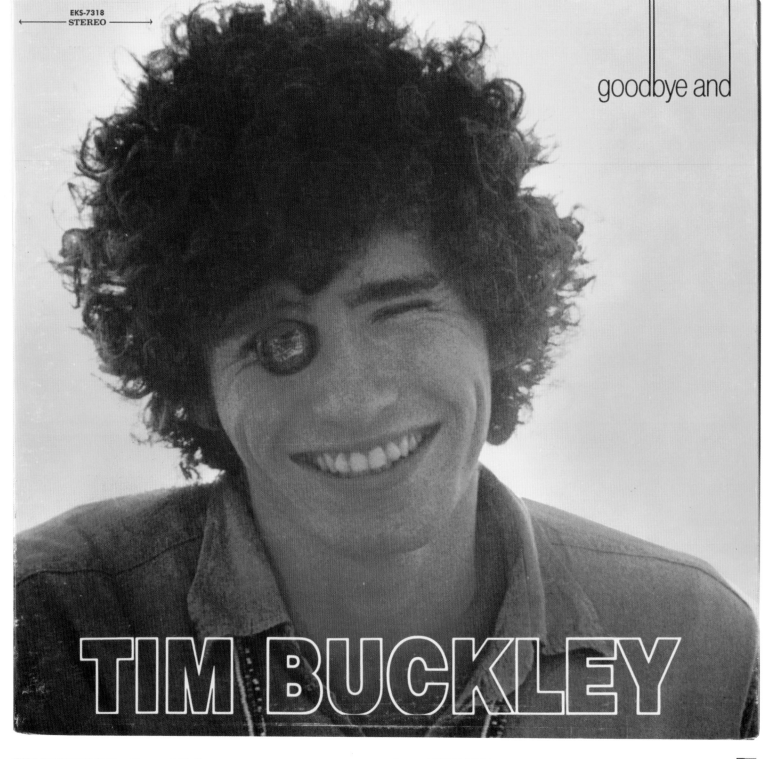

EKS-7318
← STEREO →

goodbye and

In Guy Webster's cover photo, Buckley sports a rusted Pepsi-Cola bottle cap in his eye.

TIM BUCKLEY | Goodbye and Hello

August 1967 | Elektra

A strong case could be made for including Buckley's debut LP on this list, but *Goodbye and Hello*, issued one year later, is where the young Orange County singer-songwriter found the voice that would establish him as the cherished, if deeply tragic, figure he remains. Where *Tim Buckley* was the work of a relatively straightforward post-Dylan troubadour, this album is more experimental, and thus exciting, with Buckley setting his songs within arrangements that hover between folk and jazz but always convey the intensity of rock. "No Man Can Find the War" frames his fragile, escalating narrative with propulsive congas and the sounds of gunfire and helicopters, and the poetic ramble of "I Never Asked to Be Your Mountain" is underpinned by a quasi-Bo Diddley beat produced by slashing acoustic guitar. Perhaps best of all is the phantasmagoric encounter with the mystical hobo in "Morning Glory," Buckley's voice accompanied by an

ethereal chorus on a melody of unmatched beauty. Credit Elektra Records founder Jac Holzman with the foresight to have let such a gifted artist make such a questionably commercial yet incontestably important record.

Back cover

PINK FLOYD | The Piper At The Gates Of Dawn

August 1967 | Columbia

One of many totally unprecedented records released in 1967, *Piper at the Gates of Dawn* introduced one of the few genuinely "mega-groups" groups in history and suggested new directions that rock might follow. That such sonic signposts would be pointed out by what had only moments before been an R&B covers band formed by college lads is all the more remarkable. Much of the credit accrues to the late Syd Barrett, the group's guiding spark and, initially, principal songwriter. But Rick Wright, Roger Waters and Nick Mason also deserve attention. While the San Francisco groups had been pushing hard against the instrumental envelope for a year or more, Pink Floyd was the first U.K. band to blast past the pop psychedelia of the Beatles and others and crash the jam barrier. What rendered *Piper* such a landmark was its marriage of well-anchored, if eccentric, composition with free-blowing ensemble playing. Barrett's "The

Gnome," "Bike" and "Matilda Mother" stretch conventional forms, but more spacey excursions like "Astronomy Domine," "Interstellar Overdrive" and "Lucifer Sam" firmly captured the freak-flag of British psychedelia—and, ultimately, invented progressive rock in one fell swoop.

THE PIPER AT THE GATES OF DAWN

SYD BARRETT—LEAD GUITAR & VOCALS
ROGER WATERS—BASS GUITAR & VOCALS
RICK WRIGHT—ORGAN/PIANO
NICKY MASON—DRUMS

SIDE ONE
1. ASTRONOMY DOMINÉ
   (Barrett)
2. LUCIFER SAM
   (Barrett)
3. MATILDA MOTHER
   (Barrett)
4. FLAMING
   (Barrett)
5. POW R. TOC H.
   (Barrett—Waters—Wright—Mason)
6. TAKE UP THY STETHOSCOPE
   AND WALK
   (Waters)

SIDE TWO
1. INTERSTELLAR OVERDRIVE
   (Barrett—Waters—Wright—Mason)
2. THE GNOME
   (Barrett)
3. CHAPTER 24
   (Barrett)
4. THE SCARECROW
   (Barrett)
5. BIKE
   (Barrett)

PRODUCED BY: NORMAN SMITH
Recording Engineer: Peter Bown
Front Cover Photo: Vic Singh
Rear Cover Design: Syd Barrett

℗ 1967

E.M.I RECORDS THE GRAMOPHONE COMPANY LTD.
HAYES · MIDDLESEX · ENGLAND

Made and Printed in Great Britain

Columbia

EMI

To play this **STEREO** record on a mono reproducer the
reproducer should have either a stereo pick-up wired for
mono or a suitable mono pick-up. Most pick-ups produced
recently will be suitable for this purpose. If in doubt consult
your dealer. True stereophonic reproduction will only be obtained
from a complete stereo reproducer. To keep this record clean
and dust free we recommend the regular use of **NEW EMITEX**.

6709 TPS   Printed and made by Ernest J. Day & Co. Ltd., London   SX 6157 / SCX 6157

The back cover fea-
tured an illustration
by the band's Syd
Barrett. The album
title comes from
Kenneth Grahame's
children's book *The
Wind in the Willows*.

As was often the
case with '60s
albums, stereo
and mono copies
featured different
sound mixes.

BUFFALO SPRINGFIELD | Again　　　　　　　　　　October 1967 | Atco

Following a sterling first album, Buffalo Springfield shines on this sophomore set. Never has a band on the verge of breaking apart sounded this good. If the track list is all over the musical map, the group's members are taking off in consistently interesting directions. It wouldn't be inaccurate to claim that Neil Young is *Again*'s shining star, as he not only pushes his songwriting far beyond his work on the band's debut but begins here to sketch the more expansive contours of his solo records. His "Mr. Soul," "Expecting to Fly" and "Broken Arrow" rank among the peak moments of the group's short career, but *Again* doesn't want for highlights. Stills' folk-hard-rock-banjo breakdown "Bluebird" was rightly a staple of early rock-FM radio, and "Hung Upside Down" is an especially deft negotiation between subtle melody and muscular rhythm. If Richie Furay's contributions were initially overshadowed by those of his better-

known bandmates, one listen to *Again* rectifies the slight. "Child's Claim to Fame" is bittersweet yet sprightly country-rock, "Sad Memory" one of the Springfield's most poignant ballads and "Good Time Boy" (sung by drummer Dewey Martin) the pure-fun cut that leavens the album's otherwise somber themes and concerns. The kicker is that *Again* pays off in a way that it shouldn't: all the disparity and contrasting styles somehow cohere, and make it one of the better albums of the '60s.

Buffalo Springfield Again

ATCO STEREO SD 33-226

We wish to thank the following friends, enemies & people we don't know from Adam for their influence and inspiration. The dedication is to Barry Friedman.

Hank B. Marvin
Otis Redding
Doc Watson
FRED NEIL
Hank Williams
John Herald
Rickey Nelson
Randy Backman
Joe Mara
The Ventures
Roy Orbison
Jan & Sylvia
Jimi Hendrix
Bert Jansh
Jim & Jean
Cyrus Faryar & Rusty
Gene Pitney
Buddy Miles
Mickey Mickey—
Dany Peter
Eric Clapton

The Nurk Twins & George
Ringo
Phil Spector
Lester B. Pearson
Bobby Harmelink
KEN KOBLUN
Floyd Cramer
The Five Byrds
The Dillards
Robert Johnson
Herbie Cohen
Frank Zappa
Stones
Elmer & Mario
Donovan Leicht
Enid
JIM FRIEDMAN
Rickey James Matthews Jim Fielder
The Spoons
Jerry Yester

Chet atkins
Jefferson airplane
Peter Noone
Nurit
John Lee Hooker
John Hopkins
Charlie Chin
Jimmy Reed
Flatt & Scruggs
JACK NITZCHE
Jad Diltz
Mickey Most
John Coltrane
Lisa Kindred
Tim Hardin
Ray Brown
Craig Allen
Jindy Collins
George Romney
Billie Winter
Chip Douglas

BOB GIBSON
Fidel
Jim Messina
Fort William
Robert Zimmerman
Pibefitney Pala
Steve Saunders
Albt. Grossman
Richie Havens
Eddie Miller
Peanuts Willinghan
Pete Seeger
Mort.
Chuck Berry
The Kingston Trio & John
Felix Pappalardi
The Vanilla Fudge
...and a hundred thousand more.
(spelling by The Buffalo Springfield)

Side One

MR. SOUL (2:35)
Respectfully dedicated to the ladies of The Whisky A Go Go and the women of Hollywood. Words and Music by Neil Young. Produced by Charlie and Brian with a little help from their friends. VOCALS—Neil with Steve & Richie. GUITARS—Richie & Steve, rhythm; Neil, lead.

A CHILD'S CLAIM TO FAME (2:09)
Words and Music—Richie Furay. Production—Richie Furay. VOCALS —Richie with Steve & Neil. GUITARS—Neil, Richie & Steve. DOBRO— James Burton. BASS—Bruce. DRUMS—Dewey Martin. ENGINEERING —Ross Myering.

EVERYDAYS (2:38)
Words and Music—Steve Stills. Production—Steve Stills, Neil Young and Ahmet Ertegun. VOCALS—Steve with Richie. GUITARS—Richie (rhythm)—Neil (humm). PIANO—Steve. BASS—Jim Fielder. DRUMS— Dewey. Recorded live at Gold Star.

EXPECTING TO FLY (3:39)
Words and Music—Neil Young. Produced and arranged by Jack Nitzche & Neil Young. Dedicated to Donna & Vicki. VOCALS—Neil & Richie. LEAD GUITAR—Neil Young. ELECTRIC PIANO—Jack Nitzche. GRAND PIANO—Don Randi. Engineered by Bruce Botnick.

BLUEBIRD (4:28)
Words and Music—Steve Stills. Produced by Steve with Ahmet. VOCALS—Steve & Richie. GUITARS—Steve, Neil & Richie—all 11,386 of 'em. BASS—Bobby West. DRUMS—Dewey. BANJO—Charlie Chin. ENGINEER—Bruce Botnick.

Side Two

HUNG UPSIDE DOWN (3:24)
Words and Music—Steve Stills. Production—Steve Stills. VOCALS— Richie & Steve with Neil & Richie. GUITARS—Richie, Steve (fuzz) & Neil. ORGAN—Steve. BASS—Bruce. DRUMS—Dewey. ENGINEERING —Jim Messina.

SAD MEMORY (3:00)
Words and Music—Richie Furay. Production—Richie Furay. GUITARS —Richie & Neil (lead). Recorded by William Brittan except for the lead guitar which was recorded across town by Bill Lazarus.

GOOD TIME BOY (2:11)
Words and Music—Richie Furay. Executive Producer—Dewey Martin. VOCAL—Dewey Martin. Arranged by the horn section of The American Soul Train from Louisiana. GUITAR—Steve. BASS—Bruce. DRUMS— Dewey.

ROCK & ROLL WOMAN (2:44)
Words and Music—Steve Stills. Production—Steve Stills & Neil Young. VOCALS—Steve with Richie & Neil. GUITARS—Neil, Richie & Steve (lead). ELECTRIC PIANO—Steve. ORGAN—Steve. BASS—Bruce Palmer. DRUMS—Dewey Martin. INSPIRATION—David Crosby.

BROKEN ARROW (6:13)
Words and Music—Neil Young. Production—Neil Young. PIANO—Don Randi. GUITARS—Steve, Richie & Chris. DRUMS—Dewey. BASS— Bruce. Dedicated to Ken Koblun. VOCALS—Neil & Richie. Engineered by Jim Messina.

All the songs in this album are published by Ten East, Springalo & Cotillion, BMI.

Cover illustration: Eve Babitz
Liner notes: Buffalo Springfield
Album design: Loring Eutemey
A YORK/PALA PRODUCTION

ATCO RECORDS
1841 BROADWAY, NEW YORK, NEW YORK 10023
Division of Atlantic Recording Corporation
© 1967 Atlantic Recording Corporation   Printed in U.S.A.

SD 33-226

BUFFALO SPRINGFIELD AGAIN

AT CO SIDE 1
STEREO   ATCO RECORDS

1. MR. SOUL—Neil Young
2. A CHILD'S CLAIM TO FAME
   Richie Furay
3. EVERYDAYS—Steve Stills
4. EXPECTING TO FLY
   Neil Young
5. BLUEBIRD—Steve Stills

(ST-C-671117-MO)

EKS-74013

LOVE

forever changes

LOVE | Forever Changes

November 1967 | Elektra

Even in the heated creative marathon of the late '60s when groups competed to snatch the baton from the prior month's or week's artistic champion, this record stands out by a mile. Love's folk-rock debut of two years earlier was a distant memory, but so was the band's second LP, *Da Capo*, which had moved Arthur Lee and company partially out of the garage and into loftier digs just 10 months before *Forever Changes*. Reviewing it, *Crawdaddy* magazine praised Love's third for "making a move which few have even dreamed," namely a tantalizing amalgam of "Johnny Mathis, the Tijuana Brass and Cream" laced with acid commentary and skewered romantic monologues. The program makes convivial neighbors of the most intimate acoustic reflections (the Tim Buckley-ish "Old Man") and the most scalding, over-amped excoriations ("Live and Let Live"), in the process assembling one of rock's true masterworks. The music is filled with melancholy, longing and regret, but even when the lyrics turn caustic or make only acid-head sense, the sounds here are graceful, moving and legitimately "gorgeous," with "Alone Again Or" taking the prize. This is a one-of-a-kind record that could only have come from one group working to make magic at one precious time.

Side One
1. ALONE AGAIN OR† (Maclean-Breadcrust BMI) 3:15
   BRYAN MACLEAN, vocal
2. A HOUSE IS NOT A MOTEL* 3:25
3. ANDMOREAGAIN* 3:15
4. THE DAILY PLANET* 3:25
5. OLD MAN† (Maclean-Breadcrust BMI) 2:57
   BRYAN MACLEAN, vocal
6. THE RED TELEPHONE* 4:45

Side Two
1. MAYBE THE PEOPLE WOULD BE THE TIMES
   OR BETWEEN CLARK AND HILLDALE* 3:30
2. LIVE AND LET LIVE* 5:24
3. THE GOOD HUMOR MAN
   HE SEES EVERYTHING LIKE THIS* 3:00
4. BUMMER IN THE SUMMER* 2:20
5. YOU SET THE SCENE* 6:49

LOVE is
ARTHUR LEE, guitar & vocal
JOHN ECHOLS, guitar
BRYAN MACLEAN, guitar & vocal
KEN FORSSI, bass
MICHAEL STUART, percussion

All songs written and sung by ARTHUR LEE and published by
Grass Root Music BMI, except where otherwise noted.
*Arranged by Arthur Lee, orchestrated by David Angel
†Arranged by David Angel and Bryan Maclean

Produced by ARTHUR LEE with BRUCE BOTNICK • Production Supervisor JAC HOLZMAN • Front cover art BOB PEPPER • Back cover photo RONNIE HARAN • Cover design WILLIAM S. HARVEY
ELEKTRA RECORDS • 1855 Broadway • New York City 10023

LOVE
forever changes

STEREO elektra STEREO
EKS-74013-A
SIDE ONE

LOVE
FOREVER CHANGES
1. ALONE AGAIN OR (Maclean-Breadcrust BMI) 3:15
2. A HOUSE IS NOT A MOTEL 3:25
3. ANDMOREAGAIN 3:15
4. THE DAILY PLANET 3:25
5. OLD MAN (Maclean-Breadcrust BMI) 2:57
6. THE RED TELEPHONE 4:45
All songs written by Arthur Lee and published by
Grass Roots Music BMI except where otherwise noted.

EKS-74013

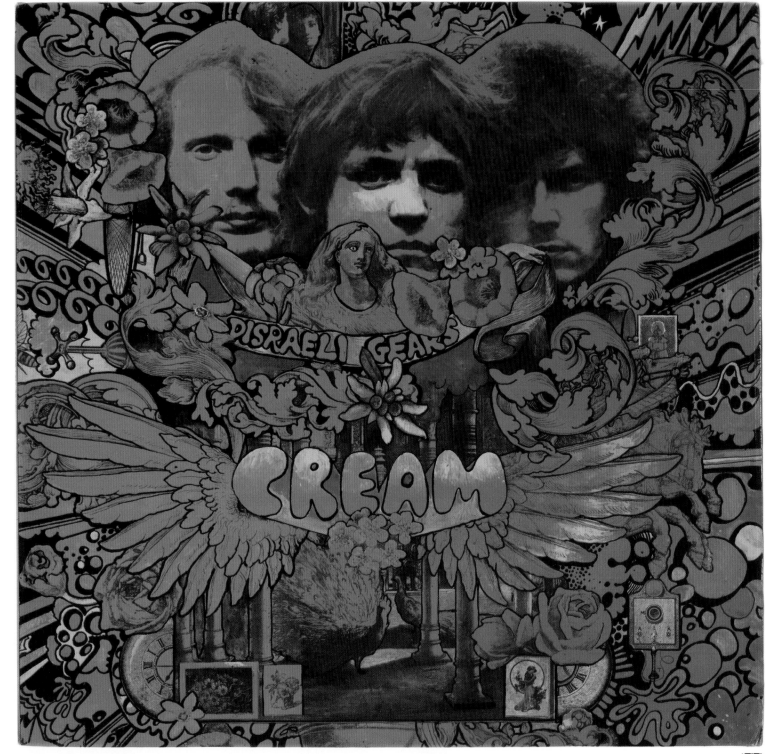

The album title is a malapropism. Guitarist Eric Clapton was discussing a racing bicycle with drummer Ginger Baker, when roadie Mick Turner noted, "It's got them Disraeli Gears," meaning "derailleur gears," but instead alluding to 19th-century British Prime Minister Benjamin Disraeli. The band thought this was hysterical, and used it for the title of their new album.

CREAM | Disraeli Gears

November 1967 | Reaction

In addition to being one of rock's most acclaimed guitarists, Eric Clapton was one of the 1960s' most antsy artists, constantly seeking escape routes from uncomfortable musical situations. After stints in the Yardbirds and John Mayall's Bluesbreakers, he settled into his longest-term relationship with Cream, pop's first acknowledged supergroup. *Disraeli Gears*, Cream's second album, is where Clapton, Jack Bruce, and Ginger Baker's collective talent became greater than the sum of its parts. The guitar hero once equated with the divine still solos, but is tethered to earth, an equal partner (and co-composer) with his singer-bassist and drummer cohorts. Though free-range blues jamming would come to characterize Cream's subsequent *Wheels of Fire*, here, discipline keeps in check any activity extraneous to the songs at hand. All parties contributed to the development of a distinct Cream style, as put forth on such rock-radio perennials as "Strange Brew," "Sunshine of Your Love," "Tales of Brave Ulysses," and "SWLABR."

Disraeli Gears is the record that turned Cream from a moderately successful favorite of music hipsters into an international attraction. That and, perhaps, the album's psyched-out Day-Glo cover, designed by Martin Sharp, who co-wrote "Tales of Brave Ulysses" with Clapton.

STEREO 594 003

DISRAELI GEARS

Produced by FELIX PAPALLARDI
In arrangement with
ROBERT STIGWOOD
Engineer TOM DOWD

Strange Brew
Sunshine of Your Love
World of Pain
Dance The Night Away
Blue Condition

Tales of Brave Ulysses
Swlabr
We're Going Wrong
Outside Woman Blues
Take It Back
Mother's Lament

reaction

The cover was designed by Australian artist Martin Sharp, who lived in the same building as Clapton and went on to design the sleeve for Cream's next album, *Wheels of Fire*. The back cover photography is by Robert Whitaker, who frequently shot The Beatles.

Disraeli Gears was the last of only three albums released on Reaction, a label owned by Cream manager Robert Stigwood.

reaction

ST 33

MADE IN ENGLAND
℗ 1967

594003
SIDE 1

DISRAELI GEARS
1. STRANGE BREW (Clapton/Collins/Papallardi)
2. SUNSHINE OF YOUR LOVE (Bruce/Brown/Clapton)
3. WORLD OF PAIN (Collins/Papallardi)
4. DANCE THE NIGHT AWAY (Bruce/Brown)
5. BLUE CONDITION (Baker)
CREAM
MCPS
1, 2, 4, 5. Dratleaf Ltd.
3. Windfall Music

TRAFFIC | Mr. Fantasy

December 1967 | Island

Mr Fantasy represents what might be described as British hippie music, as distinct from the mod, pop, blues, and spacey-psych sounds that had successively trekked up and across the U.K. charts. Formed in part by a Top-40 refugee (ex-Spencer Davis Group singer Stevie Winwood) who was glad to be free of pop's constraints, Traffic wasn't averse to jamming, but its concerns were far more song-focused than instrumentally inclined, which is not surprising, since Winwood, Dave Mason, Jim Capaldi and Chris Wood all wrote. In the spring before the Summer of Love, Island Records' Chris Blackwell sent the quartet to a cabin in Berkshire to see what might be cooked up. The band returned with one of the most appetizing long-players of the '60s, a homey, unhurried set awash in strong melodies, flowery sentiments ("Heaven Is in Your Mind"), and the warm camaraderie of musicians happy to be playing together. In the U.S.,

the tracks "Dear Mr. Fantasy," "Coloured Rain," and "Heaven Is in Your Mind" would come to occupy top slots on the playlists of the emerging FM-rock radio stations.

Mr. Fantasy

STEVE WINWOOD: Organ, Guitar, Bass Guitar, Piano, Harpsichord, Percussion and Vocals

JIM CAPALDI: Drums, Percussion and Vocals

CHRIS WOOD: Flute, Saxophone, Organ and Vocals

DAVE MASON: Guitar, Mellotron, Sitar, Tambura, Shakkai, Bass Guitar and Vocals

Recorded at Olympic Sound Studios
Engineer: Eddie Kramer
Photography: John Benton Harris
Sleeve Design: Chris Wood and CCS Advertising Associates
All songs published by Island Music Limited except "Utterly Simple" by United Artists Music and composed and arranged by the members of Traffic
PRODUCED BY: JIMMY MILLER

island
STEREO ILPS 9061

ISLAND RECORDS LIMITED 155-157 OXFORD STREET LONDON W1 ENGLAND

Back cover.

For the U.S. market, United Artists issued the album with a new title, *Heaven Is In Your Mind*, and a new cover without Dave Mason. When the song, "Dear Mr. Fantasy," became a radio hit, they changed the title back to "Mr. Fantasy."

stereo TRAFFIC • HEAVEN IS IN YOUR MIND • UNITED ARTISTS • UAS 6651

Heaven Is In Your Mind & traffic

FEATURING Mr. Fantasy

This original pressing features the collectible pink eye Island label.

MR. FANTASY
HEAVEN IS IN YOUR MIND
(Winwood—Capaldi—Wood)
BERKSHIRE POPPIES
(Winwood—Capaldi—Wood)
HOUSE FOR EVERYONE
(D. Mason)
NO FACE, NO NAME AND NO NUMBER
(Winwood—Capaldi)
DEAR MR. FANTASY
(Winwood—Capaldi—Wood)

TRAFFIC
Produced by Jimmy Miller

island
STEREO
ILPS 9061 A

89

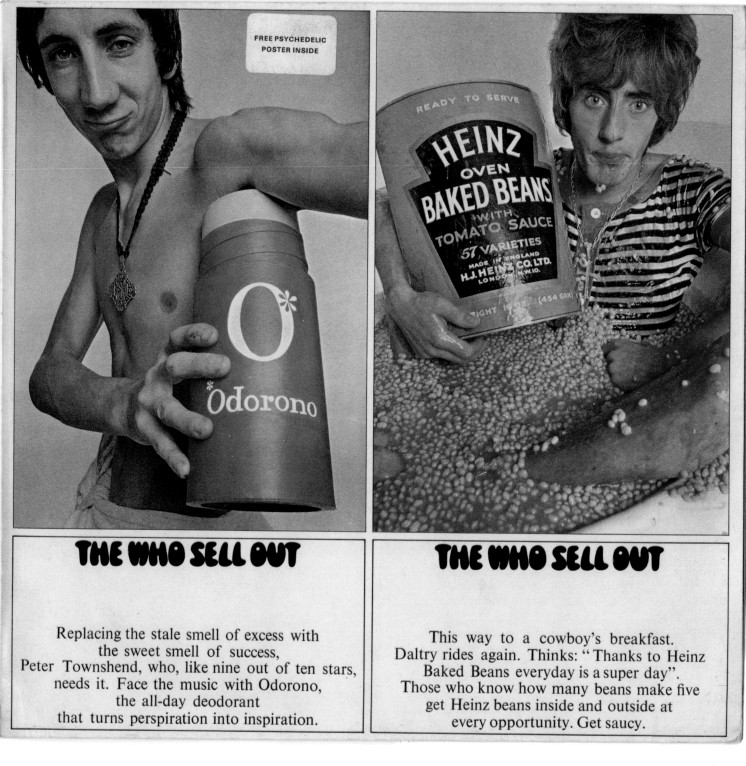

THE WHO | The Who Sell Out

December 1967 | Track

The early Who seem to have been afflicted by an extreme case of artistic restlessness. In less than two years, the group issued three albums, in the process turning itself from a mod covers-band with attitude into studio wizards whose recorded ambitions rivaled those of the Beatles and Beach Boys. *Sgt. Pepper's* was out and acclaimed and The Beach Boys' *Smile* lost in limbo by the time *The Who Sell Out* hit the shops, but the latter gets the nod as rock's first true concept set. Designed to be heard as a radio broadcast, *The Who Sell Out* utilized—and had great fun with—a familiar setting to present a fresh set of tunes. And what better group to undertake the intricate procession of songs, spots, and segues than The Who, whose previous *Happy Jack* LP had experimented with a suite ("A Quick One While He's Away"). Townshend's expansive eye for detail illuminates everything from song subjects ("Tattoo," "Mary Ann with the Shaky

Hand") to commercials that poke at youth-targeted pitches (for the acne medication "Medac": "Henry in the mirror peered/ His pimples all had disappeared"). *The Who Sell Out* gave the group its sole Top-10 hit in the U.S. ("I Can See for Miles"), but it gifted the world with an array of Who classics, among them, "Armenia City in the Sky," "I Can't Reach You," and "Our Love Was." David King and Roger Law's sleeve brought a new sophistication, and welcome humor, to the field of LP design.

THE WHO SELL OUT

There used to be a dark side to Keith Moon.
Not any more. If acne is preventing you from reaching
your acme, use Medac, the spot remover that
makes your pits flit. Put Medac on the spot now.

THE WHO SELL OUT

John Entwistle was a nine and a half stone
weakling until Charles Atlas made a man of him
at nine and three-quarter stone.
Now those huggy bear biceps bring those
beach beauties running. Put muscles
among the mussels. Tense yourself skinny.

THE WHO SELL OUT

There used to be a dark side to Keith Moon.
Not any more. If acne is preventing you from reaching
your acme, use Clearasil, the spot remover that
makes your pits flit. Put Clearasil on the spot now.

THE WHO SELL OUT

John Entwistle was a nine and a half stone
weakling until Charles Atlas made a man of him
at nine and three-quarter stone.
Now those huggy bear biceps bring those
beach beauties running. Put muscles
among the mussels. Tense yourself skinny.

Original Australian
copies had Keith
Moon applying
Clearasil, an acne
medication, instead
of the fictional
product Medac.

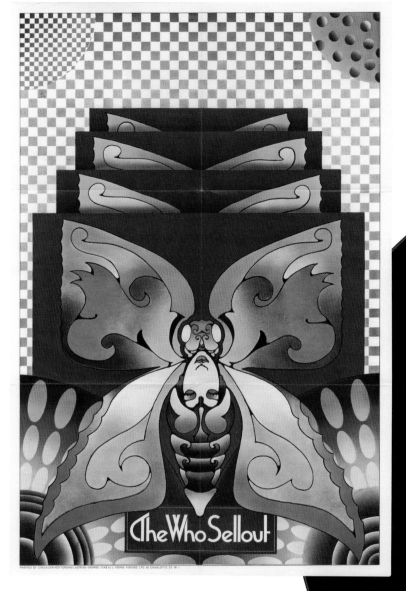

This poster,
designed by
Adrian George, was
included in the first
a thousand U.K.
copies sold.

Mono and stereo
copies of *The Who
Sell Out* have differ-
ent sound mixes.

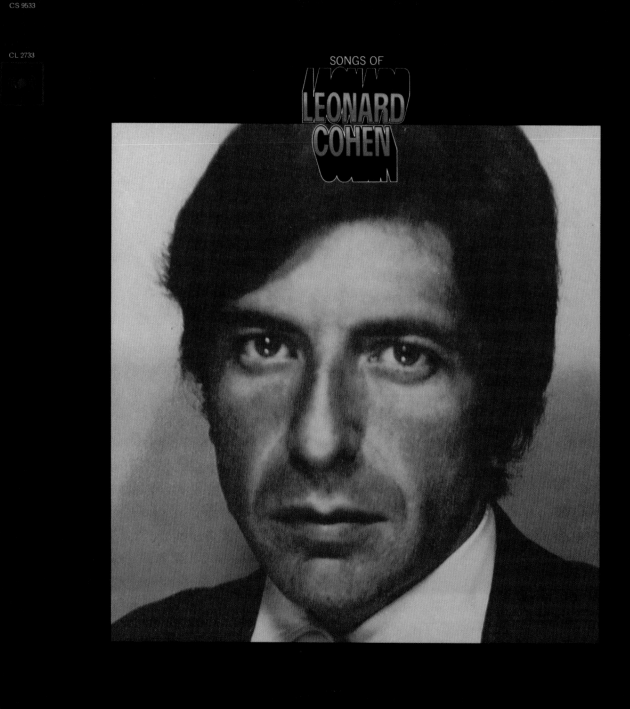

The front cover photograph was taken by a coin-operated photo booth. The credit reads "Cover Photo By Machine."

CS 9533

CL 2733

SONGS OF
LEONARD
COHEN

LEONARD COHEN | Songs of Leonard Cohen

December 1967 | Columbia

To his credit and his own bemusement, Cohen has never fit the standard uniform issued to pop stars, even in the wild and wooly '60s when he got his start. Instead, he first came to the public's attention as a poet (*The Spice-Box of the Earth*, 1961) and novelist (*Beautiful Losers*, 1966). A writer of thoughtful and deliberate songs, he was signed to Columbia Records by the legendary John Hammond (Bob Dylan, Billie Holiday, Aretha Franklin, Bruce Springsteen) and delivered *Songs of Leonard Cohen*, one of the most celebrated debuts in popular music. Though Cohen's compact, precision-cut songs were the polar opposite of Dylan's surreal ramblings, comparisons were made, which drew and continue to draw, an impressive array of singers to his material. "Suzanne" has been recorded by, among others, Judy Collins, Fairport Convention, Francoise Hardy, and Peter Gabriel; "Sisters of Mercy" by Linda Ronstadt and Emmylou Harris,

Dion, Sting and the Chieftains; "Hey, That's No Way to Say Goodbye" by Roberta Flack, Judy Collins, and the Decembrists. *Songs* marked Cohen as the first singer-songwriter not to have emerged from the ranks of folk or pop, and established highly literate standards for all who followed.

JOHN SIMON: Musical Director and Producer

Stereo CS 9533
Mono CL 2733

COLUMBIA

COVER PHOTO BY MACHINE

Manufactured by Columbia Records/CBS, Inc./51 W. 52 Street, New York, N.Y./® "Columbia," ℗ Marcas Reg. Printed in U.S.A.

COLUMBIA

LEONARD COHEN

CS 9533   SIDE 1

XSM 118903

1. SUZANNE
2. MASTER SONG
3. WINTER LADY
4. THE STRANGER SONG
5. SISTERS OF MERCY
    —L. Cohen

STEREO "360 SOUND"
® "COLUMBIA" ℗ MARCAS REG. PRINTED IN U.S.A.

The front cover has a faint black-on-black image of an arm with a skull tattoo in the bottom left corner.

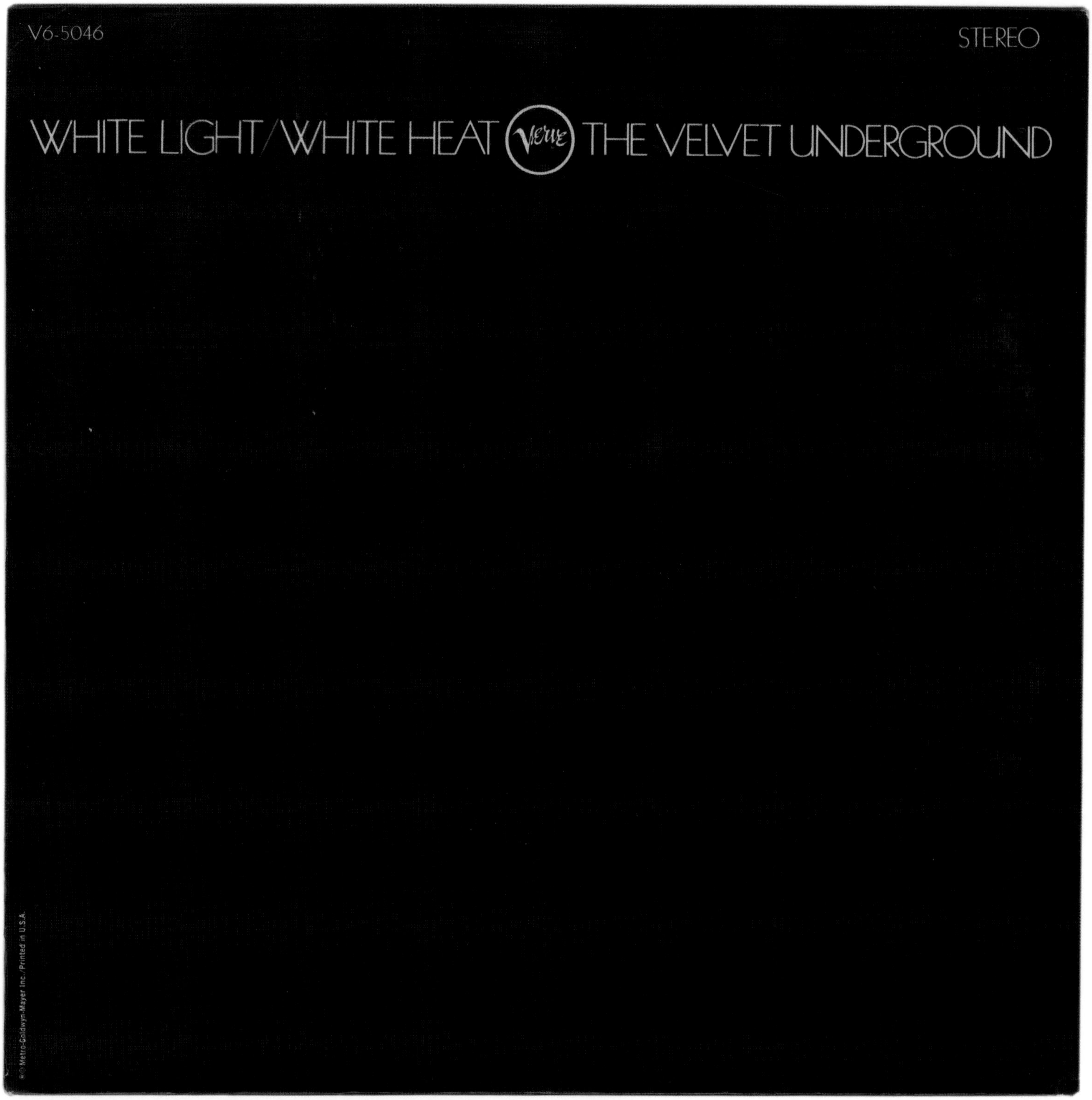

V6-5046
STEREO
WHITE LIGHT/WHITE HEAT
Verve
THE VELVET UNDERGROUND
® © Metro-Goldwyn-Mayer Inc./Printed in U.S.A.

THE VELVET UNDERGROUND | White Light/ White Heat

January 1968 | Verve

The first Velvet Underground album disclosed the group's unusual musical approach and its disdain for conventional forms of success. Encouraged, perhaps both by the positive response of its few fans and its more numerous detractors, the group pushed farther into experimental territory on *White Light/White Heat*, creating a record that John Cale, who left the band upon the record's completion, has described as "consciously anti-beauty." *White Light/White Heat* can be a challenging experience; it's as if the musicians felt they needed to disconcert the listener sufficiently to communicate just how much, as Cale put it, "everything was in turmoil then." The title track and "I Heard Her Call My Name" (whose fuzzy solo bears touches of West Coast psych) formalize Lou Reed's rockin' mode as earlier sketched in "Heroin" and "Waiting for the Man," while the Cale-narrated story-song "The Gift" and "Sister Ray" trek through less traveled, more foreboding landscapes. The latter epic, a scratchy amalgam of Stones energy and Seeds attitude that invented '80s noise-rock and No-Wave along the way, may be the defining Velvet Underground cut.

V/V6-5046

Original copies
credit Andy Warhol
for "Cover Concept"
and mistakenly title
"Here She Comes
Now" as "There
She Comes Now."

WHITE LIGHT / WHITE HEAT

Verve

THE VELVET UNDERGROUND

SIDE ONE

WHITE LIGHT / WHITE HEAT 2:44
(Words & Music: Lou Reed)

THE GIFT 8:14
(Words: Lou Reed; Music: Sterling Morrison,
John Cale, Maureen Tucker, Lou Reed)

LADY GODIVA'S OPERATION 4:52
(Words & Music: Lou Reed)

THERE SHE COMES NOW 2:00
(Words: Lou Reed; Music: Sterling Morrison,
John Cale, Maureen Tucker, Lou Reed)

SIDE TWO

I HEARD HER CALL MY NAME 4:05
(Words & Music: Lou Reed)

SISTER RAY 17:00
(Words: Lou Reed; Music: Sterling Morrison,
John Cale, Maureen Tucker, Lou Reed)

All compositions BMI

PERSONNEL:
Lou Reed: Vocal, Lead Guitar, Piano
John Cale: Vocal, Electric Viola, Organ,
  Bass Guitar
Sterling Morrison: Vocal, Guitar,
  Bass Guitar
Maureen Tucker: Percussion

Produced by Tom Wilson

Recording Engineer: Gary Kellgren
Director of Engineering: Val Valentin
Cover Photo: Billy Name
Liner Photo: Mario Anniballi
Cover Design: Acy R. Lehman
Cover Concept: Andy Warhol

This record has been engineered
and manufactured in accordance with
standards developed by the
Record Industry Association of
America, Inc., a non-profit
organization dedicated to the
betterment of recorded music
and literature.

Manufactured by MGM Records Division;
Metro-Goldwyn-Mayer Inc.
1350 Avenue of the Americas
New York, N.Y. 10019

Verve Records ®

WHITE LIGHT/
WHITE HEAT

THE VELVET
UNDERGROUND

Prod. By Tom Wilson

STEREO

V6-5046
(MGS-1258)
Side 1

1. WHITE LIGHT/WHITE HEAT—2:44
(Reed) Three Prong Music
2. THE GIFT—8:14
(Reed-Tucker-Morrison-Cale)
Three Prong Music
3. LADY GODIVA'S OPERATION—4:52
(Reed)
Three Prong Music
4. HERE SHE COMES NOW—2:00
(Morrison-Reed-Cale-Tucker)
Three Prong Music
All Selections BMI

MGM RECORDS—A DIVISION OF METRO-GOLDWYN-MAYER, INC.—Made In U.S.A.

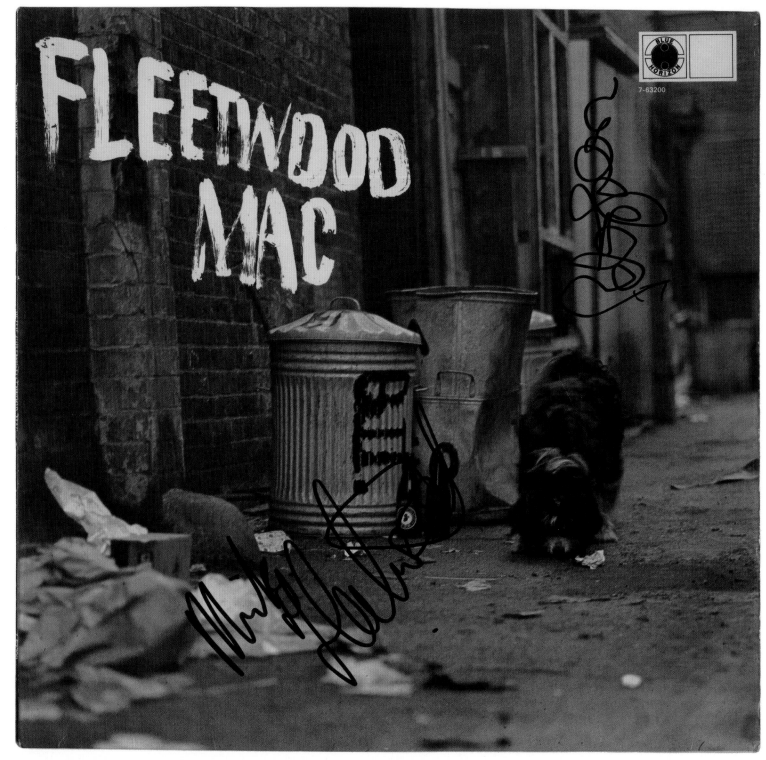

This copy of *Fleetwood Mac* is signed by guitarist Peter Green and drummer Mick Fleetwood.

7-63200

FLEETWOOD MAC | Fleetwood Mac

February 1968 | Blue Horizon

This record was groundbreaking more for its attitude than for any eruption of unconventional new sounds. Peter Green, already famous for replacing Clapton in John Mayall & the Bluesbreakers, burnishes his guitar-hero legend here, and the album serves as the cornerstone of a pop-music institution that has endured and changed vastly over four-plus decades. But *Fleetwood Mac* also marks the real start of the hugely successful genre of British blues-rock. Liberated from the more academic approach of Mayall's conservatory, yet not as eclectic or flashy as Led Zeppelin, this music found its full expression here and on late-'60s sets by Ten Years After, Free, Savoy Brown, and others. Green and second guitarist Jeremy Spencer disperse with the reverence and instead go for the groove and stay for the fun on covers of Elmore James' "Shake Your Moneymaker" and "Got to Move." Among eight band originals that rework the styles of Junior Wells,

John Lee Hooker, and Howlin' Wolf, Green's taut "Long Grey Mare" and Spencer's slow slide ballad "Cold Black Night" are highlights. The entire program is full of feeling—never maudlin or morose, and remarkably free of the overdone antics that would afflict the genre in following years. A top-10 album in Britain (without benefit of a hit single), *Fleetwood Mac* instantly put the group on the map and, soon enough, on the minds of observant music followers around the world.

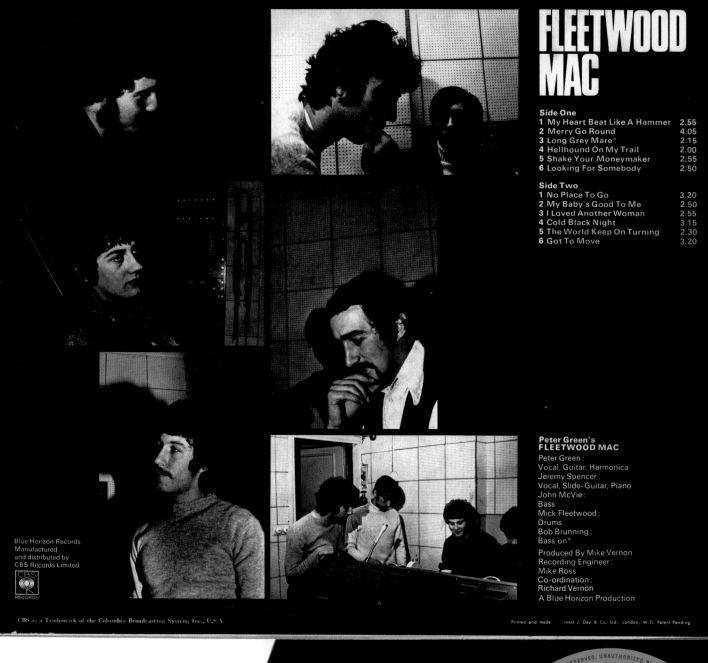

STEREO

7-63200

FLEETWOOD MAC

Side One
1 My Heart Beat Like A Hammer 2.55
2 Merry Go Round 4.05
3 Long Grey Mare* 2.15
4 Hellhound On My Trail 2.00
5 Shake Your Moneymaker 2.55
6 Looking For Somebody 2.50

Side Two
1 No Place To Go 3.20
2 My Baby's Good To Me 2.50
3 I Loved Another Woman 2.55
4 Cold Black Night 3.15
5 The World Keep On Turning 2.30
6 Got To Move 3.20

**Peter Green's
FLEETWOOD MAC**

Peter Green :
Vocal, Guitar, Harmonica
Jeremy Spencer :
Vocal, Slide-Guitar, Piano
John McVie :
Bass
Mick Fleetwood :
Drums
Bob Brunning :
Bass on*

Produced By Mike Vernon
Recording Engineer :
Mike Ross
Co-ordination :
Richard Vernon
A Blue Horizon Production

GB

Blue Horizon Records:
Manufactured
and distributed by
CBS Records Limited

CBS
RECORDS

CBS is a Trademark of the Columbia Broadcasting System, Inc., U.S.A.

Printed and made   ernest J. Day & Co. Ltd., London, W.11. Patent Pending.

FLEETWOOD MAC
PETER GREEN'S FLEETWOOD MAC

7-63200
SIDE ONE

1—4. King Music
5. Sparta Music Ltd.
6. Getaway Songs

BLUE
HORIZON

7-63200 A.
℗ 1968

1. MY HEART BEAT LIKE A HAMMER (J. Spencer)
2. MERRY GO ROUND (P. A. Green)
3. LONG GREY MARE (P. A. Green)
4. HELLHOUND ON MY TRAIL (Trad. Arr: P. A. Green)
5. SHAKE YOUR MONEYMAKER (E. James)
6. LOOKING FOR SOMEBODY (P. A. Green)
A Blue Horizon Production
Produced by Mike Vernon

MADE IN ENGLAND

The band's Mike
Heron signed this
copy, next to Robin
Williamson.

THE INCREDIBLE STRING BAND
The Hangman's Beautiful Daughter

elektra

THE INCREDIBLE STRING BAND | The Hangman's Beautiful Daughter   **March 1968 | Elektra**

The seeds planted on ISB's third long-player most recently sprouted in the winsome psych-folk of artists like Devendra Banhart and Joanna Newsom, but they likewise flowered throughout the late '60s and '70s. An impressive roster of musicians have either explicitly cited the band and this album as an inspiration, or reflected its influence in their work— among them John Lennon, Marc Bolan, Richard Thompson, the Rolling Stones (who tried to sign the group to their label), and Robert Plant, who explained Led Zeppelin's initiation into the joys of Celtic music by noting that they'd bought a copy of *The Hangman's Beautiful Daughter* and simply followed the instructions. While the group's previous LP, *The 5000 Spirits or the Layers of the Onion*, mined similar territory, this is the record that brought the String Band to the world's attention, thanks to its mix of exotic instrumentation (whistle, sitar, pan pipes, organ, dulcimer,

harpsichord), Mike Heron and Robin Williamson's idiosyncratic vocals, and the bizarre lyrics of the songs they composed ("I'm the original discriminating buffalo man / And I'll do what's wrong as long as I can"). Produced by Joe Boyd (Pink Floyd, Fairport Convention, Nick Drake), *Hangman*'s 10 tracks bundle together diverse sources to produce music that is uniquely freaky and fulfilling on "The Minotaur's Song," "Mercy I Cry City," and the 13-minute "A Very Cellular Song."

EUKS 7258
Stereo

MANUFACTURED IN THE U.K. BY POLYDOR RECORDS LTD.

U.S. Elektra used
the U.K. back cover
as the album's front
cover.

elektra

EUKS 7258
SIDE ONE
STEREO

Paradox Music
© 1968

THE HANGMAN'S BEAUTIFUL DAUGHTER
1. KOEEOADDI THERE (Williamson)
2. THE MINOTAUR'S SONG (Williamson)
3. WITCHES' HAT (Williamson)
4. A VERY CELLULAR SONG (Heron)
THE INCREDIBLE STRING BAND
Produced by Joe Boyd

Made in Gt. Britain
POLYDOR RECORDS LIMITED

David Bowie

on The Velvet Underground & Nico: *The Velvet Underground & Nico* as told to John Homans for *New York Magazine.*

Around the end of 1966, my then manager, Ken Pitt, came back from a trip to the U.S. with two albums he had been given in New York. Since they weren't particularly his cup of tea, he gave them to me to see what I made of them. The first was a great, rollicking, noisy anarchist-hippie affair by the Fugs—more fun than was healthy, and great drinking-and-getting-stoned music.

The second, a test pressing with the signature Warhol scrawled on it, was shattering. Everything I both felt and didn't know about rock music was opened to me on one unreleased disc. It was *The Velvet Underground and Nico.*

The first track glided by innocuously enough and didn't register. However, from that point on, with the opening, throbbing, sarcastic bass and guitar of "I'm Waiting For the Man," the linchpin, the keystone of my ambition was driven home. This music was so savagely indifferent to my feelings. It didn't care if I liked it or not. It could give a fuck. It was completely preoccupied with a world unseen by my suburban eyes.

Actually, though only 19, I had seen rather a lot but had accepted it quite enthusiastically as all a bit of a laugh. Apparently, the laughing was now over. I was hearing a degree of cool that I had no idea was humanly sustainable. Ravishing. One after another, tracks squirmed and slid their tentacles around my mind. Evil and sexual, the violin of "Venus in Furs," like some pre-Christian pagan-revival music. The distant, icy, "Fuck me if you want, I really don't give a damn" voice of Nico's "Femme Fatale." What an extraordinary one-two knockout punch this affair was. By the time "European Son" was done, I was so excited I couldn't move. It was late in the evening and I couldn't think of anyone to call, so I played it again and again and again.

That December, my band Buzz broke up, but not without my demanding we play "I'm Waiting For the Man" as one of the encore songs at our last gig. It was the first time a Velvet song had been covered by anyone, anywhere in the world. Lucky me.

David Bowie is a recording artist, songwriter, and actor who has sold an estimated 140 million albums. He was inducted into the Rock and Roll Hall of Fame in 1996.

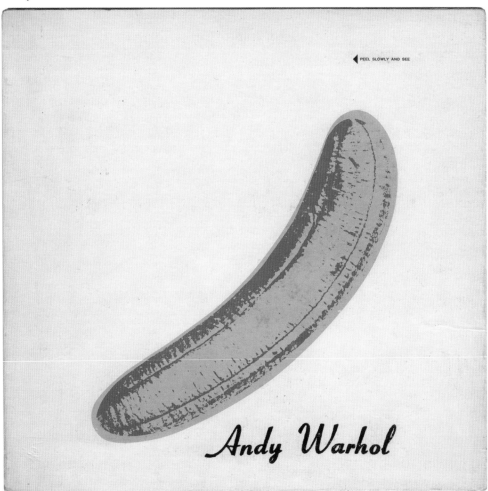

PEEL SLOWLY AND SEE

Andy Warhol

Suzanne Vega

on The Beatles: *The Beatles (White Album)* & Leonard Cohen: *Songs of Leonard Cohen*

The Beatles

I first started buying records in 1969 when I was nine years old. The first one I bought was the Beatles' *Abbey Road.* There was a record store up the street. I think I got some cash for my birthday and bought it with my own money. I was obsessed with the Beatles. Somehow I felt I had always known about the Beatles. New York had WNEW, but back then the AM stations played the Beatles also.

I don't remember how I found out about *The White Album*, probably the newspaper. I knew everything about the Beatles. I had a biography and knew it so well that I could open it to any page, look at the first word, and know what the rest of the page was about. I think my parents bought *The White Album*. I accepted all of it right away. It never occurred to me to question what they might do. It was beautiful, it meant a wild freedom of thought, a beautiful pastiche of styles, and thoughts. I liked "Dear Prudence," "Rocky Raccoon," "I'm So Tired," and "Mother Nature's Son" best.

I paid attention to the album cover and photos, too. I spent many moments staring at Paul's beautiful eyes and wondering why they let John have his picture taken with that pimple on his forehead.

Leonard Cohen

My name is Suzanne, and when I told people this, they would say, "Like the song?" For years I didn't know what they meant. Then I heard a Judy Collins album with that song "Suzanne" and "Dress Rehearsal Rag," and was so relieved and also knocked out because they were such great, unique songs. I first heard Leonard Cohen's songs while babysitting, on that Judy Collins album. Eventually I took a chance and bought *Songs of Leonard Cohen* because I wanted more. I hadn't heard it when I bought it. I had heard his work covered by others and was curious. I saw it in the record shop and I was 14, so it must have been 1974.

I became obsessed; he became my friend. I loved the sound of his voice, his nylon-string guitar, his intimate way of singing, the ethereal girls in the background, his intensity, his fearlessness of subject matter, the urban landscape. I felt that he was my good friend and that he understood the world I lived in. A complicated, mysterious, dirty world of intrigue, sex, religion, and politics.

At the time, I was listening to Top 40 radio but also to a Folkways album from 1959 that I had found in a thrift shop. He fit in just fine. Some of my friends didn't like his voice, but I didn't mind that at all. I felt that he belonged to me alone—that I was the only 15-year-old girl that ever loved him from the privacy of my room. I loved the album cover; it made me think of Joan of Arc who I already identified with. She was beautiful, she was on fire, she was in chains. He looked plain and serious, in black and white. The photo was by "Machine." So he had gone into one of those booths and had taken his own photo. It was perfect.

I first saw him at Carnegie Hall in 1988, I believe, so it was many years later. I thought of my relationship with Leonard Cohen as a private one, so I never had the urge to run out and see him perform. Besides that, I used to dance to his songs in my room. When I saw him publicly, I had to share him with others and I didn't like that so much.

I went backstage and asked to meet him. His sister, Esther, was there and said, "Oh you're Suzanne Vega. He wants to meet you." She was a big woman in a cheerful flowered dress, not a small woman dressed in black, like one would imagine Leonard's sister to be. I asked for his autograph and he wrote instead, "To my female shadow. L.C."

Since then, I have met him many times. He is what his music suggests —serious, dry, intelligent, funny, handsome, droll. Mysterious. Reserved.

Songs of Leonard Cohen is still one of my favorite albums of all time, ever. My favorites are "The Master Song," "Suzanne" (of course), and "So Long Marianne." His work influenced me very much. It made me unafraid of songs in minor keys or complicated, long songs.

Suzanne Vega is an award winning songwriter and singer whose songs "Luka" and "Tom's Diner" were worldwide hits.

Jimi Hendrix:
Record Collector

June 20, 2001 was a very late night for me, but an exciting one. I stayed up that Monday night—really Tuesday morning—until the wee hours to do some vital telephone bidding in "The Jimi Hendrix Experience Auction," held at the Bonhams and Brooks auction house in London.

A year before, in June 2000, I'd attended the opening of Seattle's *Experience Music Project*, the museum founded by Microsoft co-founder and music fanatic Paul Allen. Their collection of memorabilia, including clothes worn and instruments played by my hero, Jimi Hendrix, was astounding. But what fascinated me most was a display of albums from Hendrix's own record collection. There were a dozen or so records, mostly blues, which Jimi had owned. As a lifetime record collector, I had an emotional reaction to seeing the actual records that Jimi Hendrix had bought and listened to, the music that had inspired the master. To me, these were profoundly important, almost talismanic, objects—imbued with Hendrix's power, his inspiration, his mojo.

So when I received the catalog for the 2001 Hendrix auction, and saw Lot

130, "A Group Of Records From Jimi Hendrix's Record Collection"—twenty one of Hendrix's own albums, with provenance from his longtime girlfriend and London flatmate Kathy Etchingham--I knew I *had* to have them. And so I had a late night of telephone bidding. I made offers on some earlier items, winning some, letting others go, but Lot 130 was my top priority. When the time came, my heart was beating, but the bidding was surprisingly unspirited, and I won Hendrix's albums for a fraction of what I was prepared to pay.

A few weeks later, my hands trembled as I unpacked the FedEx box containing my new treasures. These were what collectors euphemistically call "well loved" records; they had been played many, many times, not carefully, and were covered with scratches and fingerprints. Ordinarily I would have cleaned them immediately. But these were Jimi Hendrix's records, and with Jimi Hendrix's fingerprints, cleaning them seemed like sacrilege. Instead I carefully sleeved them, put the discs in new inner sleeves (keeping the originals of course,) and cradled them, feeling almost awestruck.

The collection I'd bought included Jimi's copies of these albums:

- Acker Bilk - *Lansdowne Folio*
- The Beatles - *Sgt. Pepper's Lonely Hearts Club Band*
- Bill Cosby - *Revenge*
- Bob Dylan - *Greatest Hits*
- Bob Dylan - *Highway 61 Revisited*
- Clara Ward - *Gospel Concert*
- The Dream - *Get Dreamy*
- Elmore James - *Memorial Album*
- Howlin Wolf - *The Howlin' Wolf Album*
- Howlin Wolf - *Moanin' In The Moonlight*
- James Brown - *Showtime*
- The Jimi Hendrix Experience - *Electric Ladyland*
- John Lee Hooker - *Drifting Blues*
- Muddy Waters - *The Real Folk Blues*
- Ravi Shankar - *India's Master Musician*
- Ravi Shankar - *Portrait of a Genius*
- Robert Johnson - *King of the Delta Blues Singers*
- The Roland Kirk Quartet - *Rip, Rig and Panic*
- Wes Montgomery - *A Day In The Life*
- Various Artists - *Chicago The Blues Today*
- Various Artists - *American Folk Blues Festival '66*

Overall there were a few surprises, but if you're a Hendrix fan, the blues albums, Dylan, Ravi Shankar, and jazz titles make perfect sense. To my great delight, the copy of *Bob Dylan's Greatest Hits* had some of Hendrix's psychedelic doodling on the back cover, which the auction house somehow missed. And oddly, the copy of Dylan's *Highway 61 Revisited* had some of Jimi's dried blood on the cover, according to Etchingham the result of a cut from a wine glass.

The rarest album in the collection was *Get Dreamy*, a 1967 psychedelic LP by Norwegian quartet The Dream, featuring what has to be the earliest-ever Hendrix tribute song, "Hey Jimi" (Hendrix's debut single, "Hey Joe," was only released in December 1966.) The cover was inscribed to Hendrix by Dream guitarist (and future ECM Records jazz star) Terje Rypdal, who wrote "With all the respect we can give a fellow musician, we wrote "Hey Jimi" as a tribute to you. We hope you like it and the rest of the LP too." A highly collectible psychedelic album, copies of *Get Dreamy* have sold for $1000 (without the Hendrix association).

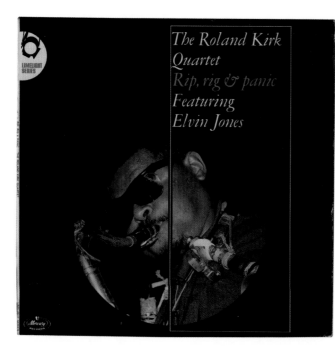

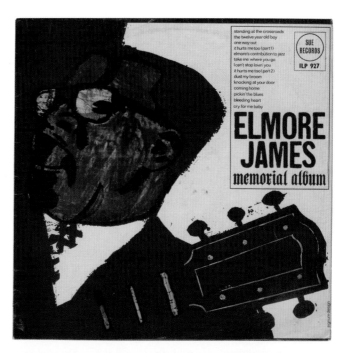

This is Howlin' Wolf's new album.
He doesn't like it.
He didn't like his electric guitar at first either.

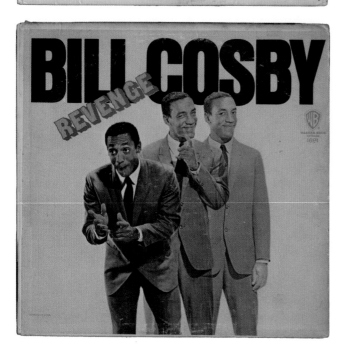

For those curious about the Experience Music Project's Hendrix LP holdings, their director of curatorial affairs, Jasen Emmons, provided this list:

- Albert King - *Live Wire-Blues Power*
- The Band - *Music From Big Pink*
- Bill Cosby - *I Started Out as a Child*
- Bob Dylan - *John Wesley Harding*
- Bob Dylan - *Blonde on Blonde*
- Canned Heat - *Canned Heat*
- Charlie Musslewhite's Southside Band - *Stand Back!*
- Cream - *Fresh Cream*
- Elmore James - *The Best Of*
- The Free Spirits - *Out of Sight and Sound*
- Friar Tuck - *And His Psychedelic Guitar*
- Howlin' Wolf - *More Real Folk Blues*
- The Jimi Hendrix Experience - *Are You Experienced*
- The Jimi Hendrix Experience - *Smash Hits*
- Jimmy Reed - *The New Jimmy Reed Album*
- Jimmy Smith & Wes Montgomery - *The Dynamic Duo*
- John Lee Hooker - *Live at Cafe Au-Go-Go*
- John Mayall - *Crusade*
- Johnny Cash - *At Folsom Prison*
- John Mayall with Eric Clapton - *Blues Breakers*
- Junior Wells - *It's My Life Baby*
- Leadbelly - *Take This Hammer*
- Lightnin' Hopkins - *Soul Blues*
- Lightnin' Hopkins - *Earth Blues*
- Lightnin' Hopkins - *Something Blue*
- Lightnin' Hopkins - *The Roots Of*
- Lightnin' Hopkins - *Lightnin' Strikes*
- Little Richard - *Vol. 2*
- Lowell Fulson - *Lowell Fulson*
- The Mothers of Invention - *Freak Out!*
- Muddy Waters - *Down On Stovall's Plantation*
- Muddy Waters - *Electric Mud*
- Original Soundtrack - *The Trip*
- Pierre Henry - *Le Voyage: D'apres le Livre des Morts Tibetian*
- Ravi Shankar - *Sound of the Sitar*
- Red Krayola - *The Parable of Arable Land*
- Sonny Boy Williamson - *Down and Out Blues*
- The Spencer Davis Group - *Autumn '66*
- Various Artists - *Blues Classics*
- Various Artists - *Chicago The Blues Today!, Vol. 1*
- Various Artists - *Heavy Heads*
- Various Artists - *Original Hits of the Great Blues Singers, Vol II*
- Various Artists - *The Original American Folk Blues Festival*
- Various Artists - *We Sing The Blues!*
- The Zodiac - *Cosmic Sounds*

Once again, few surprises here—mostly lots of blues, and some boundary challenging rock. Of course Dylan's *John Wesley Harding* LP features his original version of "All Along The Watchtower," which Jimi virtually made his own. And notice the collection contains a Lightnin' Hopkins album titled *Earth Blues*—a title Hendrix used for a song of his own, which appeared on the soundtrack to the film *Rainbow Bridge*.

I was happy to see many titles I have in my own collection. And virtually all of Jimi's picks have stood the test of time (OK, so maybe not Friar Tuck *And His Psychedelic Guitar* or The Zodiac's *Cosmic Sounds*, but a very high percentage of the albums here are true classics.) If you don't know these records and you're a Hendrix fan, you'd be well served to check out the albums in Jimi Hendrix's record collection. Unsurprisingly, the man had great taste.

THE ZOMBIES | Odessey & Oracle

April 1968 | CBS

Odessey & Oracle was issued by a band that had broken up two months before its release. True to their name, The Zombies were brought back to life, in this case by Al Kooper, who persuaded a reluctant Columbia Records (U.S.) to issue the album, which had come out in April 1968 in the U.K. *Odessey*'s June American release immediately drew rave reviews from critics and subsequently generated the band's signature hit "Time of the Season." Few albums conceived in the heat of post-*Sgt. Pepper's* passion hold up as well as *Odessey & Oracle*, which balances demanding artistic aspiration with typically tasteful, understated arrangements and performances. In terms of delivering a consistent, seamlessly textured slate of first-rate pop songs, it rightly deserves comparison to *Pet Sounds*. Rod Argent, Colin Blunstone, and compatriots were never anything less than one of rock's most tuneful aggregations,

and here they apply their melodic gifts to an array of songs that variously address war ("Butcher's Tale"), social isolation ("A Rose for Emily"), the unalloyed optimism of young romance ("This Will Be Our Year"), and the peculiar challenge of love-at-a-distance ("Care of Cell 44"). Hugely influential to this day, the Zombies can point with pride to a crowning achievement that the *New Musical Express* labeled "British psychedelia with a kaleidoscopic vision that rivals even the Beatles'."

To Jeff – this : ones a rip better than "Begin Here" thank for coming over
[signature]

STEREO

CBS
63280

SIDE ONE
Care of Cell 44
A Rose for Emily
Maybe After He's Gone
Beechwood Park
Brief Candles
Hung Up On A Dream

SIDE TWO
Changes
I Want Her She Wants Me
This Will Be Our Year
Butchers Tale (Western Front 1914)
Friends of Mine
Time Of The Season

Shakespeare said

"Be not afraid ;
The Isle is full of noises
Sound, and sweet airs that give delight and hurt not.
Sometimes a thousand twangling instruments
Will hum about mine ears ; and sometimes voices"

Really music is a very personal thing; it's the product of a person's experiences. Since no two people have been exactly alike, each writer has something unique to say. That makes anything which is not just copy of something else worth listening to.

Believing this, and laden with gifts of fruit and nuts from the Orient, we descended upon CBS chieftain Derek, and with smarm and charm extracted, astonished, the finance necessary to compose, arrange, perform, produce and cover an LP ourselves, with no outside help or interference.

This is the result :

Thanks to Terry Quirk, artist flatmate of Chris, for the cover.
Thanks to Will Shakespeare, not flatmate of Chris, for his contribution to the sleeve notes.
ROD ARGENT

CBS is a Trademark of the Columbia Broadcasting System, Inc., U.S.A.
Printed by Ernest J. Day & Co. Ltd., London W.11.

ZOMBIES

THE ZOMBIES
ODESSEY AND ORACLE

SIDE 1
STEREO
CBS
S 63280

33⅓

Veralum Music

SEPG 63280 A
℗ 1968

1. CARE OF CELL 44 (Rod Argent)
2. A ROSE FOR EMILY (Rod Argent)
3. MAYBE AFTER HE'S GONE (Chris White)
4. BEECHWOOD PARK (Chris White)
5. BRIEF CANDLES (Chris White)
6. HUNG UP ON A DREAM (Rod Argent)

MADE IN ENGLAND

The fold-open, die-cut album cover was modeled after a tobacco tin.

The top left image is the back cover and the top right image is the front cover.

SMALL FACES | Ogden's Nut Gone Flake

May 1968 | Immediate

The Faces distinguished themselves through three distinct phases of a career arc that began with mod-pop ("Sha La La La Lee" and "Itchycoo Park") and ended with rowdy bar-band rock (the Rod Stewart 'Faces' period of *A Nod's as Good as a Wink...*). Sandwiched between these endpoints was the band's psychedelic masterpiece, a post-*Pepper* extravaganza of superb pop-R&B-inflected tunes and the sidelong narrative of "Happiness Stan," which alternated full songs with snippets of monologue describing the deeds of the story's central character. Packaged in one of the most elaborate sleeves of the period—a circular 'tobacco tin' containing a die-cut, interlocking poster of the group— *Ogden's*, like the Grateful Dead's *Anthem of the Sun* (released the same month), was a forthright attempt to see just how much might be accomplished within the album format. The effort may explain some of

the record's enormous success in the U.K., but so does the presence of some of the Small Faces' most memorable songs and performances, in particular "Afterglow," "Lazy Sunday," and "Song of a Baker."

The following text appears on the record label:

IMMEDIATE
RECORD   CO. LTD.

1, Marriott, Lane
McLagan, Jones
2,4,5,6, Marriott, Lane
3, McLagan
Immediate Music

33⅓ RPM
STEREO

IMSP 012
Ⓟ 1968

IMSP 012 1Y

Side 1—OGDENS' NUT GONE FLAKE

1. OGDENS' NUT GONE FLAKE
2. AFTERGLOW
3. LONG AGOS AND WORLDS APART
4. RENE
5. SONG OF A BAKER
6. LAZY SUNDAY

SMALL FACES

Mono and stereo copies featured different sound mixes.

The album cover is a painting by Band collaborator Bob Dylan.

THE BAND | Music From Big Pink

July 1968 | Capitol

Amidst a noisy summer that rained down voltage and volume with *Cheap Thrills,* W*heels of Fire,* and *In-A-Gadda-Da-Vida*, the first album by The Band cleared the air with a refreshing lack of pretense. The product of the same five musicians who abetted Dylan's rock 'n' roll rise, *Music from Big Pink* effectively pulled the cord on guitar grandstanding and lofty lyric pronouncements, opting instead for simpler music that served the song rather than the rowdy crowd on the ballroom floor. (*Big Pink* was a factor in Eric Clapton's decision to leave Cream; he remarked that hearing the LP in 1968 "changed [his] life.") Dylan songs of then-recent *Basement Tapes* vintage provide a third of the LP's tunes ("Tears of Rage," "This Wheel's on Fire," "I Shall Be Released"), but *Big Pink* also lays its cards on the table with an earnest version of the '50s country staple "Long Black Veil" and a half dozen traditionally-rooted originals every bit as strong as

the covers. Levon Helm's vocal on "The Weight" rightly drew the most attention, but Richard Manuel's "Lonesome Suzie" is no less soulful and just as heartbreaking. *Music from Big Pink* deserves credit for two major achievements that altered the course of popular music: it introduced one of America's most important writing and performing ensembles of the late-'60s, and it embodied a less-can-be-more aesthetic that pointed pop in new directions in the 1970s, specifically in the form of country-rock and the singer-songwriter movement.

STEREO
PLAYABLE ON STEREO & MONO PHONOGRAPHS

SKAO 2955

MUSIC FROM BIG PINK

MUSIC FROM BIG PINK

RICK DANKO, LEVON HELM, GARTH HUDSON
RICHARD MANUEL, JAIME ROBBIE ROBERTSON
JOHN SIMON - PRODUCER

STEREO   SKAO-2955 1
                      (SKAO1-2955)

1. TEARS OF RAGE—ASCAP-5:16
   (B. Dylan-R. Manuel)
2. TO KINGDOM COME—ASCAP-3:20
   (J.R. Robertson)
3. IN A STATION—ASCAP-3:35 (R. Manuel)
4. CALEDONIA MISSION—ASCAP-2:54
   (J. R. Robertson)
5. THE WEIGHT—ASCAP-4:40
   (J.R. Robertson)

BIG PINK

A pink house seated in the sun
of Overlook Mountain in
West Saugerties, New York.
Big Pink bore this music and
these songs along its way.
It's the first witness of
this album that's been thought
and composed right there
inside its walls.

THE BAND

Jaime Robbie Robertson

Rick Danko

Richard Manuel

Garth Hudson

Levon Helm

John Simon, Producer

SIDE ONE

Tears of Rage 5:21
B. Dylan, R. Manuel

To Kingdom Come 3:19
J. R. Robertson

In a Station 3:31
R. Manuel

Caledonia Mission 3:53
J. R. Robertson

The Weight 4:34
J. R. Robertson

SIDE TWO

We Can Talk 3:02
R. Manuel

Long Black Veil 3:02
M. J. Wilkin, D. Dill

Chest Fever 5:15
J. R. Robertson

Lonesome Suzie 4:02
R. Manuel

This Wheels On Fire 3:11
B. Dylan, R. Danko

I Shall Be Released 3:12
B. Dylan
(All selections ASCAP except
Long Black Veil, BMI)

NEXT OF KIN

Engineers: Don Hahn, Tony May, Rex Updegraft, Shelly Yakus Cover Painting: Bob Dylan Photographs: Elliott Landy Album design: Milton Glaser Arrangements: Alb-? Grossman

111

The album cover is a painting on wood by Bill Walker that, when viewed with special glasses, appears three dimensional.

GRATEFUL DEAD | Anthem Of The Sun

July 1968 | Warner Bros.

From the outset, San Francisco groups and the labels that signed them were always plagued by the problem of getting the bands' live sounds onto vinyl. The Grateful Dead resolved the issue before anyone else, with a sophomore album that combined on-site concert tapes and studio technology to create one of the first psychedelic classics. Portions of recordings from a series of 1967-68 Dead shows, previously cut studio tracks, and fresh applications of piano, harpsichord, trumpet, and even kazoo (on "Alligator") were spliced and overlaid in a process Jerry Garcia later described as "mixing for the hallucinations." The effect is a dizzying, borderline-scary listening experience in which vocal and instrumental passages merge, rush up and recede, fading away only to reappear later in a new context, as if selected by some search engine gone awry. "Good Vibrations" might have been similarly assembled, and *Sgt. Pepper's* likewise sequenced for

seamlessness, but *Anthem of the Sun*, running on improvisational energy as much as conscious craftsmanship, stands apart. Though its fourth album, *Live Dead*, would more authentically document the group's concert sound and introduce band standards like "Dark Star" and "The Eleven," it's here that many listeners received their formal introduction to California acid rock at its most potent and mind-altering.

In 1972 the album was remixed; some copies of the new version were packaged in this alternate cover.

This white label promotional copy was made for radio stations and reviewers.

JEFF BECK | Truth

August 1968 | Columbia

Jeff Beck's first solo outing is notable for a number of reasons, not the least of which is that it brought Rod Stewart to most folks' attention. Ron Wood, pianist Nicky Hopkins, and drummer Mick Waller contributed significantly, but *Truth* remains Beck's show, a key step forward in his evolution from respected Yardbirds lead player to revered guitar hero whose only rivals were Eric Clapton and Jimi Hendrix. "[Hendrix] hit me like an earthquake," Beck has said. "I had to think long and hard about what I did next." What Beck did on *Truth* was make a masterful display of his chops without abandoning his

astute instincts for working *with,* not apart from, the singer, the songs, and the rest of his rhythm section. In the process, he and the group, most notably on "I Ain't Superstitious" and "Let Me Love You," sketched the thick outlines of blues-based "heavy" rock that would become a predominant style of early-'70s music. Despite Beck's contention that, "I don't like over-the-top heavy metal…too much volume," the power surge that is *Truth* surely foreshadowed the famous subgenre.

jeff beck

truth

SX 6293

Also available on Stereo No. SCX 6293

EMI

THE GREATEST RECORDING
ORGANISATION IN THE WORLD.

The "truth" about this album is:

Shapes Of Things—Rearranged, but the same Yardbirds hit. This must be played at maximum volume whatever phonograph you use. Makes very appropriate background music if you have Vicar over for tea.

Let Me Love You—Heavy number, tambourine played divinely by Micky Waller. *Written by Rod Stewart* Multipurpose tune.

Morning Dew—Everyone knows Tim does this wonderfully, but so do we.

You Shook Me—Probably the rudest sounds ever recorded, intended for listening to whilst angry or stoned. Last note of song is my guitar being sick-well so would you be if I smashed your guts for 2:28.

Ol' Man River—Arranged by me, but credit must go to all, everyone was super especially Rod Stewart. Again played loudly gives maximum value.

Greensleeves—(Aye that's a lovely "toon") Played on Mickie Most's guitar which by the way is the same as Elvis'.

Rock My Plimsoul—Rerecorded flipside of "Tally Man" much better feel and more spontaneity than the original.

Beck's Bolero—Not much to say about this, excuse same track on here as on the "Silver Lining" B side, but we couldn't improve on it.

Blues De Luxe—Thanks to Bert and Stan, we were able to give you a perfect example of "live" blues music that we sometimes give forth, and please let's own up about the piano solo.

I Ain't Superstitious—Stolen riff from old "Howlin' Wolf" tune, but he doesn't mind because I asked him. This number is more or less an excuse for being flash on guitar.

Well that's it Honeys, here's our first LP, called **Truth**.

—Jeff Beck

SIDE ONE

1. SHAPES OF THINGS *(Samwell-Smith)*

2. LET ME LOVE YOU *(Rod)*

3. MORNING DEW *(Rose-Dobson)*

4. YOU SHOOK ME *(Dixon)*

5. OL' MAN RIVER *(Kern)*

SIDE TWO

1. GREENSLEEVES *(Trad-arr. Rod)*

2. ROCK MY PLIMSOUL *(Rod)*

3. BECK'S BOLERO *(Page)* +

4. BLUES DE LUXE *(Rod)*

5. I AIN'T SUPERSTITIOUS *(Dixon)*

1967 +, 1968

Guitar: Jeff Beck
Vocals: Rod Stewart
Bass: Ron Wood
Drums: Mick Waller
Jeff Beck, Bass, on "Ol' Man River"
J. P. Jones, Hammond Organ, on "Ol' Man River"
Timpani by "You Know Who"
Nicky Hopkins, Piano, on "Morning Dew" and "Blues De Luxe"

Front Cover Photograph: Stephen Goldblatt.
Arranged by Jeff Beck
Recording Engineer: Ken Scott

A MICKIE MOST PRODUCTION.

E.M.I RECORDS (The Gramophone Company Ltd) HAYES·MIDDLESEX·ENGLAND

Columbia

Regd. Trade Marks of The Gramophone Company Ltd.

A COMPANY OF THE **EMI** GROUP

This mono record has been produced by the most modern techniques of processing and manufacture and conforms to the highest possible standards. It will sound even better when reproduced on stereo equipment. To keep this record clean and dust free we recommend the regular use of **NEW EMITEX**.

33⅓ R.P.M. Made and Printed in Great Britain.

6811   TPS   Printed and made by Garrod & Lofthouse Ltd. Patents Pending   CX 6293   SCX 6293

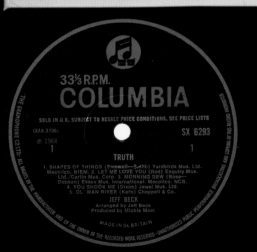

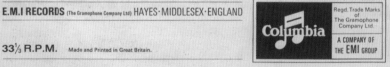

A scarce mono pressing; by the time *Truth* was issued, few albums were released in mono.

BIG BROTHER & THE HOLDING COMPANY | Cheap Thrills

August 1968 | Columbia

It's a sad fact that the tragedy at the end of Janis Joplin's life has largely obscured the music she made, which is displayed at its most impressive on this second of her two albums with Big Brother. In today's diminished music market, most new albums quickly spike in sales, then promptly fall off cliffs and out of the public's consciousness. In the summer and fall of 1968, *Cheap Thrills* was the country's top-selling LP for eight weeks, part of a year-plus run on *Billboard*'s chart. The record was a phenomenon, the most successful export from the California scene, and Joplin was an international star. Her impassioned "Piece of My Heart" was the hit, but *Cheap Thrills* also found a place in music fans' hearts for other reasons: the pain and anguish Joplin draws from "Ball and Chain," the more demure "Summertime," her part as 'one of the guys' in San Francisco's freakiest combo ("Combination of the Two"), and Robert Crumb's funky LP cover.

Joplin's arrival at such prominence even carried political significance: her non-prom-queen appearance and gutsy demeanor defied all prior notions of how women in entertainment were expected to look and act.

A very scarce mono pressing.

The front cover reproduced a 1933 artwork titled "Sweetheart of the Rodeo or Evolution of the Cowboy" by the Uruguyan-born American artist and cowboy Jo Mora.

THE BYRDS | Sweetheart Of The Rodeo

August 1968 | Columbia

While previous albums such as *Younger Than Yesterday* had hinted at the Byrds' affinity for country music, in 1968 most rock bands and their fans found tales of truck-driving men and honky-tonk angels to be anything but cool. *Sweetheart of the Rodeo* changed that, accelerating from zero to 60 rock's embrace of one of its long-estranged parent genres. Bassist Chris Hillman, who'd come to the Byrds from bluegrass, was one of the album's motivators. The other was Gram Parsons: a certified Southern hipster and zealous advocate for country music. Parsons joined the band (bringing his songs "Hickory Wind" and "One Hundred Years from Now"), sang many of *Sweetheart*'s original lead vocals, then quit. By the time of the LP's release, his vocals had been replaced by leader Roger McGuinn's. Despite the drama, and with help from guitarist Clarence White, multi-instrumentalist John Hartford and others, the Byrds produced the first real

country-rock album, tackling material by Merle Haggard and the Louvin Brothers, Bob Dylan, and Woody Guthrie, and countrifying William Bell's soul classic "You Don't Miss Your Water." *Sweetheart of the Rodeo* showed those who needed convincing just how soulful country could be, and paved the way for *Nashville Skyline* and *Exile on Main Street*, The Flying Burrito Brothers, the Eagles, and dozens of other bands.

Stereo CS 9670

COLUMBIA

THE BYRDS
SWEETHEART OF THE RODEO

Side 1
You Ain't Going Nowhere (ASCAP)
I Am a Pilgrim - Arranged by
    Roger McGuinn - Chris Hillman
The Christian Life
You Don't Miss Your Water
You're Still on My Mind
Pretty Boy Floyd

Side 2
Hickory Wind
One Hundred Years From Now
Blue Canadian Rockies
Life in Prison
Nothing Was Delivered (ASCAP)

Engineering: Roy Halee, Charlie Bragg

The selections are BMI except where noted.

Produced by Gary Usher
We would like to thank the following: Roger McGuinn - Guitar, Banjo; Chris Hillman - Bass Guitar, Mandolin;
Gram Parsons - Guitar; Kevin Kelley - Drums; Earl P. Ball - Piano; Jon Corneal - Drums; Lloyd Green - Steel
Guitar; John Hartford - Banjo, Guitar; Roy M. Huskey - Bass; Jaydee Maness - Steel Guitar; Clarence J. White - Guitar.
Album Package Design by Geller and Butler Advertising; Cover Illustration by Jo Mora, copyright 1933

COLUMBIA

THE BYRDS
SWEETHEART OF THE RODEO

CS 9670   SIDE 1
XSM 136650

STEREO

1. YOU AIN'T GOING NOWHERE - B. Dylan
2. I AM A PILGRIM - Arranged by Roger McGuinn - Chris Hillman
3. THE CHRISTIAN LIFE - I. Louvin - C. Louvin
4. YOU DON'T MISS YOUR WATER - W. Bell
5. YOU'RE STILL ON MY MIND - L. McDaniel
6. PRETTY BOY FLOYD - W. Guthrie

"360 SOUND" "360 SOUND"

® "COLUMBIA" ℗ MARCAS REG. PRINTED IN U.S.A.

THE JIMI HENDRIX EXPERIENCE ELECTRIC LADYLAND

THE JIMI HENDRIX EXPERIENCE | Electric Ladyland

October 1968 | Track

Hendrix's arrival was unprecedented, but the sheer velocity of his artistic development was just as stunning. *Electric Ladyland* was his third album in just over a year, and while it builds on the strengths of its predecessors, it also uses its four sides to boldly map out new terrain. Producing himself for the first time, and enabled by his commercial success to proceed with a full head of steam in whatever direction he desired, Hendrix delivered his masterpiece, singing and playing with more joy and confidence than ever before, adapting and eschewing conventional song form to suit the material. Inspired jazz-blues improvisation colors "Voodoo Chile" (with Steve Winwood and Jack Casady on organ and bass respectively), "Burning of the Midnight Lamp" is soaring, melodic psychedelia, and "Crosstown Traffic" a funky rhythm trip that turns on dimes. Everywhere are brilliant riffs ("1938… A Merman I Should Turn to Be") and unqualified rocking

("Crosstown Traffic," the cover of Earl King's "Come On [Let the Good Times Roll]"), as well as the definitive version of another giant's creation. "He found things [in "All Along the Watchtower"] that other people wouldn't think of finding in there," wrote Bob Dylan. "I liked his record of it, and ever since he died I've been doing it that way," Dylan noted. Add such standards as "House Burning Down" and "Long Hot Summer Night" and *Electric Ladyland* approaches the status of a Hendrix greatest-hits collection all on its own.

Side A: 1. And the Gods made love/ 2. Electric Ladyland/ 3. Crosstown traffic/ 4. Voodoo Chile
Side B: 1. Little Miss Strange/ 2. Long Hot Summer Night/
3. Come on/ 4. Gipsy eyes/ 5. Burning of the Midnight Lamp
Side C: 1. Rainy day, dream away/ 2. 1983 (A Merman I should turn to be)
3. Moon, turn the tides . . . gently gently away
Side D: 1. Still Raining Still Dreaming/ 2. House burning down/ 3. All along the Watchtower/
4. Voodoo Chile (slight return)
Produced and directed by Jimi Hendrix
Photographs by David Montgomery. Cover by David King

Electric Ladyland by The Jimi Hendrix
Experience was released in Britain with
one of the most controversial album
covers issued to date. Photographer David
Montgomery and art director David King
posed 19 young girls–reportedly non-
models recruited in London clubs–in
front of a black backdrop, and produced
a cover that offended retailers, customers,
and, reportedly, Hendrix himself. Some

THE JIMI HENDRIX EXPERIENCE   ELECTRIC LADYLAND

U.K. shops hid the album behind the counter, or turned it inside out, and Reprise, Hendrix's U.S. label, released the album in a completely different sleeve. Hendrix said of the U.K. cover, "I don't know anything about it. I don't decide which pictures will be used on my records. In the states, this album had photographs of Noel, Mitch, and me on the cover." The album pictured here is Jimi Hendrix's own copy of *Electric Ladyland*.

As double albums
were expensive
in the U.K., Track
Records released
Electric Ladyland
as two single discs,
each with a unique
cover. Above, Part
1. Below, Part 2.

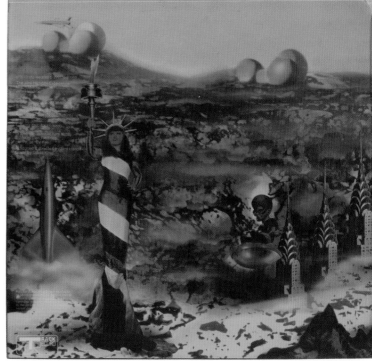

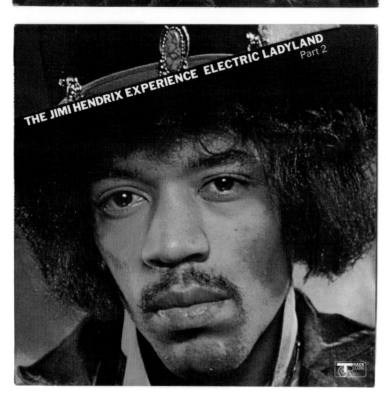

Side A: 1. And the Gods made love /2. Electric Ladyland/3. Crosstown Traffic/4. Voodoo Chile/Side B: 1. Little Miss Strange/ 2. Long Hot Summer Night/3. Come on/4. Gipsy eyes/5. Burning of the Midnight Lamp. Produced and directed by Jimi Hendrix. Cover Photograph by David Montgomery. Photographs of Mitch Mitchell and Noel Redding: Donald Silverstein.

Hendrix sent a letter to his U.S. label detailing exactly what he wanted for the American album cover; his requests were largely ignored. Above left: the blurry front cover photo is by Karl Ferris. Right: the back cover. Below: inner gatefold with liner notes by Hendrix.

STEREO

VAN MORRISON ASTRAL WEEKS

1768

Ed Thrasher's album cover features a photograph by Joel Brodsky.

VAN MORRISON | Astral Weeks

Astral Weeks wears its crown well as one of rock's most acclaimed albums some 40-plus years after release. Its immediate successors, *Moondance* and *Tupelo Honey,* placed Morrison in the vanguard of singer-songwriters (albeit one whose models were more Curtis Mayfield and Mose Allison than Dylan), but *Astral Weeks* belongs to no tradition save its own. It resides as far from "Gloria" and "Brown Eyed Girl" as from the work of Van Morrison's contemporaries. Nothing prepared the public for the album that *Mojo*'s Barney Hoskyns praised as "an attempt to outstrip language… Every breathless phrase, every gibbering cry, seems to be reaching for revelation." It may be hard to pinpoint exactly what the record's songs, six of the eight topping the five-minute mark in length, are "about," but there's no denying the intensity of feeling expressed in "Madame George," "Ballerina," "Cypress Avenue" and "The Way Young Lovers Do."

November 1968 | Warner Bros.

Unconventional string arrangements, alternately somber and swinging, assist Morrison in extracting memories from some personal reservoir filled with anguish and ecstasy. Somehow, his interpretation of those experiences, through what he later described as "the inarticulate speech of the heart," manages to touch listeners deeply. As only the best art can, *Astral Weeks* dissolves the barrier separating the personal and the shared.

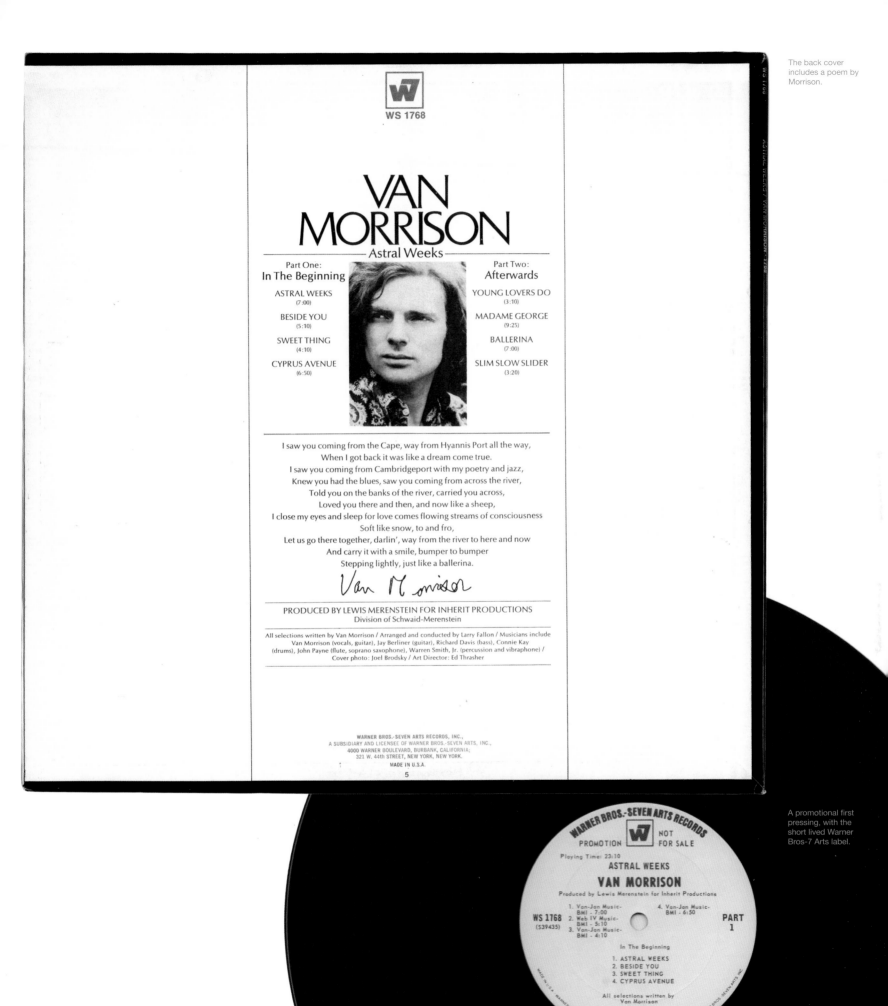

VAN MORRISON
Astral Weeks

Part One:
In The Beginning

ASTRAL WEEKS
(7:00)

BESIDE YOU
(5:10)

SWEET THING
(4:10)

CYPRUS AVENUE
(6:50)

Part Two:
Afterwards

YOUNG LOVERS DO
(3:10)

MADAME GEORGE
(9:25)

BALLERINA
(7:00)

SLIM SLOW SLIDER
(3:20)

I saw you coming from the Cape, way from Hyannis Port all the way,
When I got back it was like a dream come true.
I saw you coming from Cambridgeport with my poetry and jazz,
Knew you had the blues, saw you coming from across the river,
Told you on the banks of the river, carried you across,
Loved you there and then, and now like a sheep,
I close my eyes and sleep for love comes flowing streams of consciousness
Soft like snow, to and fro,
Let us go there together, darlin', way from the river to here and now
And carry it with a smile, bumper to bumper
Stepping lightly, just like a ballerina.

Van Morrison

PRODUCED BY LEWIS MERENSTEIN FOR INHERIT PRODUCTIONS
Division of Schwaid-Merenstein

All selections written by Van Morrison / Arranged and conducted by Larry Fallon / Musicians include
Van Morrison (vocals, guitar), Jay Berliner (guitar), Richard Davis (bass), Connie Kay
(drums), John Payne (flute, soprano saxophone), Warren Smith, Jr. (percussion and vibraphone) /
Cover photo: Joel Brodsky / Art Director: Ed Thrasher

5

The back cover includes a poem by Morrison.

A promotional first pressing, with the short lived Warner Bros-7 Arts label.

British pop artist Richard Hamilton's plain white cover was the perfect response to Peter Blake's chaotic *Sgt. Pepper's* sleeve; each copy was stamped with its own individual serial number. This is U.K. copy No. 700.

The BEATLES

Nº 0000700

THE BEATLES | The Beatles (White Album)   **November 1968 | Apple**

Only the most successful band in history could have been the one to upend the master-slave system that defined most label-artist arrangements. The first LP to be issued on the Beatles' own Apple imprint guaranteed them 100 percent creative freedom, which they took full advantage of, not just to record what they pleased and wherever they pleased, but to move unencumbered artistically. On the surface, *The White Album*'s four-sided cache of 30 tracks is more expansive than *Sgt. Pepper's Lonely Hearts Club Band*. But it's also an understated album, more a humbly offered song collection than an extravagantly staged production. Its range comprises a musical mother lode of every stylistic vein the Beatles had ever mined, plus a few new ones—gauzy psychedelia in "Dear Prudence," folky pop in "Blackbird," various shades of rock ("Revolution 1," "Helter Skelter"), retro homage ("Back in the U.S.S.R.") and brazen experimentalism ("Revolution 9"). *The White Album* also obliged fans to acknowledge the Beatles as four individual, distinctly different musicians, a fact the band itself was confronting head-on; the record came with

separate photos of each member, and many tracks feature only the song's composer, unassisted by the rest of the group (Ringo walked out midway through the sessions but returned). British pop artist Richard Hamilton devised the album's all white cover, which afforded each purchaser a unique, numbered-edition. Especially valued as collectibles are copies with low numbers, with a dozen or so U.S. copies made for executives and stamped "A0000001."

THE BEATLES
Production by GEORGE MARTIN
Orchestrations by GEORGE MARTIN

An E.M.I. Recording
33⅓
Mfd. in U.K.
SIDE 4

PMC 7068
(XEX 712)
℗ 1968

REVOLUTION 1 Northern Songs. NCB. HONEY PIE
Northern Songs. NCB. SAVOY TRUFFLE* Apple
Publishing Ltd. CRY BABY CRY Northern
Songs. NCB. REVOLUTION 9 Northern
Songs. NCB. GOOD NIGHT
Northern Songs. NCB.
(Lennon—McCartney except * G. Harrison)

A scarce mono
copy; by the time
The Beatles was
released, few
albums were issued
in mono. The mono
and stereo mixes
differ significantly.

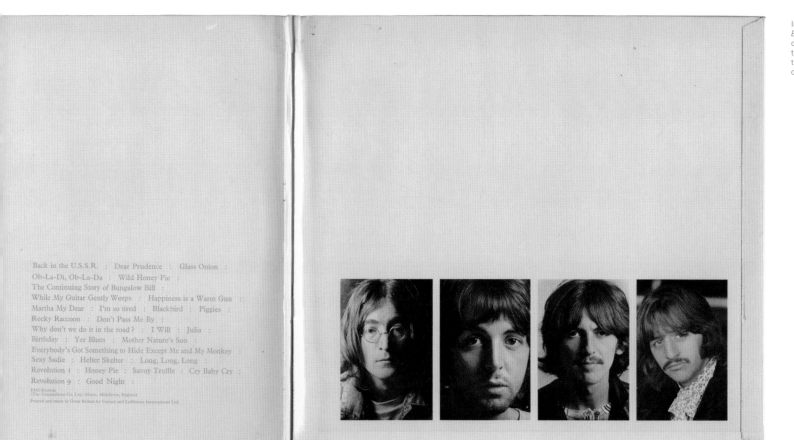

Back in the U.S.S.R. : Dear Prudence : Glass Onion :
Ob-La-Di, Ob-La-Da : Wild Honey Pic :
The Continuing Story of Bungalow Bill :
While My Guitar Gently Weeps : Happiness is a Warm Gun :
Martha My Dear : I'm so tired : Blackbird : Piggies :
Rocky Raccoon : Don't Pass Me By :
Why don't we do it in the road? : I Will : Julia :
Birthday : Yer Blues : Mother Nature's Son :
Everybody's Got Something to Hide Except Me and My Monkey :
Sexy Sadie : Helter Skelter : Long, Long, Long :
Revolution 1 : Honey Pie : Savoy Truffle : Cry Baby Cry :
Revolution 9 : Good Night :

EMI Records
(The Gramophone Co. Ltd.) Hayes, Middlesex, England
Printed and made in Great Britain by Garrod and Lofthouse International Ltd.

Inside gatefold; *The Beatles* was the only Beatles album that didn't picture them on the front cover.

THE PRETTY THINGS | S.F. Sorrow

December 1968 | Columbia

S.F. Sorrow is arguably the first rock opera. It appeared five months before The Who's *Tommy*, though a fair assessment would conclude that some of *Sorrow*'s songs and arrangements tip their hat to *The Who Sell Out*. Still, that such a smartly conceived, brilliantly executed musical narrative should emanate from a band that two years earlier was honing its Bo Diddley and Jimmy Reed chops is praiseworthy. The album recounts the rise and fall of Sebastian F. Sorrow, who, over the course of 13 tracks, is born, finds love, goes to work and war, loses love, cracks up, and resigns himself to being the world's "Loneliest Person." Individual cuts stand out, particularly the airy "She Says Good Morning," the ominous "Baron Saturday" (who introduces Sebastian to voodoo), and "Balloon Burning" (in which Sorrow's fiancée dies in the 1937 Hindenburg disaster). The Pretties' achievement is that they managed to

tell the tale clearly (much of *Sorrow*'s story is related in mini-chapters printed with the song lyrics) and make a wholly original, at times fascinating, record. The band still plays some *Sorrow* songs in concert and performed the entire album as recently as 2009.

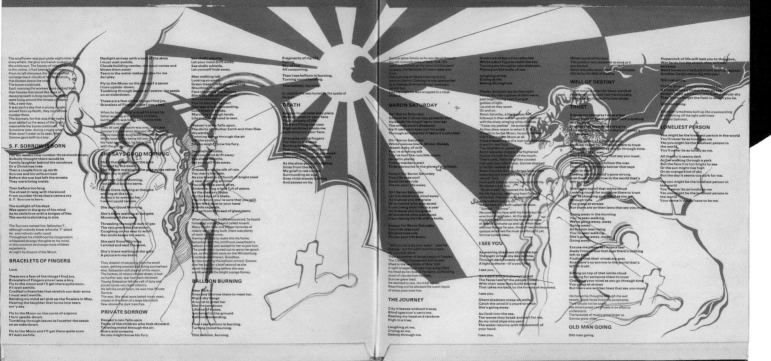

Inside gatefold with lyrics.

Back cover.

The band's U.S. label, Rare Earth, issued *S.F. Sorrow* in this strange die-cut cover meant to resemble a tombstone.

Peter Blake's sleeve for *Sweet Child* incorporated a pentagram–a five pointed star.

THE PENTANGLE | Sweet Child

December 1968 | Transatlantic

Few musical ensembles have been better named or visually represented than Pentangle. The cover of this double album, designed by Peter Blake of *Sgt. Pepper's* fame, shows all five points of the star interlocking: the perfect metaphor for how the U.K. quintet worked. Singer Jacqui McShee, guitarists Bert Jansch and John Renbourn, drummer Terry Cox, and bassist Danny Thompson mesh seamlessly on this half-concert, half-studio recording, which lit out in search of space that hadn't yet been explored by what was then designated British-folk. Where Fairport Convention expanded the genre by becoming the preeminent interpreters of a wildly eclectic songbook, Pentangle pushed the music instrumentally. The free-swinging jazz-folk heard on *Sweet Child* comprises a category the group invented and wholly owned. Highlights include the title song, instrumental "In Time" and McShee and Renbourn's brisk take on the

Furry Lewis blues "Turn Your Money Green" and her acappella "So Early in the Spring." The album remains the crown jewel of Pentangle's long, somewhat fractious career, but all five members went on to distinguished work: Jansch and Renbourn as solos, McShee in a new edition of Pentangle, Thompson backing Nick Drake on *Five Leaves Left*, and Cox contributing to such albums as *Space Oddity*, *Madman Across the Water*, and Scott Walker's *Stretch* and *We Had It All*.

The back cover features an illustration for each song.

TRA 178

Market Song Song using images inspired by a street market. Bert opens with guitar harmonics, then sings the verses and is joined by Jacqui. Danny and Terry underline the time which switches between 7/4 and 11/4 and 4/4.	**So Early In The Spring** Jacqui sings this unaccompanied traditional Scottish song.	**In Time** A group instrumental in triple time with solos by John and Bert.
No More My Lord Jacqui sings this spiritual which is also known as "Never Turn Back". It was used as a work-gang song and Terry builds up the rhythm using mallets over a riff played by Bert.	**No Exit** John and Bert play a new interpretation of a duet which first appeared on their LP 'Bert and John'.	**In Your Mind** The group sometimes call this "Over There". It features three part vocals by Bert, Jacqui and John, with Danny and Terry underlining the 7/4 rhythm.
Turn Your Money Green A blues sung by Jacqui. She heard it on an old Furry Lewis record. John accompanies her and also sings on the chorus.	**The Time Has Come** Written by Ann Briggs a traditional singer from Nottingham, and a favourite of The Pentangle.	**I've Got A Feeling** A blues sung by Jacqui in 3/4 time with Danny soloing on two choruses.
Haitian Fight Song Danny's solo interpretation of a Charles Mingus composition.	**Bruton Town** The group's arrangement of a traditional English song, with traditional ingredients—love, murder, and ghostly apparitions, as sung by Jacqui and Bert.	**The Trees They Do Grow High** Jacqui sings this group version of the traditional ballad which is also known as "Lady Mary Ann" and "Lang A Growing".
A Woman Like You A solo by Bert which Bert describes as "a cross between a love song and a black magic song". Bert uses D tuning on his guitar.	**Sweet Child** A love song sung by Bert and Jacqui with John taking the guitar lead.	**Moon Dog** This number by Terry is dedicated to a blind American street musician who used to play in the doorway of the old Basin Street Jazz Club on West 50th Street in New York City.
Goodbye Pork-Pie Hat John and Bert duet using Charles Mingus's tribute to Lester Young as a theme.	**I Loved A Lass** The Pentangle's arrangement of a traditional Scottish love song, sung by Bert.	**Hole In The Coal** Instrumental based on Ewan McColl's song "The Big Hewer" John, Terry and Danny take solos on a riff played by Bert.
3 **Three Dances** *Brentzel Gay* This is by Claude Gervaise, a 16th Century composer. *La Rotta* An Italian 14th Century estampie. *The Earle of Salisbury* This is a pavan by William Byrd, the 16th Century English composer. John on guitar. Terry on glockenspiel.	**Three Part Thing** John, Bert and Danny use a counterpoint theme composed for three instruments, with the middle section improvised on the mode. Terry backs with hand drums.	TRA 178 The Pentangle "Sweet Child" Sides 1 and 2 recorded Royal Festival Hall, London, 29 June 1968 Sides 3 and 4 recorded at IBC Studios, London, August 1968 Transatlantic Records Ltd. 120 Marylebone Lane London W1
Watch The Stars John and Jacqui sing an American childrens' Christmas song.	**Sovay** An English ballad, with unknown origins, about a female highwayman whose name could also be Sophie or Sylvie. It is sung by Jacqui.	A Shel Talmy production Engineer: Damon Lyon-Shaw Album design by Peter Blake Photography by Studio Hans Feurer Typography by Gordon House This record is STEREO. It can also be played with a modern lightweight pickup for perfect Mono reproduction. Record Sleeve printed and made by Garrod & Lofthouse Limited, London.

The Pentangle

The word unique is one that is often used out of context, however as far as The Pentangle are concerned it is a word that can honestly be applied.

No other group has so successfully knocked down musical barriers and incorporated the various types—folk, classical, blues, jazz—into their musical whole.

The two guitarists, Bert Jansch and John Renbourn, are already well established names in the folk world where their guitar styles have been particularly influential. They bring into the group elements of folk, blues and classical music and contribute much towards the Pentangle's original repertoire.

Danny Thompson, a brilliant bass player, and Terry Cox, an intelligent, understanding drummer, underpin everything expertly. These two musicians, who have names as first class session and jazz men, provide as strong a rhythm section as can be found in any group but both can take constructive solo roles in the general Pentangle pattern.

Jacqui McShee does much of the singing within the group, either working solo or dueting with Bert or John. Her clear voice can handle anything from an unaccompanied folk song to a modern blues. Jacqui is an excellent foil for the group's musicians and an integral part of The Pentangle's sound.

These five individuals, with five individual talents, have developed into a flexible musical unit and yet still able to permutate into segments giving each member a chance to expand beyond being a group entity.

Trying to describe The Pentangle's music is like trying to describe a sunset. You can talk of the colours, but the overall effect has to be seen to be appreciated. To appreciate The Pentangle, you have to listen.

Tony Wilson
Melody Maker

Terry Cox
Drums, glockenspiel and vocal
"Luckily my neighbours are deaf . . ."

Bert Jansch
Acoustic guitar and vocal
"I'm only in it for the beer."

Jacqui McShee
Vocal
"I used to sing with my sister, but we broke up the act and I replaced her with four men."

John Renbourn
Acoustic guitar and vocal
"I started off trying to play like Big Bill Broonzy, and I'm still trying."

Danny Thompson
Double bass
"I played lead trombone in the 1st Green Jackets Infantry Marching Band, then I took up the double bass and I ain't marched since."

THE SOFT MACHINE | The Soft Machine

December 1968 | Probe

Among many landscape-altering debuts in 1968, this album introduced one of rock's most steadfastly innovative and commercially dicey ensembles. Robert Wyatt, Kevin Ayers, and Mike Ratledge hailed from the same Canterbury scene that birthed Caravan, Gong, and Hatfield and the North, so the trio's inclination toward experimentalism was no surprise. But *Soft Machine* achieved something altogether its own at the crossroads of psychedelia, jazz, and pop: an ambidextrous approach that allowed the band to switch gears from extended post-Floyd keyboard excursions ("So Boot If at All") to short guitar-reverb sorties ("Joy of a Toy") and unlikely hybrids that paired somber lyric recitation with catchy, Who-like choruses ("Why Are We Sleeping"?). "We Did It Again," which the band was known to deliver 40-minute versions of in concert, uses a modified "You Really Got Me" riff under endless repetition of the title

phrase to suggest the kind of aural epics later popularized by composers like Steve Reich and Philip Glass. Tom Wilson, at the helm for the debut LPs by the Mothers and the Velvet Underground, co-produced with Chas Chandler—whose managerial and production client Jimi Hendrix the Soft Machine toured America in 1968.

THE SOFT MACHINE

CPLP-4500-A
Side 1

33⅓ RPM
STEREO

1. HOPE FOR HAPPINESS 4:10
(B. Hopper, K. Ayers, M. Ratledge)
2. JOY OF A TOY 2:49
(K. Ayers, M. Ratledge)
3. HOPE FOR HAPPINESS (reprise) 1:37
(B. Hopper, K. Ayers, M. Ratledge)
4. WHY AM I SO SHORT? 1:38
(H. Hopper, K. Ayers, M. Ratledge)
5. SO BOOT IF AT ALL 7:22
(K. Ayers, M. Ratledge, R. Wyatt)
6. A CERTAIN KIND (H. Hopper) 4:10
Above selections published by
Amm Jay Music Inc.—BMI
Produced by
Chas Chandler and Tom Wilson
Time Side I: 21:56

Back cover.

THE SOFT MACHINE

HOPE FOR HAPPINESS
JOY OF A TOY
HOPE FOR HAPPINESS (reprise)
WHY AM I SO SHORT?
SO BOOT IF AT ALL
A CERTAIN KIND
SAVE YOURSELF

PRISCILLA
LULLABYE LETTER
WE DID IT AGAIN
PLUS BELLE QU'UNE POUBELLE
WHY ARE WE SLEEPING?
BOX 25/4 LID

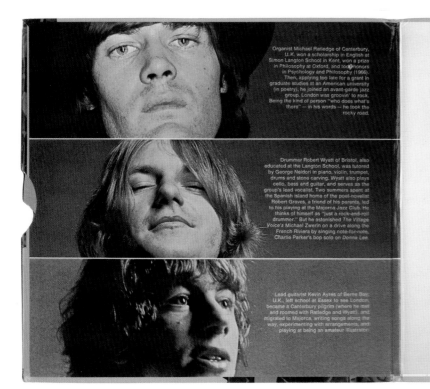

Organist Michael Ratledge of Canterbury, U.K. won a scholarship in English at Simon Langton School in Kent, won a prize in Philosophy at Oxford, and took honors in Psychology and Philosophy (1966). Then, applying too late for a grant in graduate studies at an American university (in poetry), he joined an avant-garde jazz group. London was groovin' to rock. Being the kind of person "who does what's there" — in his words — he took the rocky road.

Drummer Robert Wyatt of Bristol, also educated at the Langton School, was tutored by George Neidori in piano, violin, trumpet, drums and stone carving. Wyatt also plays cello, bass and guitar, and serves as the group's lead vocalist. Two summers spent at the Spanish island home of the poet-novelist Robert Graves, a friend of his parents, led to his playing at the Majorca Jazz Club. He thinks of himself as "just a rock-and-roll drummer." But he astonished The Village Voice's Michael Zwerin on a drive along the French Riviera by singing note-for-note, Charlie Parker's bop solo on Donna Lee.

Lead guitarist Kevin Ayres of Berne Bay, U.K., left school at Essex to see London, became a Canterbury pilgrim (where he met and roomed with Ratledge and Wyatt, and migrated to Majorca, writing songs along the way, experimenting with arrangements, and playing at being an amateur illustrator).

THE SOFT MACHINE

CPLP 4500

Close your eyes and visualize this group! Children of World War II, long hair, shades, multi-colored, paisley-patterned shirts, offbeat hats, beads, bells and bikini shorts. Three British 'drop-outs' stranded on the French Riviera and sleeping on the beaches. But they have a panel truck bulging with electronic hardware. And soon their sound fills the first half of Jean Jacques Lebel and Alan Zion's Festival Libre at St. Tropez, loosening up audiences for a play by Pablo Picasso, Desire Caught by the Tail.

Now, open your ears and listen to their music!

It's a Now sound, swings like jazz, rocks like rhythm-and-blues, hairy with fuzz-box distortion, off-the-keyboard with electronic atonalities — the sound of music updated by the music of sound.

The word-of-mouth, as well as critical panegyrics, from the south of France in American, British and French underground publications, eventually brought the group to these shores. During the past year, it has 'lived' in its panel truck, covering the underground of sound-and-light discotheques, blowing the minds of sophisticated listeners at N. Y.'s Museum of Modern Art, and co-starring with the Jimi Hendrix Experience in a record-breaking, crosscountry tour.

In this, its debut album, the contrast between the group's hippie-crude appearance and its cultivated background, is reflected in the absorbing tensions of the music. The drive is to synthesize the diverse sounds of jazz and rock in an electronic continuity. "Continuity" is the precise word, for even in personals, the group's sets are like suites, with an organ-drum interlude serving as a bridge to the next tune. The lines of succeeding numbers frequently echo, or are developments, as with Hope For Happiness in this album, of a preceding number.

"We play hour-long sets," Mike Ratledge explains, "developing a concert style. The compositions are spaced with improvisations from drum and organ and punctuated with songs. The light show diverts the eye from the mind to the bodily functions. Soon, the audience is up on its feet. As the dancers react to the organic rhythms, the regular steps modulate into free form and movement."

The music of The Soft Machine includes the shock values of unstructured composition, although many of their works are songs. Electronic devices add the impact of sensory bombardment. But these effects are mere gimmicks unless they are used with sensitivity and logic. The Soft Machine is an exciting testimonial: men need machines but machines need men and ideas to produce meaningful experience. The group creates music that is meaningful, also appealing, because it has good taste, craftsmanship, and, most of all, involvement. The track of Joy of a Toy tells it like it is!

Arnold Shaw

SIDE 1
HOPE FOR HAPPINESS
(M. Ratledge, K. Ayers, M. Ratledge) 4:22
JOY OF A TOY
(K. Ayers, M. Ratledge) 2:58
HOPE FOR HAPPINESS (reprise)
(B. Hopper, K. Ayers, M. Ratledge) 1:31
WHY AM I SO SHORT?
(H. Hopper, K. Ayers, M. Ratledge) 2:33
SO BOOT IF AT ALL
(K. Ayers, M. Ratledge, R. Wyatt) 2:33
A CERTAIN KIND
(H. Hopper) 4:00

SIDE 2
SAVE YOURSELF
(R. Wyatt) 2:26
PRISCILLA
(M. Ratledge, K. Ayers, R. Wyatt) 1:05
LULLABYE LETTER
(K. Ayers) 4:26
WE DID IT AGAIN
(K. Ayers) 3:40
PLUS BELLE QU'UNE POUBELLE
(K. Ayers) 1:55
WHY ARE WE SLEEPING?
(K. Ayers, M. Ratledge, R. Wyatt) 5:26
BOX 25/4 LID
(M. Ratledge, H. Hopper) :48

Above selections published by Amm Jay Music Inc. —BMI
Produced by Chas Chandler and Tom Wilson
Mfg. by Grand Award Record Co., Inc., a subsidiary of ABC Records Inc.
1330 Avenue of the Americas, New York, N.Y. 10019.
Cover Design Byron Goto / Eli Altman / Henry Epstein
Made in U.S.A.

CREEDENCE CLEARWATER REVIVAL | Bayou Country　　　　　**January 1969 | Fantasy**

For an artist who later had to defend himself against charges of self-plagiarism,
John Fogerty was anything but a trend follower. His compact travelin' band
began life as a Bay Area quartet that bucked the headwinds of both place and
period, eschewing solo-heavy psych tripping for an approach that circled
closer to home: a melding of rockabilly and '50s R&B. The group's second
album, *Bayou Country,* is the one that broke Creedence on the strength of
underground-FM airplay (for title track "Born on the Bayou" and the extended
"Keep on Chooglin'") and the massive single "Proud Mary." Among dozens
of versions of the tune, now a contemporary standard, are performances by
Ike & Tina Turner (an international hit in 1971), Elvis Presley, and Solomon
Burke. Creedence's deep-rooted swamp-rock coincided with the early-'70s
rock revival but has long outlived that phenomenon to become one of the most
identifiable and widely appealing styles in the history of pop music.

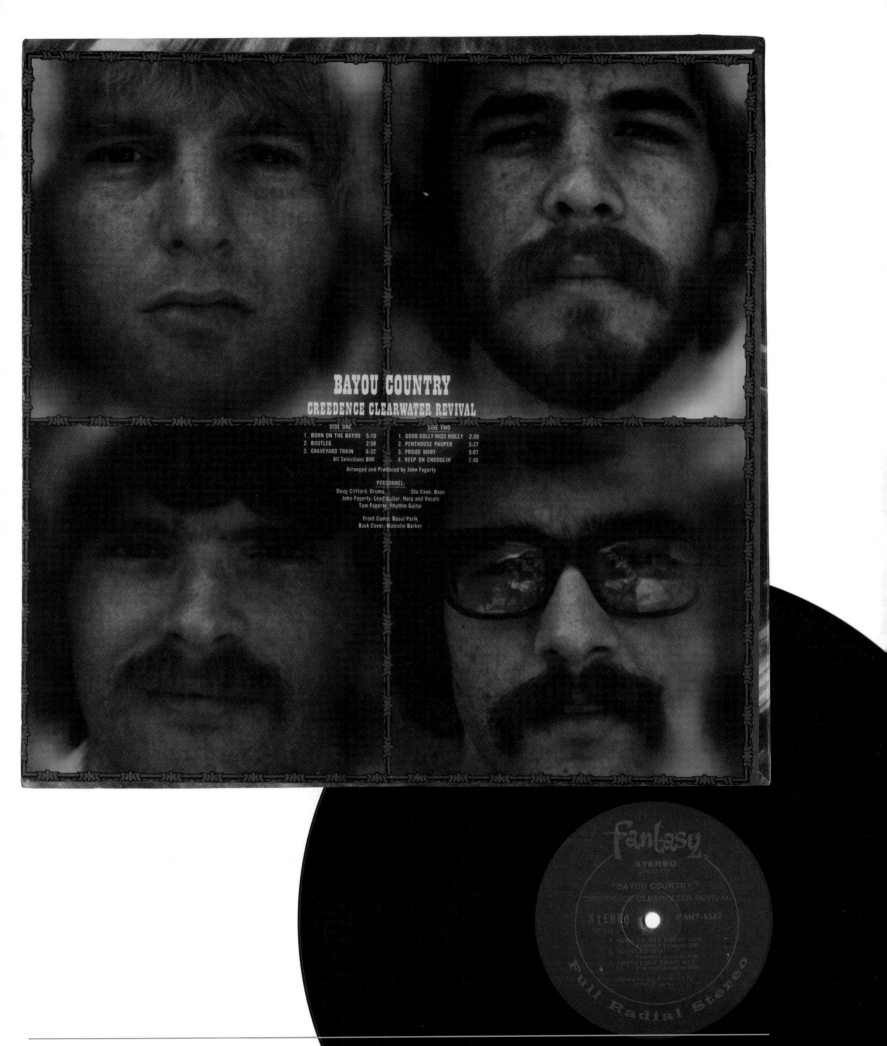

BAYOU COUNTRY
CREEDENCE CLEARWATER REVIVAL

SIDE ONE   SIDE TWO
1. BORN ON THE BAYOU   5:10   1. GOOD GOLLY MISS MOLLY   2:39
2. BOOTLEG   2:58   2. PENTHOUSE PAUPER   3:37
3. GRAVEYARD TRAIN   8:32   3. PROUD MARY   3:07
                                   4. KEEP ON CHOOGLIN'   7:40
All Selections BMI

Arranged and Produced by John Fogerty

PERSONNEL:

Doug Clifford: Drums   Stu Cook: Bass
John Fogerty: Lead Guitar, Harp and Vocals
Tom Fogerty: Rhythm Guitar

Front Cover: Basul Parik
Back Cover: Malcolm Barker

LED ZEPPELIN | Led Zeppelin

January 1969 | Atlantic

Led Zeppelin's debut made it into the Top 10 on both sides of the Atlantic and launched them into superstar status and permanent residence in the rock 'n' roll hall of fame, even before one was formally established. Clearly a shot-heard-round-the-world record, *Led Zeppelin* features the abundance of talent and inclinations that enabled Jimmy Page, Robert Plant, John Bonham, and John Paul Jones to take the ambitious next step in the evolution of British blues-rock, from Mayall purism and Stones rambunctiousness into something more dramatic. Along the way, the album's four-week stay at the top of the U.S. charts and its triple-platinum sales helped invent arena rock. Such massive popularity led to extended international tours, bigger venues, and, in this band's hands, notorious private and public behavior that luridly defined the modern myth of the all-conquering, uninhibited rock star. Underneath it all, *Led Zeppelin* remains a powerful record, its outsized presentation drawing equally from Robert Plant's vocals and the songs' arrangements, which blend feather-light acoustic passages with Jimmy Page's pummeling guitar sorties. "Communication Breakdown," "Babe I'm Gonna Leave You," and "Dazed and Confused" were staples of FM-rock playlists, and George Hardie's cover design, utilizing a photo of the Hindenburg disaster, one of the most iconic visuals in popular-music imagery.

LED ZEPPELIN

588 171 STEREO
This stereo record can be played on mono gramophones without loss of musical quality provided a stereo cartridge wired for mono sound is fitted to the pick-up. If your gramophone is a recent model it is probable that it is already fitted with a suitable cartridge. Your dealer will be able to advise you further if necessary.

JOHN BONHAM
DRUMS, TYMPANI, BACKING VOCAL

ROBERT PLANT
LEAD VOCAL, HARMONICA

Side One
1. **GOOD TIMES BAD TIMES**
(By Page, Jones & Bonham; Time: 2:43)
2. **BABE I'M GONNA LEAVE YOU**
(Traditional, arr. by Jimmy Page; Time: 6:40)
3. **YOU SHOOK ME**
(By Willie Dixon; Time: 6:30)
4. **DAZED AND CONFUSED**
(By Jimmy Page; Time: 6:27)

Side Two
1. **YOUR TIME IS GONNA COME**
(By Jimmy Page & John Paul Jones; Time: 4:41)
2. **BLACK MOUNTAIN SIDE**
(By Jimmy Page; Time: 2:06)
3. **COMMUNICATION BREAKDOWN**
(By Page, Jones, & Bonham; Time: 2:26)
4. **I CAN'T QUIT YOU BABY**
(By Willie Dixon; Time: 4:42)
5. **HOW MANY MORE TIMES**
(By Page, Jones & Bonham; Time: 3:30)

TABLA DRUMS ON BLACK MOUNTAIN SIDE
VIRAM JASANI

JIMMY PAGE
ELECTRIC GUITAR, ACOUSTIC GUITAR,
PEDAL STEEL GUITAR, BACKING VOCAL

JOHN PAUL JONES
BASS, ORGAN, BACKING VOCAL

PRODUCED BY JIMMY PAGE
Director of engineering: Glyn Johns
Executive producer: Peter Grant
Back liner photo: Chris Dreja
Cover design: George Hardie

UPTIGHT AN' OUTASIGHT is the official Atlantic Appreciation Society at 17/19, Stratford Place, London, W.1.

Under licence from Atlantic Recording Corp. USA.
Manufactured by Polydor Records Ltd., London.
Printed and made by MacNeill Press Ltd., London, S.E.1.

Publishing credits on the earliest copies credit some songs to Superhype Music.

MADE IN Gt. BRITAIN
STEREO
UNAUTHORISED PUBLIC PERFORMANCE BROADCASTING AND COPYING OF THE

LED ZEPPELIN

℗ 1969
Under licence from Atlantic Recording Corpn., U.S.A.

588171

ATLANTIC SIDE ONE

1. GOOD TIMES BAD TIMES (Page/Jones/Bonham) 2:43
2. BABE I'M GONNA LEAVE YOU (Trad. arr. Page) 6:40
3. YOU SHOOK ME (Dixon) 6:30
4. DAZED AND CONFUSED (Page) 6:27

1, 3, 4. Superhype Music
2. Jewel Music

POLYDOR RECORDS LIMITED

STEREO

A&M RECORDS

SP 4175

The Flying Burrito Bros

THE GILDED PALACE OF SIN

THE FLYING BURRITO BROS. | The Gilded Palace Of Sin　　　　**February 1969 | A&M**

Gram Parsons is the one who nudged the Byrds in the direction of country music on *Sweetheart of the Rodeo*, though he left the band before the record came out. The group's follow-up album featured a smattering of country, while Parsons' next, the debut of The Flying Burrito Brothers (co-founded with Byrds bassist Chris Hillman), barreled full-bore toward pedal-steel, Peterbilts, and sagebrush laments. Where the Byrds' countryisms were fairly straightforward, the Burritos' mixed country sincerity and sentimentality with rock-hipster awareness. The cover of *Gilded Palace of Sin* shows the band in suits, designed by cowboy tailor Nudie, festooned with marijuana leaves and drug capsules. The album's modernism is most aggressively promoted by "Hippie Boy," which sends up the tradition of the moralizing country-song monologue, but the record's best cuts take more direct and soulful approaches, led by strong Parsons

ballad performances: "Hot Burrito" (#1 and #2), "Sin City," country-rocker "Christine's Tune," and heartfelt adaptations of two R&B staples written by Dan Penn and Chips Moman, "Do Right Woman," and "Dark End of the Street." *Gilded Palace* was a highly influential album that made The Flying Burrito Brothers into something of a country-rock conservatory where practitioners of the genre trained before moving on.

THE GILDED PALACE OF SIN
THE FLYING BURRITO BROS/A & M SP 4175

A&M RECORDS

SNEEKY PETE

CHRIS HILLMAN

GRAM PARSONS

CHRIS ETHRIDGE

Gram Parsons'
Nudie suit featured
a marijuana plant,
various pills, nude
women on the la-
pels, and a crucifix
on the back of the
jacket.

SIDE ONE:

CHRISTINE'S TUNE° *3:02
(GRAM PARSONS-CHRIS HILLMAN) IRVING MUSIC BMI

SIN CITY° **4:10
(GRAM PARSONS-CHRIS HILLMAN) IRVING MUSIC BMI

DO RIGHT WOMAN° *3:56
(CHIPS MOMAN-DAN PENN) PRESS MUSIC BMI

DARK END OF THE STREET° *3:55
(SPOONER OLDHAM-DAN PENN) FAME MUSIC BMI

MY UNCLE° . . . . *†2:36
(GRAM PARSONS-CHRIS HILLMAN) IRVING MUSIC BMI

° VOCALS: GRAM PARSONS, CHRIS HILLMAN
□ VOCAL: GRAM PARSONS
× BACKGROUND VOCALS: CHRIS HILLMAN, CHRIS ETHRIDGE
• VOCAL: CHRIS HILLMAN & HOT BURRITO CHORUS

SIDE TWO:

WHEELS° ***3:02
(CHRIS HILLMAN-GRAM PARSONS) IRVING MUSIC BMI

JUANITA° *2:28
(CHRIS HILLMAN—GRAM PARSONS) IRVING MUSIC BMI

HOT BURRITO #1□ . . . . ****††3:37
(CHRIS ETHRIDGE-GRAM PARSONS) IRVING MUSIC BMI

HOT BURRITO #2□× . . . . . . ****††3:15
(CHRIS ETHRIDGE-GRAM PARSONS) IRVING MUSIC BMI

DO YOU KNOW HOW IT FEELS° **2:06
(GRAM PARSONS-GOLDBERG) GUITAR MUSIC BMI

HIPPIE BOY• ****4:55
(CHRIS HILLMAN-GRAM PARSONS) IRVING MUSIC BMI

This album is also available on stereo tapes. Write for a free full-color A&M Record Catalogue, A&M Records, 1416 N. La Brea, Hollywood, Calif. 90028.

OTHER CREDITS:

PRODUCERS: THE BURRITOS, LARRY MARKS
AND HENRY LEWY / ENGINEER: HENRY
LEWY / SPECIAL CREDITS: DRUMS: *JON
CORNEAL, **EDDIE HOH, ***SAM GOLD-
STEIN, ****POPEYE PHILLIPS / PERSONNEL:
GRAM PARSONS—RHYTHM GUITAR, KEY-
BOARD INSTRUMENTS; CHRIS HILLMAN—
RHYTHM GUITAR, MANDOLIN†; CHRIS
ETHRIDGE—BASS, PIANO††; SNEEKY PETE
—STEEL GUITAR / SPECIAL THANKS TO:
ART DIRECTOR—TOM WILKES AND THE
BOYS IN GRAPHICS / MICHAEL VOSSE / &
PHOTOGRAPHER—BARRY FEINSTEIN.

This promotional
disc was made for
radio stations and
reviewers.

THE FLYING BURRITO BROS.
THE GILDED PALACE OF SIN

1. CHRISTINE'S TUNE 3:02
(G. Parsons-C. Hillman) Irving Music Inc. (BMI)

A&M RECORDS

STEREO
SIDE 1
SP-4175
(SP-4249)
PROMOTION COPY
NOT FOR SALE

2. SIN CITY 4:10
(G. Parsons-C. Hillman) Irving Music Inc. (BMI)
3. DO RIGHT WOMAN 3:56
(C. Moman-D. Penn) Press Music (BMI)
4. DARK END OF THE STREET 3:55
(S. Oldham-D. Penn) Fame Music (BMI)
5. MY UNCLE 2:36
(G. Parsons-C. Hillman) Irving Music Inc. (BMI)

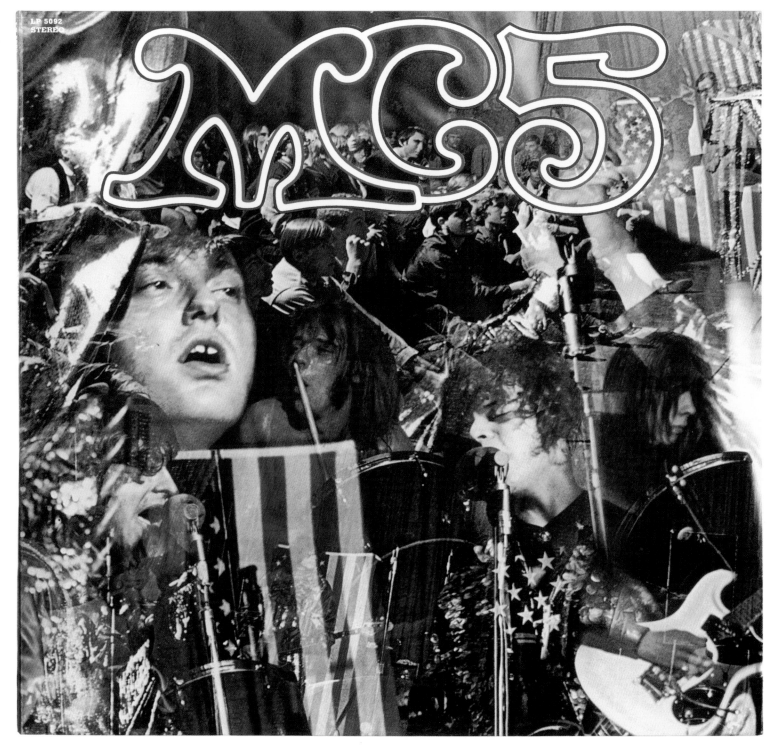

LP 5092
STEREO

MC5

MC5 | Kick Out The Jams

February 1969 | Elektra

Among the 1970s' punk rock parents, the MC5 rank alongside their Detroit "little brothers" the Stooges and New York's Velvet Underground. The quintet brings much to its debut album, which was intended to capture the high-energy quotient of the live 5 experience. Though *Kick Out the Jams* sometimes comes off loose and unstructured, there's no denying its heavy horsepower and heaping dose of attitude. The latter, best expressed in singer Rob Tyner's declaration on the opening track ("It's time to kick out the jams, motherfuckers!") joined the band in a battle with its label, which ultimately dropped the "5" after one LP. That relationship was also strained by the group's political posturing, which was even more radical and outspoken than Dylan or Country Joe & the Fish's work and inspired by a close association with band manager/local activist John Sinclair. Still, if it's about the music, then the flame-thrower intensity of cuts like "Ramblin' Rose," "Rocket Reducer No. 62 (Rama Lama Fa Fa Fa)," and "Kick Out the Jams," particularly the sonic fury of guitarists Wayne Kramer and Fred Smith, makes for a highly influential slab of late-'60s rock.

The inner gatefold featured provocative liner notes by band manager and White Panther Party Minister of Information John Sinclair.

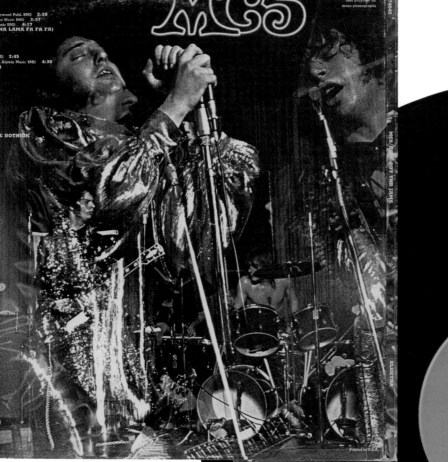

The MC5 is a whole thing. There is no way to get at the music without taking in the whole context of the music too – there is no separation. We say the MC5 is the solution to the problem of separation, because they are so together. The MC5 is totally committed to the revolution, as the revolution is totally committed to driving people out of their separate shells and into each other's arms.

I'm talking about unity, brothers and sisters, because we have to get it together. We are the solution to the problem. if we will just be that. If we can feel it. LeRoi Jones said, "feeling predicts intelligence." The MC5 will make you feel it, or leave the room. The MC5 will drive you crazy out of your head into your body. The MC5 is rock and roll. Rock and roll is the music of our bodies, of our whole lives–the resensifier. Rob Tyner calls it. We have to come together.

people, "build to a gathering," or else. Or else you are dead, and gone.

The MC5 will bring you back to your senses from wherever you have been taken to hide. They are bad. Their whole lives are totally given to this music. They are a whole thing. They are a working model of the new paleocybernetic culture in action. There is no separation. They live together to work together, they eat together, fuck together, get high together, walk down the street and through the world together. There is no separation. Just as their music will bring you together like that, if you hear it. If you will live it. And we will make sure you hear it, because we know you need it as bad as we do. We have to have it.

The music is the source and effect of our spirit flesh. The MC5 is the source and effect of the music, just as you are.

Just as I am. Just to hear the music and have it be our selves. is what we want. What we need. We are a lonely desperate people, pulled apart by the killer forces of capitalism and competition, and we need the music to hold us together. Separation is doom. We are free men, and we demand a free music, a free high energy source that will drive us wild into the streets of America yelling and screaming and tearing down everything that would keep people slaves.

The MC5 is that force. The MC5 is the revolution, in all its applications. There is no separation. Everything is everything. There is no thing to fear. The music will make you strong, as it is strong, and there is no way it can be stopped now. All power to the people! The MC5 is here now for you to hear and see and feel now! Give it up–come together –get down, brothers and sisters, it's time to testify, and what

you have here in your hands is a living testimonial to the absolute power and strength of these men. Go wild! The world is yours! Take it now, and be one with it! Kick out the jams, motherfucker! And stay alive with the MC5!

John Sinclair

Original pressings contain the exhortation, "Kick out the jams, motherfuckers;" however, complaints ensued and the offending word was replaced on subsequent pressings with "brothers and sisters."

The front cover is a collage of live photographs by Fred Lombardi.

SLY AND THE FAMILY STONE | Stand!

May 1969 | Epic

It took two years and four albums for audiences to catch up with what Sly Stone was up to, but the payoff turned out to be a win-win situation for both parties. The musical mainstream welcomed one of its most prominent innovators with *Stand!*, and Sly and his septet got their license to cover even more creative ground, which yielded some of the most distinctive and intelligent popular music of the last century. The album, and the advent of Sly & the Family Stone as an international phenomenon, is a perfect example of the adage (also coined in 1969) that "the personal is political." The multiracial group mixed rock and soul, two genres then considered separate but equal, to exhilarating effect. Its message is both implicit and explicit on *Stand!*, whose title track advocates truth in thought and action: "Stand! You've been sitting much too long / There's a permanent crease in your right and wrong." It's also ecumenical, eschewing reductive

blame games to insist that people be treated and respected as individuals ("Everyday People," "Don't Call Me Nigger, Whitey"), and full of feel-good sentiments ("Sing a Simple Song" and the band's Woodstock anthem "I Want to Take You Higher"). *Stand!* remains one of American pop's most influential albums, its psychedelic soul having been the prime motivator for the Temptations' sonic assaults under producer Norman Whitfield, and various of its tracks being widely sampled in recent years.

The back cover
juxtaposes pho-
tographs of Sly as
a baby and as an
adult.

Inside the gatefold
are lyrics and
photographs of the
band as babies and
adults.

The cover photo
was taken by pho-
tographer Frank
Bez in Topanga
Canyon, California,
circa September
1968.

NEIL YOUNG WITH CRAZY HORSE | Eveybody Knows This Is Nowhere   May 1969 | Reprise

The Neil Young that everybody knows comes into view here on his second solo outing. David Briggs replaces debut-LP producer Jack Nitzsche, and Young commences his fruitful, decades-long association with Crazy Horse. Where *Neil Young* presented the artist as a stand-alone singer-songwriter free of the bonds of a band, it often emphasized his acoustic-troubadour side. *Everybody Knows This Is Nowhere* pumps up the volume, relying more on a higher-octane rush of childlike optimism and dolorous reflection, best exemplified by "Cinnamon Girl" and "Cowgirl in the Sand." The two songs became Young classics, as did "Down by the River," which combines pop-ish harmonies and bruising electric guitar to relate a haunted "Hey Joe" tale of betrayal and revenge. The same duality characterizes the epic "Cowgirl in the Sand," with added information: Here's where Young firmly establishes his credentials as one of rock's more inventive guitar

stylists. Both underscored and egged on by the Crazy Horse rhythm section, he explores all manner of tonal and melodic terrain over the course of two solos, extracting more genuine emotion than a dozen blues shredders could summon with twice the space. On this record, Young creates a gig that he alone continues to be the most qualified to perform: the singer-songwriter whose lyrical sensitivity is matched by an equal amount of instrumental prowess and imagination.

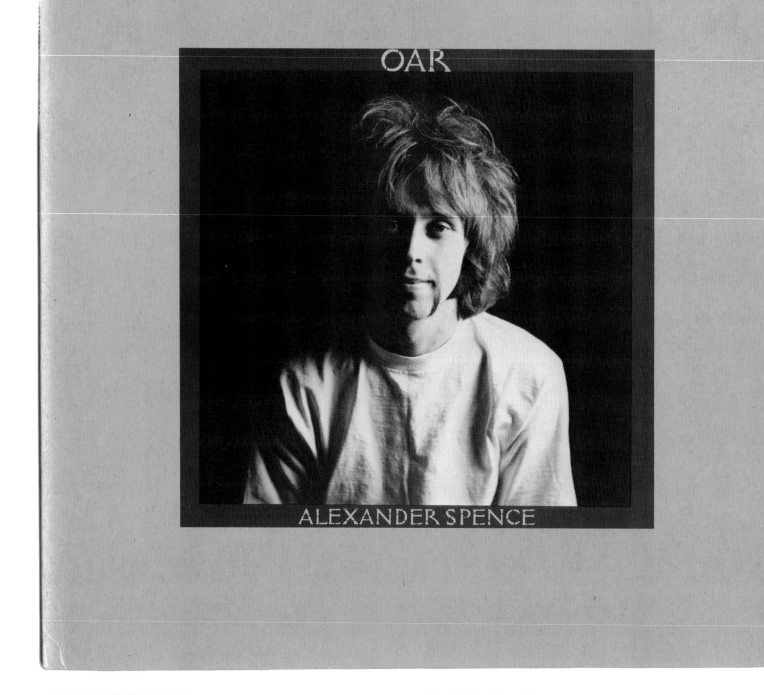

ALEXANDER SPENCE | Oar

May 1969 | Columbia

"This unique LP is bound to be forgotten," wrote Greil Marcus in his *Rolling Stone* review of this inadvertent classic, one of the most cherished cult records of all time. The contextual heavy weather surrounding it has almost overshadowed its achievement. During sessions for Moby Grape's second album, Spence, a founding member of both the Grape and Jefferson Airplane, suffered a violent LSD episode that landed him a six-month stay in New York's Bellevue Hospital. Upon his release, he repaired to Nashville to cut *Oar*. At Moby Grape producer David Rubinson's suggestion, the studio engineer simply let the tapes run, capturing whatever Spence (who played all the instruments, a full year before Paul McCartney's similarly-created debut) put down. Though Spence intended the dozen tracks as a demo for a more "produced" record, Rubinson persuaded Columbia records to issue them as they were: unadorned, imperfect, and powerfully

compelling. *Oar* is by turns warm ("Little Hands"), funny ("Dixie Peach Promenade"), and harrowing ("Grey/Afro"), the product of a disordered mind and a musician with a singular, irreducible vision of what he wants to say. If the LP was, as rumored, the worst selling in Columbia's history, it's of little consequence. *Oar*'s quiet, unsettled brilliance continues to affect listeners. A 1999 tribute album, *More Oar*, enlisted the likes of Tom Waits, Robert Plant, Robyn Hitchcock, Mudhoney, and Beck—who 10 years later posted videos of his complete version of *Oar* (assisted by Feist, members of Wilco, and others) on his website.

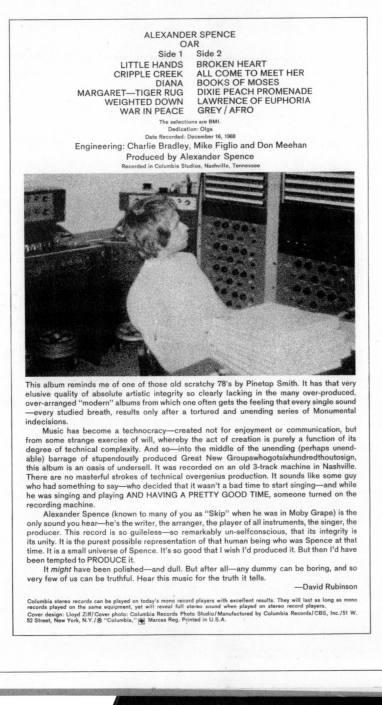

ALEXANDER SPENCE
OAR

Side 1	Side 2
LITTLE HANDS	BROKEN HEART
CRIPPLE CREEK	ALL COME TO MEET HER
DIANA	BOOKS OF MOSES
MARGARET—TIGER RUG	DIXIE PEACH PROMENADE
WEIGHTED DOWN	LAWRENCE OF EUPHORIA
WAR IN PEACE	GREY / AFRO

The selections are BMI.
Dedication: Olga
Date Recorded: December 16, 1968

Engineering: Charlie Bradley, Mike Figlio and Don Meehan

Produced by Alexander Spence
Recorded in Columbia Studios, Nashville, Tennessee

This album reminds me of one of those old scratchy 78's by Pinetop Smith. It has that very elusive quality of absolute artistic integrity so clearly lacking in the many over-produced, over-arranged "modern" albums from which one often gets the feeling that every single sound —every studied breath, results only after a tortured and unending series of Monumental indecisions.

Music has become a technocracy—created not for enjoyment or communication, but from some strange exercise of will, whereby the act of creation is purely a function of its degree of technical complexity. And so—into the middle of the unending (perhaps unend-able) barrage of stupendously produced Great New Groupswhogotsixhundredthoutosign, this album is an oasis of undersell. It was recorded on an old 3-track machine in Nashville. There are no masterful strokes of technical overgenius production. It sounds like some guy who had something to say—who decided that it wasn't a bad time to start singing—and while he was singing and playing AND HAVING A PRETTY GOOD TIME, someone turned on the recording machine.

Alexander Spence (known to many of you as "Skip" when he was in Moby Grape) is the only sound you hear—he's the writer, the arranger, the player of all instruments, the singer, the producer. This record is so guileless—so remarkably un-selfconscious, that its integrity is its unity. It is the purest possible representation of that human being who was Spence at that time. It is a small universe of Spence. It's so good that I wish I'd produced it. But then I'd have been tempted to PRODUCE it.

It *might* have been polished—and dull. But after all—any dummy can be boring, and so very few of us can be truthful. Hear this music for the truth it tells.

—David Rubinson

Columbia stereo records can be played on today's mono record players with excellent results. They will last as long as mono records played on the same equipment, yet will reveal full stereo sound when played on stereo record players.
Cover design: Lloyd Ziff / Cover photo: Columbia Records Photo Studio / Manufactured by Columbia Records / CBS, Inc. / 51 W. 52 Street, New York, N.Y. / ® "Columbia," ⬥ Marcas Reg. Printed in U.S.A.

CS 9831 Columbia

In his liner notes, Moby Grape producer David Rubinson says of *Oar*, "It's so good that I wish I'd produced it. But then I'd have been tempted to PRODUCE it."

Jon Savage

on Moby Grape: *Moby Grape* & Love: *Forever Changes*

I started buying records when I was 10 because of The Beatles. I was 10 in September 1963 and my first great love was Del Shannon's "Hey Little Girl" and "Little Town Flirt." Around the age of nine, I started getting really interested in pop music and that coincided with The Beatles. I started buying singles for myself in '63 or '64.

You could buy records in these kind of hardware and furniture shops. On the ground floor you had furniture or stuff for the home, and downstairs you had gramophones and records. My parents weren't that interested in music. My mother liked Glenn Miller but my grandfather was a huge music fan. He saw the Original Dixieland Jazz Band when they played England in 1920, and Frank Sinatra's first UK date. I've got his records in the back of this room. He was a huge jazz fan. He loved Louis Armstrong, Cab Calloway, all that stuff. And even went as far as having Elvis' '78 "Blue Suede Shoes," which he would have bought when he was in his early fifties, so he was pretty hip. It's obviously genetic, or encouraged by him, because from a very early age… you know, you're just tuned into music or you're not. And I was, and I got reinforcement from my granddad.

From '64 to '66, I used to watch the pop shows with my granddad because he wouldn't make the stupid comments that my parents would make, which were "Look at their long hair," or "They're disgusting, how can you like these," and that crap. I didn't want to hear it, I just wanted to watch the program, and I could do that with my grandfather, who understood. I'll always remember watching the Rolling Stones on *Ready, Steady, Go* in '66 and they were doing "Lady Jane." My grandfather was laughing and I said, "Shut up, shut up!" and at the end of the song I said, "Why are you laughing?" and he said, "You'll understand when you get a bit older, but it's all about a boy telling a girl that he doesn't want anything more to do with her, but he's doing it in a really clever way. He's brilliant." So he really liked The Stones, he thought they were great.

And also I was growing up at that fantastic time. The whole point about the suburbs was that they were a place where my parents' generation went to escape the war to remake their life. It was fantastic for them, but for me it was boring. There

was not a lot of culture there. And so I tuned into pop; that was how I interpreted the world. I used to listen to Radio Caroline obsessively in '65, '66, '67, and I watched *Top of the Pops* avidly every week.

Most people were not as obsessed with pop music as I was. I had a friend at school called Franklin and he and I would sing songs. I remember being on the top of the bus going to school, trying to work out the descant on "Heart Full of Soul." We would go round the other boys at our school—it was a day school—and we'd go round the other boys asking them questionnaires about whether they liked pop music, and what did they like, and why did they like, and they kind of thought we were mad because we were the only people who were really interested in pop in that obsessive way. Most people, as you know, aren't really interested in music, and huge record-sellers are the records that sell to people who don't really like music *that* much.

Moby Grape: *Moby Grape*

I've got my copy of *Moby Grape* here and I'm trying to remember when I bought it. I would have known about West Coast music from Buffalo Springfield and The Doors back in '67. But by '69, which is when I started buying this stuff, I was 15 and 16, I thought most British music sucked. It was the blues boom time, it was Jethro Tull, who I actually quite liked, but then it was Black Sabbath, who I just didn't understand at all. And then in '70 it was *Deep Purple In Rock* and all that crap, I just couldn't bear it, and that's what most of my peers were listening to. So to listen to West Coast [music] was a rebellious choice, and at my school, not many of us did that. There were about five people who did, so we actually made friends across generations.

I obviously knew about The Byrds, who I was a huge fan of, because they came to Britain in '65 and it was a huge deal. I knew about the Beach Boys as well. I was obviously aware of Los Angeles and San Francisco because there had been all that pop stuff about San Francisco in '67. I must have read about this stuff in *Zigzag* [magazine]. Also, I was really starting to haunt the secondhand record shops, and this was the kind of stuff you could pick up for 50 pence or a pound. So you'd see a picture on a record like *Moby*

Grape and you'd think, "These guys look great. I'll try these guys." I don't know how it happened, but it must have been through a combination of those things. So I got the album for something like 75 pence and it was a secondhand copy. I lived in London so I had access to record stores. I'd buy stuff like the Love single, "Laughing Stock," you know, quite unusual records.

I loved *Moby Grape* because it rocked. And a lot of the San Franciscan bands, as we know, did not rock. You listen to the equivalent albums by Jefferson Airplane and The [Grateful] Dead, and they don't rock in the same way. And Moby Grape were weird. You know, you look at that cover and I didn't realize it then, but they're obviously stoned out of their bloody minds, but they look great. They're giving off this big attitude, you know, the drummer is giving you the finger, and they just look bad. Basically it was packed with great songs, each one's a winner. At that time, don't forget, when you're a kid, you buy records and there's three or four shit tracks, but this one–every one's a fucking winner. Amazing.

And no song is over three minutes. It all whips past really quickly. You've got a multiplicity of voices, you've got basically five songwriters and five vocalists. And you've got the tunes being broken up, you've got something like "Someday," which has got an incredible break in it. You've got "Fall On You," which is a balls-out rocker. You've got ballads like "Sitting By The Window," which is a Peter Lewis song. You've got that weird track by Bob Mosley, "Lazy Me;" "I'll just lay here and decay here"–now how weird is that? You've got "Changes," which is great. It's just got lots of different moods in it. And of course you have Skip Spence, who quickly became my idol because he was so fucking weird. And I just adored "Omaha" and "Indifference," which were just so extreme and yet totally made sense.

The other thing is I also read *Rolling Stone*. You could pick up *Rolling Stone* in London from around issue 24 or 25, which would have been around late '68, and I bought it avidly. This was around the time when I started going to gigs. And I remember buying the one where Jim Morrison had been arrested. It was San Francisco-centric at that point; you got a lot of coverage of these fads. And I remember a big thing was reading Greil Marcus' very positive review of [Skip Spence's] *Oar* where he actually did this survey of Moby Grape's past. He said that Skip Spence's songs sounded like street fights, he really made it sound romantic and I just thought, "Well this is absolutely fascinating." And as I said, it was the weirder the better at that point, anything that wasn't blues.

Moby Grape is a pretty complex record, its pretty dense. It sounds as if it were made yesterday. I really loved it when I was a teenager and it stayed with me. It's one of those records that is very alive. I think it's one of the greatest records from the San Francisco scene, and probably one of the greatest American rock records ever. It's very strange what time does to these records, but at best, they still sound as alive today as they ever were, which is a lot.

Love: *Forever Changes*

I bought *Forever Changes* in the spring of 1969 when I was 15. I must have bought it because I was reading *Rolling Stone*, because I don't think *Zigzag* had started yet. I had the "Alone Again Or" single, and I was an Elektra freak and I had these little handouts that I got in '68 from Elektra. I used to collect Elektra records and newsletters. They'd give you postcards and things. Nobody else at my school had [*Forever Changes*] and I was just totally obsessed with it, really. I played it all the time.

Forever Changes was a Top 30 record in the UK, number 24, in early 1968. It was a big record. And it was one of those oddities in the way that psychedelic culture was perceived in the UK. I remember having this argument with [writer] Joel Selvin from San Francisco. Barry Miles and I were at the Rock And Roll Hall of Fame to prepare the psychedelic show ("I Want To Take You Higher") and we got into this city rivalry banter. Barry was in my ear going, "Tell Joel San Francisco groups didn't make any decent albums until 1968, and in London we were listening to the Velvet Underground and Frank Zappa." So of course, I did, and Joel went nuts. But it was true. In the British underground, the scene was as much to do with music from L.A. and New York as it was music from San Francisco. That's very important because of the way that records came over. The first Jefferson Airplane album wasn't

even released in the U.K. So *Forever Changes* was a big record in England. I remember hearing "Alone Again Or" on the radio; it must have been on Radio Caroline.

First off, you've got these guys on the cover. Come on, how cool is that? The photo on the back cover, Arthur Lee being cryptic, holding the smashed vase and then all the others kind of look stoned; they didn't have super long hair, but they look pretty out of it. I didn't think about Arthur Lee being black at all, until quite a lot later, because he wasn't signifying as black, really.

It is by far the best Love album. I mean, the first album's great, but it's very punky and quite sloppy. It's just sort of a bunch of Rolling Stones and Byrds readymades, which I really like. The second one, you've got "Revelation" on the second side, which is a bit of a bummer. And this one is the perfect one, really, isn't it? What's extraordinary now, to me, listening to it, is that it's heavy, it's rocky, but it's basically played on acoustic guitars, which is kind of weird. They're playing the two acoustic guitars together, and it's heavy! If you listen to it carefully, there's not a lot of screaming electric guitars. So when the screaming electric guitar does come, it's really powerful. Like on "Live and Let Live," which was always my favorite track.

I love "Live and Let Live" because it's got that line, "Well the snot it has caked against my pants, it has turned into crystal." When you're a teenage boy, that's pretty good. Of course you listen to it now and you hear Arthur Lee singing "Served my time, served it well, you made my soul a cell." And that's of course what eventually happened to him. He was really in tune on this album, I think. It's very prophetic. It's very deep, very acid, kind of multiple personality "I am we and you are he and we are all together" type stuff, blurring of identity, fusing with the outside world.

"Bummer in the Summer," that's the rockiest tune and that was the B-side of "Alone Again Or" in the UK. He reminded me of Dylan on that one. There are some great lines in that, where he says "I'm thinking of you, mama, when you're thinking of another man" and all that. The lyrics are really good and the way he sings them are really good throughout. I didn't even notice the strings,

in a way, in the arrangements, they're so well integrated. It's just perfect.

I think Arthur [Lee] was really onto something. He was telling it like it was. It's quite a harsh, hostile album. The brief moments when everything's kind of groovy and happy, you know, "The Good Humor Man," stuff like that, are quite rare, really. But it does have that, it isn't all dark. But it's pretty fucking dark. It's very much a black guy in LA as well, although he didn't really identify as such at the time. Most black guys in his age would have still been in suits and playing Motown soul, or just maybe beginning to get into funk.

There's not a bad track on it. "Alone Again Or" was stunning because it was such a pretty song and then he says "I will be alone again tonight my dear" and that's the payoff.

And this is one of the records I always cite. Some idiot writer in the U.K. said "hippy culture is worthless because there's no great novel to come out of that time or that movement." So I always say, "Hello? There is a great hippy novel! It's called *Forever Changes*." Because it has the depth and complexity that you'd expect from a great novel and it still releases meaning. When I hear it, forty years later... I still play it, and I'm still amazed.

Jon Savage is an English writer, broadcaster, and music journalist, perhaps best known for his award winning history of the Sex Pistols and punk music, "England's Dreaming." His other books include "The Kinks: The Official Biography" and "Teenage: The Creation of Youth Culture."

Devendra Banhart

on Davy Graham: *Folk, Blues and Beyond*, Alexander Spence: *Oar,* & Vashti Bunyan: *Just Another Diamond Day*

Davy Graham: *Folk, Blues and Beyond*

I think I bought *Folk, Blues and Beyond* at Aquarius Music in San Francisco 10 years ago. I started looking at everyone's guitar influences, it's always Bert Jansch. And then Bert's? It's Davy, you know? So you kinda keep going back and a lot of it led to Davy. The first cat who introduces new tunings to these guitar heroes, eventually Jimmy Page, everybody knows, he was listening to Bert and Davy. And Davy is one of the first people who goes and introduces the E string scale into Western traditional folk music and also introduces new sound—a tuning, DADGAD, that Keith Richards, Joni Mitchell, and everybody used for a long, long time almost exclusively. I know Joni did.

Davy also is just such a charming, cool-looking guy. He almost has this ginger afro. Kind of a very sad story, but nonetheless they appear— these strange cultural moments, and he, to me, is very much a Chet Baker kind of character. I remember at one point, Nate Russell, who's an amazing visual artist who just did the new Vetiver album cover, he sat down and played me a song with Gary Held, actually. They were like, "OK, you have to guess who this is." And I just had no clue, and it was the weirdest cover I'd ever heard and it was Davy doing a Joni Mitchell song, "Both Sides Now." I just couldn't believe it. And "Angi," this song that everybody does, it's *the* song… if you're a guitar player, if you're a cool guitar player, you gotta know that song, and that's Davy's song. Everybody has their own version of it. So Davy is predominantly known as the cat who wrote "Angi," DADGAD, and all these other things, but I've also always loved his interpretations of songs. His version of "The

Ballad of the Sad Young Men" is the best version by far. "Sally Free and Easy"–best version of that song of all time, absolutely. He's very masculine, but totally effeminate at the same time, and I've always been really turned on by characters like that.

I tried to get a hold of Davy years later and I was in contact with somebody who was kind of a caretaker, taking care of him. Davy's infamous for having booked a gig and just splittin' … you don't hear from him for months and then he just shows up. Those are things of rock 'n' roll legend. He always looked really cool, even towards the end of his life, I remember every little picture I could find, he always had his little three-piece suit or always had a good look. Also, there's a little bit of the ever-present thread of deep, deep sorrow that I also kind of get from Scott Walker. It might not even be musically, there's this demeanor of "Lord, I am your weary child," to quote Bob Marley.

Vashti Bunyan: *Just Another Diamond Day*

I've talked about Vashti Bunyan in every single interview I've done, because she's someone who's music I owe so much to, I owe my life to. I was in France at a record store. I don't think I had any money. It just happened that [the record] was in my hands suddenly. I didn't steal it, but it was one of those things where it just—I had it suddenly. And I played it and that was it. It was just, "This is it for me. This is absolutely it. This is everything that I'm looking for, and this is mine." That connection with music… I haven't had that since. And then it became this mission, "We gotta find Vashti, what is going on? I'm in love with Vashti."

At the time, my biological father had come into my life after an absence of about 18 years, and he said, "I've missed a lot of birthdays, now I'm married to this woman who works for Continental Airlines, I can offer you a ticket— where do you want to go?" So I said, "I'll go to Paris." I had no real reason, no idea, and I saved up some money, and that money ran out, and then I was really homeless. I remember going to a Sonic Youth show and saying, "Do you speak English? Anyone? Anyone?" One guy did, "Hi, let's be friends, can I please stay on your couch?" I mean, that's really how I was doing it. So at that time, if I was hungry, if I was tired, these bare human essentials—I would just turn to Vashti, and she fully satisfied those things. I don't know how that can happen. I can't imagine that happening to me again, but it definitely happened with Vashti. That was it. I was fuckin' so thirsty, and I would listen to Vashti, and it would calm that thirst.

And it just so happens that when I discovered her music, I was just sending my demos out to a couple labels and I'd make each one real nice, I'd wrap 'em up with little things, little marbles, anything I could find, whatever I could scrounge from anywhere. Eventually I was back in LA, constantly listening to Vashti, writing to Spinney, the label that had reissued her album. They actually do write back, they're like, "Well, I don't know", something vague, "But she's around, kind of, we're not sure…" but OK, it's a lead. And suddenly I play this show and my record comes out and I get my first piece of press. I'm like "Alright, well, this is such an opportunity, maybe I can communicate with her!" and it's for *NME* or Mojo, and so I write… there's somewhere in the booklet, there's a painting that says "Happy Vashti," so I write "Happy Vashti" on my shirt and I do the shot. And they don't know what that is. And I think she ended up seeing it, so we made this connection.

I remember I got her email address and I wrote her a long letter. "Dear Vashti, I love your music. I love you. And I don't know if I should do this because it doesn't seem like it's gonna pan out and all the byproducts of being a successful musician don't really interest me, and I don't think that they're attainable. This looks like a pretty rough life right now. I'm homeless, I'm broke, but I just wanna play music. Please be very, very honest with these demos. I beg you, and my life kinda depends on it." Because at that moment, I'd made a decision that if Vashti Bunyan… it isn't that she likes it, but if Vashti Bunyan's like, "Yeah, do it" then that's it. I just need her to say "Yeah, do it." Be honest, you can just think it's fuckin' horrible dribble, the most onanistic trash fuckin' music, just say "Do it" and I'll do it. I sent her music and a letter and some drawings—I was really excited—and she wrote back and said, "Yeah, do it." So it's thanks to her that I did it.

Alexander Spence: *Oar*

Skip Spence is one of those artists, kind of a Syd Barrett kind of character to me. One of the light shines through the cracks kind of vibe. I think I might have even known about Moby Grape before I knew about Skip Spence. You hear about *Oar* a lot, I think if you're just living on the sidelines, you'll find these kind of cats, and he's definitely one of those cats, someone that

influenced all these people that you know of… Tom Waits, Robert Plant, everybody knew about Skip Spence. Even the legend of the recording… he goes down in the South, locks up in a studio… Nashville, one day, playing everything… this kind of crazy Todd Rundgren-esque story.

At this point, I know the association with Jefferson Airplane, but that doesn't really turn me on. I mean, is that what it's going to be like? I'm not sure. And so, not apprehensive about it, but I know that it is this legendary story. I knew the story before I heard the record, and it was at a time when the record still isn't very ubiquitous. There had been no tribute to Skip Spence's *Oar* at that point, but you could find the reissue in the mom and pop stores.

I think just hearing "Little Hands," it was obvious that this is a hit, I mean this is a hit. "Diana" may be one of the most woeful love songs, one of the most desperate love songs I've ever heard. He's not gonna get the girl, you know? But it's for her. And I can relate to that. If you can have an album that's as cyclical as the emotional reality of the next five minutes, then you've made a really successful album to me. Bob Dylan does that. There are songs that I totally laugh at what he says. There are songs that I'm crying. There are albums that really mirror the reality of the emotional spectrum, and *Oar* does that. It goes to these extremes. And for the most part it goes to pretty dark places. But it's so fuckin' honest and pure and that's all we're really looking for. Antony [Hegarty] recently mentioned in an interview how Marc Almond said, "I don't care if I hit the notes, I just have to feel it." And I think Skip is a perfect example of that.

This is almost the genesis of the bedroom recording, where it's so personal. Rarely does somebody go into a studio and make a bedroom recording, and this is where some of that comes from and it influences so much of that stuff. In every interview I mention Skip. I've always had a list of people that I wanna talk about when I do an interview, and Skip is always there. Not to be presumptuous or disrespect the ability of music journalists, but often they don't know who I'm talking about, so they don't bother to put the person in the article. But Skip was mentioned more than a couple of times, and I remember The Pleased, which was Noah Georgeson's band with Joanna Newsom, was doing a tour with Arthur Lee and Love, and in the audience there was a woman and her son and they went up to Joanna and he said, "Hey, we listened to your records and Devendra's and Vetiver, and my dad was this guy Alexander (Skip) Spence. And we dig that you like my pop." So that was a beautiful thing, that was amazing to just feel that close to someone that is… your go-to guy, your comfort… the most obvious way of appeasing the chaos within.

Devendra Banhart is an acclaimed singer, songwriter, visual artist, and music fanatic who has collaborated with Beck, Vashti Bunyan, Caetano Veloso, and countless others.

Mick Haggerty

on Album Cover Design

I always paid attention to record covers, just being kind of a visual kid. I think the one I remember seeing earliest was the Perez Prado record, which my dad had. I can't even remember too much about it, but I remember going, "Wow! This is an amazing thing," and putting it up above his record player just to look at. Once I started sort of collecting records, I remember I had an Eddie Cochran record I bought, or I might have stolen it from a thrift store, and it didn't have a cover, so I designed my own cover. I guess that was the first one I ever did.

It was just a sleeve; I think I still have it. It was a Xeroxed picture with some sort of blue tint over it. In England, we always kind of looked down on homegrown stuff; it always had to be imported. So, from one end, you'd have all those blues covers, which were remarkable things. And then you'd have those almost homemade ones that the ska and Jamaican records came in, even the ones that were pressed in England. Those covers always just blew me away. The off-register printing and that thin glaze of shiny stuff that would peel off after about a week, and the way the flap was folded over, it had like an inch glue strip around it.

I suppose record covers must have influenced my buying decisions in one way or another. When I saw that Johnny Ace record, the one with the playing card on the cover, just bright red, I had no idea who he was, but I remember thinking "I have to have that. That looks good and needs to be in the collection." I think I have more Elvis records than I would have otherwise because I liked the covers.

Art was just an excuse to play and listen to

music. If I could have been a musician, I never would have bothered with art. Art schools were just a holding tank for musicians a lot of the time. There would be lots of music played at art schools and so for me, doing art was always about being closer to music.

For the first real album cover I did, I just took my portfolio around to Island Records—that was when they just had a second-floor flat in Notting Hill Gate and the whole record company was around one round table. Chris Blackwell, who owned it, had this theory that they shouldn't be in separate offices and they just had, like, 23 phones at a big round table. It had this folksy kind of look to it. It was actually possible to just walk in, walk upstairs, press your jeans a little bit, have your collar pressed for the day, and just say "Here's my work," and then they go, "OK, here's a record cover." It wasn't sectioned off into this business structure that it became later. I just took in my portfolio and they just said, "Oh yeah, give him a cover. Looks good." And I did the cover for Fairport Convention's *Rosie*.

The thing about an album cover is, someone gives you a tape of music, you go home and you listen to it and they say, "Bring back an image of your creation, we'll print it for you, we'll put your name on it, and then we'll distribute it pretty much all over the world." I mean, it's a joke. As an artist or someone that makes images, you just can't believe that. Not only is it your piece of art, but it has music inside. I can't think of anything better. And they pay you as well.

The axis of the world shifted when I saw Bob Seidemann's cover for *Blind Faith*. That was the moment all the rules didn't apply anymore.

The world wasn't the same. Man walking on the moon was nothing compared to seeing that cover. I have no idea how that happened. When I met Bob and found out that he'd named the band as well… I mean, I'd named a record before, but I've never named a band. That was absurd. And the degree to which Eric Clapton, as I understood it, fought for that cover. It didn't have any type on the front, it broke every single rule in the book. Pictorially, everything about it is perfect. The way it's printed, the color, the name, the girl. If it was any other girl, it would be stupid. And the record. The axis of the world just shifted for me. What do they call it? A "game changer."

In doing a cover, there's three formulas. One is some strange cassette, or sometimes just a description of a band, comes across the desk of whoever works at a record company. Then they have to farm that out to someone to produce an image for it, and it's pretty much a forgotten project. You just kinda do it, and it comes out. That's the one where you work directly with the record company and you have really no input from anybody.

At the other end of that scale is when the band calls the designer and says "We want you to do these things." You have to walk in with them and the whole project to the record company. Then there's the middle ground, which is when the musicians are working closely with a really good record company art director, and all three of you get to play—the designer, the musician, and the art director, and, well, you have to throw the management in, I guess. All four of you have to play.

I guess the first time it ever happened to me was with (legendary music business executive) Jeff Ayeroff and Supertramp on *Breakfast in America*. That was the first time I sat in a meeting with a group of people, some of whom you had to convince that a cohesive campaign, based around a particular image, style, or concept, would actually affect sales. And they were saying, "Well, I'm not so sure about that…" There was still an attitude of "just slap a picture on it that's attractive and get it out there because people really buy the music." So the idea of a cohesive campaign that could work across print and everything, that was the first time that I was able to really run with that. I worked closely with the band on that one.

Some people to collaborate with, it's just a nightmare—they can't make decisions, they're not very visual, I'd rather not work with them at all. But working with someone like David Bowie, it's a delight. He's incredibly creative and generous; he's an artist. You love having people like that call you up and they always have great ideas and there really is a synergy. There is a point when everything sort of comes together on a project and it's just a thrill; it has a real momentum to it. As long as those involved want to take risks and live by the seat of their pants, and no one's worried about retouching… "Is my hair right in this picture?" or "What suit shall I wear?" We've all done those, having to dress an artist. I always put my head in my hands, you know, like, "Really? You don't know what clothes to wear? What hope is there for you?"

I always thought *Ghost in the Machine* by The Police hit the nail on the head. Not because I was a big Police fan, that was the funny thing

about it, it was really kind of a slightly snide cover, kind of a critical cover in a way. I loved working with them and I thought Sting was incredible—I had nothing but respect for him as a person. Everyone's tastes in music are different. Jeff Ayeroff was on my case, saying, "When am I getting this portrait? You have to do this thing of The Police." I'd sit down and look at their three faces and just put my head in my hands, I didn't know what to do. I was struggling.

Meanwhile, my type house sent me a pocket calculator as a gift for my birthday or something, and the mailman folded it in half to put it through the mail slot of my studio. And because he folded it, it had died, just had this spasm and spattered out these little lines and I was looking at it and just thought…"That's it!" The Police's music is pretty calculated. It was a really kind of tongue-in-cheek image. But of course once you get the image down, you suddenly realize "Man, this has legs, this means something, it's good." Inspiration comes in all shapes and sizes, and it can come from just being absolutely furious and throwing stuff on the floor to being touched by the muse, and all the places in between.

Mick Haggerty has designed and art directed hundreds of album covers for artists including David Bowie, The Police, Jimi Hendrix, Tom Petty, Steve Winwood, Electric Light Orchestra, and Supertramp (he won the 1980 "Best Recording Package" Grammy for their "Breakfast in America"). He has directed videos for artists including Sting, John Fogerty, the B-52's, and Hall & Oats.

TOMMY
the who

The front cover panel of Mike McInnerney's triple fold sleeve.

THE WHO | Tommy

May 1969 | Track

Even in the musical renaissance that was late-'60s pop music, The Who's *Tommy* dramatically raised the bar on what might be attempted within this once spurned wing of 'the entertainment industry.' Despite precedents like the Pretty Things' *SF Sorrow* and the *The Who Sell Out*, no one in rock had thought in such grand terms as to imagine a single-narrative "rock opera" presented over four sides of a double album. Twenty-four tracks, performed solely by The Who on a variety of instruments, comprise the tale of Tommy, a "deaf, dumb and blind kid" who plays a mean pinball and inspires an admiring and destructive cult. The complexly arranged story is intriguing, whether it's absorbed in sequence or enjoyed as discreet songs—many of which became radio staples for The Who and others ("Pinball Wizard," "See Me, Feel Me," "I'm Free," "The Acid Queen," "Tommy, Can You Hear Me?"). *Tommy*

not only gained newfound respect for rock music, it catapulted The Who to a new level of superstardom and upgraded Pete Townshend's stature from pop songwriter to serious composer. It also set new design standards for long-players, with a libretto and a fold-out cover whose outer panels form three portions of a pop-art painting. The Who still performs *Tommy*, which has now been reimagined as a stage production (in 1971, 1972, and 1993), an orchestral work (1973), a film (1975), and numerous touring musicals in recent years, certifying its status as a musical landmark.

613 013/4 STEREO

Overture	3.50
It's a boy	2.07
1921	3.14
Amazing journey	3.25
Sparks	3.45
The hawker (a)	2.15
Christmas	5.30
Cousin Kevin (b)	4.03
The acid queen	3.31
Underture	9.55
Do you think its alright?	0.24
Fiddle about (b)	1.26
Pinball wizard	3.50
There's a doctor	0.25
Go to the mirror!	3.50
Tommy can you hear me?	1.35
Smash the mirror	1.20
Sensation	2.32
Miracle cure	0.10
Sally Simpson	4.10
I'm free	2.40
Welcome	4.30
Tommy's holiday camp (c)	0.57
We're not gonna take it	6.45

Opera by	*Pete Townshend*
(a) Composed by	*Sonny Boy Williamson*
(b) Composed by	*John Entwhistle*
(c) Composed by	*Keith Moon*
Producer	*Kit Lambert*
Chief Engineer	*Damon Lyon-Shaw*
Studio	*I.B.C.*
Cover Design	*Mike McInnerney*
Photos	*Barrie Meller*
Avatar	*Meher Baba*

All times approximate

Manufactured by Polydor Records Ltd., London.
Printed and made by Ernest J. Day & Co. Ltd. London. W.11
Patent pending

TRACK RECORD
POLYDOR RECORDS LTD

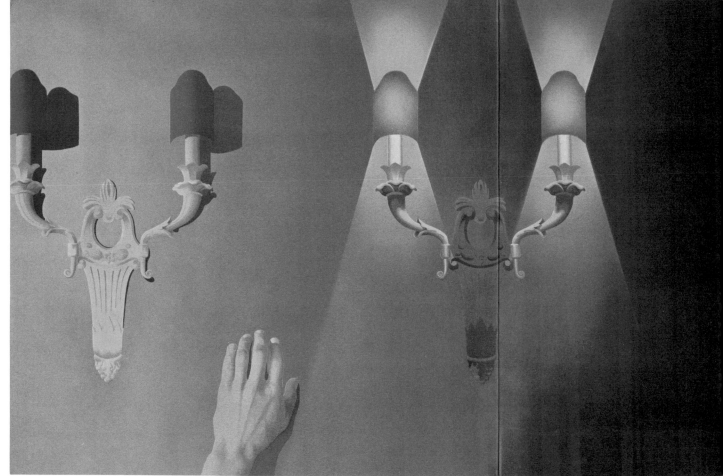

613 013-4 STEREO

Overture	3.50
It's a boy	2.07
1921	3.14
Amazing journey	3.25
Sparks	3.45
The hawker (a)	2.15
Christmas	5.30
Cousin Kevin (b)	4.03
The acid queen	3.31
Underture	9.55
Do you think its alright?	0.24
Fiddle about (b)	1.26
Pinball wizard	3.50
There's a doctor	0.25
Go to the mirror!	3.50
Tommy can you hear me?	1.35
Smash the mirror	1.20
Sensation	2.32
Miracle cure	0.10
Sally Simpson	4.10
I'm free	2.40
Welcome	4.30
Tommy's holiday camp (c)	0.57
We're not gonna take it	6.45

Opera by	Pete Townshend
(a) Composed by	Sonny Boy Williamson
(b) Composed by	John Entwhistle
(c) Composed by	Keith Moon
Producer	Kit Lambert
Chief Engineer	Damon Lyon-Shaw
Studio	I.B.C.
Cover Design	Mike McInnerney
Photos	Barrie Meller
Avatar	Meher Baba

All times approximate

Manufactured by Polydor Records Ltd., London
Printed and made by Ernest J. Day & Co. Ltd. London W.11
Patent pending

The inside gatefold.
Original U.K. cop-
ies came with a
numbered, limited
edition booklet con-
taining lyrics and
illustrations.

Deaf Dumb and blind boy.
He's in a quiet vibration land
Strange as it seems his musical dreams
Ain't quite so bad.

Ten years old
With thoughts as bold as thought can be
Loving life and becoming wise
In simplicity.

Sickness will surely take the mind
Where minds can't usually go.
Come on the amazing journey
And learn all you should know.

A vague haze of delerium
creeps up on me.
All at once a tall stranger I suddenly see.
He's dressed in a silver sparked
Glittering gown
And His golden beard flows
Nearly down to the ground.

Nothing to say and nothing to hear
And nothing to see.
Each sensation makes a note in my symphony.

Sickness will surely take the mind
Where minds can't usually go.
Come on the amazing journey
And learn all you should know.

His eyes are the eyes that
Transmit all they know.
Sparkle warm crystalline glances to show
That he is your leader
And he is your guide.
On the amazing journey together you'll ride.

CROSBY, STILLS & NASH

CROSBY, STILLS & NASH | Crosby, Stills & Nash

May 1969 | Atlantic

The first offering by Crosby, Stills & Nash is both an embarrassment of artistic riches and a significant milestone along the path of 20th century popular music. In the latter category, the trio gets the nod as not only one of the first supergroups (its members hailing from the Byrds, Buffalo Springfield, and The Hollies), but one whose mutual musical ambitions obliged them to cross international borders. Their coming-together furthered rock globalism and served as a harbinger of the acoustic-oriented singer-songwriter trend that would prevail throughout the early '70s. While *Crosby, Stills & Nash* became one of the biggest sellers of its era, a four-time platinum LP that spent more than 100 weeks on the charts, its genesis was creative rather than commercial: The trio simply wanted to make music together, unfettered by what each member saw as the limitations of his previous group. The album yielded classics like "Suite: Judy Blue

Eyes," "Wooden Ships," "Marrakesh Express," "Guinnevere," and "Long Time Gone," and its harmonic tales of love and politics have inspired artists as diverse as Jackson Browne, the Eagles, The Who, Yes, and Fleet Foxes. Crosby, Stills, & Nash and later associate Neil Young continue to enjoy a rich and growing legacy together and apart, on the radio, touring, and recording. The cover photo of the musicians seated on the porch of a house, shot days before the trio adopted its official name, famously shows the group in reverse order. When photographer Henry Diltz and C,S&N returned to the site to retake the shot, the house had been demolished. The original photo was used.

Drummer Dallas Taylor, absent from the original photoshoot, was retouched into the photo and appears on the back cover peering from behind the door.

ATLANTIC RECORDING CORPORATION 1841 BROADWAY, NEW YORK, NEW YORK 10023

The inner gatefold was shot in Big Bear, California.

The lyric insert.

Photographer Ed Caraeff and designer Cal Schenkel's pictured Captain Beefheart wearing an actual carp head over his face.

STRAIGHT STEREO STS 1053

TROUT MASK REPLICA

CAPTAIN BEEFHEART & HIS MAGIC BAND

CAPTAIN BEEFHEART & HIS MAGIC BAND | Trout Mask Replica   **June 1969 | Straight**

If, in 1969, they'd held a class reunion of all the blues bands of the mid-'60s, Captain Beefheart would have surely copped the prize for having traveled the furthest. Frank Zappa's early compatriot didn't share the head Mother's multiple inspirations. Instead, Don Van Vliet homed in on a single genre—Delta-derived Chicago blues—which he remade and remodeled extensively on *Safe as Milk* (1967) and *Strictly Personal* (1968). The following year brought *Trout Mask Replica*, a double-LP sporting perhaps pop's most confounding album cover to date. The music within was no less challenging. Saturated in surreal imagery, disjointed rhythms, and Beefheart's bellowing vocals, it showed just how quickly and completely Beefheart had outdistanced most other rock artists, including himself, in the wild-ideas department. Nor are cuts like "Ella Guru," "Ant Man Bee," and "Moonlight on Vermont" weird for weirdness' sake. *Trout*

Mask Replica is the result of a gifted artist going his own way all the way, doing the hard work of fashioning a universe from one of music's most basic forms. Beefheart doesn't just find the pain and pathos that most musicians find in blues, but the deep and humorous awareness that illuminates life itself ("My Human Gets Me Blues"). His confident, uncompromised expression of all that has earned *Trout Mask Replica* the enduring praise of punk rockers, classicists, minimalists, and word-jazzers the world over. "I heard echoes of his music in some of the records I listened to last week," said radio programmer John Peel, "I'll hear more echoes in records that I listen to this week. If there has ever been such a thing as a genius in the history of popular music, it's Beefheart."

STRAIGHT
STRAIGHT

CAPTAIN BEEFHEART AND HIS MAGIC BAND
TROUT MASK REPLICA

STEREO
2 STS 1053
Side 3

All selections copyrighted
for the world by Beefheart
Music, BMI

Produced by Frank Zappa

1. HAIR PIE: BAKE II 2:23
2. PENA 2:31
3. WELL 2:05
4. WHEN BIG JOAN SETS UP 5:19
5. FALLIN' DITCH 2:03
6. SUGAR 'N SPIKES 2:29
7. ANT MAN BEE 3:55

All music and lyrics by
Don Van Vliet

The back cover
pictures Beefheart
and the Magic
Band near their
communal home
in Woodland Hills,
California.

The lyric booklet
cover, with a photo
of a young Don
Van Vliet, later to
become Captain
Beefheart.

TROUT MASK REPLICA
CAPTAIN BEEFHEART

Bob Seidemann shot the controversal album cover, featuring a pubescent girl holding a phallic spaceship. While she was rumoured to be a groupie or drummer Ginger Baker's illegitimate daughter, she was actually a London girl who posed with her parent's permission, for a fee. Blind Faith was the first album cover with no writing or credits on the front or back covers.

BLIND FAITH | Blind Faith

August 1969 | Polydor

The term "supergroup" quickly became a debased coinage once it got applied to lesser lights, but the 1969 formation of Blind Faith surely deserved the appellation. Having just exited Cream, Eric Clapton and Ginger Baker were at their peak of popular and critical acclaim, as was Steve Winwood, whose most recent album as a member of Traffic (*Last Exit*) was an American hit. Bassist Rich Grech's group, Family, had just scored a Top-10 LP in Britain with *Family Entertainment*. Blind Faith may have been short-lived, comprising one album (produced by Jimmy Miller) and an American tour on which the group headlined at Madison Square Garden, but it bequeathed music fans this lively, unpretentious collection. *Blind Faith* brings together the pastoral yet soulful elements of Traffic and the blues-fueled energy of Cream to create something altogether fresh: music that's remarkably free of the self-importance and grandstanding

impulses that might be expected from such high-profile players. "Can't Find My Way Home" and "Presence of the Lord" became FM-rock standards, and the band's rootsy reworking of Buddy Holly's "Well All Right" points directly toward Clapton's next venture, Derek and the Dominos. Bob Seidemann's photo for the front-sleeve of the U.K. edition of *Blind Faith* stirred up much controversy, which prompted the band's American label to issue the album with two covers: the original and one featuring a more conventional portrait.

Back cover.

The band's U.S. label, Atco, released the album with two covers; the original and this clean version.

New York artist Jimmy Grashow created woodblock prints for the *Stand Up* cover.

JETHRO TULL | Stand Up

August 1969 | Island

Eric Clapton may have been the first, but not the last, guitarist to take a hike from a band because it was diverging from its blues origins. Mick Abrahams, a founding member of Jethro Tull, found himself making the same move in 1968, in part because co-founder Ian Anderson wished to light out for groovier pastures (a not uncommon impulse in those heady days). *Stand Up* was the band's second album, and it is where Jethro Tull, under the uncontested artistic direction of Anderson, grew into one of the 70s' most popular groups, one whose name grew to be almost synonymous with progressive and 'classic' rock. Blues still show up on *Stand Up* (the opening track, "A New Day Yesterday"), but so do Celtic folk elements and a hard-swinging jazz sound, particularly on cuts like "Nothing Is Easy" (with solos from Anderson's flute and Martin Barre's guitar) and "Look Into the Sun," which treads on the pastoral-psychedelic turf of early Traffic. Arena tours, FM airplay, and "Living in the Past" were still to come, but *Stand Up* gave Tull its signature sound, one that would eventually lead to superstardom. Initial editions of the LP featured James Grashow's intricate woodcut portraits of the band and cut-outs that "stood up" as the cover was opened.

168

The inner gatefold
featured a pop-up
Jethro Tull.

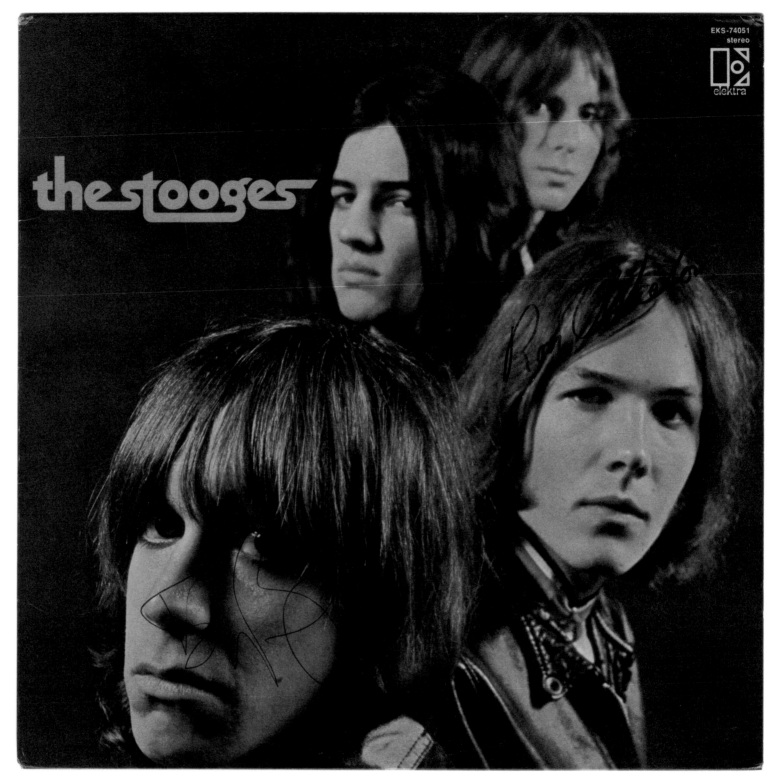

EKS-74051
stereo

elektra

THE STOOGES | The Stooges   **August 1969 | Elektra**

A good three years before Lenny Kaye's *Nuggets* compilation brought the phrase "punk rock" into the musical conversation, there was this record. Unlike many albums of its day, it didn't come with an impressionistic cover portrait of the band, its lyrics betrayed no hint of cosmic consciousness or big-issue awareness, and it was devoid of displays of technical virtuosity. Instead, *The Stooges* confronted the listener with four insolent-looking post-teens, a cache of monosyllabic song titles, and just over half an hour's worth of stripped-down rock 'n' roll—the kind of music that achievements like *Sgt. Pepper's*, *Bookends,* and *A Piper at the Gates of Dawn* were thought to have vanquished for good. Granting the Velvet Underground, New York Dolls, and MC5 their due, this band and this album are what provided the principal blueprint for '70s punk, both musically and attitudinally. Its aggressive bent, lack of sentiment, and preoccupation with

bad vibes and boredom sketched out a whole new direction for popular music, one that went ignored for half a decade. But connect it did, with Iggy's savage vocals and Ron Asheton's brutal guitar bashing out tracks that are now well placed in the canon of late-period rock 'n' roll: "1969," "No Fun," "Real Cool Time," "I Wanna Be Your Dog."

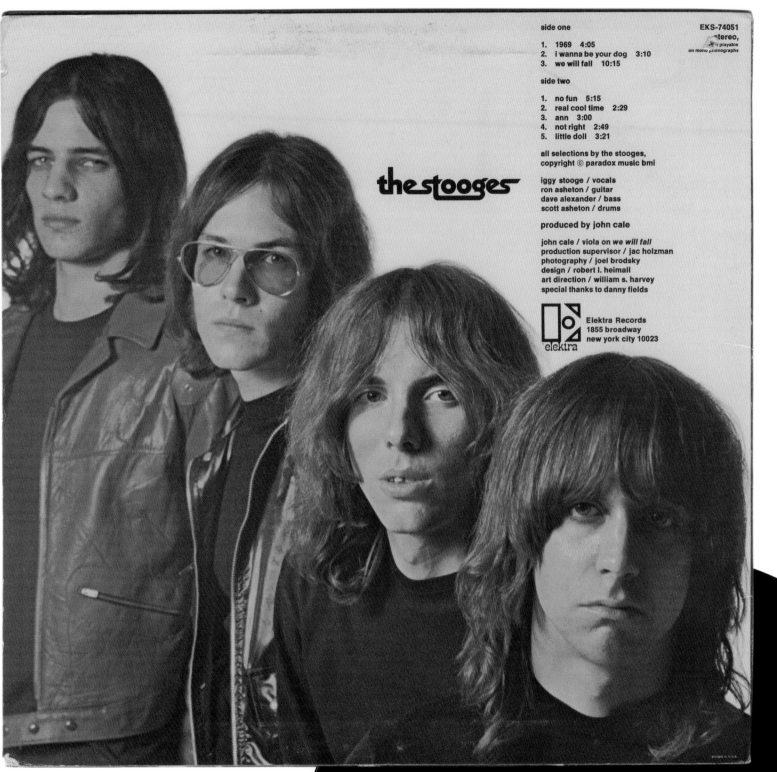

side one

EKS-74051

stereo,
playable
on mono phonographs

1. 1969   4:05
2. i wanna be your dog   3:10
3. we will fall   10:15

side two

1. no fun   5:15
2. real cool time   2:29
3. ann   3:00
4. not right   2:49
5. little doll   3:21

all selections by the stooges,
copyright © paradox music bmi

the stooges

iggy stooge / vocals
ron asheton / guitar
dave alexander / bass
scott asheton / drums

produced by john cale

john cale / viola on *we will fall*
production supervisor / jac holzman
photography / joel brodsky
design / robert l. heimall
art direction / william s. harvey
special thanks to danny fields

Elektra Records
1855 broadway
new york city 10023

A rare white label
promotional copy,
sent to radio and
reviewers.

the stooges

PROMOTIONAL COPY
NOT FOR SALE

side one eks-74071-a stereo

elektra

fun house

1. down on the street   3:42
2. loose   3:33
3. t.v. eye   4:17
4. dirt   7:00

Elektra Records, 15 Columbus Circle, New York City 10023

produced by don gallucci

NICK DRAKE | Five Leaves Left

September 1969 | Island

"Fame is but a fruit tree, so very unsound/ It can never flourish till its stalk is in the ground." The line, from this British singer-songwriter's debut album, was chillingly prescient. Despite issuing three LPs, he refused to perform live or do interviews, thus almost permanently assuring his sub-cult status—until 2000, when, 26 years after his death, his "Pink Moon" was used in a TV commercial for Volkswagen. Viewers clamored for information on the singer and the song, and within a month Drake's catalog sold more than it had in the preceding 30 years. *Five Leaves Left* is the work of an idiosyncratic yet accessible artist who is best categorized as British-folk; Fairport Convention's Richard Thompson and Pentangle's Danny Thompson accompany Drake here. But the temperament of songs like "River Man," "Way to Blue," and "The Thoughts of Mary Jane" is just as closely aligned with the sedate, often somber sounds of cool jazz.

The isolation and sense of detachment in "Man in a Shed" and "Fruit Tree" are especially poignant, particularly the latter's string arrangement by Robert Kirby (whose credits include records with Elton John, Elvis Costello, John Cale, and Vashti Bunyan). Producer Joe Boyd has kept all three of Drake's albums in print, which helps explain the singer's enduring popularity among such musicians as the Cure's Robert Smith, REM's Peter Buck, Kate Bush, and The Dream Academy, whose 1985 hit "Life in a Northern Town" was about Drake's life. While virtually ignored during his lifetime, Drake now ranks among the most acclaimed of all English singer-songwriters.

This rare first pressing has the collectible pink block Island label.

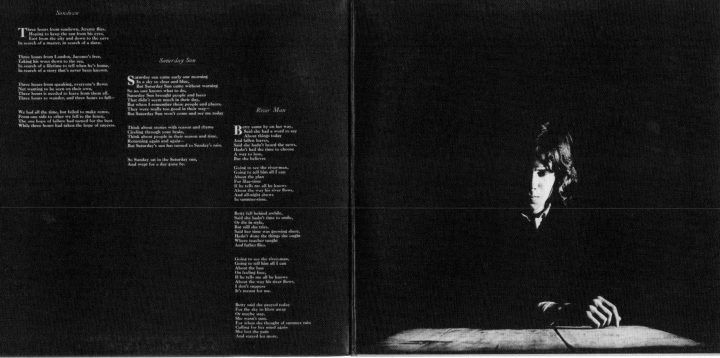

The cover painting is by Barry Godber, a computer programmer who died of a heart attack soon after the album's release. It was his only painting. It is now owned by Crimson founder Robert Fripp who said the face on the outside is the Schizoid Man, and the one on the inside is the Crimson King. If you cover the smiling face, the eyes reveal an incredible sadness. "What can one add? It reflects the music."

KING CRIMSON | In The Court Of The Crimson King

October 1969 | Island

As the '60s began to wind down, psychedelic music galloped off in many directions, morphing into the blues and progressive rock that would characterize much of the 1970s. King Crimson was one of the first British groups out of the prog gate, and the band sprinted ahead of the pack by producing the genre's first true masterwork, *In the Court of the Crimson King*. Under the leadership of guitarist Robert Fripp, King Crimson abandoned most of rock's R&B roots to embrace a kind of guitar and mellotron-based, crypto-classical style that went well beyond what Procol Harum and the Moody Blues had previously attempted. Lyricist Pete Sinfield supplies the oblique wordplay ("rusted chains of prison moons") and bassist Greg Lake (later of Emerson, Lake & Palmer) the vocals, while Fripp and reeds/keyboard player Ian McDonald unleash lush melodies and big ponderous riffs—as on the classic "21st Century

Schizoid Man" and the suites "Epitaph" and "The Court of the Crimson King," the LP's other most "rock" track.

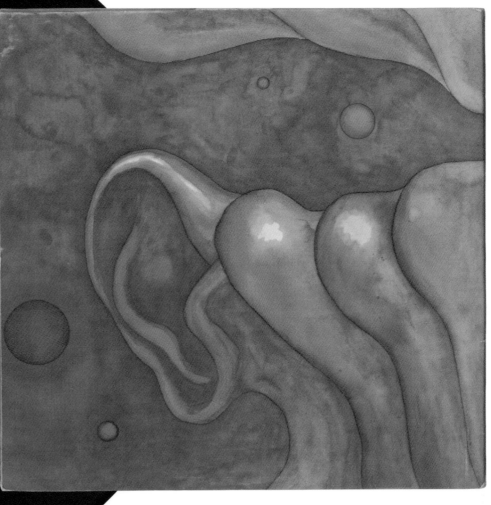

The disc features the rare pink "i" Island label.

FAIRPORT CONVENTION | Liege & Lief

December 1969 | Island

"Making English folk music fashionable was an extraordinary accomplishment," wrote producer Joe Boyd in his autobiography, *White Bicycles*. It was indeed an achievement, especially considering Fairport Convention's early disinclination toward un-American models. Boyd also reveals that drummer Dave Mattacks wanted to ape Levon Helm's *Big Pink* drum sound and that the group intended to cut *Liege & Lief* at L.A.'s Gold Star studio in homage to Phil Spector (several tracks were recorded but remain unissued). The third of three Fairport LPs released in 1969, *Liege & Lief* was a major turning point for Sandy Denny, Richard Thompson, and company. They abandoned their standard practice of mixing group compositions with (imaginative) covers of songs by Dylan and Joni Mitchell to make an album exclusively derived from Celtic or British-folk sources. This is perhaps *the* major U.K. folk-rock record, as it strongly

affirms both descriptors on the driving "Tam Lin" and a pair of death-haunted classics: "Crazy Man Michael" and "Matty Groves," the latter sporting fiery fiddle and electric-guitar interplay from Dave Swarbrick and Thompson. At BBC Radio 2's folk awards ceremony in 2006, *Liege & Lief* was named the Most Influential Folk Album of All Time.

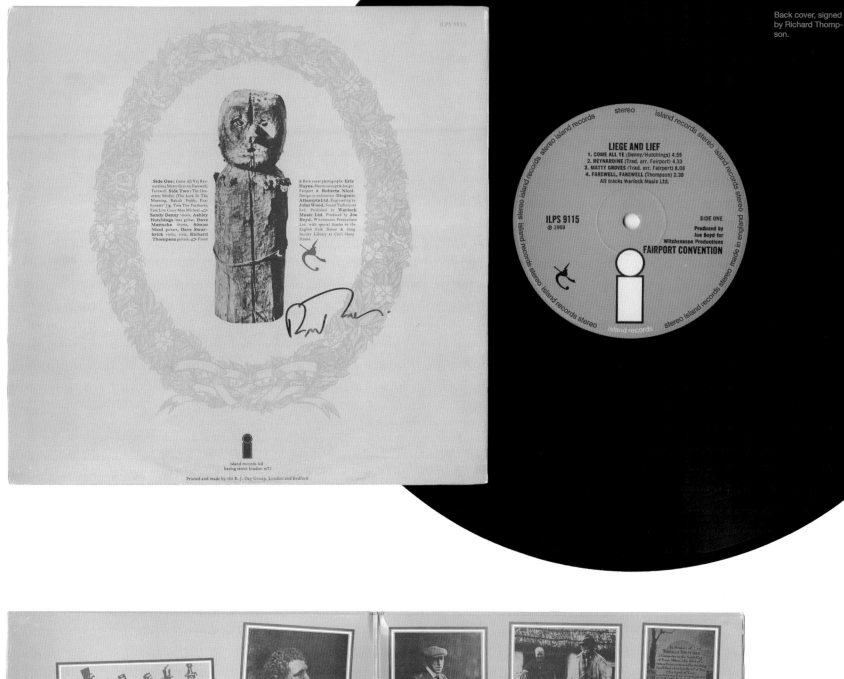

Back cover, signed
by Richard Thompson.

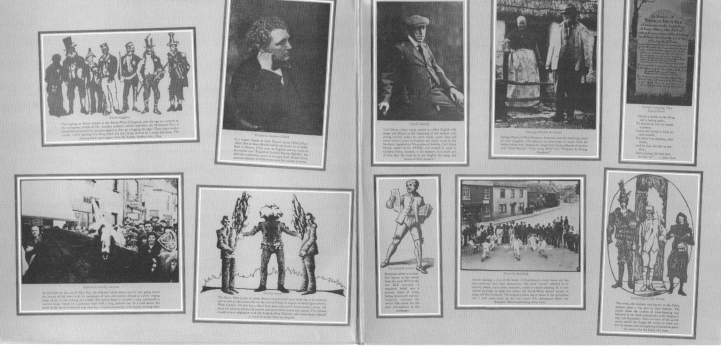

VASHTI BUNYAN | Just Another Diamond Day

Early 1970 | Philips

British singer-songwriter Vashti Bunyan took a circuitous route to cult stardom, not unlike her contemporary Nick Drake. Originally one of several "pretty young things" on London's mid-'60s scene, she cut two singles (the first an unreleased Jagger-Richards song produced by Stones manager Andrew Loog Oldham). The experience left her with a strong distaste for pop music and led to a self-imposed exile, during which she traveled rural Britain with her boyfriend in a horse-drawn cart. At the end of 1969, she returned to the city and cut this folky, altogether original debut with producer Joe Boyd (Pink Floyd, Fairport Convention, Incredible String Band) and a support crew that included Incredible String Band's Robin Williamson and Fairport's Dave Swarbrick. Bunyan's captivating vocal style might be described as a more reticent Joni Mitchell, but it's all her own, its hushed presence drawing the listener into its tales of nature ("Glow Worms"), everyday euphoria ("Diamond Day"), and surreal

experience ("Timothy Grub"). The LP's commercial failure didn't prevent its rediscovery 30 years later by a new generation of similarly inclined performers of intimate music, including Devendra Banhart, Joanna Newsom, and Animal Collective—several of whom played on Bunyan's sophomore set, *Lookaftering*, in 2005.

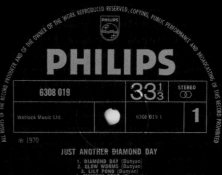

THE MOVE | Shazam

February 1970 | Regal Zonophone

The second Move album is an all-Roy-Wood show, in part a staging ground for his next experiment, the Electric Light Orchestra, but also a unique assemblage of styles that holds its shape together. The achievement is all the more laudable in that *Shazam* is divided in half, with mostly Wood originals sharing space with diverse material by some first-rate song-crafters. Tom Paxton's folk chestnut "The Last Thing on My Mind" is remade into a heavy-psych opus, while Mann and Weil's "Don't Make My Baby Blue," best known as an easy-listening ballad by Frankie Laine, gets buffed up with bruising, minor-chord riffage. These sit comfortably alongside "Cherry Blossom Clinic Revisited," which recasts the Move's "Cherry Blossom Clinic" in a Black-Sabbath-does-"Penny Lane" mode, the pre-E.L.O. delicacy of "Beautiful Daughter," and the pastiche that is "Hello Susie," a track that seems to toss old rock 'n' roll, brontosaurus-

heavy metal and the vocal yelp of Slade's Noddy Holder (whose star hadn't quite yet risen) into a heavenly pop spin-cycle. Wood knew whereof he spoke in the epic "Fields of People," when he read the line "Strange new ideas fill the air." Adding to *Shazam*'s period charm are the intra-track dialogues that crop up throughout the album.

SLRZ 1012
(1E 062 © 91011)
stereo

'SHAZAM'

SIDE ONE
1. HELLO SUSIE (Wood)
2. BEAUTIFUL DAUGHTER (Wood)
3. CHERRY BLOSSOM CLINIC REVISITED (Wood)

SIDE TWO
1. FIELDS OF PEOPLE (Day-Pierson)
2. DON'T MAKE MY BABY BLUE (Mann-Weil)
3. THE LAST THING ON MY MIND (Paxton)

℗ 1970

Recorded at Advision Studios
Produced by Roy Wood, Carl Wayne, Rick Price, in conjunction with
Gerald Chevin for Straight Ahead Productions
Cover Design by NICKLEBY
Back Cover Photos: London Photo Agency

E.M.I RECORDS (The Gramophone Co.Ltd.) HAYES MIDDLESEX ENGLAND

REGAL
ZONOPHONE
A COMPANY OF
THE EMI GROUP

33⅓ R.P.M.

7003 TPS Printed and made by Garrod & Lofthouse Ltd. SLRZ 1012

REGAL
ZONOPHONE

STEREO
(YCARX.63) 33⅓
1

SLRZ 1012
℗ 1970
1

SHAZAM
1. HELLO SUSIE
2. BEAUTIFUL DAUGHTER
3. CHERRY BLOSSOM CLINIC REVISITED
(Wood) Essex International, Mecolico. BIEM, NCB

THE MOVE
PRODUCED BY ROY WOOD, CARL WAYNE, RICK PRICE
IN CONJUNCTION WITH GERALD CHEVIN FOR
STRAIGHT AHEAD PRODUCTIONS

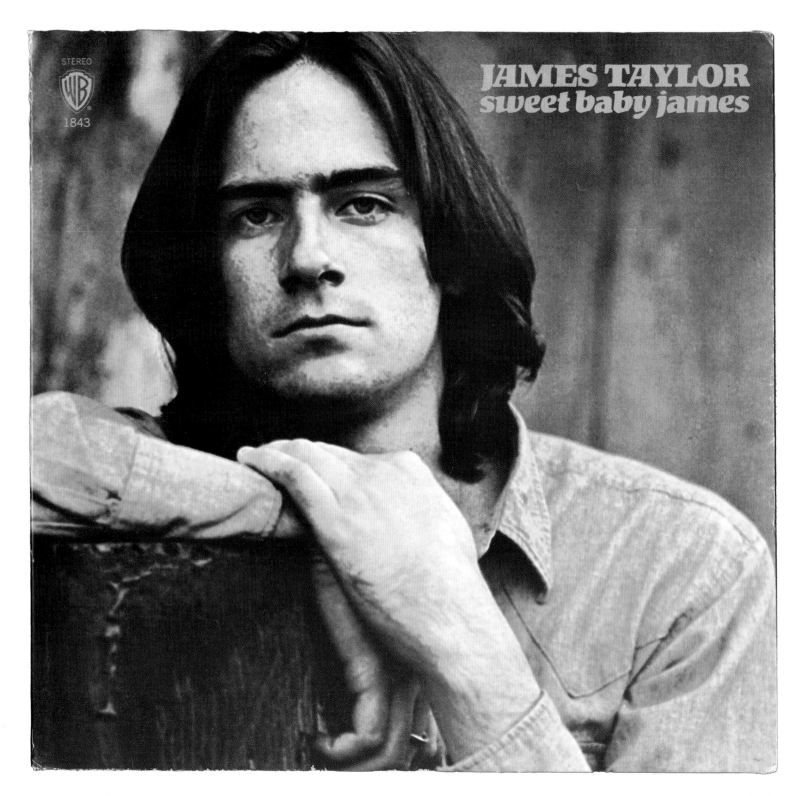

JAMES TAYLOR | Sweet Baby James

February 1970 | Warner Bros.

Taylor's second album, his breakthrough record, is both an evocative document of its time and an ageless artifact whose sentiments have no sell-by date. The album's autumnal, mostly acoustic tone proved to be a much-needed tonic—the public displayed an almost insatiable appetite for it, keeping it on the *Billboard* chart for just under two years. *Sweet Baby James* is where Taylor connects as one of America's most skilled and conscientious song-crafters and as a figure whose candidly expressed journey through "Fire and Rain" renders him someone worth listening to and rooting for. The album officially launched Taylor's career and the 70s' singer-songwriter movement, which now resides as a permanent tradition within mainstream and alternative music. "Fire and Rain," "Country Road," "Steamroller," and "Lo and Behold" became Taylor standards and have been recorded by numerous pop, soul, and country artists. The album's success paved the way for his biggest single, the anthem "You've Got a Friend," which brought its writer, Carole King, international recognition.

Sweet Baby James
Lo and Behold
Sunny Skies
Steamroller
Country Road
Oh Susannah
Fire and Rain
Blossom
Anywhere Like Heaven
Oh Baby, Don't You Loose
Your Lip on Me
Suite for 20G

James Taylor (guitar)
Danny Kootch (guitar)
Carole King (piano)
Russ Kunkel (drums)
Randy Meisner (bass)
Bobby West (bass)
John London (bass)
Red Rhodes (steel guitar)
Jack Bielan (brass arrangements)
Chris Darrow (fiddle)

Recorded at
Sunset Sound, December '69
Written and sung by
James Taylor (except "Oh Susannah"
which was written by
Stephen Foster)

Produced By Peter Asher
for Marylebone Productions, Inc.
Published By
Country Road Music Inc. BMI/Blackwood Music, Inc.
Engineered By Bill Lazerus
Photography By Henry Diltz
Art Direction By Ed Thrasher

Warner Bros. Records Inc.,
a Subsidiary & Licensee of
Warner Bros. Inc.,
4000 Warner Blvd., Burbank, Calif.
488 Madison Ave., New York, N.Y.
Made in U.S.A.

WARNER BROS. RECORDS

SWEET BABY JAMES
JAMES TAYLOR
Produced by Peter Asher for
Marylebone Productions, Inc.

WS 1843
(S39618)

SIDE
1

1. SWEET BABY JAMES (James Taylor)
2. LO AND BEHOLD (James Taylor)
3. SUNNY SKIES (James Taylor)
4. STEAMROLLER (James Taylor)
5. COUNTRY ROAD (James Taylor)
6. OH, SUSANNA (Stephen Foster)

STEREO

BLACK SABBATH | Black Sabbath

February 1970 | Vertigo

There were precedents—most notably the 1968 arrivals of Led Zeppelin and Blue Cheer—but the first Black Sabbath album is where one of the two most resilient strains in post-Beatles popular music was born. At the same time that James Taylor and a host of acoustic troubadours were crafting the outlines of the singer-songwriter genre, Ozzy Osbourne, Tony Iommi, Bill Ward, and Geezer Butler were forging great chunks of guitar into the similarly basic, but considerably louder, style known as heavy metal. Sabbath's genius was in reducing hard rock to its instrumental essentials—few bands of the time, save Deep Purple, let single riffs so dominate their sound—and then layering on lyrics. The latter element conjured a foreboding world of wizards, demons, and nightmares that has defined heavy metal and its innumerable subgenres for four decades. The British and American editions of *Black Sabbath* vary somewhat, most

noticeably in that the U.S. version replaces "Evil Woman," the group's cover of the American band Crow's 1969 hit, with the Sabbath original "Wicked World." Not only did Sabbath's debut define a genre and launch a group that, initially derided, would evolve into an institution, but the music's no-frills approach laid the groundwork for the advent of punk rock later in the decade.

First pressings on the highly collect- ible Vertigo label featured the credit "A Philips Record Product."

Inside gatefold, with an inverted cross.

EMERSON LAKE & PALMER | Emerson Lake & Palmer

November 1970 | Island

As flag-wavers for progressive rock, no one raised the banner higher than Emerson, Lake & Palmer. An English supergroup (comprised of former members of, respectively, The Nice, King Crimson, and Atomic Rooster), the group preceded its only real competition, Yes, onto the public stage with this debut LP, which was a fixture on *Billboard*'s chart for nearly a year. The trio combines an informed affection for classical sources with an enthusiasm for improvisation that proved irresistible to the early-'70s audiences who delighted in its technical virtuosity and flair for dramatic presentation. "Lucky Man," written by guitarist-vocalist Greg Lake when he was 12, gave the band its hit single, and the extended "Take a Pebble" became a fast favorite on FM-rock radio. Flashy showmanship drove the group's concerts, but energy and a knack for dynamic arrangements abound here as well, as on "Knife-Edge," where Emerson's roiling keyboard work rocks Bach and Czech composer Leos Janacek, and "The Barbarian," which is sliced into portions by Lake's rough guitar riff and Emerson's breakneck Brubeck piano-playing.

ILPS 9132

Side One

The Barbarian
Emerson, Lake and Palmer

Take a Pebble
Lake

Knife-Edge
Emerson, Lake and Fraser

Side Two

The Three Fates:

Clotho Royal Festival Hall Organ
Emerson

Lachesis Piano Solo
Emerson

Atropos Piano Trio
Emerson

Tank
Emerson and Palmer

Lucky Man
Lake

Recorded at Advision   Engineer: Eddie Offord
Production: Greg Lake   Arranged & Directed: Emerson, Lake & Palmer for E.G. Records
All Songs Published by E.G. Music ©1970
Cover Painting: Nic Dartnell
Printed and made by the E.J. Day Group London and Bedford

island records ltd
basing street london w11

stereo

EMERSON, LAKE & PALMER

1. THE BARBARIAN (Emerson/Lake & Palmer)
2. TAKE A PEBBLE (Lake)
3. KNIFE-EDGE (Emerson/Lake & Fraser)
All songs published by E.G. Music

ILPS-9132
℗ 1970

SIDE ONE

EMERSON, LAKE & PALMER
Produced by: GREG LAKE
for E.G. Records

On the cover, Bowie wore a "man's dress" by British designer Mr. Fish. The cover proved so controversial that Bowie's German and American labels created their own covers. This copy is signed by Bowie, guitarist Mick Ronson, and bassist/producer Tony Visconti.

DAVID BOWIE | The Man Who Sold The World

November 1970 | Mercury

Bowie's most consistent character trait has, oddly enough, been his changeability. The stylistic diversity of his catalog is dizzying, littered with parts he played and discarded in service of specific songs and album concepts and trends he instigated and abandoned before others seized them. *The Man Who Sold the World*, his third album, is the first on which Bowie comes across as an artist fully confident of his vision, accessorizing dark subject matter (insanity, the Vietnam war, malevolent computers) with a singular musical approach. This inventive brand of hard rock was created with his new associate, guitarist Mick Ronson, whose playing and arranging would subsequently yield the pair's masterpiece, *The Rise and Fall of Ziggy Stardust and the Spiders from Mars*. In place of his previous pop and Anthony Newley affectations, Bowie, singing better than ever, sets his song puzzles against a backdrop suggestive of Black Sabbath ("Black

Country Rock," "She Shook Me Cold"), The Who ("Running Gun Blues") and Hendrix-styled psychedelia (The Width of a Circle"). Though not a big seller, the album proved influential—on such bands as Nirvana (who covered the title cut), Nine Inch Nails, the Cure, and Siouxsie and the Banshees. The cover of the original U.K. pressing, picturing Bowie in a Greta Garbo-esque pose, wearing a "man's dress," is perhaps the earliest manifestation of glam-rock.

SIDE 1
THE WIDTH OF A CIRCLE . . . 8 : 07
ALL THE MADMEN . . . 5 : 38
BLACK COUNTRY ROCK . . . 3 : 33
AFTER ALL . . . 3 : 52

SIDE 2
RUNNING GUN BLUES . . . . 3 : 12
SAVIOUR MACHINE . . . 4 : 27
SHE SHOOK ME COLD . . . . 4 : 13
THE MAN WHO SOLD THE WORLD . . . 3 : 58
THE SUPERMEN . . . 3 : 39

ALL SELECTIONS WRITTEN BY DAVID BOWIE
ALL SELECTIONS PUBLISHED BY TITANIC MUSIC LTD/CHRYSALIS MUSIC LTD
PRODUCED BY TONY VISCONTI

DAVID BOWIE : GUITAR, VOCALS
TONY VISCONTI : ELECTRIC BASS, PIANO, GUITAR
MICK RONSON : GUITAR
MICK WOODMANSLEY : DRUMS
RALPH MACE : MOOG SYNTHESIZER

RECORDED AT TRIDENT STUDIOS AND ADVISION STUDIOS
REMIX AT TRIDENT STUDIOS
MANY THANKS TO OUR ENGINEER, KEN

ALBUM DESIGNED AND PHOTOGRAPHED BY KEEF

This stereo record can be played on mono reproducers provided either a compatible
or stereo cartridge wired for mono is fitted. Recent equipment may already be
fitted with a suitable cartridge. If in doubt, consult your dealer.

6338041

SBL
PRICE
CODE

The earliest copies
mistakenly credit
producer Tony
Visconti as Tonny
Visconti.

German Mercury released the album in a cover that folds open into a 24" circle.

U.S. Mercury released the album with this cartoon cover by Bowie's friend Michael J. Weller.

In 1972, U.S. RCA reissued *The Man Who Sold The World* with a contemporary photograph on the cover.

CAT STEVENS | Tea For The Tillerman

November 1970 | Island

Stevens' capacity for reinvention long preceded his 1979 adoption of the name Yusuf Islam. The artist formerly known as Steven Demetre Georgiou had morphed into Cat Stevens slightly more than a decade earlier and began enjoying success in the U.K.—both as a solo performer and as the composer of hits by P.P. Arnold ("The First Cut Is the Deepest"), the Tremeloes ("Here Comes My Baby"), and others. But it was *Tea for the Tillerman*, produced by ex-Yardbird Paul Samwell-Smith, that broke Stevens and enabled him to quickly rise to the crest of the wave of the emerging singer-songwriter movement. Unlike his American counterparts, Stevens came less from the acoustic folk-music tradition than from the hook-laden school of British pop, which served him extremely well. *Tea for the Tillerman* is almost overstocked with memorable melodies whose catchiness underpins simply stated ruminations on social anxieties ("Where

Do the Children Play?") and more personal concerns ("Miles from Nowhere," "Sad Lisa," "On the Road to Find Out"). The album formally introduced an artist whose work would literally define much of popular music of the early-to-mid-'70s on the subsequent albums *Teaser and the Firecat, Catch Bull at Four,* and *Buddha and the Chocolate Box*.

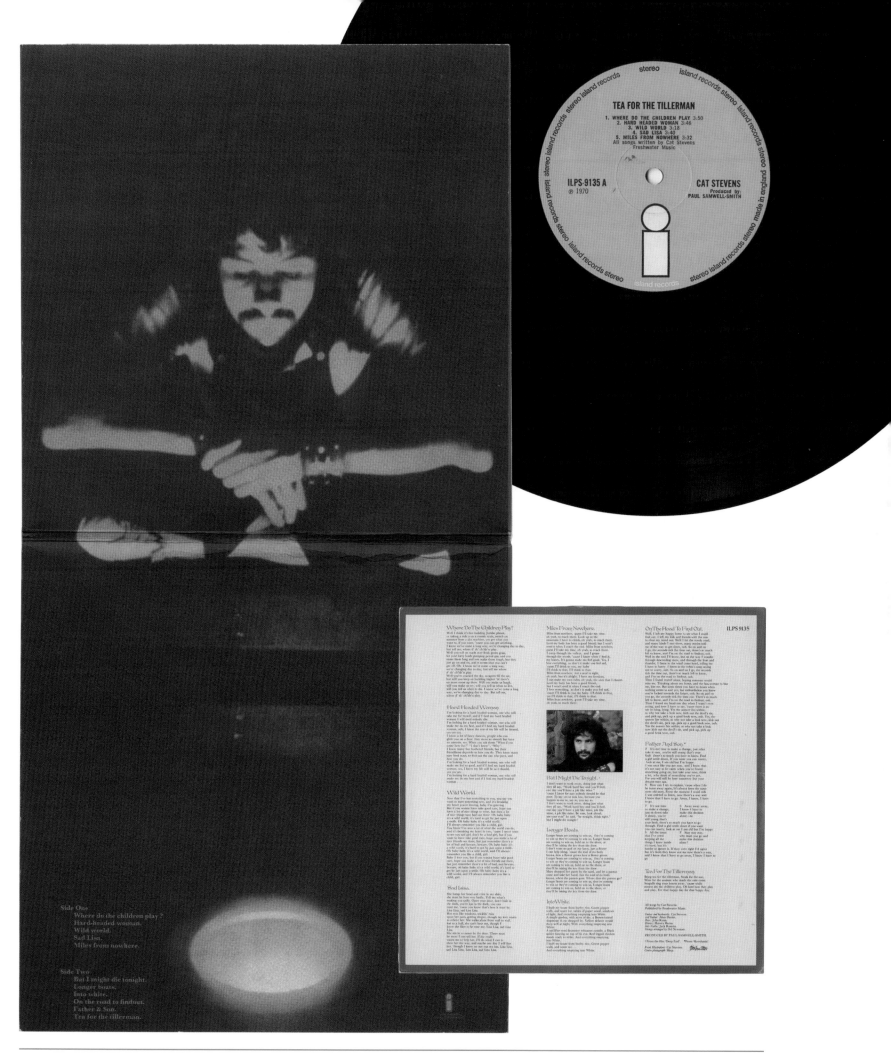

CAROLE KING | Tapestry

February 1971 | Ode

An era-defining record, as much a fixture in homes of the time as macramé flower pot hangers and herbal tea, King's second album is inextricably bound up with the '70s singer-songwriter movement it inaugurated. James Taylor's liner notes from a 1999 reissue convey what it was about *Tapestry* that touched enough hearts to make it America's favorite album for 15 consecutive weeks and, ultimately, a 25-million-seller: the songs, he wrote, were "very accessible, very personal statements, built from the ground up with a simple, elegant architecture." A decade after her '60s heyday as one of pop's most commercial tunesmiths, King applied her talents to becoming a performing artist in an autobiographical, alternately grateful and bittersweet LP that yielded no less than three No. 1 singles: "It's Too Late," "I Feel the Earth Move," and James Taylor's version of "You've Got a Friend." "So Far Away," "Smackwater Jack," and "Where You Lead" were likewise hits for King. *Tapestry* helped kick-start the singer-writer and inspired countless women to become artists of the front-and-center variety—not merely group singers or producer-directed mannequins. An unqualified pop-music classic, *Tapestry* boasted a support crew that included Taylor, Joni Mitchell, and Merry "Gimme Shelter" Clayton on backing vocals, and David Campbell (Beck's father) on cello and viola.

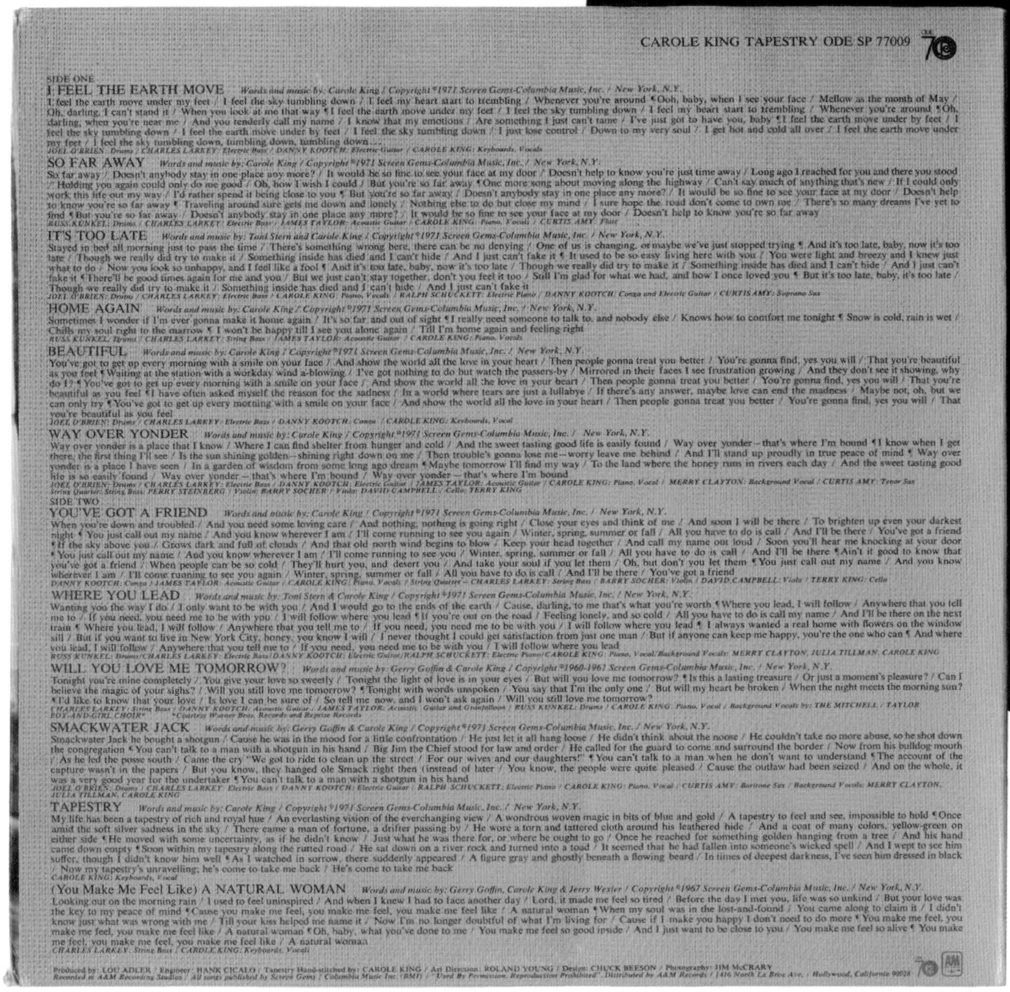

SIDE ONE

I FEEL THE EARTH MOVE *Words and music by: Carole King / Copyright ©1971 Screen Gems-Columbia Music, Inc. / New York, N.Y.*
I feel the earth move under my feet / I feel the sky tumbling down / I feel my heart start to trembling / Whenever you're around / Ooh, baby, when I see your face / Mellow as the month of May / Oh, darling, I can't stand it / When you look at me that way ¶ I feel the sky tumbling down / Whenever you're around ¶ Oh, darling, when you're near me / And you tenderly call my name / I know that my emotions / Are something I just can't tame / I've just got to have you, baby ¶ I feel the earth move under my feet / I feel the sky tumbling down / I feel the earth move under my feet / I feel the sky tumbling down / I feel my heart start to trembling / Whenever you're around / Oh, baby / I feel the earth move / I just lose control / Down to my very soul / I get hot and cold all over / I feel the earth move under my feet / I feel the sky tumbling down, tumbling down, tumbling down...
JOEL O'BRIEN: Drums / CHARLES LARKEY: Electric Bass / DANNY KOOTCH: Electric Guitar / CAROLE KING: Keyboards, Vocals

SO FAR AWAY *Words and music by: Carole King / Copyright ©1971 Screen Gems-Columbia Music, Inc. / New York, N.Y.*
So far away / Doesn't anybody stay in one place any more? / It would be so fine to see your face at my door / Doesn't help to know you're just time away / Long ago I reached for you and there you stood / Holding you again could only do me good / Oh, how I wish I could / But you're so far away / One more song about moving along the highway / Can't say much of anything that's new / If I could only work this life out my way / I'd rather spend it being close to you / But you're so far away / Doesn't anybody stay in one place any more? / It would be so fine to see your face at my door / Doesn't help to know you're so far away / Traveling around sure gets me down and lonely / Nothing else to do but close my mind / I sure hope the road don't come to own me / There's so many dreams I've yet to find / But you're so far away / Doesn't anybody stay in one place any more? / It would be so fine to see your face at my door / Doesn't help to know you're so far away
RUSS KUNKEL: Drums / CHARLES LARKEY: Electric Bass / JAMES TAYLOR: Acoustic Guitar / CURTIS AMY: Flute

IT'S TOO LATE *Words and music by: Toni Stern and Carole King / Copyright ©1971 Screen Gems-Columbia Music, Inc. / New York, N.Y.*
Stayed in bed all morning just to pass the time / There's something wrong here, there can be no denying / One of us is changing, or maybe we've just stopped trying / And it's too late, baby, now it's too late / Though we really did try to make it / Something inside has died and I can't hide / And I just can't fake it / It used to be so easy living here with you / You were light and breezy and I knew just what to do / Now you look so unhappy and I feel like a fool / And it's too late, baby, now it's too late / Though we really did try to make it / Something inside has died and I can't hide / And I just can't fake it ¶ There'll be good times again for me and you / But we just can't stay together, don't you feel it too / Still I'm glad for what we had, and how I once loved you / But it's too late, baby, it's too late / Though we really did try to make it / And I just can't fake it
JOEL O'BRIEN: Drums / CHARLES LARKEY: Electric Bass / DANNY KOOTCH: Conga and Electric Guitar / CURTIS AMY: Soprano Sax

HOME AGAIN *Words and music by: Carole King / Copyright ©1971 Screen Gems-Columbia Music, Inc. / New York, N.Y.*
Sometimes I wonder if I'm ever gonna make it home again / It's so far and out of sight / I really need someone to talk to, and nobody else / Knows how to comfort me tonight ¶ Snow is cold, rain is wet / Chills my soul right to the marrow ¶ I won't be happy till I see you alone again / Till I'm home again and feeling right
RUSS KUNKEL: Drums / CHARLES LARKEY: Electric Bass / JAMES TAYLOR: Acoustic Guitar / CAROLE KING: Piano, Vocals

BEAUTIFUL *Words and music by: Carole King / Copyright ©1971 Screen Gems-Columbia Music, Inc. / New York, N.Y.*
You've got to get up every morning with a smile on your face / And show the world all the love in your heart / Then people gonna treat you better / You're gonna find, yes you will / That you're beautiful as you feel ¶ Waiting at the station with a workday wind a-blowing / I've got nothing to do but watch the passers-by / Mirrored on their faces I see frustration growing / And they don't see it showing, why do I ¶ You've got to get up every morning with a smile on your face / And show the world all the love in your heart / Then people gonna treat you better / You're gonna find, yes you will / That you're beautiful as you feel ¶ I have often asked myself the reason for the sadness / In a world where tears are just a lullaby / If there's any answer, maybe love can end the madness / Maybe not, oh, but we can only try ¶ You've got to get up every morning with a smile on your face / And show the world all the love in your heart / Then people gonna treat you better / You're gonna find, yes you will / That you're beautiful as you feel
JOEL O'BRIEN: Drums / CHARLES LARKEY: Electric Bass / DANNY KOOTCH: Conga / CAROLE KING: Keyboards, Vocal

WAY OVER YONDER *Words and music by: Carole King / Copyright ©1971 Screen Gems-Columbia Music, Inc. / New York, N.Y.*
Way over yonder is a place that I know / Where I can find shelter from hunger and cold / And the sweet tasting good life is easily found / Way over yonder — that's where I'm bound ¶ I know when I get there, the first thing I'll see / Is the sun shining golden — shining right down on me / Then trouble's gonna lose me — worry leave me behind / And I'll stand up proudly in true peace of mind ¶ Way over yonder is a place I have seen / In a garden of wisdom from some long ago dream / Maybe tomorrow I'll find my way / To the land where the honey runs in rivers each day / And the sweet tasting good life is so easily found / Way over yonder — that's where I'm bound / Way over yonder — that's where I'm bound
JOEL O'BRIEN: Drums / CHARLES LARKEY: Electric Bass / DANNY KOOTCH: Acoustic Guitar / JAMES TAYLOR: Acoustic Guitar / CAROLE KING: Piano, Vocal / MERRY CLAYTON: Background Vocal / CURTIS AMY: Tenor Sax / String Quartet: String Bass; PERRY STEINBERG / Violin: BARRY SOCHER / Viola: DAVID CAMPBELL / Cello: TERRY KING

SIDE TWO

YOU'VE GOT A FRIEND *Words and music by: Carole King / Copyright ©1971 Screen Gems-Columbia Music, Inc. / New York, N.Y.*
When you're down and troubled / And you need some loving care / And nothing, nothing is going right / Close your eyes and think of me / And soon I will be there / To brighten up even your darkest night ¶ You just call out my name / And you know wherever I am / I'll come running to see you again / Winter, spring, summer or fall / All you have to do is call / And I'll be there / You've got a friend ¶ If the sky above you / Grows dark and full of clouds / And that old north wind begins to blow / Keep your head together / And call my name out loud / Soon you'll hear me knocking at your door ¶ You just call out my name / And you know wherever I am / I'll come running to see you again / Winter, spring, summer or fall / All you have to do is call / And I'll be there / Ain't it good to know that you've got a friend ¶ When people can be so cold? / They'll hurt you, and desert you / And take your soul if you let them / Oh, but don't you let them ¶ You just call out my name / And you know wherever I am / I'll come running to see you again / Winter, spring, summer or fall / All you have to do is call / And I'll be there / You've got a friend
DANNY KOOTCH: Electric Guitar / JAMES TAYLOR: Acoustic Guitar / CAROLE KING: Piano, Vocal / MERRY CLAYTON: Background Vocal

WHERE YOU LEAD *Words and music by: Toni Stern & Carole King / Copyright ©1971 Screen Gems-Columbia Music, Inc. / New York, N.Y.*
Wanting you the way I do / I only want to be with you / And I would go to the ends of the earth / Cause, darling, to me that's what you're worth ¶ Where you lead, I will follow / Anywhere that you tell me to / If you need, you need me to be with you / I will follow where you lead ¶ At times I wanted / To live in New York City, honey, you know I will / I never thought I could get satisfaction from just one man / But if anyone can keep me happy, you're the one who can ¶ And where you lead, I will follow / Anywhere that you tell me to / If you need, you need me to be with you / I will follow where you lead
RUSS KUNKEL: Drums / CHARLES LARKEY: Electric Bass / DANNY KOOTCH: Electric Guitar / RALPH SCHUCKETT: Electric Piano / CAROLE KING: Piano, Vocal / Background Vocals: MERRY CLAYTON, JULIA TILLMAN, CAROLE KING

WILL YOU LOVE ME TOMORROW *Words and music by: Gerry Goffin & Carole King / Copyright ©1960-1971 Screen Gems-Columbia Music, Inc. / New York, N.Y.*
Tonight you're mine completely / You give your love so sweetly / Tonight the light of love is in your eyes / But will you love me tomorrow? ¶ Is this a lasting treasure / Or just a moment's pleasure? / Can I believe the magic of your sighs? / Will you still love me tomorrow? ¶ Tonight with words unspoken / You say that I'm the only one / But will my heart be broken / When the night meets the morning sun? ¶ I'd like to know that your love / Is love I can be sure of / So tell me now, and I won't ask again / Will you still love me tomorrow?
CHARLES LARKEY: String Bass / DANNY KOOTCH: Acoustic Guitar / JAMES TAYLOR: Acoustic Guitar and Orchidlion / RUSS KUNKEL: Drums / CAROLE KING: Piano, Vocal / Background Vocals by: THE MITCHELLS / TAYLOR BOYS AND GIRL CHOIR

SMACKWATER JACK *Words and music by: Gerry Goffin & Carole King / Copyright ©1971 Screen Gems-Columbia Music, Inc. / New York, N.Y.*
Smackwater Jack he bought a shotgun / 'Cause he was in the mood for a little confrontation / He just let it all hang loose / He didn't think about the noose / He couldn't take no more abuse, so he shot down the congregation ¶ You can't talk to a man with a shotgun in his hand / Big Jim the Chief stood for law and order / He called for the guard to come and surround the border / Now from his bulldog mouth / As he led the posse south / Came the cry 'We got to ride to clean up the street' / For our wives and our daughters' ¶ You can't talk to a man when he don't want to understand ¶ The account of the capture wasn't in the papers / But you know, they hanged ole Smack right then (instead of later / You know, the people were quite pleased / 'Cause the outlaw had been seized / And on the whole, it was a very good year for the undertaker ¶ You can't talk to a man with a shotgun in his hand
JOEL O'BRIEN: Drums / CHARLES LARKEY: Electric Bass / DANNY KOOTCH: Electric Guitar / RALPH SCHUCKETT: Electric Piano / CAROLE KING: Piano, Vocal / CURTIS AMY: Baritone Sax / Background Vocals: MERRY CLAYTON, JULIA TILLMAN, CAROLE KING

TAPESTRY *Words and music by: Carole King / Copyright ©1971 Screen Gems-Columbia Music, Inc. / New York, N.Y.*
My life has been a tapestry of rich and royal hue / An everlasting vision of the everchanging view / A wondrous woven magic in bits of blue and gold / A tapestry to feel and see, impossible to hold ¶ Once amid the soft silver sadness in the sky / There came a man of fortune, a drifter passing by / He wore a torn and tattered cloth around his feathered hide / And a coat of many colors, yellow-green on either side ¶ He moved with some uncertainty, as if he didn't know / Just what he was there for, or where he ought to go / Once he reached for something golden hanging from a tree / And his hand came down empty ¶ Soon within my tapestry along the rutted road / He sat down on a river rock, and turned into a toad / It seemed that he had fallen into someone's wicked spell / And I wept to see him suffer, though I didn't know him well ¶ As I watched in sorrow, there suddenly appeared / A figure gray and ghostly beneath a flowing beard / In times of deepest darkness, I've seen him dressed in black / Now my tapestry's unravelling; he's come to take me back
CAROLE KING: Keyboards, Vocal

(You Make Me Feel Like) A NATURAL WOMAN *Words and music by: Gerry Goffin, Carole King & Jerry Wexler / Copyright ©1967 Screen Gems-Columbia Music, Inc. / New York, N.Y.*
Looking out on the morning rain / I used to feel uninspired / And when I knew I had to face another day / Lord, it made me feel so tired / Before the day I met you, life was so unkind / But your love was the key to my peace of mind ¶ 'Cause you make me feel, you make me feel, you make me feel like / A natural woman ¶ When my soul was in the lost-and-found / You came along to claim it / I didn't know just what was wrong with me / 'Til your kiss helped me name it / Now I'm no longer doubtful of what I'm living for / Cause if I make you happy I don't need to do more ¶ You make me feel, you make me feel, you make me feel like / A natural woman ¶ Oh, baby, what you've done to me / You make me feel so good inside / And I just want to be close to you / You make me feel so alive ¶ You make me feel, you make me feel, you make me feel like / A natural woman
CHARLES LARKEY: String Bass / CAROLE KING: Keyboards, Vocals

Produced by: LOU ADLER / Engineer: HANK CICALO / Tapestry Hand-stitched by: CAROLE KING / Art Direction: ROLAND YOUNG / Design: CHUCK BEESON / Photographer: JIM McCRARY / Recorded at A&M Recording Studios / All songs published by Screen Gems / Columbia Music Inc. (BMI)

STEREO
SIDE 1
SP-77009
(SP-77017)

TAPESTRY
CAROLE KING

1. I Feel The Earth Move 2:57 (Carole King)
2. So Far Away 3:55 (Carole King)
3. It's Too Late 3:51 (Carole King-Toni Stern)
4. Home Again 2:27 (Carole King)
5. Beautiful 3:05 (Carole King)
6. Way Over Yonder 4:42 (Carole King)

All tunes published by Screen Gems/Columbia Music, Inc. (BMI)

Produced by LOU ADLER

DISTRIBUTED BY A&M RECORDS · 1416 N. LA BREA, HOLLYWOOD, CALIFORNIA 90028

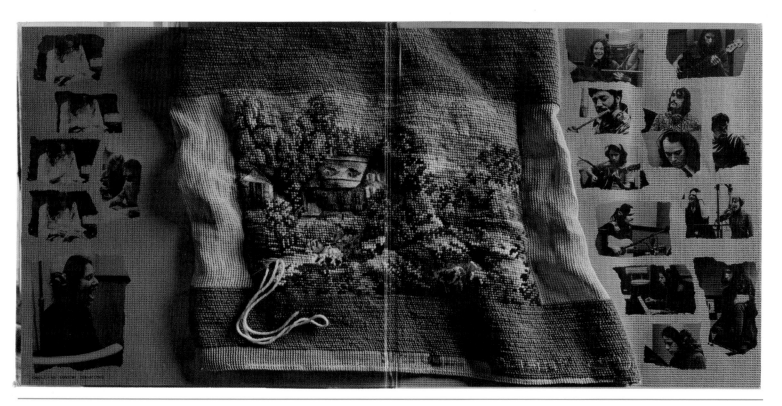

A tapestry stiched by King appears inside the gatefold.

CAN | Tago Mago

February 1971 | United Artists

"I saw the mushroom head, I was born and I was dead." Even by prog-rock standards, a song whose lyrics largely consist of that phrase repeated 30 times in four minutes might constitute a challenge for listeners. But Holger Czukay and his krautrock quintet never had easy listening on their minds, as proved by Can's third LP, a double album that ranks as one of the genre's most liberating and avant-garde. On *Tago Mago*, Czukay, in the manner of Frank Zappa, spliced finished session tracks with surreptitiously recorded jam and practice tapes he dubbed "in-between-recordings." This collaging mixed sturdy funk rhythms and electronic effects with psychedelic guitar-keyboard digressions that often occupy an entire side of the album, as on "Halleluhwah" and "Aumgn." The cherry atop *Tago Mago*'s experimental instrumentation is vocalist Damo Suzuki, a Japanese busker the band met in Munich and invited into the band. Suzuki's vocals,

delivered in limited English on such tracks as "Paperhouse," "Mushroom," and "Oh Yeah," only add to the aura of strangeness that permeates the entirety of *Tago Mago*. The record may be an acquired taste, but it's been acquired by many, including Radiohead, the Fall, John Lydon, and the Jesus and Mary Chain.

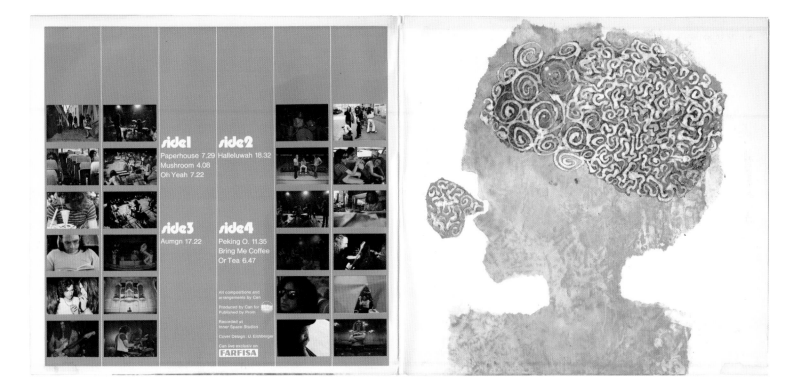

Can's British label released the album with a different cover, aiming for the rock audience.

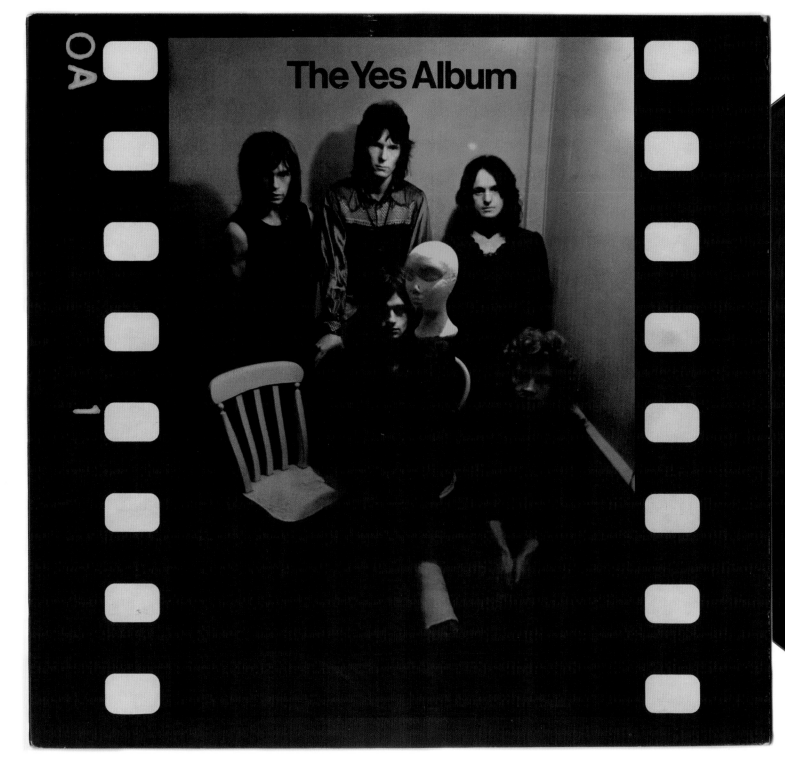

YES | The Yes Album

February 1971 | Atlantic

Yes was the first progressive group to experience major mainstream success in both the U.S. and the U.K., and this, its third long-player, was the vehicle that paved the way forward to *Fragile, Close to the Edge,* and five other Top-10 albums. Where those sets lean toward the sidelong marathons that endeared the group to its most ardent fans, *The Yes Album* divides evenly between long-form and more concise pieces—all constructed with as keen an eye toward melody as on virtuoso performances. The first Yes LP to feature guitar hero Steve Howe and the last to feature original keyboardist Tony Banks (until a decade later), *The Yes Album* showcases the writing contributions of all members; bassist Chris Squire penned the FM staple "All Good People" and vocalist Jon Anderson the Top-40 single "Your Move." With Howe, Squire and Anderson composed the three-part "Starship Trooper," which was inspired by Robert Heinlein's 1959 sci-fi novel *Starship Troopers.* Forty years after the *Village Voice* praised *The Yes Album* for its "arty eclecticism," the band continues to tour and record.

The Yes Album

Side one:
1. Yours is no disgrace /Yes
2. The Clap /Howe *
3. Starship trooper:
   a. Life seeker /Anderson
   b. Disillusion /Squire
   c. Wurm /Howe

Side two:
1. I've seen all good people:
   a. Your move /Anderson
   b. All good people /Squire
2. A venture /Anderson
3. Perpetual change /Anderson/Squire

Personnel:
John Anderson: vocals/percussion
Chris Squire: bass guitars/vocals
Steve Howe: electric & acoustic guitars/vachalia/ vocal
Tony Kaye: piano/organ/moog
Bill Bruford: drums/percussion

Recorders on 'Your move': Colin Goldring

Produced by Yes & Eddie Offord
at Advision Studios, London
Autumn 1970
Engineer: Eddie Offord
Co-ordination: Brian Lane
Thanks to Tom Dowd

*Recorded live, Lyceum, London

Photography: Phil Franks
   & Barry Wentzell
Design: Jon Goodchild

All titles by Yessongs Limited

Under licence from:
Atlantic Recording Corporation USA
Manufactured by Polydor
Records Limited
Sleeve printed and made by
MacNeill Press Ltd., London, S.E.

JONI MITCHELL

JONI MITCHELL | Blue

June 1971 | Reprise

Blue's immediate predecessors *Clouds* and *Ladies of the Canyon* had already created fans for Mitchell's songs and singing. So had prominent covers of her material by Judy Collins, Crosby, Stills, Nash & Young ("Woodstock"), and others. But *Blue* is the record that instantly connected Mitchell to the larger audience the critics had always insisted she deserved. The *New York Times* proclaimed it one of the most significant albums of the last century, crediting it with "ushering in the confessional mode for pop songwriting." "Carey" and "All I Want" are among the isolated bright spots in a program that consists mostly of downbeat, wholly frank admissions about romantic entanglements and ideals that didn't work out. This isn't surprising since the LP, which Mitchell described as coming from a period in which "[she] had no personal defenses," followed her painful breakup with Graham Nash. The album's theme carries over to Tim Considine's

moody front-sleeve photo of Mitchell, a likely visual allusion to *Kind of Blue*, Miles' Davis' landmark LP whose compositions, like those on *Blue*, relied on unconventional tunings. Mitchell is accompanied here by James Taylor on guitar ("A Case of You," "All I Want," and "California") and Stephen Stills, who plays guitar and bass on "Carey."

This white label promotional copy was made for radio and reviewers.

Joe Boyd

on The Incredible String Band & Nick Drake

I grew up with music and spent my teenage years listening to records that were made 30 or 20 or 10 years before. So I was very conscious of a historical perspective, and when I was making records, I was always conscious of producing them in a way where I could say, "I think I will be happy to listen to this in 50 years. I won't be embarrassed, and that hopefully other people will listen to this in 50 years." I didn't let anybody pan and phase the guitar from right to left, because I just thought, that would date it. I always had an eye on posterity when I was producing at the time.

The Incredible String Band

When I first saw Robin Williamson and Clive Palmer, I just took one look at Robin, heard him sing, and thought, "This guy's a star." This was 1965, before Dylan went electric, the days when you could think, well, folk music, you can be a star. Dylan blew that idea out of the water. So that was my first thought, just: "He's a star." Not anything more sophisticated or complicated in terms of the marketing plan.

Then when I heard Mike Heron, the three of them, and they started singing their own songs, I thought, "These songs are fabulous. I've got to record them. It's great stuff, we'll figure it out later." And later, when I heard the songs for the second album, and I heard them perform, using sitar and gimbri, and start to go off in these directions. I just said, even before we made the *5000 Spirits* album, "I gotta get them out of the folk clubs, I don't want them ever to play another folk club." Only play rock clubs, basically. They are a psychedelic band, they just happen to not be electric. And I think they were a little perplexed because they were used to the folk world, in a way, and I suddenly had them opening for Pink Floyd at Saville Theatre. The cover of *5000 Spirits* was a totally cynical ploy to wave a big flag and say, "This is a psychedelic act." So I think by the

second album, I was consciously steering it in a certain direction from the get go. And it worked.

I think that *The Hangman's Beautiful Daughter* has some of the best things they ever did. "Koeeoaddi There" and "A Very Cellular Song" are their masterpieces. But I also think there are some weak things on it. But sonically, it's definitely one of [engineer] John Woods' great moments.

Nick Drake

It's quite wrong to say that Nick Drake's music was just stumbling along in its level of obscurity until suddenly, the Volkswagen ad came along. Initially, the albums sold a couple thousand each. I had Island put together the *Fruit Tree* box set, which was in about '78 or '79. And that caused a few ripples in England, but I don't think they exported many to America. But they only made, you know, 500, a thousand. And so when I started Hannibal, I needed some stuff in the catalogue and was conscious of the fact that, although Island had three Nick Drake original albums available in England, they were not available in the U.S., and the box set was not available. So I went to Island and said, "Can I put these out?" And they said, "OK, sure." This guy from Long Island, Frank Kornelussen, had been pestering me about Sandy Denny. He was spending the summer in England and I agreed to pay him a fee to help out on the Sandy box. And in those days, you could actually walk through the Island tape stacks. One day he just walked in and he had a box and he said, "Hey, look, here's some Nick Drake stuff." And I said "Oh, yeah, I remember that, 'Clothes of Sand.'"

We started talking about putting together a Nick outtakes thing, which led to *Time of No Reply*, and reissuing the box set with the three original albums and this. Around the same time, there was a wave of critical response in the press,

some important articles, they stirred something up. And basically in the years leading up to the Volkswagen commercial, every year, sales doubled. There was a real upward curve from '79 through '89, a real surge, and then Volkswagen took it to another level, but the surge was already happening before Volkswagen came along.

I remember being stunned when the publishing people told me there's a chance to put a Nick Drake song in a Volkswagen ad. I said, "Oh I don't think so, that sounds like a really bad idea." They said, "Just take a look at the storyboard," so I did and thought, "Hm, that's kind of interesting" because it's seems more like an ad for Nick Drake than an ad for Volkswagen. I said, "Just check back, is it really true that they're not going to have any sales pitch over Nick's music?" and they came back and said, "Yeah, that's true, there'll be no voiceover."

I then sent it off to Gabrielle [Nick Drake's sister] and we talked about it. We met with the advertising people about it… and this guy, this obvious stoner, came in with a kind of L.L. Bean lumberjack shirt on and one of those knit caps, and he was the guy. And evidently, they'd done the whole storyboard, the whole thing had been prepared around another track. It was the night before the pitch meeting and he was at home smoking a joint and he listened to "Pink Moon" and he goes, "Shit. Fuck me. This could work." So he comes in the next morning and gets his colleagues together and plays them "Pink Moon" and says "Let's pitch this, too," and that's how it came about.

Joe Boyd is an American record producer, manager, and label founder who recorded Pink Floyd, Nick Drake, Fairport Convention, The Incredible String Band, Vashti Bunyan, and many others.

Johnny Marr

on Iggy & The Stooges: *Raw Power*

The Stooges: *Raw Power*

I was pretty young when I bought my first record—nine, I think. I got "Jeepster" by T.Rex on a 45rpm 7". It was a cool start and the band were my first love, but the truth is I got it because the label had a great photo of Marc Bolan and Mickey Finn on it, so I was snagged by that. I was really into the pop singles of the day, which were all the UK glam stuff: Roxy Music, Bowie, The Sweet, everything.

My parents were really into records, still are— my mother made up her own pop chart and compared it with the official one each week. They would have opinions about what I was buying and what was coming out. Records were the main thing in the house. As I got into my teens I checked out the rock bands who were around, but I wasn't crazy about a lot of it. My friends were into Led Zeppelin and Deep Purple and even though it was very guitar-based, I didn't take to it too much. It seemed quite drab.

I got into *Raw Power* by Iggy and The Stooges because a friend of mine who was a little older, Billy Duffy, now of The Cult, heard me playing a riff I'd written, and he kept saying that it sounded like James Williamson from The Stooges, who I had never heard. There were quite a few guys in my neighborhood who played guitar and hung out together, sort of competitive, but a very healthy scene. I was one of about five or six teenage boys, and we all had our own thing. One guy was really into Neil Young, another was into Nils Lofgren, another Pete Townshend and Paul Kossoff, and I was into Rory Gallagher, and then I discovered Johnny Thunders in a big way.

I thought I'd better check this *Raw Power* record out as it sounded intriguing, just the words "Iggy and The Stooges" and "Raw Power," so I went to find it. I was always looking through the racks in the record shops in Manchester, and when I came across it I got an actual physical jolt from the cover and vibe of it. I went back a week later and bought it for about £3.50. On the bus ride home, I just stared at it in awe.

I'd heard "I Wanna Be Your Dog" by the early Stooges lineup and I thought it was great. I knew *Raw Power* had something else going on because of James Williamson's guitar playing and maybe Bowie's odd production. Even though it had a famously messed-up mix, the rawness of it didn't phase me because the earlier stuff is actually more basic sounding. What first struck me about *Raw Power* was a beautiful darkness to it, a sophistication almost. It delivered exactly what was on the cover: other-worldly druggy rock' n' roll, sex, violence, but strangely beautiful somehow. From then on, I just climbed into a world with that record.

The David Bowie mix of *Raw Power* was obviously eccentric and a little "messed up." Things would lurch forward and some other things were too quiet. It was pretty muddy, but even though I could hear it could be better, I just went with it, and got used to it pretty quickly.

It was just all part of it, and it actually added to the strangeness and singularity of it. It was outside of everything, but still had killer singing and guitar playing.

"Gimme Danger" was the riff that Billy thought sounded like my playing, and he was right. When I first heard it, I knew what he meant and more importantly, I knew I was on the right track, in a big way, so that's always been a big track for me. I love the tune too. I spent an entire winter playing guitar along with the album in my bedroom, in the dark, orange street lights coming through the windows, when I was sixteen. Its influence came out on the Smiths album *The Queen Is Dead*. I was obsessed with "I Need Somebody" and I ended doing that song live with The Healers in 2002 and 2003. I got into all of it. "Penetration" is one of the best vocal performances I've ever heard, and "Search And Destroy" is pretty much definitive.

I got the first two Stooges albums immediately after I got *Raw Power,* and I know every note and word on them. I know plenty of people who think the first two albums are the best, or more important and influential, and even though I love them, I love *Raw Power* more. I've often been asked who my favorite guitar player is, and I always answer "James Williamson." I like different guitar players for different reasons, obviously, but when push comes to shove, James has it all in my book.

I've missed the Stooges reunion shows because our schedules haven't worked out. James and I keep in touch, and we're getting together for the first time next week. I've come across Iggy a couple of times. I had a car crash in '87 and he sent a message to me to see if I was OK, which I found amazing and so nice. I saw him in Brixton around '89, me and Matt Johnson from The The were in his dressing room. Iggy must have sensed that Matt and I had some chemistry, because he said, "You two should work together," so we did. He was right.

I've picked up a few copies of *Raw Power* over the years. My friend Jon Savage is also a huge fan, and he and I both treasure our original vinyl versions and we kind of geek out over it. I still play it—on vinyl, on anything.

Johnny Marr is a legendary English guitarist and songwriter best known for founding The Smiths with Morrissey. He has also been a member of Electronic, The The, and Modest Mouse.

Peter Buck

On Patti Smith: *Horses* & Record Collecting

Patti Smith: *Horses*

My father built his own little stereo from Heathkit, but I think he aspired to have a really nice one, so he subscribed to Stereo Review. A journalist named Steve Simels was writing about Patti Smith in 1973, he wrote about her very first things. I knew who [her guitarist and collaborator] Lenny Kaye was because I bought the *Nuggets* album. So every month he wrote something about Patti Smith, or it seemed like it, and I went and bought her record the first day it came out. I was probably the only person in Georgia who special ordered it. Honestly, I didn't meet anyone who had that record for three or four years. It just seemed like in the early 70s, it was all over. In retrospect, there was great music, but The Beatles broke up and *Goats Head Soup* came out after *Exile on Main Street*. Every band that you loved was doing lesser work and bands were breaking up, and the radio got really horrible. There were a few things like Roxy Music and Todd Rundgren that were talking about the future, and Al Green was still making great records—there was a lot of great soul music—but *Horses* just felt like the first blast in whatever was coming. It just felt like if you'd taken classic rock 'n' roll stuff like "Gloria" and "Land of 1000 Dances" and totally re-contextualized it in this way that felt completely modern and forward looking.

I just didn't have any clue as to what it would sound like. I'd read about it, but he kept mentioning she did poetry and "Gloria," and I'm thinking, "OK, maybe it's a garage band, I don't know." At the time, it was really hard to understand. I remember playing it and going, "Well, that's different…" and playing the record again and looking at the picture on the cover, and then flipping it over. Her version of "Gloria" really hit home right away because I knew that song, and I think I had actually played it at that point. Some of the longer, more improvisatory stuff, I was just starting to learn about jazz and I think I kind of hooked it up. It's a record that came out in the fall of '75, and within a month or two, I was playing it every day, and it meant a huge amount to me. Luckily enough, she came

and did a four night stand in, I think, February of '76 in Atlanta—two sets a night—and I went and saw every single show.

[*Horses* producer and Velvet Undeground co-founder] John Cale came out for one song each night and he played "My Generation" and smashed his bass. Then I'd go back the next day and he'd have the same bass all taped up and they'd do "My Generation" again, and he smash his bass. They hadn't really done many shows outside of New York. I talked to Patti later and she said that they'd done something in Los Angeles, but basically they were a New York band and it was their first tour and these were their first shows. They didn't have enough material to do two sets, so they were totally improvising, and there was no one there. It was maybe a hundred people. It was pretty unbelievable.

This guy I met said, "Hey I'm writing for" and he named some magazine, and he goes, "I have a table right up front." It was a bar that had tables. I was there at 9 o'clock every day for the 11 o'clock show so I said, "Well can I sit with you? I'll buy you drinks." He was into White Russians, he'd drink White Russians and go upstairs. He said, "You wanna come up there?" "Yeah sure." So in between sets we walked up and he introduced me to Patti, I was just so shy, I'm like, "Uh, hi…" I told her later when we were playing together, "You know, I don't know if you remember, but I met you in Atlanta in 1976. I was too shy to say it, but you didn't have a bass player at the time and I would have given 10 years of my life to be your bass player." And Patti turns over and looks at Lenny and she goes, "Yeah, and if you were cute you coulda got the job." Think how my life would have changed if I would have been the bass player for the Patti Smith Group. I wouldn't have been a good enough bass player to do it, but it's a fantasy that I like to have.

Her shows were totally seat-of-the-pants improv, which I really love. The very first night she came out and did the first set and then came out for the second set and started the first song, she looks at me and goes, "Wait a minute, are you the same

crowd that was here for the last show?" "Yeah!" She goes, "Well, in New York they always get rid of the crowd and you have a different crowd, and we don't really know that many songs. But we'll see what we can do, we'll make some stuff up." So, she read poetry, they did a Ronettes song that obviously they'd never rehearsed. They did this huge jam where they did [The Doors'] "Horse Latitudes" and she improvised a poem about Jim Morrison. It was great, and she said, "I wrote this song, but I didn't show it to the guys" and she sang this kind of Ronettes-y song that she had of her own called, I think, "Alone in a Crowd." It was a great show; you could just tell it was like, "We only know an hour of material, and we gotta play two and a half hours? Uh oh." In one of the local reviews, the main part of the review was, "I have never seen a woman spit on the stage before."

I don't know if you can listen to our records and tell that we were influenced by Patti because so much of what she is is an intellectual influence. The freedom and the poetry, but in particular I really like the way that she combines things that would be considered kind of high art-ish with, you know, "Louie Louie." When R.E.M. was being put together, it was kind of like "I love this kind of stuff because I don't mind the trashy aspect of it either." We were a rock band and as much as people thought we were really art-y, we were a total unstaged garage band.

On Collecting Records

Everyone always says, "Oh, I always listened to Iggy and the Stooges and the Velvet Underground." Well, I did. I was 14 years old and I loved the Beatles and the Beach Boys, but I loved the Velvet Underground, and then I discovered Iggy and the Stooges. I bought *Funhouse* for a quarter from this DJ that I knew, and loved it. I was reading *Creem* magazine, so I bought *Raw Power* and I hitchhiked to the record store when I was 15 to buy *Exile on Main Street*.

I hadn't really begun to understand jazz until maybe the end of the '70s. And I hate to say it, but I wasn't listening to a lot of soul music. The black music I listened to was blues and I was just discovering Chicago blues. And there were some country blues records, I didn't even know what that was. You couldn't really read about it. But I was trying to educate myself about this stuff, and I'd read interviews with people I liked. I read this interview with Pete Townsend where he said his favorite guitar player was Steve Cropper from Booker T and the MG's. So, I found a Booker T and the MG's record for a dollar that I really liked. When I started working in record stores, all of a sudden all this stuff kind of made sense. There were more and more connections between blues and garage rock, country blues and folk music, and Bob Dylan and country music. Unfortunately, jazz in my era was fusion, and I hated that stuff. But I started finding out about earlier Miles Davis and John Coltrane and started going to the farther out stuff. I was just in the process of learning about all that.

I remember playing one of the [Pink Floyd founder] Syd Barrett records to someone, I think it was *The Madcap Laughs* and they were like, "He's stopping songs in the middle." I didn't understand it, necessarily, but I'd read a review of it that sounded interesting and I bought an import. So basically when punk rock came along, it wasn't any shock to me, because it was stuff I knew about. I could tell who had listened to the Stooges and the [New York] Dolls. I actually saw the New York Dolls when I was 15.

I was definitely influenced by The Byrds, but by everything else, too. But I guess when *Murmur* came out, I remember, I bought tons of records, and nothing else sounded like it that year. I'm quite proud that it was really out of time in its own way.

I worked at a record store in Atlanta and I hated it because it was a Top 40 store. I helped a little with ordering, I could put out import stuff. I'm pretty sure it was the first place in Atlanta that had the Clash record. Honestly, it was just soul destroying to go in there every day and sell 50 copies of *Saturday Night Fever*, 50 *Grease*, 50 *Frampton*

Comes Alive. It was a really bad time for retail. I ended up moving to Athens to work at Wuxtry, which was a used records store. All the new things we had were country blues and punk rock, so that was right up my alley.

I went into Wuxtry and said, "I really like your store. I work in another record store and come in here and spend fully half my weekly paycheck buying punk records and import singles. I'd like to work with you guys." Mark, the guy who runs the place said, "You know, most people that come in here are just record store queers and I hate them. You don't seem like too much of an asshole, you're kind of normal. So if you can move to Athens by Tuesday, you've got a job." And Athens was about 60 miles away. I said, "I can do that." I called a friend who lived there and said, "Can I come crash on your floor?"

Wuxtry was the place where the 80 hipsters in town would check in fairly regularly to see if there were any good new records or if anyone knew about shows. So I met everyone in the whole scene within a month. The guy from Pylon would come in and put up their posters, and I was kind of shy, but we'd start talking. In those days, the shows were not in traditional venues; Pylon was playing in a loft with one light bulb. It was like, "Well, can I go to something like that?" I was really nervous, but I went, and I just met everybody. I started meeting women that way, and seeing all the local bands, and I thought, "Well, I'll be in a band, too."

At the time, Wuxtry was really tiny, smaller than my bedroom. But we did try to get the good stuff, and there was another record store that was a little bigger. For local bands there were really only two or three places where you could put up posters— in the record stores and there were two poles downtown. And there were only three bands. But that's how we met everyone.

For finding out about music, there was *New York Rocker*, and the college station in Athens, and the college station in Atlanta, which other people could hear, and word of mouth. There were

fanzines and a lot of bands toured, so we'd trudge to Atlanta. Things started going through Atlanta; it wasn't yet a big hub or anything, but it was also a smaller world. And occasionally you'd get a *Melody Maker* or something.

I don't buy and play vinyl as much as I used to because I travel so much. There's a used record store in Portland called Mississippi Records, they put out compilations and I buy a handful of those. But I buy lots of CDs. An iPod works for me. It used to be hell traveling when records came in. You'd go on the road for a long time and never be able to hear good new music. With a CD at least you can pack a suitcase full of stuff. I listen to music in my car, when I'm walking, on airplanes, but yeah, I still buy vinyl, and it just is a matter of how much space I have and what my attention span is. I still like 45 rpm singles; I buy a lot of those.

If I'm buying vinyl, I only buy it in stores like Mississippi in Portland. I buy interesting stuff from the '50s and '60s—I really like mono 45s, they just sound great. I must have 10,000 singles and at least the same amount of albums and probably 15,000 CDs. I've probably got a record store's worth of CDs. For me, the whole searching for records thing started just because things were out of print. There was a day when all the Lovin' Spoonful records were out of print, all The Yardbirds records, and then you realize there are a bunch of Yardbirds singles that aren't on any of the albums, even when you can find the albums. "We Love You" by The [Rolling] Stones isn't available in any way except a 45, and it's one of my favorite Stones songs, "Child of the Moon" the same thing. It was a matter of looking at the B-sides of singles and finding albums you didn't even know existed.

Peter Buck is a guitarist and co-founder of REM. In his numerous "side-project" bands he has played and toured with Robyn Hitchcock, Warren Zevon, Steve Wynn, Billy Bragg, Glenn Tilbrook and many others. He has produced records for a number of bands including Uncle Tupelo, The Fleshtones, and The Feelies.

CENSORED!

As early as 1957, album covers were causing controversy. The Five Keys' *On Stage!* featured a studio shot of the R&B vocal quintet in profile, and some overly sensitive consumers complained the barely visible forefinger of singer Rudy West resembled a penis—causing their label, Capitol, to airbrush out the offending digit.

In the ensuing years, numerous album covers have been censored, modified, or banned outright for a variety of reasons. Record companies have refused to issue albums with covers submitted by their artists, stores have refused to stock "controversial" covers, overzealous cultural commentators have perfected the art of the media driven album cover protest, and in the case of Lynyrd Skynyrd's *Street Survivors*, a tragic accident necessitated a change.

In 1966, something as innocent as a toilet could get your album cover banned. Copies of The Mama's and the Papa's *If You Can Believe Your Eyes and Ears* with the "toilet cover" are very rare.

In 1966, Capitol Records printed approximately 750,000 copies of the Beatles' *Yesterday And Today* album with the notorious "butcher cover" before deciding not to release it. A few got out, but most were pasted over with a less controversial cover, resulting in thousands of teenagers trying to steam off or otherwise remove the "trunk cover." Sealed original butcher covers have sold for as much as $30,000.

Drummer Don Stevenson is "flipping the bird" on the cover of Moby Grape's 1967 debut album; when complaints were received, Columbia Records airbrushed out the offending digit.

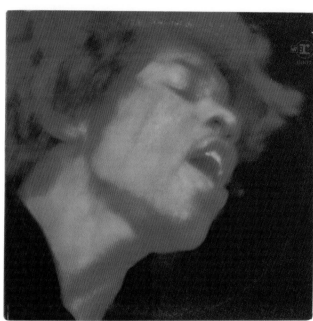

The original 1968 U.K. issue of *Electric Ladyland* by The Jimi Hendrix Experience featured 19 nude girls on the cover; the design generated enormous controversy and Hendrix's U.S. label, Reprise, designed a completely different cover.

John Lennon and Yoko Ono's 1968 album *Unfinished Music No. 1: Two Virgins* is best known for its cover, sold in the U.S. in a brown paper wrapper. Despite this precaution, copies were confiscated as obscene in a number of cities. Lennon commented that the controversy might have had more to do with the pair being unattractive, describing it as a photo of "two slightly overweight ex-junkies."

For the cover of
their 1968 album,
Beggars Banquet,
Keith Richards
and Mick Jagger
scribbled on a real
life bathroom wall
belonging to the
Porsche mechanic
of their art director.
Their U.K. based la-
bel, Decca, refused
to use the cover,
and a months-long
stalemate ensued.
Eventually, the
Stones gave in,
and the album was
issued in a cover
resembling an en-
graved invitation.

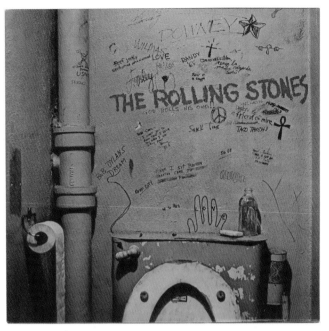

The controversal
cover for *Blind Faith*
(1968) featured an
underage girl hold-
ing a phallic space-
ship. The band's
U.S. label, Atco,
released the album
with two covers; the
original and a clean
version with the
band's photo.

Roxy Music's 1974
album, *Country Life*,
was originally sold
sealed in opaque
green shrink wrap.
That precaution
wasn't enough,
however, and a
second cover,
without the girls,
was issued.

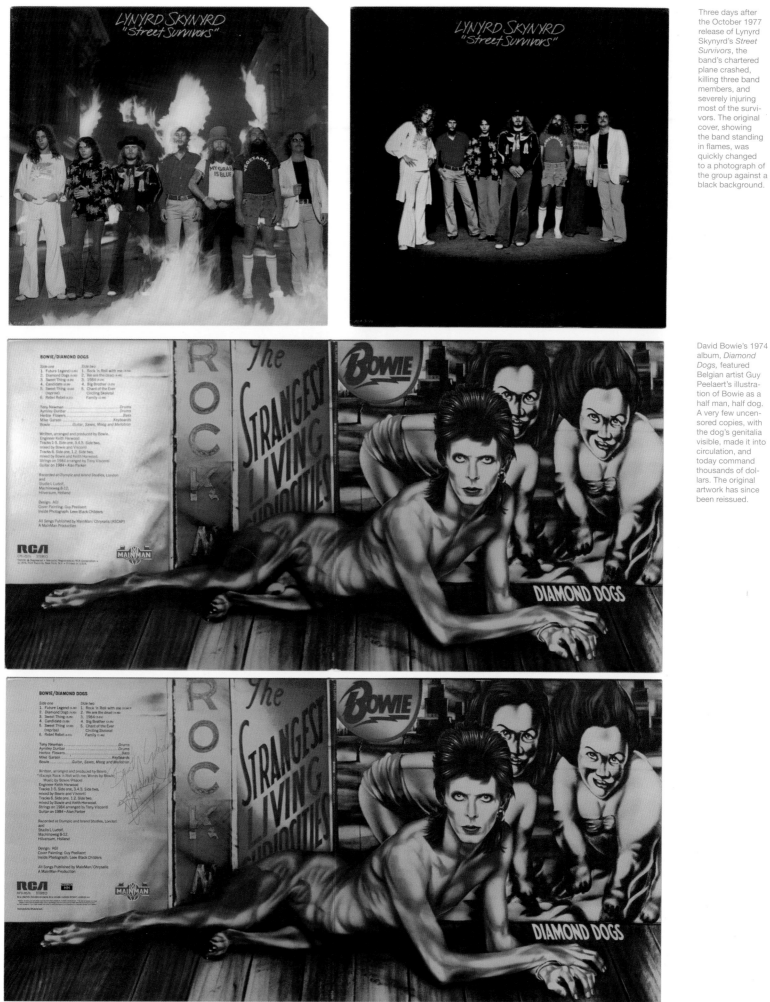

Three days after the October 1977 release of Lynyrd Skynyrd's *Street Survivors*, the band's chartered plane crashed, killing three band members, and severely injuring most of the survivors. The original cover, showing the band standing in flames, was quickly changed to a photograph of the group against a black background.

David Bowie's 1974 album, *Diamond Dogs*, featured Belgian artist Guy Peelaert's illustration of Bowie as a half man, half dog. A very few uncensored copies, with the dog's genitalia visible, made it into circulation, and today command thousands of dollars. The original artwork has since been reissued.

Jim Marshall's cover pictures the Allman Brothers against a brick wall in Macon, Georgia, moments after Duane Allman scored drugs from a local dealer who happened to be passing by.

THE ALLMAN BROTHERS BAND | At Fillmore East

July 1971 | Capricorn

Southern rock begins with this record. Tearing a page from the West Coast psych playbook, the Allmans applied ensemble unity and virtuoso turns to basic blues, extending the form into marathons that swung like mad. It helped that the excursions were led by two distinctly different but complimentary guitar stylists, the more lyrical Dickey Betts and the brazenly creative Duane Allman, who'd already distinguished himself in Eric Clapton's Derek & the Dominos and on landmark records by Wilson Pickett, Aretha Franklin, and others. This double LP broke the band (after two well-received albums), with a bristling mix of incendiary jams, most notably "You Don't Love Me" and the FM-radio staples "Whipping Post" and "In Memory of Elizabeth Reed," and soul-inflected, yet subtle, vocals from keyboardist Gregg Allman. One of America's great 'survivor bands,' the Allmans soldier on, touring the world and recording despite the twin tragedies of Duane and bassist Berry Oakley's deaths (1971 and 1972). Jim Marshall's documentary-style cover photo perfectly captures the good-humored, band-on-the-job attitude of musicians who showed up and worked hard to make magic night after night. "This ain't no fashion show," *Mojo* quoted Duane Allman as saying, "We came here to play."

Capricorn records was co-owned by Allmans manager, Phil Walden.

The back cover shows the band's roadies, drinking Pabst Blue Ribbon beer provided by Marshall as a reward for stacking the band's equipment cases.

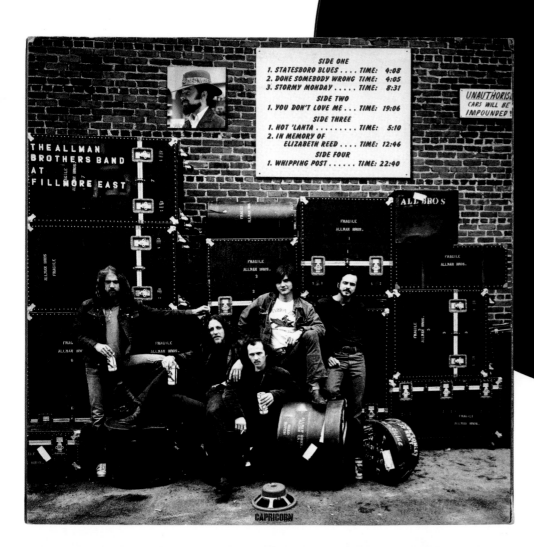

SIDE ONE
1. STATESBORO BLUES .... TIME: 4:08
2. DONE SOMEBODY WRONG TIME: 4:05
3. STORMY MONDAY ..... TIME: 8:31

SIDE TWO
1. YOU DON'T LOVE ME ... TIME: 19:06

SIDE THREE
1. HOT 'LANTA .... TIME: 5:10
2. IN MEMORY OF
   ELIZABETH REED .... TIME: 12:46

SIDE FOUR
1. WHIPPING POST ..... TIME: 22:40

THE ALLMAN BROTHERS BAND AT FILLMORE EAST

UNAUTHORISE
CARS WILL BE
IMPOUNDED

CAPRICORN

SD 2-802
THE ALLMAN
BROTHERS BAND
AT FILLMORE EAST

STEREO   ONE

1. STATESBORO BLUES (4:08)
   Will McTell
2. DONE SOMEBODY WRONG (4:05)
   Thomas-Lewis-James-Robinson
3. STORMY MONDAY (8:31)
   T. Bone Walker

(ST-CAP-712223-MO)

DIST. BY ATCO, DIV. OF ATLANTIC RECORDING CORP., 1841 B'WAY, N.Y, N.Y.

GENESIS | Nursery Cryme

November 1971 | Charisma

While many art-rock and prog-rock groups of the era bent their heads to their keyboards to wander in search of lost chords, Genesis offered something different. As heard on *Nursery Cryme*, their third LP but the first to feature the familiar Gabriel-Collins-Hackett-Banks-Rutherford lineup, the band is just as instrumentally capable as its peers but conspicuously more literate and humorous. "The Musical Box" and "The Return of the Giant Hogweed" are multi-parted epics, replete with changing prog tempos, but they're also narratives told with whimsy and mordant wit: the former a Victorian tale of a young girl who, among other things, whacks her young suitor's head with a croquet mallet, the latter an account of England being subjugated by a viral weed imported from Russia. More compact but equally odd is the perky story of "Harold the Barrel," a restaurateur who cuts off and serves his toes to his customers before committing suicide.

The album staked Genesis' claim to a uniquely clever brand of smart-rock, one that served it well through *Foxtrot, Selling England by the Pound, The Lamb Lies Down on Broadway,* and Peter Gabriel's solo career.

An original pressing with the rare Charisma pink scroll label.

Faust's debut album had a transparent disc and cover; producer Uwe Nettelbeck is credited with album design, and Andy Hertel as the fist model.

Faust's debut album had a transparent disc and cover; producer Uwe Nettelbeck is credited with album design, and Andy Hertel as the fist model.

FAUST | Faust

Circa November 1971 | Polydor

"It's what's inside that counts," goes the old adage. For many rock fans, though, it was the striking outside of German band Faust's first album that sparked curiosity and beckoned them in for a closer look. Pressed on clear vinyl, the band's name embossed on a silver label, with a translucent sleeve depicting an X-ray of a clenched hand, *Faust* (German for "fist") breached the farthest boundaries of progressive rock at the time of its release. The sextet relies on various keyboards, sax, and guitar to generate instrumental storms that fade in like transmissions from space, then erupt into violent collages of electronic zaps, fuzz guitar, surreal dialogue, and, particularly on the 16-minute "Miss Fortune," multiple rhythms playing against each other. Amazingly, it all works, the album's three tracks constituting a head-trip whose ultimate "meaning" remains deliciously ungraspable. No less an authority than Julien Cope, British rock musician and author of the definitive *Krautrocksampler*, said, "There is no band more mysterious than Faust."

I can't get no satisf...
you need... love

...goose
...on your
...trick

Ben setzte sich in einen Sessel. Jill nahm zu seinen Füßen im Gras Platz. Ihnen gegenüber stand ein 3-D-Gerät, das als Aquarium getarnt war. Als Ben es anschaltete, verschwanden die Zierfische: "A pregnant 25-year old mother of three was fatally shot by an upstairs neighbor in her apartment house when she complained about noise the woman was making, police reported. Mrs. Joyce Walker, 3445 South La Brea Avenue, was hit in the abdomen by a 22-caliber derringer bullet and died an hour and 20 minutes later in Central Receiving Hospital. Booked on suspicion of ... was the neighbor, Helen Holloway, ..." ließ ein Truck... ansah... und Er schien... men. "Bitte... mer du... des FBI in Los Ang... ing." Er ...schoß förmlich aus seinem Mustang heraus. Im ...annte Licht, und die singenden Mädchen ...auf die Straße zu hören. Er klingel- ...niemand meldete, stieß er die Tür ...schlug ihm der Geruch von Blut ...Zimmer war leer. Er schaltete ...arat aus. Jetzt erst bemerkte ...unter der Couch. "Wie reizend ...rte sie. Er war am Rande des ...lasse Ihnen Badewasser ein- ...en und ...etwas Calgon Bath Oil hinzu. ...wird Sie ...pannen", schlug er erstickt ...zurück. Ihre Augen verdreh- ...sie ihre Hände auf die be- ...Produzenten legte. "Ich mag ...sagte sie. "Wie heißen Sie", ...ne", antwortete sie, "Daphne ...in Tänzerin, aber ich arbeite zur Zei... Ich wohne mit meinem Freund ...Beverly Hills Hotel." "Oh", sagte er ent- ...erher führte er sie zur Sauna. Er ...en Himmel. "Soll ich Ihnen noch ein- ...n Geschlechtsteil zeigen", fragte sie ...end mit ihrer tiefen, aufgerauhten und in- ...en Stimme, wobei ihr sagenhafter Busen ge- nau auf ihn zeigte und ihn blenden zu wollen ...schien. Oberst John Damon, der aus zweifelhaf- ten Gründen seine Frauenkleider noch nicht abgelegt hatte, griff ebenfalls zum Telefon. Er war Kommandeur der Flugbasis Homestead im Süden von Miami. Diese Militärdienststelle arbeitete eng mit der CIA zusammen. Daphne La Salle ruht in einem Grab des Westwood Friedhofs. Die Trauerfeier, ein unwirkliches, heimliches Begräbnis unter einem strahlend hellen Himmel, hatte keine zehn Minuten gedauert. Ben sagte zu Jill: "Auch die heißeste Nachrichtensendung geht einmal zu Ende."

Polydor
FAUST
GEMA
Made in Germany
MISS FORTUNE (Faust) 17:55
Produced by Uwe Nettelbeck

Side 1:
Why don't you ...
Meadow Meal

Werner Diermaier
Joachim Irmler
Arnulf Meifert
Jean-Hervé Peron
Rudolf Sosna
Gunther Wüsthoff

Kurt Graupner
Andy Hertel

Uwe Nettelbeck

Stereo, also playable mono
Manufactured by
Deutsche Grammophon, Hamburg
Printed in Germany,
Imprimé en Allemagne by
Dyrbye & Hartmann, Hamburg

...recorded ...1971

Big Star took their name from a Memphis area grocery store chain; Carole Manning designed the literal album cover, featuring a neon star by Memphis artist Ron Pekar.

BIG STAR | #1 Record

From the beginning, Alex Chilton's post-Box Tops enterprise seems to have been destined for both obscurity and fame. The Memphis group's second LP was issued on the fledgling rock imprint of a major soul label and lost in a promotional limbo: AM stations found Big Star's amalgam of Byrds, Beach Boys, and Brit Invasion too darkly quirky, while FM-ers heavily invested in "heavy" prog and overcooked blues-rock dismissed it as too pop. But the band's introduction, at the 1973 Rock Writers' Convention in Memphis, lit a long fuse on a career that burned slowly and intensely for decades. Critical praise and word-of-mouth testimonials for the band's hyper-melodic music and left-of-center lyrics turned Big Star into the prime example of a cult band whose circle of influence far outstripped its sales figures. *Radio City* quickly became an out-of-print item, but throughout the years, copies circulated widely among the cognoscenti.

April 1972 | Ardent

Knowing "September Gurls" and "Mod Lang" was the secret handshake that bonded together a growing community of fans, many of whom later used what they heard to fashion power-pop and alternative rock. R.E.M., Cheap Trick, the Replacements, Primal Scream, Posies, Teenage Fanclub, and Wilco are just a few groups whose music has reflected the influence of Big Star and its most beloved record.

Legendary photographer Robert Frank shot the Stones with an 8 millimeter movie camera for the *Exile* cover, pulling frames from the film footage and combining them with older photographs he'd taken on a road trip across America.

THE ROLLING STONES | Exile On Main St.

May 1972 | Rolling Stones

Handing it an A+ grade upon release, the *Village Voice*'s reviewer wrote that *Exile* was a "difficult masterpiece," with Mick Jagger's voice often submerged under layers of "studio murk." He also proclaimed it a unique record that "rocks with extra power and concentration." Who knew then that the album's dense air and attitude would exert such a tug that, within a decade, it would be heralded as the quintessential Stones album. Coming from a band that has always prized economy, *Exile* sprawls and tumbles across four sides, exhibiting a raw, improvisational feel that betrays the circumstances of its creation. These are mostly substance-enhanced sessions conducted in the basement of a decrepit manse in the south of France. Miraculously, it all coheres: the woozy country of "Sweet Virginia" and careening '50s rock of "Rip This Joint," the churchy "Shine a Light," and the slide-fueled "Stop Breaking Down." Two hit singles debuted on *Exile*, both largely Keith Richards' compositions, the certified Stones classic "Tumbling Dice" and "Happy." The support cast is star-filled (Billy Preston, Doctor John, Nicky Hopkins, Bobby Keys, Clydie King, and Vanetta Fields), but the achievement is the Stones' alone, from the free-range patchwork of songs down to the selection of Robert Frank's cover photography of freaks and outcasts. This is a classic in every respect.

Exile was released on the band's own label, Rolling Stones Records.

The inner sleeves combined Frank's photos and Mick Jagger's handwritten credits.

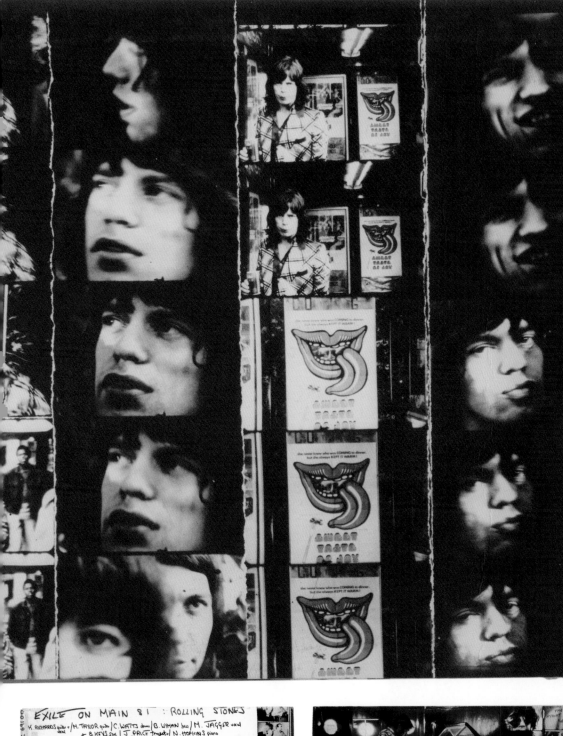

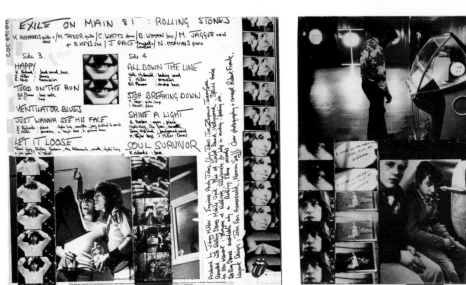

The album included a set of 12 postcards, with photograps by Norman Seeff.

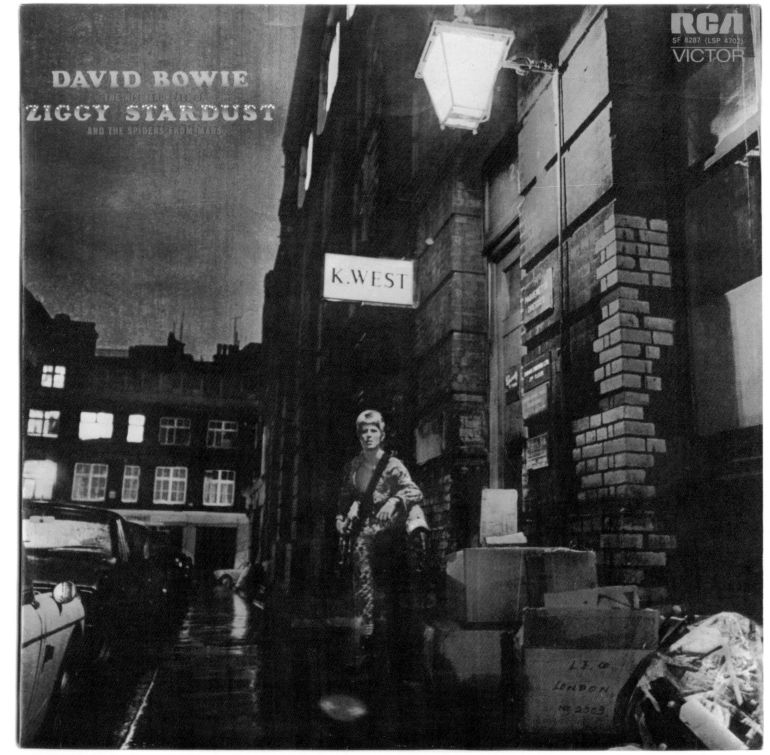

DAVID BOWIE
The Rise And Fall Of Ziggy Stardust And The Spiders From Mars

June 1972 | RCA

The fifth time proved the charm for Bowie. All of his previous albums, in particular *David Bowie* (*Space Oddity), The Man Who Sold the World*, and *Hunky Dory*, led to this place, where his fascination with role-playing and musical shape-shifting firmly congealed. He effectively presents Ziggy Stardust as a character (the alien-turned-idealized rock star), a concept album, a performing attraction at the head of a fully staged touring production, and an enduring, near-mythic piece of pop-music arcana. Ziggy's tale is told on a cache of tracks that traverse everything from first-generation rock 'n' roll ("Hang on to Yourself," which rechannels Eddie Cochran, and "Suffragette City") and neo-doowop ("Rock and Roll Suicide") to sci-fi balladry ("Starman") and Beatles-esque musings ("Moonage Daydream"). Co-conspirator Mick Ronson (guitar, piano, vocals, arranging) helped Bowie achieve his

vision, one that yielded an international best-selling LP, invented glam-rock and launched Bowie on an irreversible path to superstardom. Not the least consequential aspect of *Ziggy*'s success was that it led to the rerelease of his back catalog, which made fresh hit singles of "Changes" and "Space Oddity." The album also sparked pop's momentary fling with androgyny and eccentric hairstyles, further testimony to its having created an honest-to-goodness pop-cultural moment.

DAVID BOWIE
ZIGGY STARDUST

A GEM PRODUCTION

SIDE 1.

FIVE YEARS (4:42)
SOUL LOVE (3:34)
MOONAGE DAYDREAM (4:40)
STARMAN (4:10)
IT AIN'T EASY (2:58)

SIDE 2.

LADY STARDUST (3:22)
STAR (2:47)
HANG ON TO YOURSELF (2:40)
ZIGGY STARDUST (3:13)
SUFFRAGETTE CITY (3:25)
ROCK 'n' ROLL SUICIDE (2:58)

THE MUSICIANS ARE:
DAVID BOWIE-GUITAR, SAX AND VOCALS.
MICK RONSON-GUITAR, PIANO AND VOCALS.
TREVOR BOLDER-BASS.
MICK WOODMANSEY-DRUMS.

ARRANGEMENTS:
DAVID BOWIE AND MICK RONSON.

ALBUM PRODUCTION:
DAVID BOWIE AND KEN SCOTT
AT TRIDENT STUDIOS, LONDON.

PHOTOGRAPHS:
BRIAN WARD.

ART WORK:
TERRY PASTOR OF MAIN ARTERY.

TO BE PLAYED AT MAXIMUM VOLUME.

"Stereo records give full stereo reproduction when played on a stereo record player. They can be played on most modern mono record players fitted with a lightweight tone arm and pick-up head and the sound reproduction will be monaural. If you have doubts and wish to avoid damaging your equipment or records, consult your dealer."

RCA
SF 8287 (LSP 4702)
VICTOR

© 1972 RCA LIMITED   Printed in England by Robert Stace

RCA LIMITED, RECORD DIVISION, RCA HOUSE, CURZON STREET, LONDON W1

At the bottom of the back cover is the message "To Be Played At Maximum Volume."

The inner sleeve with band photos.

Original discs carry the credit "A Gem Production."

223

The front cover featured only Mick Rock's classic photo of Iggy Pop.

IGGY AND THE STOOGES | Raw Power

February 1973 | Columbia

It says something about rock's ascent to the status of serious art that, by the 1980s and '90s, many landmark albums were being reissued with additional material, scholarly annotation and, in some cases, remixes that addressed the audio shortcomings of their original editions. Iggy's 1997 re-do of *Raw Power* fits into this category, and, while his version improves upon David Bowie's original, overly brittle-sounding version of the album, there was never any question about the fundamental strength of the songs and performances that comprised this record. Bowie's imprimatur, though, along with legendarily wild stage shows, is what brought Iggy to the attention of most music fans and effectively transformed him from critical cult favorite to certified pop icon. The album only furthers and intensifies the furious sound that earlier stunned critics and cognoscenti on *The Stooges* and *Fun House*. And the tunes, among them "Search and

Destroy," "Shake Appeal," and "Gimme Danger," provide the footbridge that allowed the band to sprint from its isolated perch as the lone artisans of fierce minimalist rock 'n' roll to the forefront of one of music's most revolutionary genres: punk. *Raw Power* remains a recording of undeniable sonic power and raw, unyielding artistic vision.

IGGY AND THE STOOGES
RAW POWER

SIDE 1
Search And Destroy
Gimme Danger
Your Pretty Face Is Going To Hell
   (Originally titled "Hard To Beat")
Penetration

SIDE 2
Raw Power
I Need Somebody
Shake Appeal
Death Trip

All tunes were written by Iggy Pop
and James Williamson.
Iggy Pop—vocals
James Williamson—guitars
Ron Asheton—bass and vocals
Scott Asheton—drums

Produced by Iggy Pop for MainMan.
A MainMan Production.
Mixed by David Bowie
and Iggy Pop. All selections
published by MainMan, Ltd. (ASCAP)
Recorded at CBS Studios, London.
Mixed at Western Sound, Hollywood.
Photography: Mick Rock.
Iggy and The Stooges represented
exclusively by MainMan, Ltd.

32111

IGGY AND
THE STOOGES
RAW POWER

KC 32111   SIDE 1
STEREO   AL 32111
                          ℗ 1973 CBS, Inc.

1. SEARCH AND DESTROY 3:26
2. GIMME DANGER 3:28
3. YOUR PRETTY FACE IS
   GOING TO HELL 4:52
4. PENETRATION 3:35

- I. Pop - J. Williamson -

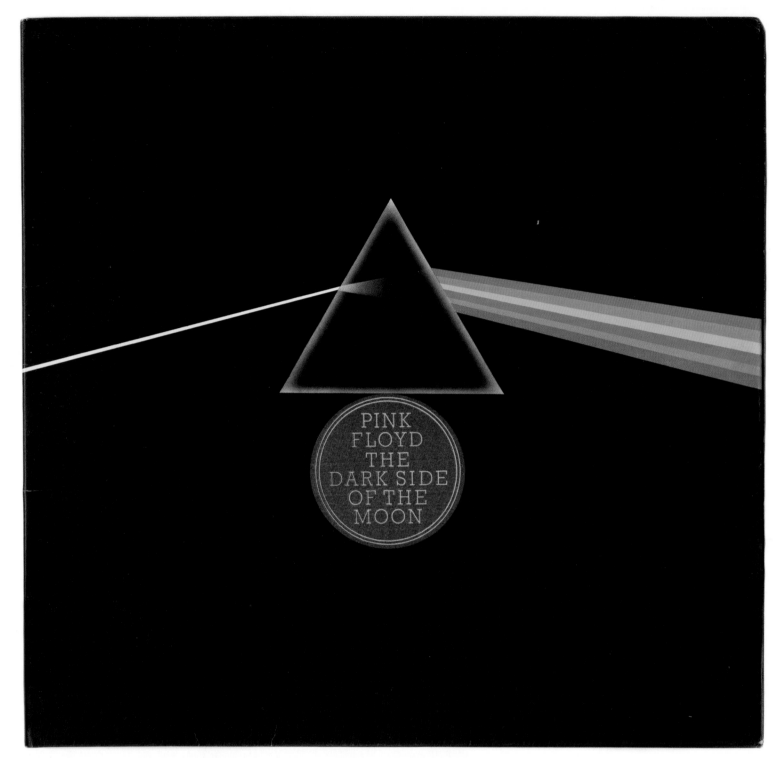

The cover by Hipgnosis and George Hardie had no type; early copies were stickered with band name and album title.

PINK FLOYD | The Dark Side of the Moon   **March 1973 | Harvest**

Much like *Sgt. Pepper's Lonely Hearts Club Band* or *Tapestry*, Pink Floyd's eighth album occupied a prized place in a great many households: more than 45 million to date. One of the best-selling LPs of all time, *Dark Side* reshaped public perception about a prog quartet whose long-form instrumental music was characterized by its own guitarist (David Gilmour) as "psychedelic noodling." The album spent more than 14 years on *Billboard*'s chart—proof of an appeal that, unlike other momentarily popular blockbusters, spanned more than one pop-music generation. Pink Floyd still flexes its marathon muscles here ("Time" and the ominous "Us and Them"), but the album, whose subjects include greed, isolation, and madness, is also anchored by earthbound roots—Clare Torry's post-Aretha gospelisms on "The Great Gig in the Sky," and "Money," which burnishes a riff on loan from Sonny Boy Williamson's "Help Me." "Money" became

a Top-40 and FM-radio staple and still spins as a grandfathered-in track on oldies formats. Notwithstanding the subsequent successes of *The Wall* and *The Division Bell*, *Dark Side of the Moon* defined Pink Floyd as an indefatigable brand built on high concepts, provocative packaging, and an ensemble identity. The persistent, though since dispelled myth that the album was intended as an after-the-fact soundtrack to *The Wizard of Oz* only added to the aura of mystery that has always surrounded the band.

On the label:

THE GRAMOPHONE CO LTD. ALL RIGHTS OF THE MANUFACTURER AND OF THE OWNER OF THE RECORDED WORK RESERVED

EMI · Harvest

PINK FLOYD

SIDE 1
(P) 1973
The Gramophone
Company Limited

STEREO
SHVL 804
(04A) 33⅓

World Copyrights Ltd.
Lyrics by Roger Waters
Music by Pink Floyd
Produced by Pink Floyd

UNAUTHORISED PUBLIC PERFORMANCE BROADCASTING AND COPYING OF THIS RECORD PROHIBITED

MADE IN GT BRITAIN

On the sleeve:

SHVL 804
(JE 054 + 05249)
stereo

Highly collectible
first pressings
feature labels with a
solid blue triangle.

The album package also included two posters.

Two pyramid stickers were included in the package.

Inside gatefold.

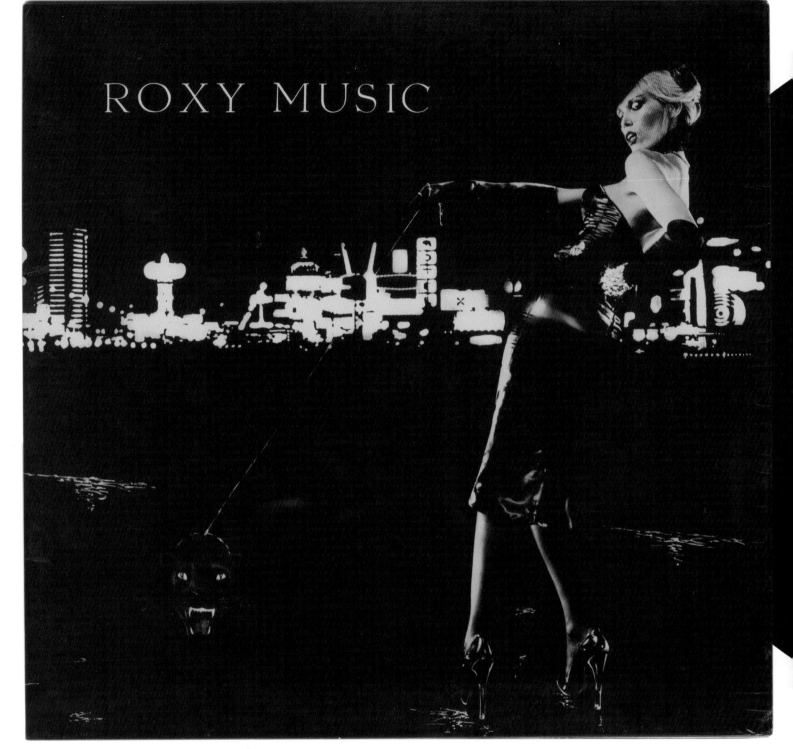

ROXY MUSIC | For Your Pleasure

March 1973 | Island

An assemblage of wholly diverse parts that manages to be elegantly original, Roxy Music prefigured contemporary "mash-ups" by three decades. Ferry's Forties matinee-idol suavity, Andrew Mackay's bleating '50s sax playing, and Phil Manzanera's scratchy, Stones-meets-Velvets guitar playing connect for unprecedented effect in the band's 1973 sophomore set. The futuristic, rule-busting contributions of the band came from its most influential member, Brian Eno, whose synthesizer work layers the record with a pervasive, and compelling strangeness. "Do the Strand" and "Editions of You" set forth utterly fresh ways to "rock." The ballads "Beauty Queen" and "For Your Pleasure" oddly blend romance and irony, and on "In Every Dream Home a Heartache" Ferry couches his critique of modern living in an ode to an inflatable doll. The net result: *For Your Pleasure* created a

self-contained musical universe that challenged Roxy's successors to go heavy on the ideas without forsaking the essential groove.

FOR YOUR PLEASURE
THE SECOND ROXY MUSIC ALBUM

1. DO THE STRAND (4.00)
2. BEAUTY QUEEN (4.35)
3. STRICTLY CONFIDENTIAL (3.42)
4. EDITIONS OF YOU (3.40)
5. IN EVERY DREAM HOME A HEARTACHE (4.25)

All songs written by Bryan Ferry
Published by ◉ Music Ltd. © 1973
Produced by Chris Thomas and Roxy Music for ◉ Records Ltd.

ROXY MUSIC   ILPS-9232-A

℗ 1973 Island
Records Ltd

ISLAND

ILPS 9232

The back cover
featured Ferry as
Lear's chauffeur.

This first pressing
has Island's pink
rim label.

The inner gatefold,
signed by band
members (left to
right) Brian Eno,
Phil Manzanera,
Bryan Ferry, Andy
Mackay, and Paul
Thompson, with
bassist John Porter
at bottom.

FOR YOUR PLEASURE...
The second Roxy Music Album

Photography – Karl Stoecker
Art direction – Nicholas de Ville
Artwork – C.C.S.
Amanda's clothes; hair and
make-up – Anthony Price
Roxy hair – Smile
Crew – Jennings and Hort
© Island Records 1973

SIDE ONE
Do the Strand
Beauty Queen
Strictly Confidential
Editions of You
In every Dream Home a Heartache

SIDE TWO
The Bogus Man
Grey Lagoons
For your Pleasure

Words and Music by Bryan Ferry

Bryan Ferry – Voice and Keyboards
Andrew Mackay – Oboe and Saxophone
Eno – Synthesizer and Tapes
Paul Thompson – Drums
Phil Manzanera – Guitar
Guest artiste : John Porter – Bass

Recorded at AIR Studios
London, February 1973
Engineers: John Middleton and John Punter
Produced by Chris Thomas and Roxy Music
for E.G. Records
Special thanks to John Anthony
All songs arranged by Roxy Music
All songs published by E. G. Music Ltd.℗ 1973

231

Stereo SRM.1.675

NEW YORK DOLLS | New York Dolls

July 1973 | Mercury

Despite isolated islands of hope like Stooges' *Raw Power* and the Velvets' *Loaded*, the early 1970s weren't an especially fruitful period for basic rock 'n' roll. New music that adhered to the noisy principles of '50s and '60s form was rare when metal, prog, country-rock, and singer-songwriters ruled the day. Then, the Dolls arrived. The band's startling image drew the most attention, but this Todd Rundgren-produced debut, a critical fave and a commercial dud, had a far greater subliminal, and subversive, effect than sales figures suggested. David Johansen's Jagger-ish vocals and Johnny Thunders' crashing guitar animate a slate of ragged originals (plus a cover of Bo Diddley's "Pills") that pay homage to girl-group pop ("Trash," "Lookin' for a Kiss") and early Stones ("Personality Crisis," "Subway Train") in a stateside version of the kind of good-times rock being made in the U.K. by the Faces. The Dolls would have the last laugh on

their detractors, though. Before the decade ended, they'd be hailed as a major inspiration for the Ramones and the Sex Pistols (the latter's manager, Malcom McLaren, had once performed the same role for the Dolls).

Side 1: Personality Crisis/Looking For A Kiss/Vietnamese Baby/Lonely Planet Boy/Frankenstein (Orig.)
Side 2: Trash/Bad Girl/Subway Train/Pills/Private World/Jet Boy

℗ 1973 Phonogram Inc. All selections published by Seldak Music Corp./Hanenshaw Pub., Inc.(ASCAP) except "Pills" published by Arc Music Corp. (BMI)

Produced by Todd Rundgren
Engineers: Jack Douglas & Ed Sprigg • Mastering: Sterling Sound • Recorded at Record Plant Studios, New York
The Dolls are:
Johnny Thunders–Guitar, Vocals • Sylvain Sylvain–Guitar, Piano, Vocals • David Jo Hansen–Vocals, Harmonica, Gong
Arthur Harold Kane–Bass • Jerry Nolan–Drums
All arrangements by The New York Dolls
Additional Piano & Moog–Todd Rundgren • Saxophone–The Fantastic Buddy Bowser
Photography: Toshi • Hair: Shin • Makeup: Dave O'Grady • Cover Coordination: Album Graphics, Inc.
Executive Producers: Marty Thau, Steve Leber, David Krebs, Paul Nelson
The New York Dolls are represented exclusively by Dollhouse, Inc.
Special thanks: Paul Nelson, Bud Scoppa, Betty Thau, Peter Jordan, Max, Keeth, Christian, Desmond
A Dollhouse, Inc. Production • 575 Lexington Ave., New York City, N.Y. 10022
This album is dedicated to Billy Doll

Also available on Musikassette and Stereo 8 Tapes MCR-4-1-675–MC-8-1-675   Manufactured and Distributed by Phonogram, Inc., One IBM Plaza, Chicago, Illinois 60611

The back cover
was shot in front of
Gem Spa in New
York City.

The custom inner
sleeve.

Mercury Records
gave the Dolls this
custom record
label.

German painter and poet Emil Schult created the *Autobahn* cover and many others for Kraftwerk. He also co-wrote lyrics for them and breifly played guitar in the band. The blue and white Autobahn logo is on a sticker.

KRAFTWERK | Autobahn

November 1974 | Philips

Krautrock's first bestseller had an unlikely genesis that served art by nakedly engaging with commerce. Where Bob Dylan had negotiated the time-space continuum by dividing "Like a Rolling Stone" into two halves of a 45-rpm single, Kraftwerk answered the challenge by cutting the 22 minutes of the side-long "Autobahn" down to a three-minute single. The result was an unlikely hit that introduced the world to a high-concept, mostly electronic German quartet that had run on cruise-control through three LPs of experimental, decidedly non-pop music. *Autobahn* changed that with an infectiously droning Moog-driven program designed as an audio simulation of a road trip. "Autobahn" is one of five tracks that separate the journey into alternately restful and incrementally busier moods. It would be hard to overestimate the influence of Kraftwerk in general, and *Autobahn* in particular, on popular music. Both have had an undeniable,

continuing impact on genres as disparate as disco and New Wave, trance and ambient music and electronica, and on the work of such artists as David Bowie, Blondie, Depeche Mode, Afrika Bambaataa, Jay-Z, Duran Duran, Coldplay, and Joy Division.

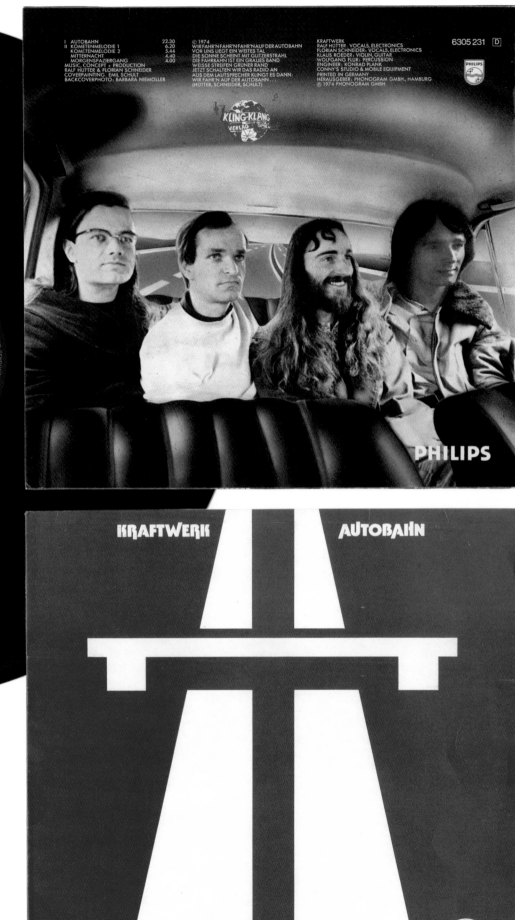

I   AUTOBAHN   22.30
II KOMETENMELODIE 1   6.20
    KOMETENMELODIE 2   5.44
    MITTERNACHT   4.40
    MORGENSPAZIERGANG   4.00
MUSIC, CONCEPT + PRODUCTION
RALF HÜTTER & FLORIAN SCHNEIDER
COVERPAINTING: EMIL SCHULT
BACKCOVERPHOTO: BARBARA NIEMÖLLER

℗ 1974
WIR FAHR'N FAHR'N FAHR'N AUF DER AUTOBAHN
VOR UNS LIEGT EIN WEITES TAL
DIE SONNE SCHEINT MIT GLITZERSTRAHL
DIE FAHRBAHN IST EIN GRAUES BAND
WEISSE STREIFEN GRÜNER RAND
JETZT SCHALTEN WIR DAS RADIO AN
AUS DEM LAUTSPRECHER KLINGT ES DANN:
WIR FAHR'N AUF DER AUTOBAHN . . .
(HÜTTER, SCHNEIDER, SCHULT)

KRAFTWERK
RALF HÜTTER: VOCALS, ELECTRONICS
FLORIAN SCHNEIDER: VOCALS, ELECTRONICS
KLAUS ROEDER: VIOLIN, GUITAR
WOLFGANG FLUR: PERCUSSION
ENGINEER: KONRAD PLANK
CONNY'S STUDIO & MOBILE EQUIPMENT
PRINTED IN GERMANY
HERAUSGEBER: PHONOGRAM GMBH., HAMBURG
℗ 1974 PHONOGRAM GMBH

6305 231 D

KLING-KLANG
VERLAG GMBH

PHILIPS

PHILIPS
STEREO 33⅓ ∞
GEMA   6305 231
          AA 6305 231.1 Y   1
          Made in Germany

Autobahn
Autobahn
(R. Hütter/F. Schneider) 22:30
KRAFTWERK
℗ 1974 PHONOGRAM GmbH

KRAFTWERK   AUTOBAHN

VERTIGO

U.K. Vertigo released *Autobahn* with this cover.

For the *Born To Run* cover, photographer Eric Meola shot 900 photographs of Springsteen in a 3 hour session. Meola noted, "Other things happened, but when we saw the contact sheets, that one just sort of popped. Instantly we knew that was the shot."

BRUCE SPRINGSTEEN | Born To Run

August 1975 | Columbia

"I saw rock and roll's future, and its name is Bruce Springsteen." The testimony was critic Jon Landau's, uttered in May of 1974. Landau's proclamation came true just over a year later, with the release of this album. *Born to Run* launched a phenomenon, built an empire, and established one of the most influential figures in modern pop. It was also a profoundly radical record; in the pre-punk '70s, the heyday of introspective singer-songwriters and chest-pounding metallurgists, Springsteen reinvented rock with what *Rolling Stone*'s Greil Marcus called "a magnificent album…a '57 Chevy running on melted down Crystals records." Onstage or on vinyl, Springsteen's performances of "Thunder Road," "Born to Run," and "Jungleland" were impossible not to get swept up in: big, romantic, heart-pumping narratives whose very sound was liberating—and powerful enough to shut out the rest of the world as long as they played. This is

direct, impassioned music-making without a single disingenuous or merely expedient note. It all seems to matter to Springsteen, who is intent on communicating precisely that to the audience. Even its dark themes (aging, compromised ethics, lowered expectations) are delivered with abundant energy and hope. These songs still inform Springsteen's set lists more than three decades later, suggesting the immeasurable impact *Born to Run* had and continues to have.

Inside gatefold.

Advance test pressings were sent out with this alternate sleeve, known as the script cover. Mint copies have sold for over $1,500.

Back cover; the album was designed by John Berg and Andy Engel.

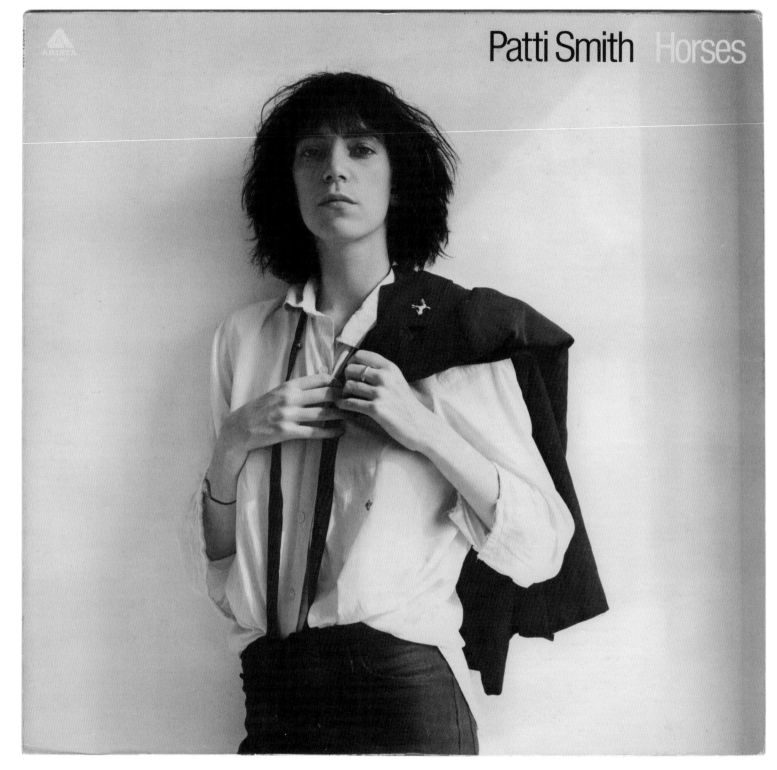

PATTI SMITH | Horses

December 1975 | Arista

Smith's debut album is noteworthy in several respects. *Horses* brought forth a totally original artist whose vision melded the visceral energy of rock 'n' roll with a literate, even poetic, sensibility and established several historical precedents. Not the least of these was Smith's pioneering stance as a woman fronting a hard-rock band—something that had been in short supply ever since Grace Slick and Janis Joplin first supplanted the girl-group singers of the early '60s. Smith's charismatic presence, her role in the band (penning all the songs save two covers) and the group's performances inspired subsequent female performers and helped spark New York's incipient punk scene. Fervid readings of Van Morrison's "Gloria," and her own "Land" and "Free Money," highlight a set that deftly yolks early Velvet Underground style to the shamanistic ramblings of Jim Morrison and points toward the fortified primitivism of the Ramones, whose debut was then four months distant. *Horses* got FM airplay and reams of positive press (the *Village Voice* praised her "revolutionary" singing and the band's "minimalist fury"), and made permanent fans of R.E.M.'s Peter Buck and Michael Stipe, the Smiths' Morrissey and Johnny Marr, U2, and Siouxsie and the Banshees.

AL 4066

richard sohl: piano

lenny kaye: lead guitar

ivan kral: guitar, bass

jay dee daugherty: drums

compacted awareness . . gems flattening . . long streams of resin tools . . kool system of destine wax sculpt . . drums tongue and waves slapping . . the feel of horses long before horses enter the scene . . molten tar stud dead w/bones and glass and the teeth of women . . . veins filled w/existance . . beyond race gender baptism mathmatics poli-tricks . . . assassinating rythum . . c-rude transending . . soul-ar energy in the shape of a laughing pack of scarabs dressed in coats of milk armour . . grace greased w/merc and henna . . . hair wires . . neither the desire nor the ability to stop i plop on the bed pink electric immediate some human light bulb these bands around my neck should reveal what state i'm in . . only history (gentle rocking mona lisa) seals . . only histoire is responsible for the ultimate cannonizing . . as for me i am truly totally ready to go . . .

sonic klein man its me my shape burnt in the sky its me the memoire of me racing thru the eye of the mer thru the eye of the sea thru the arm of the needle merging and jacking new filaments new risks etched forever in a cold system of wax . . horses groping for a sign for a breath . . .

charms. sweet angels—you have made me no longer afraid of death.

gloria/redondo beach/birdland/free money
kimberly/break it up/land/elegie

produced by: john cale

executive producer: wartoke records inc.
engineering: bernie kirsh
assistant engineer: frank d'augusta

recorded and mixed at electric lady studios nyc
mastered by bernie kirsh and bob ludwig at sterling sound inc.
guitars on break it up: tom verlaine (television)
guitars on elegie: allen lanier* (blue oyster cult)
birdland was inspired by peter reich and huey smith
*allen lanier appears through the courtesy of columbia records

photography: robert mapplethorpe   design: bob heimall

patti smith is exclusively managed by the wartoke concern inc. nyc

special thanks to jane friedman who knew . . .
de l'ame pour l'ame

ARISTA

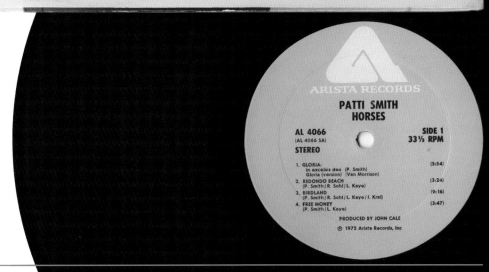

ARISTA RECORDS

PATTI SMITH
HORSES

AL 4066   SIDE 1
(AL 4066 SA)   33⅓ RPM
STEREO

1. GLORIA:
   in excelsis deo (P. Smith)   (5:54)
   Gloria (version) (Van Morrison)
2. REDONDO BEACH   (3:24)
   (P. Smith / R. Sohl / L. Kaye)
3. BIRDLAND   (9:16)
   (P. Smith / R. Sohl / L. Kaye / I. Kral)
4. FREE MONEY   (3:47)
   (P. Smith / L. Kaye)

PRODUCED BY JOHN CALE

℗ 1975 Arista Records, Inc

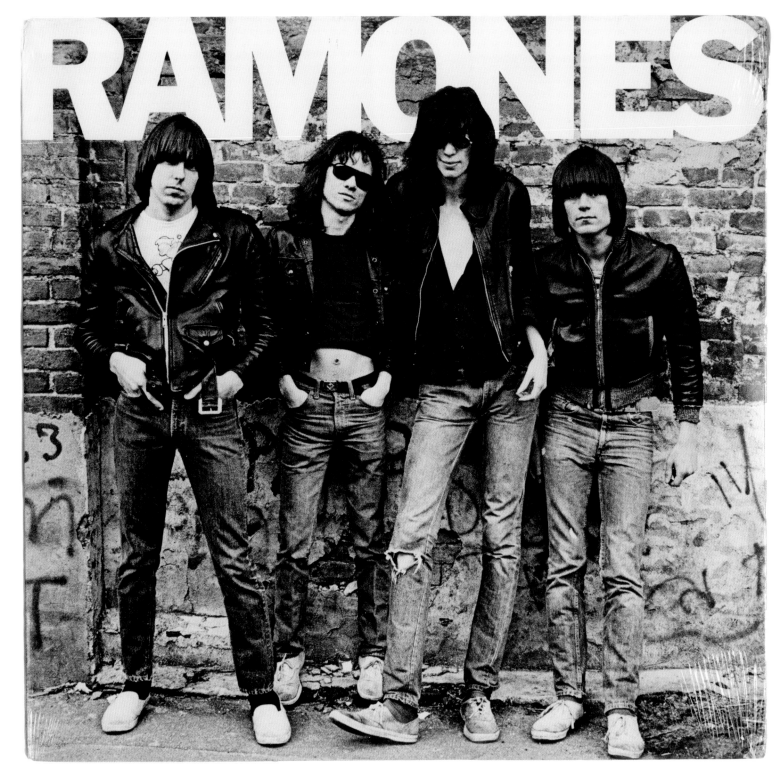

RAMONES | Ramones

April 1976 | Sire

A revolutionary record by one of popular music's most original bands, *Ramones* sold poorly but influenced widely. This was, as critic Jon Savage put it, "the one record that could truly be called a paradigm shift." It invented '70s punk, thereby bringing forth the anarchic British edition, as well as New Wave, post-punk, and the next generation's indie and alternative genres. From its black and white, leather-and-Levis cover to the 14 one and two-minute song performances within, *Ramones* is the work of a group that knew exactly what it wanted to do: restore the basic energy, rebelliousness, and humor that had gradually been bred out of rock since the early '70s. The Ramones use many of the same roots as Springsteen ('60s pop, Brill Building melodies, a romanticized urban orientation), place them in a Stooges-powered Veg-O-Matic, and pour out something completely different. The concoction was high-concept, from the names

the band members took to the breathless performances, faux-Brit accents, even down to the inclusion of that '70s-album fixture, the lyric sheet, to illuminate songs whose entire text could be "You're a loudmouth baby/ You better shut it up/ I'm gonna beat you up." Words weren't really the point. On "Blitzkrieg Bop," "Judy Is a Punk," "Now I Wanna Sniff Some Glue," and the rest, the point was to make liberating noise in service of that most radical, and elusive, of qualities: simple fun.

Side One

BLITZKRIEG BOP (2:12)

BEAT ON THE BRAT (2:30)

JUDY IS A PUNK (1:30)

I WANNA BE YOUR BOYFRIEND (2:24)

CHAIN SAW (1:55)

NOW I WANNA SNIFF
    SOME GLUE (1:34)

I DON'T WANNA GO DOWN TO
    THE BASEMENT (2:35)

Side Two

LOUDMOUTH (2:14)

HAVANA AFFAIR (2:00)

LISTEN TO MY HEART (1:56)

53rd & 3rd (2:19)

LET'S DANCE (BMI) (1:51)

I DON'T WANNA WALK
    AROUND WITH YOU (1:43)

TODAY YOUR LOVE, TOMORROW
    THE WORLD (2:09)

All songs written by The Ramones except
    "Let's Dance" written by Jim Lee.

All songs ASCAP except where indicated.

Johnny Ramone: Guitar

Joey Ramone: Lead Vocals

DeeDee Ramone: Bass

Tommy Ramone: Drums

Produced by CRAIG LEON

Associate Producer: T. Erdelyi

Recorded at Plaza Sound, Radio City
    Music Hall, New York

Engineered by Rob Freeman

Assistant Engineer: Don Hunerburg

Mastered at Sterling Sound by Greg Calbi

Ramones Management: Danny Fields

Special Thanks to: Lisa and Richard Robinson
    Linda and Seymour Stein

Front cover photography: Roberta Bayley
    (Courtesy Punk Magazine)

Back cover photography: Arturo Vega

SIRE

Ramones collaborator Arturo Vega shot a belt buckle in a passport photo machine for the back cover.

First pressings had a credit for ABC Records at the bottom of the label.

SIRE

"RAMONES"
RAMONES

SIDE A
STEREO

SASD-7520
(SASD-7520-A)

1. BLITZKRIEG BOP 2:12
2. BEAT IS ON THE BRAT 2:30
3. JUDY IS A PUNK 1:30
4. I WANNA BE YOUR BOYFRIEND 2:24
5. CHAIN SAW 1:55
6. NOW I WANNA SNIFF SOME GLUE 1:34
7. I DON'T WANNA GO DOWN TO THE BASEMENT 2:35

All selections written by the Ramones
and published by Taco Tunes /
Bleu Disque Music (ASCAP)

PRODUCED BY CRAIG LEON

©1976 SIRE
RECORDS, INC.

SIRE RECORDS INC. MARKETED BY ABC RECORDS INC. L.A. CALIF 90048 N.Y. N.Y. 10019 PRINTED IN U.S.A.

The Modern Lovers was originally issued on the Home of the Hits label; it was later reissued on Beserkely Records.

THE MODERN LOVERS | The Modern Lovers

August 1976 | Home of the Hits

"Suppose they gave a war and nobody came?" That phrase, the title of a lost film farce from 1970, could well be applied to the Modern Lovers. Jonathan Richman's Boston quartet valiantly took the field in 1971 and '72 to fire some of the first shots of what would become punk/New Wave (keyboardist Jerry Harrison later co-founded Talking Heads, drummer David Robinson The Cars). The recordings that comprise *The Modern Lovers*—produced by John Cale—were not officially issued until 1976, but their unaffected, back-to-basics style set the stage for much of what was to come. Richman, vocally emulating his hero Lou Reed, marries garage-riff minimalism with a provocative sensibility that praises contemporary suburbia ("Modern World"), disdains hippie ethics ("I'm Straight"), and serves up a brace of songs that turned into post-punk classics. "Pablo Picasso" was covered by David Bowie, Iggy, and John

Cale, and "Roadrunner" has been variously interpreted by the Sex Pistols and Joan Jett. *The Modern Lovers* not only provided some of the kindling that ignited a revolution, it remains an uncompromised, genuinely one-of-a-kind record.

the modern lovers

GLOUCESTER HIGH

ghs auditorium   **fri. march 16**

Ernie Brooks
bass, bg vocals

Jerry Harrison
piano, organ, bg vocals

Jonathan Richman
vocalist and guitarist

David Robinson
drums, bg vocals

"Roadrunner," "Astral Plane," "Old World,"
"Pablo Picasso," "She Cracked" and
"Someone I Care About" produced by
John Cale—16 track demo for
Warner Brothers 1971

"Hospital" donated by Jerry Harrison
recorded at Intermedia Sound, Boston

"Girl Friend" and "Modern World"
recorded by Robert Appere
and Alan Mason

Remix by Gary Phillips, Matthew King Kaufman
and Glen Kolotkin

LP compiled by Matthew King Kaufman
LP co-ordination—Jim Blodgett
LP assistance—T. Lubin
Mastering—G. Horn

Side One	Side Two
Roadrunner	She Cracked
Astral Plane	Hospital
Old World	Someone I Care About
Pablo Picasso	Girl Friend
	Modern World

All songs written by Jonathan Richman

All songs © Modern Love Songs

P & © 1976
"Home of
the Hits"
HH 1910

"Home of
the Hits"

℗ 1976
Home of
the Hits

HH-1910-A
Side One

the modern lovers

1. Roadrunner
2. Astral Plane
3. Old World
4. Pablo Picasso

AC/DC | Dirty Deeds Done Dirt Cheap

September 1976 | Albert Productions

Once punk broke, a musical culture-war broke out between followers of the upstart genre and those of the older, more established heavy-metal style. Into the breach came this record, which magically seemed to mollify both camps. *Dirty Deeds Done Dirt Cheap* was a record that carried all the crunching power and requisite boogie thrust of metal, but also embodied the verve and irreverent humor put forth by the best punk rock. Singer Bon Scott and guitarist Angus Young lead the proceedings, which for the most part entail broad, double-entendre lyrics ("Big Balls," "Squealer") over indestructible riffs (rather like Slade with guitar solos). The album, AC/DC's third, initially flew under the radar in the States, where import copies of the original Australian record and an international edition had to serve fans until Atlantic Records issued it here in 1981 (following the mega-success of the group's *Highway to Hell* and *Back in Black* LPs). The American version

became an instant hit and the title cut an album-radio smash. *Dirty Deeds* was produced by former Easybeats Harry Vanda and George Young, older brother of Angus and rhythm guitarist Malcolm Young.

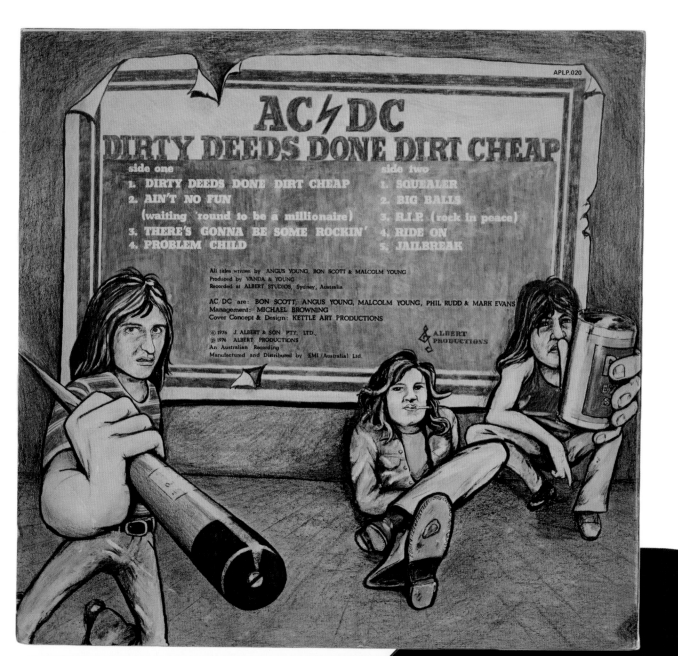

FLEETWOOD MAC | Rumours

February 1977 | Warner Bros.

What Carole King's *Tapestry* was to the early '70s, *Rumours* was to the later '70s: a touchstone record that every mainstream music fan either owned or heard everywhere. Its stats are staggering: 40 million copies sold worldwide, top honors for 31 weeks on *Billboard*'s chart, where it resided for two and a half years, four Top-10 singles, and a Grammy for Album of the Year in 1978. Coming on the heels of the *Fleetwood Mac* LP, itself a mini blockbuster, *Rumours* generated anticipation, but neither the group nor the music industry was prepared for the reception it got—especially for an outfit that had formed nine years and 10 albums earlier as a blues band. But the band now included Lindsey Buckingham and Stevie Nicks and singer-writer Christine McVie. Their contributions made *Rumour*s an amalgam of jangling folk-rock (Buckingham's "Go Your Own Way"), atmospheric ballads (Nicks' "Dreams"), and infectious pop

(McVie's "You Make Loving Fun" and "Don't Stop," which was used as the theme song for Bill Clinton's 1992 presidential campaign). If *Rumours'* success impelled the music business to expect mega-million sellers as the new normal (which they only briefly were), it moved the band's creative director Buckingham to risk even more the next time out. *Rumours'* successor, *Tusk,* was a challenging double LP—rawer, more rocking, and notoriously experimental for a superstar act.

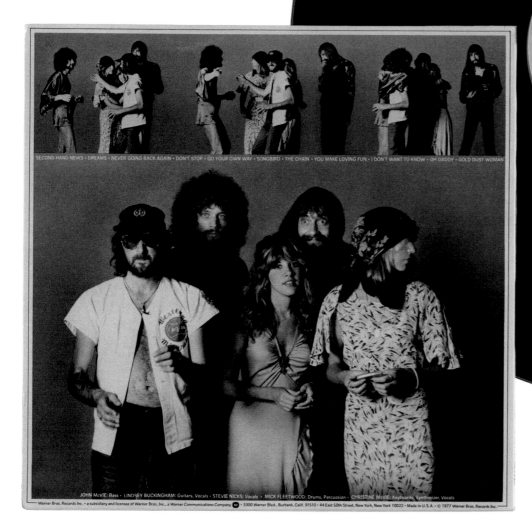

The original disc, with the classic Warner Bros palm tree label.

Back cover.

The insert, with lyrics on reverse.

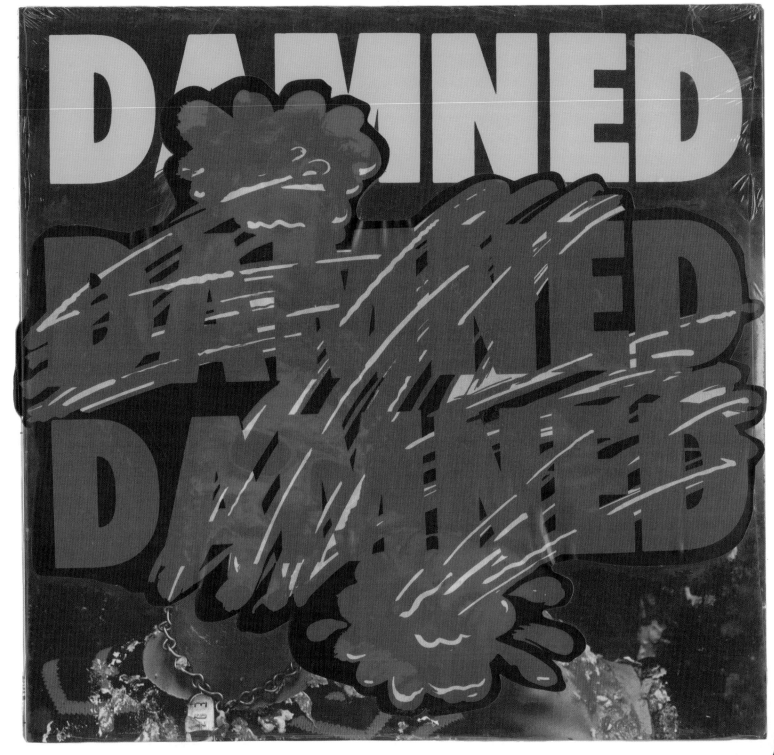

THE DAMNED | The Damned   **February 1977 | Stiff**

"I saw the Pistols play and thought that they had a shambolic charm," Damned bassist Captain Sensible told a journalist, "but we could actually play our instruments. We simply wanted to play as fast and as loud and as chaotically as possible. I didn't see the Pistols as being remotely in that genre." The first British punk band to release a single ("New Rose") and an album (this one, produced by Nick Lowe) had few peers in the fast-and-furious competition to draft the blueprint for the music's U.K. edition. Taking its cue almost exclusively from the Ramones and the Stooges (whose "1970" is covered here as "I Feel Alright"), the band tears through a dozen songs in half an hour, most penned by guitarist Brian James. The pace slackens only for the creep-show ballad "Feel the Pain," a clear precursor to '80s goth-rock. Otherwise, it's an unrelieved torrent of powerfully primitive rock 'n' roll, commencing with the lightning strike of "Neat Neat Neat" and thundering through "Born to Kill," "Stab Your Back," "New Rose," and "So Messed Up."

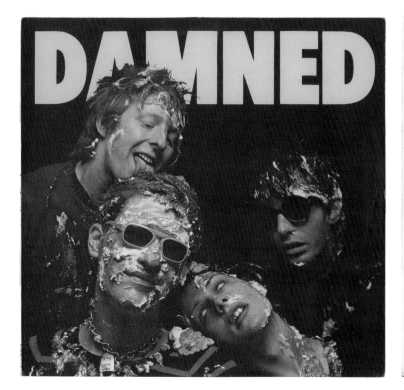

The original cover, without the shrink wrap.

Stiff Records loved promotional stunts; for the Damned's debut, they made a small number of album covers that "mistakenly" pictured Eddie and the Hot Rods instead of the Damned, and added an "erratum" sticker–creating an instant collector's item.

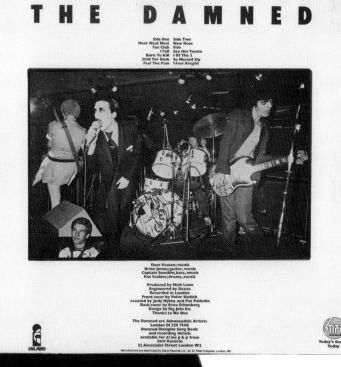

The "official" back cover.

THE CLASH | The Clash   **April 1977 | CBS**

The Ramones may have invented punk and the Sex Pistols infused it with a sense of danger, but The Clash brought social consciousness to the music. Issued barely two months after the Damned's debut, *The Clash* was the first major-label album by a British punk band, and it sold respectably. The album's real achievement, though, was to expand the vocabulary of the new genre, both in terms of the subjects it might address and the musical styles it might appropriate to do so. "White Riot" and "Career Opportunities" employ a Ramones-ish blitz to protest Britain's labor problems, while "I'm So Bored with the U.S.A." re-channels MC5 righteousness to rage against the Americanization of culture. A cover of Junior Murvin's "Police & Thieves" uses quasi-dub style to decry the violence of both society's insiders and its outcasts. The band's perspective here is populist, an attempt to champion the man-in-the-street over the

politically powerful, and thus not dissimilar to Bruce Springsteen's outlook. The album's musical range hints at The Clash's determination not to be hemmed in by the orthodoxies that were already forming in punk. The subsequent albums, *Give 'Em Enough Rope, London Calling, Sandinista!,* and *Combat Rock* found the band utilizing rockabilly, reggae, metal, and even sound collages to state its musical and political cases.

The back cover was shot during a riot at London's Notting Hill Carnival, the inspiration for the album's "White Riot."

S i d e 1

JANIE JONES
REMOTE CONTROL
I'M SO BORED WITH THE U.S.A.
WHITE RIOT
HATE & WAR
WHAT'S MY NAME*
DENY
LONDON'S BURNING

S i d e 2

CAREER OPPORTUNITIES
CHEAT
PROTEX BLUE
POLICE & THIEVES**
48 HOURS
GARAGELAND

THE CLASH   Mick Jones - guitar, vocals
             Joe Strummer - guitar, vocals
             Paul Simonon - bass guitar
             Tory Crimes - drums

All songs written by Strummer/Jones
except *Strummer/Jones/K.Levine and ** Murvin/Perry.
All songs copyright control except ** Blue Mountain Music Ltd.
Photographs: Front Cover - Kate Simon; Back Cover - Rocco Macauley.

©1977 CBS Records
℗1977 CBS Records

WARNING - Copyright subsists in all CBS recordings. Any unauthorized broadcasting, public performance, copying or re-recording in any manner whatsoever will constitute infringement of such copyright. Licences for the use of records for public performance may be obtained from Phonographic Performance Ltd., Evelyn House, 62 Oxford Street, W.1.

is a Registered Trademark of CBS Inc.
Shorepak by Shorewood Packaging Co. Ltd., England

Stereo
CBS
82000

THE CLASH

S CBS 82000 A°   33⅓ RPM
STEREO   S CBS 82000
                                  ℗1977 CBS Records

1. JANIE JONES (Strummer/Jones) (2.05)
2. REMOTE CONTROL (Strummer/Jones) (3.00)
3. I'M SO BORED WITH THE U.S.A. (Strummer/Jones) (2.24)
4. WHITE RIOT (Strummer/Jones) (1.55)
5. HATE & WAR (Strummer/Jones) (2.04)
6. WHAT'S MY NAME (Strummer/Jones/K. Levine) (1.40)
7. DENY (Strummer/Jones) (3.03)
8. LONDON'S BURNING (Strummer/Jones) (2.10)
Produced by Micky Foote
1-8 Copyright Control
Original sound recording made by CBS Records

MADE IN ENGLAND

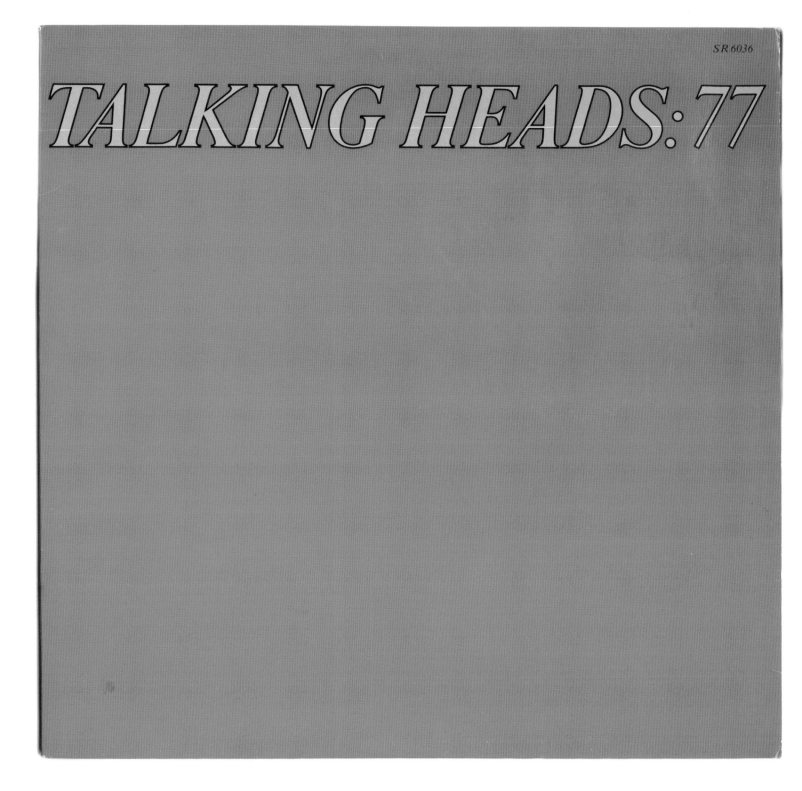

SR 6036

TALKING HEADS | Talking Heads: 77

September 1977 | Sire

Just as the "San Francisco sound" of an earlier decade proved less homogeneous than its handle, New York's downtown rock scene of the mid-'70s resisted one-size-fits-all categorization. Talking Heads played the same clubs as the hyper-speed Ramones, the '60s-popped Blondie, and the uptown-soul-obsessed Mink Deville, but had little else in common with these bands. *Talking Heads 77* revealed the quartet as progenitors of what came to be labeled as "art-rock": angular guitar rhythms, David Byrne's eccentric voicing, odd syntax, and subject matter that veered from musings on the mundane to surreal metaphors. "Pulled Up" expresses gratitude for good parenting, "Psycho Killer" spools out the interior monologue of a madman, and in "The Book I Read," Byrne compares love to a book he's just read. Buried within the songs' off-kilter rhythms are premonitions of the band's fascination with funk, which would surface in its 1979 hit

cover of Al Green's "Take Me to the River" and bassist Tina Weymouth and drummer Chris Frantz's '80s side project the Tom Tom Club—as well as in the music of numerous post-punk ensembles who heard something inspirational in *Talking Heads 77*.

UH-OH, LOVE COMES TO TOWN
NEW FEELING
TENTATIVE DECISIONS
HAPPY DAY
WHO IS IT?
NO COMPASSION

THE BOOK I READ
DON'T WORRY ABOUT THE GOVERNMENT
FIRST WEEK/LAST WEEK . . . CAREFREE
PSYCHO KILLER
PULLED UP

Left to Right:
MARTINA WEYMOUTH: BASS PLAYER
JERRY HARRISON: GUITAR AND KEYBOARD PLAYER, 2ND SINGER
DAVID BYRNE: GUITAR PLAYER AND SINGER
CHRIS FRANTZ: DRUMMER
PRODUCED BY TONY BONGIOVI, LANCE QUINN AND TALKING HEADS, ENGINEERED BY ED STASIUM. SIRE RECORDS 165 WEST 74 ST. N.Y., N.Y. 10023

SIRE

SIRE®

TALKING HEADS '77
TALKING HEADS
Produced by Tony Bongiovi, Lance Quinn &
Talking Heads

SR 6036   SIDE I

1. UH-OH, LOVE COMES TO TOWN   2:48
2. NEW FEELING   3:09
3. TENTATIVE DECISIONS   3:04
4. HAPPY DAY   3:55
5. WHO IS IT?   1:41
6. NO COMPASSION   4:47

All selections written by David Byrne
All selections published by Bleu Disque Music
Co., Inc./Index Music-ASCAP

© 1977 Sire
Records, Inc.

Sire Records, Inc. Marketed by Warner Bros. Records Inc. Made in U.S.A.

NEVER MIND
THE BOLLOCKS

HERE'S THE

Sex PisTOLs

SEX PISTOLS | Never Mind The Bollocks Here's The Sex Pistols   **October 1977 | Virgin**

The most important punk rock album ever was also the most commercially successful and one that has lost little of its punch over three decades. It's arrival was highly anticipated, and it was preceded by an outlandish narrative scripted by band manager Malcolm McLaren: the Pistols' notorious TV interview with Bill Grundy, their tour cancellation, getting dropped by EMI, picked up and sacked by A&M, signing with Virgin, and the controversies over "Anarchy in the U.K." and "God Save the Queen." But *Never Mind the Bollocks* is more than a luridly-packaged "event" record. The album is a sonic fireball packed with searing performances by Johnny Rotten and cohorts; it's a major rock album—of its time but still capable of throwing sparks—fit to serve right alongside the best of the Stones, Hendrix, or Dylan. On "Pretty Vacant," "No Feelings," and "Problems," lyrics, sound, and attitude mesh perfectly to form a justifiably

intemperate response to Britain's mid-'70s political hypocrisy, dead-end economy, and contempt for non-conforming subjects. *Never Mind the Bollocks* was no slapdash affair—producer Chris Thomas, who'd worked on *The White Album* and LPs by Roxy Music and Procol Harum, helped the band craft a thunderous, uncompromised record that fully achieved the impact its creators intended.

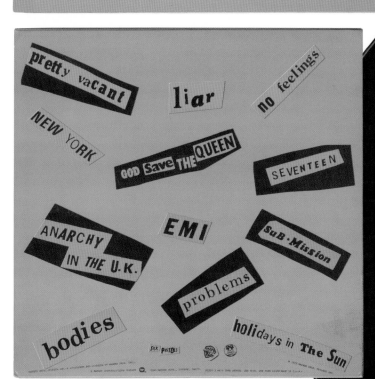

The first copies had no track listing on the back cover.

A track listing was added to later covers.

The earliest copies included eleven tracks, however the band soon changed their mind and added "Submission." Some copies came with a one-sided "Submission" single.

THE VINYL MYSTIQUE

by Ken Barnes

It all started with a girl, of course. And an electric 12-string guitar.

Actually, it started with a driver's license and a long-overdue realization. I had been a devoted radio listener since 1960, soaking up the surf records and R&B, the girl groups and British Invaders. But it was not until June 1965, when I acquired the legal authorization to hit the road, that a basic notion, known to everyone except the cloistered and the brain-dead, clicked in my head. Those songs I loved on the radio were available to purchase in stores on vinyl albums and singles.

So my 13-year-old brother and I pooled our paltry cash reserves, I drove us out to Music City in West Covina, California, and we bought two albums: *Mr. Tambourine Man* by the Byrds, because of the 12-string intro to the title track, which had electrified me more than any song up to that time, and *Marianne Faithfull*, because I had a major crush on the British singer. I would buy my first single a few months later ("Too Many People" by L.A. folk-rockers The Leaves,) and singles later became my primary collecting obsession. But I gravitated toward albums for the first purchase, even though they were about four times as expensive. In the case of Faithfull, I'm pretty sure the cover shot sold me, but with The Byrds it must have been the hope that it might contain 10 other songs as good as "Mr. Tambourine Man." Fortunately, that was pretty much the case, so I set upon a lifelong quest for more perfect albums.

In Boston for a family visit that summer, my brother and I added three more albums to our hoard: *All Summer Long* and *Today* by the Beach Boys, and another LP I cannot recall, which means it must have been a disappointment, sorely undercutting my conviction that all album tracks would be as memorable as their radio hits. Still, four out of five albums had been big winners, so my course was fixed.

The main problem was money. It had never occurred to me in all those years of dedicated radio listening to ask my parents for records, or money to buy them, since I hadn't clearly grasped the concept yet. I never did directly resort to that desperate measure. But as a jobless and impoverished high school student, I had a cash crisis.

I partially solved it by the simple expedient of cutting my lunch expenses at the school cafeteria to 11 cents a day, this sum purchasing a frozen orange-juice bar and a dinner roll (I compensated by scarfing everything remotely edible in the refrigerator once I got home from school.) But I could still afford only a few records, even with the aid of my brother's likewise scanty funds (We theoretically owned the records in common, a pledge terminated a few years later when he relinquished most of them to me for convenience's sake).

So, unable to acquire everything in sight (a philosophy employed only after I was employed, some years later), I had to have a strategy for buying albums. Often I'd hear a single on the radio and look for the album, other times I'd avail myself of friends' recommendations. Bob Dylan arrived by that method. But I'd frequently just buy an album if the cover looked good or I liked the name of the band.

I'm pretty sure I bought the first Love album because the cover appealed to me. I also fell prey to the irresistible allure of British imports—a friend had the *Kinks Kontroversy* album, with its colorful laminated sleeve. I asked him where he got it, and eventually he drove us all the way from my San Gabriel Valley suburb into Hollywood (a nearly incalculable distance, not so much physically as psychically) to a tiny store called Lewin's Record Paradise, which featured luminous, imported albums by the Beatles, Rolling Stones, Spencer Davis Group and more. It was here, I think, that the intrinsic aesthetic value of the album-as-arti-

fact was seared into my brainstem once and for all (I bought only a few records at Lewin's over the next couple of years, since imports cost more than double the price of domestic LPs, but I spent a *lot* of time in the choosing.)

There was one import album I was desperate to buy. Ever since I saw a mimed performance of "I Can't Explain" on the daily *Where the Action Is* TV show some time in the first half of 1965, the Who had become my new favorite band, replacing even the Byrds (who were big stars by then; as always, it was more fun to root for an act no one had heard of.) I ordered copies of that single and its even more astonishing follow-up, "Anyway, Anyhow, Anywhere," from a Pasadena record store. Somehow I stumbled on a mail-order operation in England, the Heanor Record Centre, that would send you UK records if you could scrape up the price plus postage. And they sent catalogs, which conjured all sorts of tantalizing, unaffordable possibilities. So, after some industrious and nutritionally inadvisable scraping, we ordered British copies of "Anyway" (it had a different B-side!) and the new Who single, "My Generation."

But where was the album? An examination of the British top 10 lists printed in the local radio station music paper, the *KRLA Beat*, indicated that all three of the Who's singles were hits. But my first visit to Lewin's turned up no trace of a Who album. What on earth was taking them so long? Another visit—nothing. These trips, with gas costs, time considerations and the lingering cultural timidity of a suburban teen venturing to Hollywood, were not undertaken lightly. And yet another, equally fruitless, early in 1966, a year after *I Can't Explain* was released, when the album surely must have been released (it had been, in fact, just before Christmas in the UK, but had not reached the distant outpost of Lewin's yet).

Finally, sometime in the spring, it was there, in

all its menacing glory. It cost something like $7.50, a few weeks of lunch money, but it looked gorgeous and sounded fantastic. The *My Generation* album instantly became my No. 1 (and, largely thanks to the expanded CD reissue that I must admit is a welcome by-product of modern technology, still ranks near the top).

But the completion of that quest only whetted my appetite for more elusive imports. Lewin's was inconveniently located, and I couldn't afford the prices. Same thing for the Heanor mail-order catalogs. Besides the expense, the records took months to arrive by low-cost sea mail, ratcheting up the anticipation but negating the crucial instant gratification of spotting a desirable record and buying it on the spot. By careful budgeting, I could scare up sufficient funds to order a few import singles, but albums seemed too risky.

So, even six years after the Who album purchase, when I was out of school and had an ill-paying job in San Jose, California, that still provided some discretionary income, my '60s import collection languished. I knew by then that import albums not only looked cooler but often had tracks not found on their American equivalents. Imagine, then, my bogglement when I walked into a Palo Alto used-record store in 1972 and found no less than four immaculate British Hollies albums, plus both UK Them LPs, for $2.50 apiece. It was a Grail moment, amplified a few weeks later when a discount department store yielded the Pretty Things' *Get the Picture* and two Troggs albums, *Trogglodynamite* and *Cellophane*.

By then I was a seasoned, knowledgeable record shopper, but the days of buying albums on impulse were mostly over. I missed the thrill of buying an album just because I liked the band's name. The best result of that incautious approach came at college in early 1967, when with a few bucks left over from the monthly food-and-rent budget I stumbled on the first Velvet Under-

ground LP. The Warhol peel-off banana cover did nothing for me, and I'd never heard of the group, but I liked that name. Good instinct.

Up until about 1968, you didn't need good instincts for impulse buying. If you were concentrating on rock albums, there were so few released (compared to today's tens of thousands annually) and the average quality level was so high that you could take a blind flyer and have a good chance of coming up with a gem.

That changed as albums began to eclipse singles as moneymakers and labels leaped to cash in on the new "underground" rock boom, with the not-unpredictable outcome of a severe overall quality drop. And by 1968, if you were an avid reader and listener, it became harder to fly blind anyway. As the sixties waned, between the new FM rock radio stations and the underground weeklies and actual ROCK PUBLICATIONS (*Rolling Stone, Crawdaddy*), you could get a pretty good idea of what was out there and what it sounded like. You still held out hope that each new album you bought would constitute musical perfection, but the sheer joy of pure, out-of-nowhere discovery was elusive once you'd heard a track or read an item about the artist. And if you hadn't heard of an album, it only took one or two mistakes to cure your gambling ways.

One other contemporary method I used was buying records because of the label that issued them, a tactic that hasn't gone away. It worked for collectors with Chess records in the '50s, Motown in the '60s, Stiff in the '80s, Sub Pop in the '90s, and any number of niche/indie labels today … up to a point. There always would come a time when that reliable source of fine music would start faltering.

The label I was most willing to take a chance on during my early album-buying years was Elektra. The covers were always striking and the music varied in style but was always interesting. Love

was the first (I started with Elektra's rock era, passing on most of the folk material, to my later regret). Liking that a lot, I took a shot on the Doors and Tim Buckley, following with more obscure favorites such as the Dillards and Steve Noonan. Finally, after one too many Ars Novas or Earth Operas, I had to stop buying Elektra releases unheard, but it was a great run.

My Elektra complex also illustrates the key role artwork had in establishing the album as cherished artifact. Elektra albums (likewise Blue Note, if you were a jazz fan), or those glossy British imports, were records you were proud to display, enjoyed looking at while listening, absorbing aesthetic appeal along with liner note information.

The fact that thousands of unregenerate vinyl fetishists have burbled over the years at great length about the tactile and visual superiority of the record to the cassette/8-track/CD/MP3/enclouded song file doesn't make it any less true. Records are innately cool in a way subsequent configurations can't match, as the steady rise in vinyl sales over the last decade and the not-unrelated increase in younger vinyl buyers illustrate. Records have been a way of life for me forever, and I'm not about to stop. As REM said, "If death is pretty final, I'm buying vinyl."

Ken Barnes has written about music for seminal publications such as Bomp, Phonograph Record Magazine, Creem *and* Rolling Stone. *He is the former music editor of* USA Today, *and the former Senior VP/Editor at* Radio & Records. *His massive record collection focuses on 45's, which number over 110,000.*

Credits

Essays as told to Jeff Gold:
>   Devendra Banhart on Vashti Bunyan, Davy Graham and Skip Spence
>   Joe Boyd on Nick Drake and The Incredible String Band
>   Peter Buck on Patti Smith
>   Nels Cline on Jimi Hendrix
>   Mick Haggerty on Album Cover Design
>   Robyn Hitchcock on The Beatles, Bob Dylan and Pink Floyd
>   Jon Savage on Love and Moby Grape

Essays written by the contributors:
>   Ken Barnes on Record Collecting
>   Jac Holzman on the History of the LP
>   Johnny Marr on Iggy & The Stooges
>   Graham Nash on The Beatles and Joni Mitchell
>   Iggy Pop on The Mothers of Invention and Them
>   Suzanne Vega on The Beatles and Leonard Cohen

Album essays written by Gene Sculatti in consultation with Jeff Gold.
>   Gene Sculatti is a writer, editor, and broadcaster who has written about
>   music for *Rolling Stone, Billboard, Radio and Records* and numerous
>   other publications. His books include *The Catalog of Cool, Too Cool,*
>   and *San Francisco Nights: The Psychedelic Music Trip.*

The frontispiece shows Jimi Hendrix displaying his own copy of *Electric Ladyland* in his London home. Happily, he left no bite marks. An enlarged photo of his copy of the album may be seen on pages 122 and 123.

Acknowledgements

For Jody, Ella and Cleo.
You are everything to me.

Thank you:

Bryan Ray Turcotte, for making this a reality.

Clint Woodside, Chelsea Hodson, and Ron Fleming, for your design and editing expertise.

Devendra Banhart, Ken Barnes, Joe Boyd, Peter Buck, Nels Cline, Mick Haggerty, Robyn Hitchcock, Jac Holzman, Johnny Marr, Graham Nash, Iggy Pop, Jon Savage, Gene Sculatti and Suzanne Vega, for sharing your insights.

Lee Kaplan, for giving me the idea.

Geoffrey Weiss and Gary Johnson for your peerless record collecting wisdom, and for loaning me albums I could find nowhere else.

Gene Sculatti, for your exceptional words.

Zach Cowie, Jon Savage, Mark Goldstein and Jeff Ayeroff, without whom this would have been a much lesser enterprise.

Steve Ades, Bill Allerton, Mark Arevalo, Colin Baker, Steven Baker, Gary Borman, David Bressler, Beverly Brown, Rosemary Carroll, Larry Clemens, Art Collins, Perry Cox, Bertis Downs, Jasen Emmons, Richard Foos, Gil Friesen, The Gold Family, Ken Gold, Yuri Grishin, Robin Hurley, Denise Kaufman, Howard Kramer, Margaret Kramer, Wayne Kramer, Howard Krumholtz, Harvey Kubernik, Johan Kugelberg, Barry Ollman, Kevin O'Neil, Andrew Roth and The Book of 101 Books, Bob Say, Richard Silverston, Gary Stewart, Gregg Turner, David Weinhart, Vicious Sloth (Peter, Ange & Glenn).